ι

DATE DUE

219	Fax Request		

FOETAL *and* NEONATAL PHYSIOLOGY

Million years ago

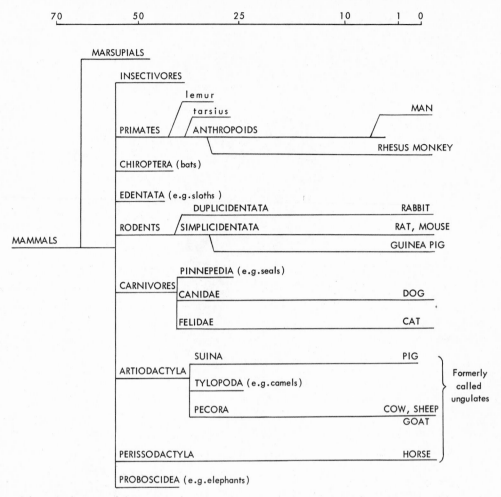

Schematic diagram of the origins of some common mammals as deduced from the geological record.

Foetal AND Neonatal
Physiology

A Comparative Study of the Changes at Birth

GEOFFREY S. DAWES, D.M.

*Director of the Nuffield Institute for Medical Research,
University of Oxford*

YEAR BOOK MEDICAL PUBLISHERS, INC.

35 EAST WACKER DRIVE • CHICAGO

Preface

THE MAIN THEME of this book is the development in the foetus and newborn of the integrated responses which are needed to conserve their energy supply for maintenance of their internal environment, growth and development. For some years it has been apparent that the large and rapidly increasing literature in this field requires a more general treatment than is possible within the scope of a review article. I have attempted to cover the main features of the cardiovascular and respiratory systems, some relevant aspects of energy metabolism, temperature control and growth, and their integration by hormonal and nervous mechanisms. The evidence available is like an unfinished patchwork quilt, derived from many species and incomplete in part. There are other aspects of the physiology of this period of life which have been excluded, such as the development of sex differentiation and immunological tolerance, not because I think they are unimportant, but because they are peripheral to the main topic.

The great increase in the number and size of scientific journals nowadays presents all would-be reviewers with an appalling task. This is my excuse —if I have failed to cover some researches—while I am indebted to many friends and colleagues who have drawn my attention to work of which I was not previously aware. They have most generously given time and thought and allowed me to quote their unpublished observations.

In particular I am indebted to Dr. Julius Comroe, who made it possible for me to spend a sabbatical leave in his department and placed its admirable facilities at my disposal. I have especially valued the friendly and informed criticism of the many experts in different fields who work there.

I also acknowledge with gratitude the kindness of colleagues and publishers who have allowed me to reproduce illustrations, the artistry of Helen Gee who drew all the new and original figures, and the patience of Mrs. Ginna Bunker and her assistants who have typed the manuscript. Finally, I owe a particular debt of gratitude to my Oxford colleagues and my secretary who made it possible for me to escape from other commitments and to concentrate on this task, and who have all contributed so notably to the work described in the following pages.

GEOFFREY S. DAWES

Cardiovascular Research Institute
University of California Medical Center
San Francisco

Table of Contents

1

Introduction

THE YOUNG of different species are often said to be of different maturity at birth. Even if we limit consideration to those whose physiology has been investigated most extensively this is obviously true. For, whereas the rat, rabbit and human infants are born naked and can only right themselves with difficulty, the guinea pig and the lamb have well-developed hairy or woolen coats, can walk, if somewhat unsteadily, as soon as they are born and, though they are capable of independent movement, rapidly develop a close association with their mother. In the latter species mobility at birth must be accompanied by the establishment of a firm maternal link in order to ensure survival, and this requires well-developed special sense organs and brain. Yet all the animals which we shall consider, and the human infant, whether in this sense mature at birth or not, have one thing in common; they all must have developed by the time they are born a circulation and lungs which are fully capable of maintaining independent existence. At first glance one might suppose that the task imposed on its heart and lungs by the newborn lamb, for instance, which toddles around after its mother, would be far greater than that in the rabbit, which lies comparatively quiescent in its nest. Yet the tasks are not dissimilar. The metabolic rate of a newborn rabbit under optimal thermal conditions is even greater than that of a newborn lamb, and its ability to increase its O_2 uptake on exposure to cold is staggering. In these terms, therefore, the cardiovascular and respiratory systems of all these species are remarkably mature at birth.

Yet there are differences which are plain to see. The distribution of the cardiac output to the various organs must differ according to need. In the lamb it may be that the skeletal muscles are of special importance, while the newborn rabbit, because it is small and naked, requires a large blood supply to those tissues, such as brown adipose tissue, which are especially developed for heat production. The human infant has a particularly large brain. So, while the circulation and lungs need to be mature at birth, the analogy between different species cannot be pressed too far. There is here the prospect of an interesting exercise in comparative physiology, in which general principles should hold in every species, but with particular adaptation to particular needs.

A broad attack on these problems in a number of species is attractive for other reasons. Some of these species lend themselves well to particular types of study; the foetal lamb, for instance, because it is relatively large at birth and because the uterus of the sheep does not at once contract and expel the placenta on caesarean section; or the newborn rabbit, because it is cheap and readily obtained, and thus can be used for experiments in which large numbers are required for statistical reasons; or the rhesus monkey, because its brain is more closely related to that of the human infant at birth. Yet the combined wealth of experience of those who have studied the human infant far exceeds that of anyone who works with animals—in this sense, that a physiologist may study 150 or so sheep in a year and, if he is fortunate, find 2 or 3 answers to specific questions which he has decided to present. But a paediatrician is presented with the natural vagaries of development and disease in a community, and if he is observant and critical, can grasp the many opportunities which offer themselves. Both types of research are complementary.

For instance, I remember with a little chagrin contemplating experiments to determine the effect of nephrectomy on amniotic fluid formation and on foetal growth and development in the sheep. Later,

TABLE 1.—Extracted from the Registrar General's Statistical Review of England and Wales

Year	1930	1960	1964
Total population (million)	39.8	45.8	47.5
Total live births registered	648,811	785,005	875,972
Stillbirths (per 1,000 total births)	41	20	16
Infant mortality (<1 yr: per 1,000 live births)	60	22	20
Deaths			
0–6 days	14,267	10,475	10,537
7 days–1 year	24,641	6,643	6,908
Next 6 years	20,646	3,080	3,175

in the same year, I went to a meeting on the placenta (Villee, 1958) at which Edith Potter described the morbid anatomical appearances in renal agenesis in 6 human infants which had been born alive at term. There was little amniotic fluid on delivery, but development had been normal apart from some distortion of the limbs which was attributed to pressure by the wall of the uterus. So the experiment had already been done, naturally. Many conditions are relatively so rare that, though the natural disease may occur in animals, it is not practicable as an experimental project. I have not seen a case of patent ductus arteriosus in sheep outside the immediate newborn period, though there is one pathological report in the literature. The labour in examining large numbers of animals for such conditions would be too great to be worth while. There are other considerations. Deliberately planned experimental studies on animals usually answer only the questions asked, though there is occasionally a delightful and unexpected bonus. The careful study of a large community often reveals unexpected problems, which may lead to the generation of new ideas, but analysis is often impeded by ethical and technical considerations. Therefore, both types of research are necessary. Fundamental work needs no apologia, yet it is sometimes useful to take stock of where we stand.

One way of doing this is to take a brief look at mortality rates in the perinatal period. Table 1 illustrates the observation, common to all countries of Western Europe and North America, that in the past 30 years the human stillbirth and infant mortality rate has greatly decreased. But the greatest advance has been achieved in the treatment of sick children after the first 7 days of life. Indeed, the figures show that more children now die of natural causes in the first 7 days of life than in the next 7 years. The death rate (per 1,000 live births) in the

first 7 days has fallen only from 22 in 1930 to 13 in 1960, and to 12 in 1964. The reason for this is that the principal medical advance during this period of time has been in the treatment of infections, and these are of less importance in the newborn period than are the hazards of transition from foetal to neonatal life. Some of the infants which die are born with anomalies which preclude normal independent life or at an age at which they are not viable. There is a limit which one would not wish to exceed in striving too officiously to keep these infants alive. What is more important is the idea now being examined that some of the infants which subsequently are found to be deficient in one respect or another have acquired this defect as a result of events at or shortly after birth. To assess the probability of the truth of this idea, a very large investigation is required.

The veterinary profession has an even more formidable perinatal problem, as can be seen from Table 2. In the smaller animals the high neonatal mortality rate may sometimes be exaggerated by maternal infanticide and neglect in unnatural surroundings, but this is not always so. Many other sources, too numerous to quote in detail, support the conclusion that these are representative figures. There is a similar problem which can reach com-

TABLE 2.—Infant Losses in Some Animal Species

	Stillbirths (% of All Births)	Deaths before Weaning (% of Liveborn)
Rats	1–2	22–56
Rabbits		7–26
Hamsters		10–48
Pigs	4–12	6–9 (in first 24 hrs)
Sheep		12–27

Sources: Russell (1948); Thomson and Aitken (1959); Duncan, Lodge, and Baskett (1960).

TABLE 3.—Weights of Mothers and Young, and Lengths of Gestation, in Man and Some Common Laboratory Species

Species	Maternal Weight Kg	Birth Weight Gm	Birth Weight in Terms of Maternal Weight (%) Single Foetus	Whole Litter	Usual Number of Young	Length of Gestation Days	Sources (Apart from Personal)
Man	56	3,200	5.7	5.7	1	280	Leitch, Hytten, and Billewicz (1959)
Pig	130	1,200	1.1	6.8	8	114	Duncan, Lodge, and Baskett (1960); Leitch, Hytten, and Billewicz (1959)
Sheep (Hampshire)	70	4,000	5.7	11.4	2	147	
Dog (Beagle)	8.4	270	3.2	16.1	5	59	Hosein (personal communication, 1966)
Rhesus monkey	8	500	6.3	6.3	1	168	
Cat	3	100	3.3	13.2	4	63	
Rabbit	2.5	50	2.0	14.0	7	31	
Guinea pig	0.7	85	12.1	36.3	3	67	
Rat	0.15	5	3.3	23.4	7	22	Russell (1948)
Mouse	0.03	1.4	4.7	37.3	8	19	Altman and Dittmer (1962)

The values quoted are only intended to give a general indication; there is great variation in different races and varieties, and with the number of foetuses.

parable dimensions in livestock, such as cattle and thoroughbred horses. Better housing, better feeding, and more obstetrical and postnatal care can reduce perinatal mortality in these species, but there is a large residual loss which still appears to be much greater than that in man. Infection appears to play only a minor part. Of course, if a farmer were to give his stock the same care which his wife receives he might have more sheep and cattle, but he would soon be bankrupt. On the other hand, he can use selective breeding, and an increase in productivity can sometimes be achieved by simple measures. Since newborn piglets were found to be particularly susceptible to heat loss, the death rate has been reduced by littering in warm sheds.

It is hardly surprising that the pathological problems of late foetal life, placental function, delivery, and survival after birth appear essentially the same in man and animals, though there are variations which draw attention to particular aspects more in some species than in others. The respiratory distress syndrome of the newborn was described in man before it was noticed in animals. But runts were described as a recognizeable variation from the normal in domestic animals many centuries before "dysmature" or "small-for-dates" babies (a more polite term) were distinguished in the human species. Evidently each has something to offer.

Table 3 shows a number of points. The maternal weights vary over a thousandfold range and, generally speaking, the smaller the mother the shorter is the period of gestation. Leitch, Hytten, and Bil-

lewicz (1959) pointed out that the total weight of the young at birth is relatively greater the less the average maternal weight of a given species, as shown in Figure 1. In our particular group of species this trend is not uniform (Table 3), possibly because the domestic pig and sheep have been selectively bred for large carcass size and multiple births. All these species have been subjected to selective breeding for one purpose or another, apart from man, the rhesus monkey, and perhaps the cat, and of these only the monkey is not domesticated. The implication is that

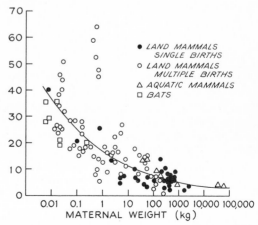

Fig. 1.—Relation between maternal and neonatal weights in different species. (Redrawn from Leitch, Hytten, and Billewicz, 1959.)

TOTAL NEWBORN WEIGHT AS A PERCENTAGE OF MATERNAL WEIGHT

- LAND MAMMALS SINGLE BIRTHS
○ LAND MAMMALS MULTIPLE BIRTHS
△ AQUATIC MAMMALS
□ BATS

MATERNAL WEIGHT (kg)

the processes of natural selection have been varied from what they would otherwise have been, and even though this variation is comparatively recent in evolutionary terms, we are now dealing with specially selected material. Thus in selecting sheep or pigs for more wool or better carcasses the farmer may also, unconsciously, have selected for associated intrauterine or placental characteristics which may be more or less favourable ultimately. The gross measure of total productivity may well conceal many physiological and pathological variables.

There is another general biological problem to be faced at birth in warm-blooded creatures. The smaller the animal, the larger is the ratio of surface area to body mass and the more difficult does thermoregulation become. Thus in mothers of relatively low weight, if the young at birth are smaller in direct proportion, their survival will be more dependent on the provision of metabolic fuel to tide over the first few days, or of a warm nest, burrow, or bassinette, or on close contact with the mother for warmth in a temperate climate (as with the rhesus monkey), or in an extreme case the provision of a marsupial pouch. Figure 1 suggests that, in general, small mothers have a relatively larger conceptus, which may be a small contribution to the physical problem of thermoregulation in the newborn. But there is obviously a limit which cannot be exceeded, determined on the physiological side by the strain on the mother's metabolism, circulation, and skeletal structure, and on the ecological side by the restriction of her mobility during pregnancy.

Table 3 shows that the total litter weight varies from 6 to 37% of the maternal weight in the species considered. Man, with a figure of 6%, is favourably placed in comparison with the guinea pig. Although the stillbirth and perinatal mortality rates increase in any species with increasing litter size, strict interspecies comparisons do not appear to have been made. It may well be that the guinea pig is as well adapted to bear such a large extra mass of living tissue as other species are to bear their relatively smaller burdens. But the physiological adaptations of the maternal guinea pig's circulation might repay study, as an exaggerated model of what must happen in all species. There is another feature of such interspecies comparisons of viability which is curious. In man a great deal of attention has been given to premature delivery as a cause of perinatal mortality and morbidity, but it is hard to find a single reference to prematurity in animals. Large scale statistical analyses of prematurity have not been undertaken, and yet it is difficult to believe that premature delivery is not a contributory factor in perinatal problems in other species as in man.

Lastly, it is worth taking a brief glance at the relative organ weights at birth in the species with which we shall be concerned (Table 4). There are some remarkable and perhaps unexpected differences. It is not surprising to find that the brain of a human infant born at term can be up to 13% of its body weight. It is a still greater proportion of total body weight on premature delivery. Nor is it surprising that the lamb's brain is only 1.3% of body

TABLE 4.—ORGAN WEIGHTS IN NEWBORN ANIMALS, EXPRESSED AS A PERCENTAGE OF BIRTH WEIGHT

Species	Brain	Liver	Skeletal Muscle	Skeleton	Skin	Heart	Lungs	Sources:
Man	10–13	3.5–4.3	18	14	—	0.5–0.65	1.5–1.8	Gruenwald and Minh (1960); Altman and Dittmer (1962)
Pig	3.7	4.7	30	24	10.5	1.0	2.2	McMeekan (1940)
Sheep	1.3	2.1	22	23	11*	1.0	1.8	Carlyle (1948); Shelley and Personal
Dog	3.3	9.6	—	—	—	1.5	2.7	Hosein (personal communication)
Rhesus monkey	12	3.3	25	—	12.6	0.6	1.0	Personal and Shelley
Cat	3.3	4.1	30	12	—	0.9	2.5	Altman and Dittmer (1962)
Rabbit	2.9	6.6	15	—	19	—	2.6	Dawkins and Hull (1964); Cockburn and Harding, and Shelley (personal communications, 1966)
Guinea pig	—	4.8	14–16	—	16	0.5	1.5	Altman and Dittmer (1962); Shelley (personal communication)
Rat	5	6.3	15	—	15	0.5	—	Altman and Dittmer (1962); Cockburn (personal communication)
Mouse	6.3	4.3	—	—	—	0.5	1.4	Altman and Dittmer (1962)

* Shaved.

TABLE 5.—To Illustrate the Effect of Body Size on Relative Brain Size in Adults of Related Vertebrate Species

Species	Adult Body Weight (Kg)	Brain Weight in Terms of Body Weight (%)
House cat	3.3	0.94
Lion	119.5	0.18
Marmoset	0.33	3.82
Gibbon	9.5	1.37
Orang-utan	73.5	0.54

weight at birth. From this point of view, the rhesus monkey (with 12%) is a better model of man, e.g., for studying the distribution of cardiac output in the foetus. What may be unexpected is the high proportion of brain in the newborn rat and mouse (5–6.3%), which results from the fact that their period of gestation is relatively short. It may also result in part from the operation of Haller's Law, which states that in adults of related vertebrate species relative brain size increases as body size decreases (Table 5; Schutz, 1926). The range of variation in the proportionate weights of other organs is less, but not negligible. The liver varies from 2 to 6.6% and contains a very high concentration of glycogen, which is rapidly mobilized at birth. A large proportion of body weight is skeletal muscle, and this varies from 14 to 30%. The skeleton is well developed in the pig and sheep, species which are large and fairly mobile at birth. The skin is a large proportion of the whole in small animals, as was to be expected. The heart (0.5–1.0%) and lungs (1.4–2.6%) form only a small and rather invariable percentage of the total body mass. This is consistent with the view that the cardiovascular and respiratory systems must be mature at birth, and that their tasks are not very different in different species.

The range of different characteristics in these species, their difference in habits, domestication, nutrition, and length of gestation; in weight at birth, relative organ weights, blood pressure, growth rate, and maturity (which is hard to define and impossible to measure quantitatively), all these have advantages as well as disadvantages. These variations are not so much an impediment to rational classification of knowledge as a challenge and opportunity to exploit species characteristics, in the belief that good physiological principles apply in every species.

References

Altman, P. A., and Dittmer, A. S.: *Growth* (Washington, D. C.: Federation of American Societies for Experimental Biology, 1962).

Carlyle, A.: An integration of the total oxygen consumption of the sheep foetus from that of the tissues, J. Physiol. 107:355-364, 1948.

Dawkins, M. J. R., and Hull, D.: Brown adipose tissue and the response of new-born rabbits to cold, J. Physiol. 172:216-238, 1964.

Duncan, D. L.; Lodge, G. A., and Baskett, R. G.: *Diet in Relation to Reproduction and the Viability of the Young. Part III. Pigs* (Bucks, England: Commonwealth Agricultural Bureau, 1960).

Gruenwald, P., and Minh, H. N.: Evaluation of body and organ weights in perinatal pathology, Am. J. Clin. Path. 34:247-253, 1960.

Leitch, I.; Hytten, F. C., and Billewicz, W. Z.: The maternal and neonatal weights of some mammalia, Proc. Zool. Soc. London 133:11–28, 1959.

McMeekan, C. P.: Growth and development in the pig, with special reference to carcass quality characters, J. Agric. Sc. 30:276–343, 1940.

Russell, F. C.: Diet in relation to reproduction and viability of the young. Part I. Rats and other laboratory animals, Commonwealth Bureau Animal Nutrition, Tech. Comm. 16, 1948.

Schutz, A. H.: Fetal growth of man and other primates, Quart. Rev. Biol. 1:465–521, 1926.

Thomson, W., and Aitken, F. C.: *Diet in Relation to Reproduction and Viability of the Young. Part II. Sheep* (Bucks, England: Commonwealth Agricultural Bureau, 1959).

Villee, C. A.: *The Placenta and Fetal Membranes* (Baltimore: The Williams & Wilkins Company, 1958).

2

The Comparative Anatomy of the Placenta

FROM THE POINT OF VIEW of the physiologist interested in gas exchange across the placenta there are three aspects to the comparative anatomy of this organ which require to be examined. These concern first the relative directions of blood flow on the maternal and foetal sides of the membrane which separates the two circulations within the area of gaseous exchange; secondly, the quantitative measurement of the various elements within the placenta which are essential to the interpretation of gas exchange measurements (e.g., the area of the membrane, the distance between maternal and foetal red cells, the volume of placental tissue in and outside the region of gas exchange); and thirdly, the detailed structure of this fascinating and complex membrane, its variation between species and with gestational age within a species.

The Relative Directions of Blood Flow

It will be rather easier to discuss placental vascular structure if we already have in mind the various theoretical models which, in the last few years, have been considered as possible individual elements, which may be combined in different proportions to compose a placenta. Blood flow in contiguous maternal and foetal vascular channels could be countercurrent (Fig. 2, *A*), concurrent (Fig. 2, *B*), or crosscurrent (Fig. 2, *C*; this is described by Bartels, Moll, and Metcalfe, 1962, as multivillous). If the maternal blood enters a large space in which it is exposed to foetal capillaries, one could have a pool flow (Fig. 2, *D*), provided that mixing within the pool was sufficient to distinguish this from a crosscurrent flow system. With these possibilities in mind we may consider placental vascular structure in different species.

In man and the higher subhuman primates the maternal tissues are eroded above the decidual plate (Fig. 3). The spiral arterioles which bring blood from the uterine arteries to the maternal side of the placenta open into the intervillous space, described by Bartels, Moll, and Metcalfe (1962) as a "disorderly system of communicating crevices between the villar trees wherein the blood flows according to the haemodynamic pressure gradient." The crevices have been estimated as about 50 μ wide (Bartels and

Fig. 2.—Diagrams of possible arrangements in maternal and foetal vascular channels in the area of gas exchange of a placenta.

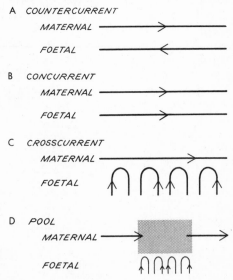

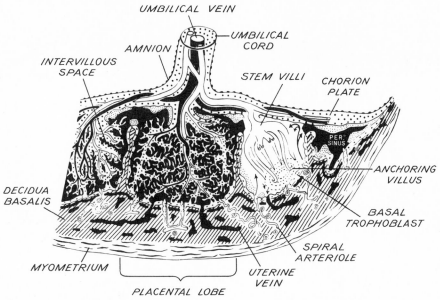

Fig. 3.—The architectural plan of the human placenta. (After Strauss, Goldenberg, Hirota, and Okudaira, 1965.)

Moll, 1964). The maternal arteries and veins which open into and out of the intervillous space are disposed all over the surface of the basal plate (Ramsey, 1962). And Ramsey and her colleagues have shown that on injecting the placentas of rhesus monkeys *in situ*, the maternal arterial blood enters under high pressure and spreads up to the chorionic plate before much lateral dispersion takes place. Similar observations have been made, also by cineangiography, in man. Crawford (1962) has pointed out that the human placenta has a regular arrangement within each cotyledonary lobe which will permit just such a regular distribution of maternal flow. He suggests that maternal blood, after reaching the chorionic plate, disperses laterally and downward past the capillary bed of the foetal villi to reach the basal plate. The foetal capillary bed is a continuous supple three-dimensional structure, neither rigid nor anywhere free-floating, because the terminal portions of the villi are anchored to the basal plate. Thus, despite the irregular appearance of the intervillous space, its structure could impose an orderly distribution of flow upon the maternal blood stream.

Within the intervillous space the relation of foetal to maternal blood flow could adopt any of the forms illustrated in Figure 2, but there is general agreement that countercurrent and concurrent flows are unlikely (Wilkin, 1958; Crawford, 1962; Ramsey,

1962; Bartels, Moll, and Metcalfe, 1962). There is less enthusiasm for pool flow (Fig. 2, *D*) and more for crosscurrent (Fig. 2, *C*). Anatomical investigation has not distinguished between the possibilities with absolute certainty, and possibly cannot, and there are too many other variables which enter the interpretation of physiological data to make them relevant. There are two further points. First, if the current interpretation of the anatomy given by Crawford (1962) and Ramsey (1962) is correct, then maternal flow in some parts of the intervillous space is undoubtedly pulsatile. Foetal flow is probably pulsatile. As the maternal and foetal heart rates are unequal, these pulsations are usually out of phase. Secondly, there may be some points at which a stream of maternal arterial blood is projected against an area of foetal capillaries, rather than flowing smoothly across it. This is likely to raise a different condition for gas transfer than those envisaged in Figure 1, and would contribute even more to the heterogeneous character of the human placenta.

In contrast, the first anatomical observations upon the placentas of some common laboratory animals suggested that their vascular organization was orderly and well arranged for countercurrent flow (Tafani, 1887; Mossman, 1926), a design which would facilitate gas transfer. The detailed anatomical work of Mossman on the rabbit, and of Barcroft and Barron (1946) on the sheep showed that the foetal and maternal villi interdigitated, presumably in order that the vessels on both sides could be brought into close apposition. In these species the maternal blood is not emptied into an intervillous space between the foetal capillaries, but remains in vascular channels throughout its course through the placenta. The arteries within the foetal villi extend to the end of the villus and supply blood to the capillaries on its outer surface. The arteries on the maternal side do the same. Barcroft and Barron (1946) claimed that there were veins only at the base of the villi in the sheep, so that maternal and foetal blood would be brought in close contact, flowing in their capillaries in opposite directions on the surface of interdigitating maternal and foetal villi (Fig. 4).

There are two grounds for questioning this anatomical evidence. First, in 1950 Wimsatt showed that the foetal villus of the sheep contained veins not only in its base but throughout its length. This has been confirmed by Gwen Barer in the Nuffield Institute in unpublished observations made in 1960–63 and by Steven (1966). Clearly, the presence of these veins must mean that blood from foetal arterioles is exposed in a foetal capillary on a small part of the villus surface only. There are no veins in the substance of a maternal villus, but only in its base. Consequently, the vascular arrangement must resemble Figure 2, *C* (crosscurrent) rather than Figure 2, *A* (countercurrent).

Secondly, even this may be regarded as an oversimplification of the true state of affairs when we consider that gas transfer must be taking place between two opposing contiguous sheets of capillaries. Examination of these capillary networks in fixed and cleared specimens shows that their orientation is disorderly. It seems highly improbable that flow is unidirectional. The basic idea of gas exchange between a single maternal vascular unit to a contiguous foetal unit (or units), whose orientation is fixed (as implied in Fig. 2), is too simple. We should think in terms of gas transfer between two contiguous surface areas through which the capillaries are running in every direction. Steven (1966) illustrates this complex arrangement by diagrams of the foetal (Fig. 5, *A*) and maternal (Fig. 5, *B*) villous trees which interlock with one another to form the placenta in a sheep.

There is some physiological evidence which bears on the question of whether placental flow is countercurrent or otherwise in the rabbit and sheep. In the rabbit, Barron and Meschia (1954) reported that uterine venous Po_2 (25 mm Hg) was less than that in the umbilical vein (48 mm Hg); this might suggest that placental flow was countercurrent. Yet the Po_2 in maternal placental venous blood is not necessarily identical with that in uterine venous blood and there are usually several foetuses in each rabbit uterus. It is particularly difficult to get umbilical venous blood samples from foetal rabbits ($\sim$50 Gm at term) in conditions which can be shown to be steady, and without altering umbilical flow. It is not stated whether the maternal and foetal blood samples were taken simultaneously; if they were not, the conclusion is uncertain unless the physiological state was steady. Yet even with these reservations as to interpretation, the observations are provocative and deserve clarification.

In the sheep, Metcalfe, Moll, Bartels, Hilpert, and Parer (1965) have produced functional evidence to show that placental flow is not countercurrent. They perfused sheep placentas *in situ* through the foetal umbilical vessels with a dextran solution containing carbon monoxide and nitrous oxide. It was calculated that 81% of umbilical flow passed through the area of gas exchange (assuming that all the carbon monoxide was removed there and none elsewhere); the remainder was taken to represent "shunted umbilical flow." This shunted flow was taken into consideration when the direction of perfusion of the umbilical arteries and veins was reversed. The proportion of nitrous oxide removed was not altered by reversal of perfusion, as would have been expected if flow were countercurrent. Such experiments are easier in sheep than in rabbits or rhesus monkeys, but the technical problems are

Fig. 4.—Plan of the circulation in the sheep's placental cotyledon. (After Barcroft and Barron, 1946.)

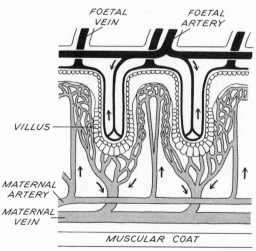

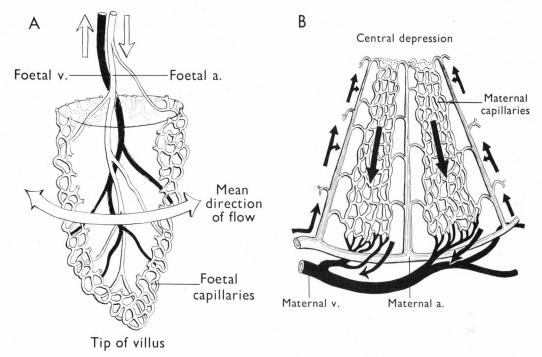

Fig. 5.—Plan of the circulation in the sheep's placental cotyledon. (By Steven, 1966, showing the foetal **(A)** and maternal **(B)** vasculature.)

not insuperable, and in view of the apparent anatomical differences it would be good to have information of this type on other species.

Placental Morphometry

Morphometry as a word is a bit of a mouthful, but it has come to stay. The Anglo-Saxon equivalents have too much bare strength (shape-count, form-size), reminiscent of the Icelandic sagas. The traditional method of planimetry was tedious when used on histological sections and not easily adapted to larger structures. Newer methods have proved more adaptable, more rapid, and more susceptible to statistical control. The degree of folding of a complex structure within a solid object may be estimated by the number of times a traversing line is intercepted, the mean linear intercept method. And the proportions by volume occupied by different types of tissue can be measured by superimposing a grid of equidistant points over the cut surface, an idea which was derived from a method used by geologists to determine the composition of the face of a cliff. These methods, when applied to the lung, rapidly produced a great deal of new quantitative informa-

tion, and it looks as if they are going to be as useful for the placenta, where even less information was previously available.

Aherne and Dunnill (1966a, b) have made a radical departure from previous investigators by dividing the volume of placentas into two main morphological components, the parenchyma, composed of the villi and intervillous space, and the non-parenchyma, composed of chorionic and decidual plates, foetal vessels exceeding 1 mm in diameter, and intercotyledonary septa. In 10 normal human placentas at term the non-parenchymatous fraction was ~21% of the *total* volume (mean volume 488 ml; range 391–723). This represents tissue which is outside the area of gas exchange, whose metabolism must be provided for separately from the maternal or foetal circulations.

The parenchyma was divided into intervillous space (36%), villi (58%), and fibrin (4%). The intervillous space, which averaged 144 ml in volume, is one of the compartments most susceptible to change by blood loss on delivery, and this should probably be regarded as a minimal figure. It might be twice as great *in vivo*. The foetal capillaries occupied only 12% of the parenchyma, equivalent to a total volume of 45 ml. Presumably, there was also loss of foetal blood. Even so, the figures might suggest that at any one time there was more blood within the maternal than the foetal areas. Perhaps part of the maternal area, the intervillous space, should be regarded as an extension of the adjacent arteries and veins rather than as a place in which gas transfer is proceeding. The gas exchange area would then look more like Figure 2, *C* rather than Figure 2, *D*, and we would also have to exercise caution as to the interpretation of blood samples withdrawn from the intervillous space, which might be taken at random from the inlet or outlet spaces rather than the area of gas exchange. A good deal of this is speculative because of possible artifacts, but this is the best material available.

The total surface area of the villi in the normal human placenta is linearly related to placental volume; at term the area is probably about 11 m² (Aherne and Dunnill, 1966a). This makes allowance for the fact that not all of the placenta is parenchyma, but does not take into account the elaboration of the villous surface by microvilli. The capillaries pursue a sinuous course and approach the surface of a villus more or less closely at different points, so that it is not easy to define the area of exposure. This area ("the vasculo-syncytial membrane") was estimated by Aherne and Dunnill to increase from 0.4 m² at 28 weeks gestation to 1.8 m² at term. As in the lung, the area of gas exchange may not be wholly confined to the capillaries, though the rapidly increasing distances for diffusion must restrict this to a small region on either side. It is interesting to compare the effective area of gaseous exchange (i.e., that area in which the capillaries approach the intervillous space or alveoli) in a human placenta at term and in the lung after birth (Table 6). The least quantity of O_2 required to be moved per minute through unit area of membrane is greater in the placenta than in a newborn human infant or adult man at rest, but much less than when the infant is exposed to cold or the man takes vigorous exercise. When the greater length of the diffusion path in the placenta is taken into account, its functional task for O_2 transfer is not very different from that of the lung.

The length of the diffusion path between the maternal and foetal vascular channels is more difficult to measure than in the lung. An O_2 molecule (Fig. 6) must be detached from a maternal haemoglobin molecule and pass through the intracellular fluid and membrane of the maternal erythrocyte, a layer of plasma, the syncytial trophoblast, basement membranes, and the endothelium of the foetal capillary, another layer of plasma and the membrane and intracellular fluid of the foetal erythrocyte, before it can reach and combine with the foetal haemoglobin molecule. This is the most favourable situation. In many areas the foetal capillaries are separated from the maternal intervillous space by a variable mass of tissue including the Langhans' cells (Fig. 6). Also the vascular morphology changes with increasing gestational age. The terminal villi become smaller, the capillaries within each villus become larger in number and more closely applied to the surface of the villous wall (Fig. 7). The syncytial trophoblast which overlies the capillaries may become very thin and in many places devoid of nuclei. The minimum membrane thickness at term is about 3.5 μ according to electromicrograph studies by Aherne and Dunnill (1966). This is not very different from the estimates of Wulf (1962) and others (Wilkin, 1958). The height of the microvilli may add another μ, and the layers of plasma on either side perhaps 2 μ each. The thickness is probably greater earlier in gestation (Wilkin, 1958). It would also be

---

TABLE 6.—COMPARISON OF O_2 TRANSFER ACROSS THE PLACENTA AT TERM AND IN THE LUNG OF NEWBORN AND ADULT MAN

	HUMAN PLACENTA AT TERM	HUMAN INFANT AT BIRTH		ADULT MAN	
		IN WARM	IN COLD	AT REST	ON EXERCISE
Diffusion area, (M²)‡	1.8	2.8	2.8	75	75
VO₂, (ml/min)	16*	16*	42†	240	3600
VO₂/M²	8.9	5.7	15.0	3.4	51
Minimum length of diffusion path (μ) excluding plasma and red cells	~3.5	~2.5	~2.5	~0.5	~0.5

* Calculated as 4.6 ml/kg/min in a 3.5 kg infant.
† Calculated as 12 ml/kg/min in a 3.5 kg infant.
‡ Calculated as vascular area in each case (vasculo-syncytial or capillary-alveolar) (Dunnill, 1962).

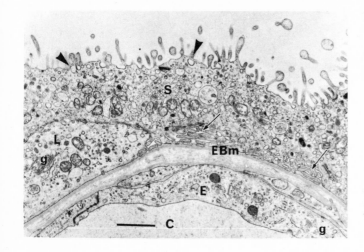

Fig. 6.—Electron micrograph to show the gas exchange area of a third trimester human placenta. (Strauss *et. al.*, 1965. C, foetal capillary; *E*, capillary endothelium; *EBm*, basement membrane; *L*, Langhans' cell; *S*, syncytial trophoblast. Scale: 1μ.)

useful to have some information about the mean lengths of the capillary path within the effective area of gas exchange; this is not yet available.

In experimental animals such as rhesus monkeys, sheep, or rabbits, there is no published information on placental morphometry comparable with that in man, though some is being collected. There are a few estimates of the length of the diffusion path in the sheep and cat in the literature, but these were all made more than 10 years ago, using methods of computation which are not comparable with those quoted in man. All that can be said is that the path lengths appear to be a little longer than in man; more detailed quantitative measurements are needed on every aspect of placental morphometry. This is particularly necessary for comparison between species because the gross appearance and the detailed histology are so variable. Only quantitative

morphometry can provide a sound basis for comparing measurements of placental gas transfer in different species. A longer diffusion pathway might be partly offset by a larger diffusion area for instance.

Gross Comparative Morphology

The gross appearance of the allanto-chorionic placenta across which gas transfer takes place in eutherian mammals (i.e., those with placentas) differs greatly in different species. All are composed of smaller units called cotyledons. In man these cotyledons are combined to form a single flat plate or cake. The word is derived from the Greek for cake, and shows a strong anthropocentric bias; it certainly would not have been used to describe the placenta of a dog or sheep. The placenta looks much

Fig. 7.—Changes in the appearance of terminal villi with gestational age in the human placenta. (Strauss *et al.*, 1965. **A,** first trimester; **B,** third trimester. Haematoxylin and eosin, ×440.)

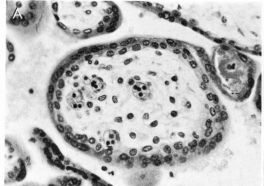

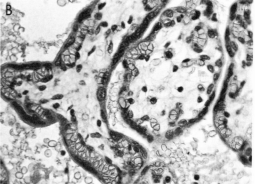

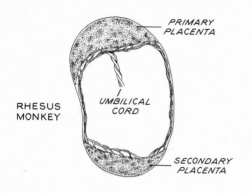

RHESUS
MONKEY

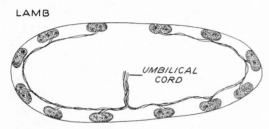

LAMB

Fig. 8.—Sectional views of uterus to show the two placentas in the rhesus monkey and the arrangement of the placental cotyledons in sheep.

band which encircles the foetus and complicates an intrauterine surgical approach.

In the sheep, goat, and cow the placenta is cotyledonary. The cotyledons (30–80 in number), instead of being brought together in a single structure, are dispersed across a wide area of the uterus (Fig. 8). The point of attachment of the foetal element is determined by specialized areas known as caruncles, which are scattered over the horns of the uterus mainly along the medial sides. The umbilical vessels break up into a large number of cotyledonary branches which are distributed each to a separate cotyledon. This arrangement has many advantages from the point of the experimental physiologist. A cotyledonary umbilical artery or vein can be tied, and catheters can be introduced into the main trunks with little disturbance and the loss of function of only one cotyledon. However, these cotyledonary vessels go into spasm very readily and need careful handling.

There are some other important features about these cotyledonary placentas. The venous drainage from the maternal side of each cotyledon in the sheep is joined by small branches which drain the myometrium. But it is possible to tie these off, or even better, to use one of them to introduce a fine catheter so that blood samples can be removed from a maternal vein uncontaminated by myometrial

the same in the baboon as in man. In the rhesus monkey (which has been used a great deal for experimental work in the past, and is likely to be used even more in the future) it is usually in two parts. The umbilical cord supplies the primary placenta, and then gives off a variable number of vessels of varying size which run within the foetal membranes to supply the secondary placenta (Fig. 8). The primary placenta is usually, but not always, larger than the secondary; they are sometimes loosely attached to one another. This anatomical arrangement is useful to experimental workers because it is possible to obtain umbilical arterial and venous blood samples from the vessels joining the two parts, without opening the amniotic cavity. But this can be done only at the risk of sacrificing some placental tissue, because vascular connections between the several cotyledons which make up each part are of very variable size. In the rhesus monkey, the separation between each cotyledon is easier to discern on the surface of the placenta than in man. Otherwise the structure is very similar.

In many other laboratory species, the rabbit, guinea pig, rat, and mouse, the placenta also is a single disc as in man. In the cat and dog it is zonary, that is to say, it consists of a comparatively narrow

Fig. 9.—Sectional diagram of a sheep's placental cotyledon **(above)** and plans of the foetal and maternal aspects **(below)**.

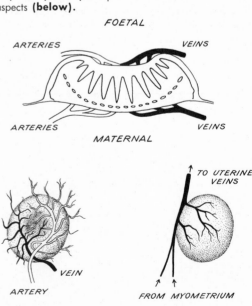

blood (Fig. 9). This can be done through a uterine incision less than 2 cm long, with very little disturbance, in more than one cotyledon at a time. The foetal side of the placental cotyledon is less easy to reach; it is usually necessary to deliver the foetus. A single cotyledon is often supplied by more than one umbilical cotyledonary artery and more than one vein. The vascular arrangement is also complicated by the fact that the umbilical vessels supply the large capillary network of the extracotyledonary chorionic membrane and the vessels which are applied to the surface of the amnion. Therefore, if one wishes to obtain a sample of cotyledonary umbilical (i.e., foetal) venous blood, uncontaminated by the venous drainage from the membranes, the connecting vessels at the edge of the foetal side of the cotyledon must be destroyed; they are quite easily cauterized. Ultimately, it may be possible, with improved methods of handling, to perfuse a single sheep's cotyledon from both maternal and foetal sides, and to study the effect of changing flows on gas transfer. This has not yet been attempted; the vessels readily go into spasm, and we have insufficient experience of the behaviour of the cotyledons *in vivo* by which to judge whether the preparation is good.

We may also briefly consider the relative changes in foetal and placental weight. In all the species for which data are available, the weight of the placenta increases much more rapidly than that of the foetus early in gestation. Then, at a later date, the growth of the placenta slows down while that of the foetus continues. The result is that somewhere about mid-

TABLE 7.—THE WEIGHTS OF THE FOETUS, COTYLEDONS, AND FOETAL MEMBRANES IN THE SHEEP DURING THE LAST HALF OF GESTATION (MEANS ± S.E.)

GESTATION AGE (Days)	NUMBER	FOETAL WEIGHT (Kg)	COTYLEDONARY WEIGHT (Gm)	MEMBRANE WEIGHT (Gm)
86–98	21	0.65	562 ± 25	125 ± 7
110–127	23	2.29	409 ± 23	167 ± 13
130–143	30	3.54	402 ± 9	224 ± 11

gestation, but varying in time with each species, the weight of the foetus comes to exceed that of the placenta. The placental cotyledons reach their maximal weight just over halfway through gestation in goats and sheep (Table 7; Cloete, 1939; Barcroft, 1946). In the rat, mouse, and guinea pig placental weight reaches a maximum rather later and appears to decline at the very end (Flexner and Pohl, 1941; McLaren, 1965). It also appeared to decline in the rabbit (Barcroft and Rothschild, 1932), though more numerous measurements have thrown doubt on this conclusion (Harding and Shelley, unpublished). In man and the rhesus monkey, mean placental weight continues to increase until term. Figure 10 illustrates these changes in man and the guinea pig. These relations become important when we consider the relative O_2 consumptions of foetus and placenta at different gestational ages and in different species. At term the mean weight of the placenta (excluding the membranes) varies greatly when expressed as a proportion of the foetal weight,

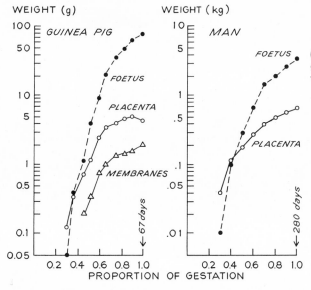

Fig. 10.—Growth of the foetus and placenta. (In man, from the data of Walker, 1954, and guinea pig, from the data of Ibsen, 1929; the weights are plotted on logarithmic scales.)

TABLE 8.—WEIGHTS OF FOETUS AND PLACENTA AT BIRTH IN MAN AND SOME COMMON LABORATORY SPECIES

AUTHORS	SPECIES	WEIGHT OF FOETUS AT BIRTH (GM)	WEIGHT OF PLACENTA AT TERM (GM)	PLACENTAL: FOETAL WEIGHT (%)
Duncan, Lodge, and Baskett (1960)	Man	3,500	500	14
	Pig	1,300	200	15
	Sheep	4,500	350*	8
	Rhesus monkey	500	100	20
Pohl and Flexner (1941)	Cat	100	15.5	15
Harding and Shelley (unpublished)	Rabbit	50	4	8
Eckstein, McKeown, and Record (1955)	Guinea pig	85	5	6
Campbell, Innes, and Kosterlitz (1953)	Rat	4	0.45	11
McLaren (1965)	Mouse	1	0.09	9

* Placentomes only (i.e., excluding membranes).

from ~6% in the guinea pig to ~20% in the rhesus monkey (Table 8). In man it is ~14%. Without more information it is not possible to interpret these facts. They could be due in part to the difference in the amounts of maternal tissue or of blood remaining in the placentas of different species. It is not always clear whether the foetus was weighed after its fur or wool had dried (although this is unlikely to introduce a serious error), or whether the differences are due to variations in the water contents of placenta or foetus. Weight alone is likely to be an imprecise measure of placental function (even when infarcts are excluded), but other morphometric variables (e.g., the effective area of gas exchange, the "vasculo-syncytial membrane" of Aherne and Dunnill in man) are expressed in terms of placental volume or weight. Perhaps they should also be expressed in terms of dry weight, or of amino-nitrogen before and after washing out the blood, to provide a basis for comparison which might be less dependent upon the casual events of delivery.

Comparative Histology

There are many good descriptions of the species variations in placental histology, and it is easy to see why this work has been done. The organization of maternal and foetal tissues within the placenta of different species constituted a challenging problem, which bore upon the origins of viviparity and was a source of material on which to base ideas about the evolution of species. The efforts of his-

tologists were, therefore, directed first toward a description and analysis of placental cytology, then to classification, and latterly to histochemistry and the improvement of detailed information by the use of the electron microscope. It is no exaggeration to say that more and more excellent work has been done on the comparative histology of the placenta than on most other aspects. And if the information available is not always what physiologists or other experimentalists need for new purposes (e.g., in quantitative terms), they have only themselves to blame for not asking.

In 1909, Grosser introduced a new unifying concept which had a great influence. He divided placentas (chorio-allantoic placentas) into four types, differing in the presence or absence of the maternal tissues, and hence in the number of tissue layers that were left to form the placental membrane between maternal and foetal blood. Placentas in which all layers were present were called epithelio-chorial (Table 9). Those in which the maternal surface epithelium was absent were called syndesmochorial. Those in which only the endometrial vessel walls were present were called endotheliochorial, while those in which even the vessel walls were gone, so that the chorionic villi were bathed in maternal blood, were called haemochorial. To this list, subsequent authors added further types, of which the most important, from our point of view, is the haemoendothelial, in which the chorionic trophoderm is absent as well as the maternal tissues, leaving only the foetal capillary walls between the two

TABLE 9.—HISTOLOGICAL CLASSIFICATION OF PLACENTAS

TISSUES SEPARATING FOETAL AND MATERNAL BLOOD

	MATERNAL TISSUE (UTERINE MUCOUS MEMBRANE)			FOETAL TISSUE			
HISTOLOGICAL TYPE	Endothelium	Connective Tissue	Epithelium	Tropho-blast	Connective Tissue	Endo-thelium	TYPICAL SPECIES
Epitheliochorial	+	+	+	+	+	+	Pig
Syndesmochorial	+	+	−	+	+	+	Sheep, goat, cow
Endotheliochorial	+	−	−	+	+	+	Cat, dog
Haemochorial	−	−	−	+	+	+	Man, rhesus monkey
Haemoendothelial	−	−	−	−	±	+	Rabbit, guinea pig, rat, mouse

Based on Amoroso (1952).

circulations (Amoroso, 1952; Wimsatt, 1962). With more information and better methods the classification of species has undergone some revision with time. The species with which we are presently concerned are now classified as in Table 9.

From the time when this histological classification was first introduced it greatly influenced the ideas of anatomists, and of the rather few physiologists who concerned themselves with the placenta, because it was thought that the number of tissue layers within the placental membrane determined its thickness and permeability. Haemochorial or haemoendothelial placentas were considered likely to be the most efficient, and epitheliochorial or syndesmochorial the least efficient. However, methods for measuring placental efficiency were not available. Subsequent investigations showed that the organization of the membrane was much more variable than was at first supposed, even within a single placenta. Some parts of the placental membrane, particularly those at which the vascular channels of one side approach those of the other side, are much thinner than other parts. Consequently, "parts of the placental membrane in epithelio- syndesmo- and endothelio-chorial placentas may actually be no thicker or involve any more layers than the barrier in many haemochorial placentas, but there may, of course, be quantitative differences between species in the amount of surface represented by such thin areas" (Wimsatt, 1962). Within a single species, the placenta may change its histological class during gestation. The rabbit starts off with an epitheliochorial placenta, and it is not until the last three days of gestation that this becomes a predominantly haemoendothelial placenta (Amoroso, 1952). So the views of histologists have gradually changed, and Dempsey (1960) has written that "the physiological inference

that the epitheliochorial placenta is inefficient, whereas the haemochorial placenta is efficient, is hardly supported by measurements of the rates of growth of the foetuses in the different species." This is certainly true.

Yet there is one important series of observations which lend some support to the possible functional significance of the Grosser classification. In 1941, Pohl and Flexner showed that the transfer rates of a radioisotope of sodium per unit weight of guinea pig or rat (haemochorial) placenta was much greater than that in the cat (endotheliochorial). To some extent this difference was compensated for by a relatively larger placenta in the cat. There may be other factors involved (e.g., different blood flow rates on either side of the area of exchange in the various species). More information is needed, but the results are interesting.

Although the Grosser classification is of uncertain value for physiology, no better system of classification has been devised. The work which its formulation engendered has been of great value in providing excellent histological studies of the placenta in many different species. The placenta is a complex organ, which is concerned not only with gas transfer by simple diffusion. It is also involved in the maintenance of osmotic equilibrium between the maternal and foetal circulations, and with the facilitated transport of some material (e.g., glucose and possibly amino acids; Widdas, 1961). It maintains a differential permeability to salts and a potential gradient between its surfaces, said to be as much as 30 mv (the foetal circulation being negative). It modifies or elaborates the structure of hormones and has a considerable O_2 consumption. It contains several different cell types which may be concerned with different synthetic or transfer functions. The diffusion of oxygen and carbon dioxide across this complex structure is bound to be affected by these other activities which, however, may take place mainly in areas other than those which are primarily concerned with gas exchange. The question of whether the placenta is in this sense made up of different functional units is still unresolved.

REFERENCES

Aherne, W., and Dunnill, M. S.: Morphometry of the human placenta, Brit. M. Bull. 22:5–8, 1966,a.

Aherne, W., and Dunnill, M. S.: Quantitative aspects of placental structure, J. Path. & Bact. 91:123–140, 1966,b.

Amoroso, E. C.: Placentation, in Parkes, A. S. (ed.): *Marshall's Physiology of Reproduction* (3d ed.; London: Longmans, Green & Co., Ltd., 1952), vol. 2, pp. 127–311.

Barcroft, J.: *Researches on Pre-Natal Life* (Oxford: Blackwell Scientific Publications, 1946).

Barcroft, J., and Barron, D. H.: Observations on the form and relations of the maternal and fetal vessels in the placenta of the sheep, Anat. Rec. 94:569–595, 1946.

Barcroft, J., and Rothschild, P.: The volume of blood in the uterus during pregnancy, J. Physiol. 76:447–459, 1932.

Barron, D. H., and Meschia, G.: A comparative study of the exchange of the respiratory gases across the placenta, Cold Spring, Harb. Symp. Quant. Biol. 19:93–101, 1954.

Bartels, H., and Moll, W.: Passage of inert substances and oxygen in the human placenta, Pflüger's Arch. ges Physiol. 280:165–177, 1964.

Bartels, H.; Moll, W., and Metcalfe, J.: Physiology of gas exchange in the human placenta, Am. J. Obst. & Gynec. 84:1714–1730, 1962.

Cloete, J. H. L.: Prenatal growth in the merino sheep, Onderstepoort J. Vet. Sc. 13:417–558, 1939.

Crawford, J. M.: Vascular anatomy of the human placenta, Am. J. Obst. & Gynec. 84:1543–1567, 1962.

Dempsey, E. W.: Histophysical Considerations, in Villee, C. A. (ed.): *The Placenta and Fetal Membranes* (Baltimore: The Williams & Wilkins Company, 1960), pp. 29–35.

Dunnill, M. S.: Postnatal growth of the lung, Thorax 17:329–333, 1962.

Flexner, L. B., and Pohl, H. A.: The transfer of radioactive sodium across the placenta of the white rat, J. Cell. & Comp. Physiol. 18:49–59, 1941.

Grosser, O.: *Vergleichende Anatomie und Entwicklungsgeschichte der Eihäute und der Placenta mit besonderer Berücksichtigung des Menschen* (Vienna: Braumüller, 1909).

Ibsen, H. L.: Prenatal growth in guinea pigs with special reference to environmental factors affecting weight at birth, J. Exper. Zool. 51:51–91, 1929.

McLaren, A.: Placental weight loss in late pregnancy, J. Reprod. Fertil. 9:343–346, 1965.

Metcalfe, J.; Moll, W.; Bartels, H.; Hilpert, P., and Parer, J. T.: Transfer of carbon monoxide and nitrous oxide in the artificially perfused sheep placenta, Circulation Res. 16:95–101, 1965.

Mossman, H. W.: The rabbit placenta and the problem of placental transmission, Am. J. Anat. 37:433–497, 1926.

Ramsey, E. M.: Circulation in the intervillous space of the primate placenta, Am. J. Obst. & Gynec. 84:1649–1663, 1962.

Steven, D. H.: Further observations on placental circulation in the sheep, J. Physiol. 183:13–15, 1966.

Strauss, L.; Goldenberg, N.; Hirota, K., and Okudaira, Y.: Structure of the human placenta; with observations on ultrastructure of the terminal chorionic villus. Birth defects, original article series, The National Foundation 1:13–26, 1965.

Tafani, A.: La circulation dans le placenta de quelques mammifères, Arch. ital. Biol. 7:49–57, 1887.

Walker, J.: Weight of the human fetus and of its placenta, Cold Spring Harb. Symp. Quant. Biol. 19:39–40, 1954.

Widdas, W. F.: Transport mechanisms in the foetus, Brit. M. Bull. 17:107–111, 1961.

Wilkin, P.: Etude des facteurs physiques conditionnant les échanges transplacentaires, in Snoeck, J. (ed.): *Le Placenta Humain* (Paris: Masson & Cie, 1958), pp. 194–211.

Wimsatt, W. A.: New histological observations on the placenta of the sheep, Am. J. Anat. 87:391–458, 1950.

Wimsatt, W. A.: Some aspects of the comparative anatomy of the mammalian placenta, Am. J. Obst. & Gynec. 84:1568–1594, 1962.

Wulf, H.: Der Gasaustausch in der reifen Plazenta des Menschen, Ztschr. Geburtsh. u. Gynäk. 158:117–134, 269–319, 1962.

3

Oxygen Transfer Across the Placenta

Observations *In Vivo*

THE RESPIRATORY FUNCTION
OF THE BLOOD

IN 1930, Anselmino and Hoffman and Eastman separately drew attention to the fact that the changes in the blood of a human infant after birth are very like those in an acclimatized mountaineer descending to sea level. At birth the haemoglobin concentration (Williamson, 1916) and the O_2 carrying capacity of the blood is high and the O_2 affinity is greater than that in the adult. During the next few weeks, in a normal infant born at term, both the O_2 carrying capacity and the O_2 affinity of the blood fall. This suggested that the Po_2 in foetal arterial blood was relatively low, as the work of Huggett (1927) on foetal goats, and of Eastman (1930) and Haselhorst and Stromberger (1931) on the cord blood of human infants showed. The stage was thus set for the very reasonable hypothesis that these haematological changes represent a necessary and biologically important adaptation. These are some of the few facts that are usually taught to medical and veterinary students about placental gas exchange. They are important facts, as an understanding of the respiratory function of the blood is a necessary prerequisite for any discussion of gas exchange. But they are not the only facts, and in some species and at most gestational ages it may be that they are less important than other facts.

Let us consider the O_2 carrying capacity (which may be equated with the haemoglobin concentration multiplied by a constant factor) of foetal blood.

In man and sheep, the O_2 carrying capacity of blood rises rapidly early in gestation, and more slowly during the last third. At term, it usually exceeds that of adults. The scatter between individual foetal observations is large (e.g., Barcroft, 1946; Born, Dawes, and Mott, 1956), in part because the O_2 carrying capacity is labile; for instance, it rises at once during hypoxaemia. In the rhesus monkey and rabbit there is no great difference between the O_2 carrying capacity of foetal blood at term and that of adult blood. The rises in haemoglobin concentration during gestation in man and pig are contrasted in Figure 11; that of man increases earlier and to a higher value. Table 10 shows that there is a wide variation in the relative haemoglobin concentration as between the infant at birth and the adult; in some species that of the newborn is greater, in others (e.g., pig and rat) it is less. So it is not true that in all species the infant at term is better off than the adult in this respect, nor is it true of any species early in gestation. On the other hand, in all these species there is a fall in haemoglobin concentration in the two weeks after birth. This corresponds to the time of physiological jaundice and (in some species) of rapid increase in weight (e.g., in the rat and rabbit), so interpretation is complicated. The relatively low Po_2 of the foetal environment may have acted as a stimulus to haematopoiesis, but the significance of this for survival is not as sure as at first appeared. Some rats (born with a relatively low haemoglobin) are stillborn or runts, but so are some sheep (born with a high haemoglobin). Some human foetuses survive until 34 weeks' gestation, although their haemoglo-

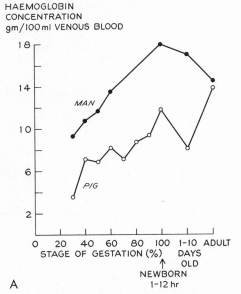

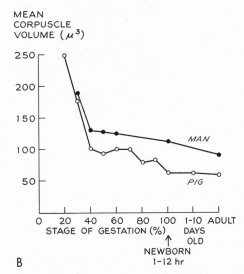

Fig. 11.—Changes in haemoglobin concentration and mean corpuscular volume with age in man and pigs. (From Dittmer and Grebe [eds.], 1958, 1959.)

bin concentration has been reduced by erythroblastosis to 4 gm/100 ml or less; it is normally at least 15 gm/100 ml by then. So, although a high haemoglobin concentration is helpful in enabling the same quantity of foetal blood to carry more O_2, it is not decisive. This is just one of many factors which must be considered.

One of the factors which might be important early in gestation is the size of the red cells. The mean corpuscular volume is large during the first third of gestation (Fig. 11) and it seems likely that more force would be needed to push large cells through capillaries. On the other hand, at this age the number of red cells per unit volume of blood is low.

The haemoglobin-oxygen dissociation curves are different in foetal and maternal bloods. Solutions of human foetal and maternal haemoglobins, separated from their respective cells, when dialyzed against a common solution have identical O_2 dissociation curves (Allen, Wyman, and Smith, 1953). So the difference must reside in the electrolyte content, total base content, or carbonic anhydrase activity of the cellular environment (Nechtman and Huisman, 1964), rather than in the different properties of the foetal or adult haemoglobin molecule.

TABLE 10.—HAEMOGLOBIN CONCENTRATIONS IN NEWBORNS AND ADULTS
OF DIFFERENT SPECIES

	HAEMOGLOBIN (GM/100 ML WHOLE BLOOD)		
SPECIES	Newborn at Term	Adult	SOURCES
Man	18	15	Albritton (1952); Dittmer and Grebe (1958, 1959)
Pig	11.8	13.8	Wintrobe and Schumacker (1936)
Sheep	15	10	Cross, Dawes, and Mott (1959)
Cat	12	12	Wintrobe and Schumacker (1936)
Rabbit	14.5	12.8–14.7	Mott (1965)
Rat	7.6–10.3	12.8–14.9	Nicholas (1928); Wintrobe and Schumacker (1936); Brumer, Eyre, and Carlson (1938)
Goat	11	13	Albritton (1952)

This is common ground; what is uncertain is the biological significance which may be attached to the difference. Human foetuses with erythroblastosis can survive and continue to grow to a normal size for their age after a transfusion of adult red cells, sufficient to replace most of their own haemolysed red cells. But we don't yet know whether the former, after exposure to the foetal intravascular environment, still have the same HbO_2 dissociation curve as they had before transfusion.

As Barron and Meschia (1954) have pointed out, there are large differences in the relative positions of the maternal and foetal HbO_2 dissociation curves *in vitro* in different species. The difference is large in the sheep and small in the rabbit (Fig. 12); it is negligible in the elephant halfway through gestation (Bartels, 1964). Interpretation *in vivo* is complicated by the Bohr shift, the displacement of the HbO_2 dissociation curve to the left with increasing pH, which thereby increases the amount of O_2 which can be taken up at a given partial pressure, e.g., as a result of release of CO_2 during passage of foetal blood through the umbilical capillaries. Conversely, the maternal HbO_2 dissociation curve is displaced in the opposite direction (as a result of CO_2 uptake) and this leads to a greater loss of O_2 at the same Po_2. The effect of these changes, in opposing directions in maternal and foetal bloods, could be large, and Bartels, Moll, and Metcalfe (1962) calculated that because of them and the higher O_2 affinity of foetal blood, that blood is

$\sim$13% more saturated with O_2 at the same O_2 pressure. Their computations were based on values for umbilical arterial (pH 7.24) and venous (pH 7.32) bloods on human vaginal delivery which are lower than many would accept as representative of normal intrauterine life. The arteriovenous difference (0.08 pH units) is greater than that usually observed in foetal animals (0.03 pH units) in a steady state; it now seems likely that their large difference was due to an unsteady state due to the conditions of delivery.

There is no doubt that these mechanisms act advantageously to the foetus, and we need to understand them thoroughly, but they may not play so large a part as has been generally supposed. It would be interesting if the haemoglobin concentration and O_2 affinity of foetal blood rose more rapidly in foetuses, part of whose placenta was removed early in gestation. Can the foetus thus compensate for the loss of placental tissue? And does the remainder of the placenta also compensate by further growth and development as does the liver?

HISTORICAL

In the 1930s two facts seemed sure. First, that though the normal foetus had a sufficient supply of O_2 it was at a low partial pressure, a circumstance which led someone, probably Barcroft or Eastman (but perhaps derived from the provocative paper by Anselmino and Hoffman) to coin the phrase "Mount Everest *in utero*." Secondly, it was thought that the anatomy of the placental vessels indicated that flow was countercurrent, and the high O_2 carrying capacity and high O_2 affinity of foetal blood at term also favoured placental gas exchange. But if the conditions for placental gas exchange were so favourable, how did it come about that the foetal Po_2 was so low? It was in order to explain this fact that the hypothesis was proposed that the placental membrane was relatively impermeable to oxygen.

The placental membrane is not only a complex structure through which some substances diffuse and others may receive a helping hand in passing. It is also an almost complete barrier against the transfer of red cells between the maternal and foetal bloodstreams, not perfect perhaps, but so nearly perfect as to deserve the word "barrier." This word was then adopted as a synonym for the placental "membrane," and for the past 30 years either has been used almost without distinction. The idea that the placental membrane is relatively impermeable

Fig. 12.—Haemoglobin-oxygen dissociation curves of foetal and maternal blood in sheep and rabbits. (Redrawn from Barron and Meschia, 1954.)

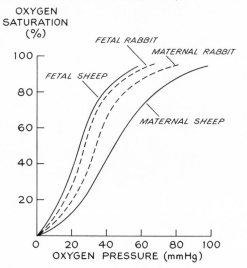

to oxygen, which was first formulated to explain an awkward set of facts, was given a respectable and important position by this use of words. It is an idea which has never been tested by direct experiment, as Barron (1960) has pointed out, and yet has had a great influence upon obstetricians and physiologists. It has not been tested because it is difficult to make the necessary measurements, and especially to be sure that the results depend solely on the permeability of the placental membrane uninfluenced by any other physiological circumstance.

Barron and Meschia (1954) estimated the mean Po_2 diffusion gradient across the placenta, assuming that the blood samples which they obtained from uterine and umbilical arteries and veins were representative of blood entering or leaving the area of gas exchange and that the direction of flow on the two sides was wholly countercurrent. They used a Bohr integration method to calculate the mean Po_2 and made the explicit assumption that all the O_2 which left the maternal blood entered the foetal blood. They found a mean diffusion gradient of 9–14 mm Hg in the rabbit and of 33–48 mm Hg in the sheep near term. An analogous, but not identical, method of calculation in man was based on the measurement of the Po_2 in intervillous space blood samples. This gave a diffusion gradient of ∼20 mm Hg. It can be challenged on the ground that such intervillous samples may have been taken from anywhere in the space, and indeed repeated samples from different areas give variable results. However, it is also true that such variations as have been recorded will not affect the estimated diffusion gradient greatly.

These large species differences in the calculated Po_2 diffusion gradients were not challenged; they were accepted (as silence gave consent) as reasonable estimates, and they were explained as a result of differences in placental types. Now, looking back at this evidence critically, the very large differences do raise some suspicion as to the validity of the measurements. Were the experimental subjects really in a steady state and, in each species, in a comparable (not necessarily a "normal") condition? It is more difficult to handle foetal rabbits (weighing 30–50 Gm) than foetal sheep (3–5 kg) and to get good blood samples from them without disturbing their condition unduly. These are difficult experiments to do and, in the days before gas analysis was simplified by the use of polarographic electrodes, it involved much painstaking work and the use of comparatively large blood samples. Also the low values recorded by Barron and Meschia in

the uterine venous blood of rabbits at term (O_2 saturation 19–37%; mean Po_2 25 mm Hg) is surprising, and it would be worth repeating these observations with serial measurements of arterial pH to demonstrate that both mother and foetus were in a physiologically normal and steady state. It was noticed by Harding and Shelley (unpublished) that foetal rabbits delivered by caesarean section under general anaesthesia with minimal handling had blood lactate concentrations of 3–6 mEq/1 (normal ∼1 mg/1), rising sequentially with each littermate delivered; this is convincing evidence of progressive hypoxaemia.

The apparent large diffusion gradients for oxygen could still be regarded as circumstantial evidence for a relative impermeability of the placental membrane but for four things:

1. The evidence for countercurrent flow is under heavy attack, as explained in the preceding chapter.

2. The O_2 consumption of the placental tissue itself is far from negligible.

3. No account was taken of the possibility of uneven distribution of flow in the maternal and foetal circulations, i.e., of a perfusion:perfusion ratio (on the analogy of the pulmonary ventilation:perfusion ratio) which was not ideal.

4. Equilibrium of gas transfer might not be reached during a single passage of the placental capillary bed.

Longo, Power, and Forster (1965) calculated a placental diffusion coefficient in 5 anaesthetized sheep near term for carbon monoxide of 0.50±0.14 (S.D.) ml/mm Hg per kg foetal weight, whereas that for oxygen was much less, only 0.12 ± 0.04. This at once suggests that the transfer of O_2 across the placenta is far from being a matter of diffusion between two blood streams, uncomplicated by other physiological considerations. The difference between CO and O_2 was ascribed to a possible combination of errors in measurement of foetal (and perhaps placental) O_2 consumption, of vascular shunts, and an uneven distribution of blood flow. All these are certainly strong candidates for consideration.

The O_2 Consumption of the Placenta

In 1952, Huggett and Hammond considered the possibility that the large O_2 gradient across the placenta was due to active placental tissue metabolism, of which there is now much evidence. They concluded from measurements in the literature of the O_2 consumption of placental tissue slices that this was of the same order as that of other active organs such as the pancreas and kidney, but that "it is impossible to say it is sufficient or insufficient to impair oxygen diffusion." The problem was to determine whether this local consumption of O_2 was likely to modify the Po_2 gradient for the diffusion of O_2 across the placenta.

The O_2 consumption of the placental tissue might be both in series and in parallel with the area of gas exchange. If it were in series the principal effect expected would be to cause an apparent increase in the Po_2 gradient across the placental membrane between the maternal and foetal blood streams. This might be modified to a small extent if some placental O_2 consumption were to take place not only within the area of gas exchange but also along the vessels leading to and from this area (Fig. 13, A). This seems plausible on histological grounds; in the lung gas exchange is not limited to the vessels of the alveolar membrane. If some of the O_2 consumption of the placental tissue were in parallel with the area of gas exchange (Fig. 13, B), the effect expected on the maternal side would be a loss of O_2 from the

Fig. 13.—Schematic diagram of possible sites of placental O_2 uptake (stippled area) in series, **A**, or in parallel, **B**, with the area of gas exchange.

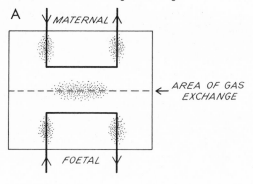

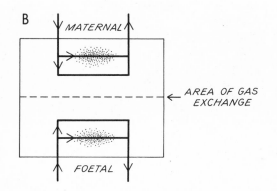

total volume of maternal blood passing through the placenta without a decrease in the effective transplacental Po_2 gradient. On the foetal side, O_2 consumption in parallel may be regarded as a small addition to foetal O_2 consumption. Within the placenta there must be O_2 consumption in the supporting structures (which Aherne and Dunnill call nonparenchyma), and much of this may be supplied by vessels in parallel with those going to and from the area of gas exchange. The consequences of the complex arrangements shown in Figure 13, A and B, both of which probably exist in the placenta, are not easy to predict. Much would depend on the relative size of foetal and placental O_2 consumption. So it seemed better to proceed empirically at first, by planning an experiment which might indicate whether the effect of placental O_2 consumption was likely to be small or large.

A study of hypothetical diagrams, such as those of Figure 13, suggested that one simplification could be made by experimental means, i.e., by eliminating the O_2 consumption of the foetus. Mature foetal lambs were delivered by caesarean section under chloralose anaesthesia (Campbell, Dawes, Fishman, Hyman, and James, 1966). The foetus was removed and replaced by a pump, the placenta and membranes being left *in situ*. When the pump was started, the umbilical arterial and venous blood soon came into equilibrium at a Po_2 much below that in the maternal arterial blood. When the maternal Po_2 was ~90 mm Hg, umbilical Po_2 was ~50 mm Hg. When the mother was given O_2 to breathe in place of air her arterial Po_2 rose to ~300 mm Hg; umbilical Po_2 came into equilibrium within a few minutes at ~90 mm Hg (Fig. 14). The difference between these results can be attributed to the shape of the HbO_2 dissociation curve. The removal of the same quantity of O_2 from the maternal blood by the placental tissues will cause a greater absolute fall in Po_2 when the maternal arterial Po_2 is 300 mm Hg than when it is 90 mm Hg. It is also possible that both maternal placental flow and placental O_2 consumption may have altered when the ewe was given O_2 to breathe in place of air.

The essential feature of these observations was that gas exchange was studied when foetal O_2 uptake from the placenta was reduced to zero; i.e., when the O_2 content of umbilical arterial and venous blood was identical. The latter result can be achieved with less surgical interference, by ventilating the foetus (still attached to an intact placenta *in situ*) and adjusting the ventilation. In practice,

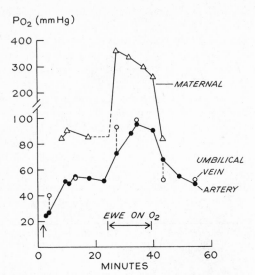

Fig. 14.—Sheep's placenta *in situ* at 141 days' gestation, perfused by a pump (started at the arrow) through the umbilical vessels with heparinised foetal blood. The umbilical arterial (●) and venous (○) P_{O_2} rapidly came into equilibrium at a value much below that in maternal arterial blood (△), whether the ewe was ventilated with air or O_2 (Campbell *et al.*, 1966).

measurement of O_2 content takes a little while, and it is easier to use the P_{O_2} (which must be measured in any event) at equal pH and P_{CO_2} as a measure of O_2 content. So the foetus was ventilated with a gas mixture containing ~5% CO_2 and a variable quantity of O_2 (21–50%) in N_2. It then proved comparatively easy to adjust the P_{O_2} and P_{CO_2} of umbilical arterial and venous bloods to be equal, whether the whole foetus was delivered from the uterus or only its neck (to give access to the trachea). The results obtained with this preparation were no different from those when the foetus was replaced with a pump, except that it was now possible to maintain a much higher umbilical blood flow, closer to that observed in the intact, unventilated foetus. In both types of preparation, when the O_2 uptake of the foetus from the placenta was zero, the P_{O_2} of umbilical blood was much less than that of maternal arterial blood (Fig. 15). In these circumstances, the P_{O_2} of maternal cotyledonary placental venous blood (uncontaminated with myometrial venous blood) also was low, much lower than that of maternal arterial blood, a fact which clearly indicated that a considerable quantity of O_2 was being removed by the placenta.

The O_2 consumption of the placenta and foetal membranes *in situ* were measured. At the end of an

experiment in which the foetus was replaced by a pump, the ewe was killed by severing the aorta, so that the maternal blood supply to the placenta was quickly arrested. The P_{O_2} in the 350 ml blood circulating through the foetal side of the placenta fell over 7 minutes from 58 to less than 10 mm Hg, as O_2 was removed by the placenta and foetal membranes from the umbilical vessels. This suggested that steady state measurements could be obtained if the umbilical O_2 supply was maintained by a ventilated foetus. In subsequent experiments a mature foetal lamb was delivered, but was left attached to the placenta by an intact umbilical cord. The lamb was ventilated, the ewe was killed, and the O_2 consumption of the placenta and foetal membranes was calculated either as the difference between the O_2 uptake of the lamb (measured from a closed circuit) before and after occlusion of the umbilical cord, or as the product of umbilical blood flow (measured with a cannulated electromagnetic flowmeter) and arteriovenous O_2 difference. These two methods agreed well. In 5 lambs of 137–143 days gestation (foetal weight 4.1 ± 0.4 kg; term is ~147 days), the mean O_2 consumption of the lambs was 20.1 ± 1.5 (S.E.) ml/min, while that of the placenta and membranes was 8.4 ± 1.0 ml/min. The O_2 consumption of the placenta and membranes together was 30–72% of that of the foetus. The mean O_2 consumption of the foetus agreed well with that of previous estimates by other methods, and also with that observed in newly delivered unanaesthetized lambs at term in a neutral thermal environment.

The O_2 consumption of single placental cotyledons (separated from the extra-cotyledonary chorion) was measured as the product of venous outflow and arteriovenous O_2 difference, after tying off the maternal blood supply to the cotyledon. This gave a figure of 1.04 ± 0.10 ml/100 Gm wet weight per minute. It may be an underestimate because of surface cooling, exposure, and handling, and the uncertainty of whether all the maternal portions of the cotyledon were adequately oxygenated. The many estimates in the literature, using placental tissue slices in several species, and the few measurements on isolated perfused human placentas (usually with rather low rates of umbilical flow) give a range of O_2 consumption whose upper values coincide with this figure of ~1 ml/100 Gm min (for references see Campbell *et al.*, 1966). The agreement is good when the differences in species and methods are considered. The mean figure of 8.4 ± 1.0 ml O_2/min quoted in the preceding paragraph for whole intact sheep's placenta and membranes at term *in situ* is rather more than would be expected on this basis, possibly because the placenta and membranes were kept warm within the uterus and were not handled.

So far, then, the results are reasonably consistent and support the view that the O_2 consumption of the placental tissue is, under the experimental conditions, far from negligible. It is possible that blood flow through the maternal side of the placenta was less than it might have been under other circumstances; this would have led to a relatively lower umbilical Po_2 and a larger transplacental Po_2 gradient in the absence of foetal O_2 uptake from the placenta. The effect of changes in maternal blood flow would certainly be well worth further investigation.

The fact that there is a large transplacental Po_2 gradient in a single cotyledon, isolated from the surrounding membranes, and in which O_2 uptake by the umbilical vessels is zero, suggests that placental O_2 consumption may be largely in series with the area of gas exchange. It is unlikely that such a large gradient could be explained by consumption in parallel on the foetal side. The effect of placental metabolism has been discussed in terms of O_2 consumption rather than CO_2 production because O_2 is less diffusible, and the gradient for O_2 is greater and will be disturbed less by local production of acid metabolites. With these reservations the arguments should also apply to CO_2 diffusion from the foetal to the maternal blood stream.

There are a number of interesting aspects to placental O_2 consumption which remain to be explored. In all species at some period of gestation there is more placenta than foetus. In the sheep, the placental cotyledons weigh as much as the foetus at 80–90 days gestation (a little over half way to term); in man, the curves of foetal and placental weight cross at about 17 weeks gestation (just under half way to term). There is then a real possibility that the O_2 consumption of the placenta may be as great or greater than that of the foetus. This possibility is reinforced by the fact that the O_2 consumption of human placental tissue slices falls by more than 50% during the last half of gestation (Tremblay, Sybulski, and Maughan, 1965). It is also possible that the

Fig. 15.—Maternal arterial Po_2, and umbilical arterial and venous Po_2 when equalized either by mechanical perfusion of the placenta ($\triangle$), or by ventilation of the sheep foetus after delivery ($\circ$), or *in utero* ($\bullet$). The maternal arterial Po_2 is always greater, the difference increasing as maternal arterial Po_2 is raised even though foetal O_2 uptake from the placenta is zero. (Redrawn from Campbell *et al.*, 1966, to the same scale as Fig. 16.)

Fig. 16.—The normal relation between foetal and maternal arterial blood Po_2 in the sheep foetus. Simultaneous measurements were made with the ewes breathing air ($\bullet$), receiving additional O_2 ($\triangle$), or ventilated with 3, 6 or 10% O_2 ($\circ$). (Redrawn from Comline, Silver, and Silver, 1965.)

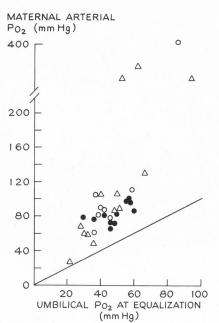

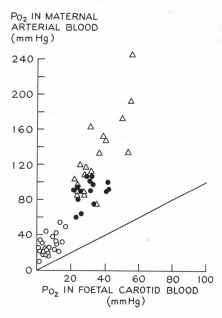

O_2 consumption of the placenta may be altered by hormones or drugs. And one may suppose that under conditions of maternal hypoxaemia (as on sudden exposure to a rarified atmosphere) or reduction in maternal placental flow (during maternal haemorrhage or traumatic shock) the placental tissues may be supplied with O_2 in preference to the foetus. The placenta may survive such conditions although the foetus dies.

Finally, the relatively high O_2 consumption of the placenta, combined with the slope of the maternal HbO_2 dissociation curve, provides a reasonable explanation of the fact that a large rise in maternal Po_2, as on breathing 100% O_2, causes only a comparatively small rise in foetal Po_2 (uneven distribution of blood flow in the placenta is an additional reason; see below). And conversely, it helps to explain the comparatively small fall in foetal Po_2 during maternal hypoxaemia. There is a striking resemblance between Figure 15, which shows the relation between maternal arterial and umbilical Po_2 when foetal O_2 uptake from the placenta was zero, and Figure 16, which shows the relation between maternal arterial and foetal carotid Po_2 in sheep under normal circumstances (Comline, Silver, and Silver, 1965). Barron (1960) observed that foetal lambs in the Peruvian Andes (with a maternal arterial Po_2 of about 47 mm Hg at 15,000 feet) had an arterial Po_2 within the range of those at sea level, and quoted similar conclusions by Kaiser, Cummings, Reynolds, and Marbarger (1958) who placed pregnant ewes in a low-pressure chamber at 385 mm Hg for 10 days. He interpreted his observations by saying that "we are confronted by evidence indicating that the fetus maintains the oxygen tension in its blood at a low level; that it is not a victim of its environment," and suggested that the foetus elects to develop in a low oxygen tension. It now seems that, as a result of the functional organization of the placenta, the foetus has little choice in the matter.

Yet there is an aspect of the situation which Barron's provocative discussion first raised. Why is the foetus placed in this particular type of environment? It is hard to believe that a low foetal Po_2 should be a necessary and inescapable feature of any conceivable placental design. For instance, with a less complex placental membrane and a more efficient vascular arrangement, foetal Po_2 might be increased considerably. There are various possible explanations which may be suggested. A higher foetal arterial Po_2 (60–80 mm Hg) might be undesirable, because of toxic effects or for circulatory

reasons, such as premature constriction of the ductus arteriosus or vasodilatation in the lungs. Or the necessary increase in placental size and complexity may have been incompatible with other aspects of placental structure, such as rapid growth, hormone production, transfer functions, and detachment after birth. Or perhaps it was just unnecessary. Provided there is a large enough systemic blood flow to the foetal tissues, providing the O_2 carrying capacity of its blood is great enough, the O_2 saturation of foetal blood is clearly sufficient to supply tissue needs with some margin of safety.

UNEVEN DISTRIBUTION OF PLACENTAL FLOWS

Uneven distribution of blood flow, as between the maternal and foetal sides of different areas of gas exchange within the placenta, will lead to an increase in the net transplacental Po_2 gradient just as certainly as does maldistribution of ventilation and perfusion in the lung. This concept raises a number of interesting questions.

If flow in the maternal blood spaces and the foetal villi within the placenta is pulsatile, there might be moment-to-moment variations in the perfusion : perfusion ratio because the maternal and foetal heart rates are usually out of phase. On both sides, arterial inflow is certainly pulsatile. On the venous side, flow in the common umbilical vein in the abdomen of a foetal lamb is almost non-pulsatile; but this is a long way from the cotyledonary veins, the intervening vessels are very distensible and likely to damp out pulsations, and the path lengths from individual cotyledons to each umbilical vein are different. It may not be easy to obtain direct evidence as to whether flow in the placenta is pulsatile. One possible method might be to make it non-pulsatile on one side and look for rhythmic changes in the blood gases in the venous effluent from that side. For instance, umbilical vessels might be perfused at constant flow and a search might be made for rhythmic variations in umbilical venous Po_2 in time with the maternal heart rate. There is also the possibility that volume changes on one side of the placental vascular bed might influence the other side, if the supporting structures of the cotyledon are sufficiently rigid. If this were so, pressure variations on the maternal side might be transmitted to and detected on the foetal side, perfused at constant flow.

There is as yet no evidence of a local mechanism for the regulation of umbilical : maternal flow within a cotyledon. When the maternal flow to a single sheep's cotyledon was tied off while umbilical venous outflow was being measured there was no immediate change in umbilical flow, other than that attributable to the unavoidable mechanical disturbance. Umbilical arterial pressure was unchanged. The umbilical venous outflow gradually decreased over the next half hour, but this appeared to be more the result of visible spasm in the umbilical cotyledonary vessels than maternal ischaemia, since it began in some cotyledons even before the maternal vessels were tied. In the lung, this experiment would have been equivalent to stopping ventilation to a lobe of the lung and would have led to a rapid rise in local pulmonary vascular resistance and diversion of blood flow away from the unventilated area. Similarly, provided the foetus is ventilated so that it does not become asphyxiated, killing the mother by exsanguination causes little immediate alteration in total umbilical blood flow (to both cotyledons and membranes).

Power, Longo, Wagner, Kuhl, and Forster (1966) have measured relative blood flow in various placental regions by injection of macroaggregated albumin particles labeled with I^{125} or I^{131} into sheep. One isotope was injected into the ewe and the other into the lamb, and the distribution of the particles caught in the maternal and foetal villous capillaries was examined. They calculated that the ratios of maternal to foetal flow in a single cotyledon varied up to tenfold. They concluded that the maternal and foetal blood flows were unevenly distributed to their respective placental capillaries, and that the ratio of maternal to foetal capillary flow was not uniform. The validity of the latter conclusion (which, if correct, is important) depends on whether sufficient account was taken of the fact that the placental cotyledons are not homogeneous structures. They consist of both gas-exchanging areas (parenchyma) and supporting structures (non-parenchyma). Thus, it is not surprising that the ratio of flows in some areas of a cotyledon varied greatly; what is important is the ratio of flows in contiguous sheets of maternal and foetal capillaries. It is uncertain from the brief abstract quoted whether the method used was of adequate discrimination for this purpose. If the macroaggregated albumin particles were too large to pass through capillaries they cannot have reached them, and it must be difficult to decide what tissues they would have reached if they had been able to pass further, parenchyma or non-parenchyma.

To summarise, maldistribution of flow may exist within the placenta. There are theoretical reasons for supposing it may and no mechanism yet known which would adjust umbilical to maternal flow or *vice versa*. Direct experimental evidence is inconclusive. As yet, few experiments have been done on this interesting problem, which might have a considerable influence on the transplacental Po_2 gradient.

Placental Models

Understanding of placental physiology depends not only on physiological measurements *in vivo,* under as natural conditions as possible, but also on the construction of model systems whose properties may be examined for their approximation to reality. Such models have been designed to study the equilibration of gas transfer by graphical analysis, and to examine the factors which determine transplacental Po_2 gradients.

EQUILIBRATION OF GAS TRANSFER

In the lung of a normal man at rest, gas equilibration takes place well before the blood has passed the full length of the alveolar capillary. In the placenta, we do not know for sure whether or not equilibration is achieved during passage of the villous capillaries, but there is some evidence which bears on the point at issue.

Let us begin by considering what might be regarded as reasonable evidence of equilibration. This will depend on interpretation of the anatomical and physiological evidence as to the relative directions of flow on either side of the placenta, and on the location of the principal sites of O_2 consumption within the placental tissues. Only if flow is wholly concurrent must the Po_2 of maternal placental and umbilical venous blood be identical on equilibration. In the sheep, the Po_2 of maternal cotyledonary venous blood and of umbilical venous blood was not identical, even when foetal O_2 uptake from the placenta was reduced to zero (i.e., when gaseous diffusion across the placental membrane was minimal); the difference between the two varied from -11 to $+15$ mm Hg. So this approach is unlikely to be profitable.

The problem also is aggravated by the fact that at any given time there is only a limited quantity of oxygen in the maternal blood within the area of exchange. A small increase in the quantity of O_2 diffusing across the placenta must cause a fall in the maternal blood Po_2. Hence, if umbilical flow is increased, O_2 uptake into foetal blood from the placenta will reach a plateau whose height is determined by the fall in mean maternal Po_2 and the increased velocity of umbilical flow. Some other approach seemed desirable.

Ross (1967) has applied the method of graphical analysis of gas exchange to the placenta, and produced a model which may be useful in this connection. He assumed that the exchange of O_2 and CO_2 occurred in the same ratio in maternal and foetal blood (i.e., unaltered by the metabolism of intervening placental tissue or by exchange of nonvolatile acids or gases). Using nomograms for human foetal and maternal blood he drew lines on a Po_2:Pco_2 diagram to indicate the possible changes in Po_2 and Pco_2 at a series of different respiratory exchange ratios from 0.7–1.0. These lines radiate from the maternal and umbilical arterial points to intersect at partial pressures of Po_2 and Pco_2 intermediate between those in the maternal and umbilical arteries (Fig. 17). If the assumed respiratory exchange ratio was too low or too high the lines failed to intersect; thus, with the assumptions already stated, the range of possible exchange ratios was less than that from 0.7–1.0. The point of intersection of maternal and foetal lines of identical R (respiratory exchange ratio) value represents the theoretical point of equilibrium. If equilibrium is not attained, or if blood is shunted on either side of the placenta,

the effluent blood should have gas tensions deviating from the equilibrium point along the appropriate maternal and foetal R lines.

Ross found little published evidence suitable for comparison with his model. However, some of the data from human deliveries gave values for umbilical venous blood close to the theoretical equilibrium point (Fig. 17, UV), suggesting that in these instances equilibration had been achieved. Others gave respiratory exchange ratios outside the theoretical range, perhaps because of an unsteady state on delivery, because samples were not drawn simultaneously, or because of errors in analysis or other causes. The observation that in some instances there is a prima facie case for believing that equilibration is achieved is interesting in itself. The method of analysis is valuable as a different way of thinking about placental gas exchange.

MODELS OF BLOOD FLOW AND O_2 TRANSFER

Several models of placental blood flow and O_2 exchange have been considered (Noer, 1946; Lamport, 1954; Wilkin, 1958; Wulf, 1962; Bartels and Moll, 1964). The most useful function of these models has been to compare the relative efficiency for O_2 transfer of the various blood flow systems. Bartels and Moll used equations originally derived

Fig. 17.—Pco_2:Po_2 diagram of human maternal and foetal blood to show equal R (respiratory exchange ratio, 0.7–1.0) lines drawn from the maternal (MA) and umbilical (UA) arterial points. The point of intersection (e.g., at UV) indicates the point of theoretical equilibrium. If the umbilical vein blood coincides with this point, it could suggest that equilibrium is attained. The presence of maternal or foetal shunts would move the equilibrium point away from this along the respective maternal or foetal lines. (Redrawn from Ross, 1967.)

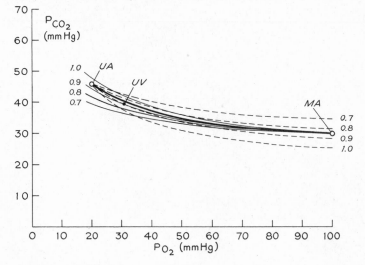

for studying heat transfer to perform the necessary calculations under defined and simplified conditions. They decided to ignore the O_2 consumption of the placenta and the effects of shunts and of uneven distribution of flow. The placenta was visualized as a uniform structure in which gas transfer was directly dependent on the difference in partial pressures between maternal and foetal blood. The results of these calculations are shown diagrammatically in Figure 18. The ordinate is the ratio of the difference in umbilical arteriovenous Po_2 to the difference between maternal and foetal arterial Po_2. The abscissa is the ratio of the diffusion capacity of the placental membrane for O_2 (D_p) to the transport capacity of foetal blood (TC_F). [The diffusion capacity is defined as the amount of gas diffusing through the membrane per unit time and per unit of Po_2 difference between the two sides; the transport capacity is the product of placental flow and effective O_2 solubility, i.e., the quantity of O_2 transported to and from the placenta per unit time and per unit of Po_2 change in maternal or foetal blood.] The steeply rising curve of the countercurrent flow system (Fig. 18) shows that the foetal Po_2 will approach that of the maternal blood if the diffusion capacity of the membrane is sufficiently large in relation to the transport capacity of the blood on either side of the placenta. This is the most efficient transport system. The pool and concurrent flow systems are the least efficient, while the crosscurrent flow system is intermediate. It is particularly interesting to observe that if the diffusion capacity is low or the transport capacity is high, the differences between the efficiencies of these flow systems are much reduced. In fact, under the very conditions when efficiency is most needed, with a small or infarcted placenta and a baby continuing to grow rapidly, the teleological significance of countercurrent flow is least. This is a rather astonishing conclusion to be reached after all that has been written about the importance of countercurrent flow in the last 30 years.

It is a great temptation to put actual measured values into the equations in order to compare the O_2 diffusion capacities of the placental membranes in different species. I think this temptation should be resisted at present. Too little is yet known of the way in which other variables, such as placental O_2 consumption, uneven distribution of flow, and particularly the experimental conditions, may have affected the measurements. Without more information it is not possible to allow for these, and the comparison would probably be very misleading.

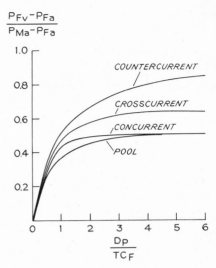

Fig. 18.—Theoretical comparison of the efficiency for O_2 transfer in different placental models; for description see text. The more efficient, the higher the ordinate value. If the diffusion capacity (D_p) is low or the foetal transport capacity for O_2 (TC_F) high, the systems are of almost equal efficiency. Otherwise the countercurrent and crosscurrent systems are better. (Redrawn from Bartels and Moll, 1964.)

Also a fair comparison must depend on measurements of the effective area of gas exchange.

Conclusion

The ultimate aim of physiological studies of placental gas exchange must be to identify the principal factors involved and to express them in quantitative terms. There is a long way to go. All that has been achieved so far is the definition of some of the issues. Progress in the past 40 years, since Huggett, Anselmino and Hoffman, Eastman, Haselhorst and Stromberger, and Barcroft and his colleagues gave the subject a start, has been very slow. It has been slow not because there were no tools available (for the methods of pulmonary physiology are readily adapted to these purposes) but because there have not been many people interested in the placenta. In the past few years, there has been a considerable increase in interest, and there is little doubt that greater use of inert gas, radioisotopes, rapid freezing of tissues, and the like will make progress speedier.

Even now there seems to be a general conclusion taking shape. Whereas formerly the foetus was regarded as a creature which was inadequately supplied with oxygen, it is now believed normally to have enough oxygen and to spare for its purposes and under its special conditions of life. The concept of the placenta as an esoteric organ, across which gas transfer is effected by highly specialized devices, dependent on countercurrent flow, a high O_2 carrying capacity and an unusual HbO_2 dissociation curve, is being replaced by another image, that of a rather rough-and-ready device which works well enough under normal circumstances. Different species with placentas of apparently different structures may have developed them for reasons other than efficiency of gas transfer. Provided that enough foetal blood is exposed to enough maternal blood long enough and over a large enough area, the details of the system used may not be of great biological importance.

Perhaps this change in attitude to the placenta may derive partly from a change in attitude in physiology generally. Many examples may be quoted, but two will suffice. First, the baroreceptors of the carotid sinus and aortic arch were once thought to be the only systemic baroreceptors. We now know there are many such receptors scattered up and down the heart and great vessels, and their removal makes comparatively little difference to an animal's behaviour. Its responses are not mainly determined by a single simple input, and perhaps this is just as well. Second, regional blood flow through the adult lung is variable, according to the height above the heart. The lung is not organized so delicately as once was thought, but on a more robust pattern. So future work on the placenta as an organ of gas exchange may be more rewarding when directed to the general plan of its behaviour rather than to the possible teleological significance of some of the details.

REFERENCES

Albritton, E. C. (ed.): *Standard Values in Blood* (Philadelphia: W. B. Saunders Company, 1952).

Allen, D. W.; Wyman, J., and Smith, C. A.: The oxygen equilibrium of fetal and adult human hemoglobin, J. Biol. Chem. 203:81–87, 1953.

Anselmino, K. J., and Hoffman, F.: Die Ursachen des Icterus neonatorum, Arch. Gynäk. 143:477–499, 1930.

Barcroft, J.: *Researches on Prenatal Life* (Oxford: Blackwell Scientific Publications, 1946).

Barron, D. H.: Homeostasis of the Foetus, in Fishbein, E. (ed.): *Congenital Malformations* (Philadelphia: J. B. Lippincott Company, 1960), pp. 247–252.

Barron, D. H., and Meschia, G.: A comparative study of the exchange of the respiratory gases across the placenta, Cold Spring Harb. Symp. Quant. Biol. 19:93–101, 1954.

Bartels, H.: Comparative physiology of oxygen transport in mammals, Lancet 2:599–604, 1964.

Bartels, H., and Moll, W.: Passage of inert substances and oxygen in the human placenta, Pflüger's Arch. ges. Physiol. 280:165–177, 1964.

Bartels, H.; Moll, W., and Metcalfe, J.: Physiology of gas exchange in the human placenta, Am. J. Obst. & Gynec. 84:1714–1730, 1962.

Born, G. V. R.; Dawes, G. S., and Mott, J. C.: Oxygen lack and autonomic nervous control of the foetal circulation in the lamb, J. Physiol. 134:149–166, 1956.

Brumer, H. D.; Eyre, J., van de, and Carlson, A. J.: The blood picture of rats from birth to twenty-four days of age, Am. J. Physiol. 124:620–626, 1938.

Campbell, A. G. M.; Dawes, G. S.; Fishman, A. P.; Hyman, A. I., and James, G. B.: The oxygen consumption of the placenta and foetal membranes in the sheep, J. Physiol. 182:439–464, 1966.

Comline, R. S.; Silver, I. A., and Silver, M.: Factors responsible for the stimulation of the adrenal medulla during asphyxia in the foetal lamb, J. Physiol. 178:211–238, 1965.

Cross, K. W.; Dawes, G. S., and Mott, J. C.: Anoxia, oxygen consumption and cardiac output in new-born lambs and adult sheep, J. Physiol. 146:316–343, 1959.

Dittmer, D. S., and Grebe, R. M. (eds.): *Handbook of Respiration* (Philadelphia: W. B. Saunders Company, 1958).

Dittmer, D. S., and Grebe, R. M. (eds.): *Handbook of Circulation* (Philadelphia: W. B. Saunders Company, 1959).

Eastman, N. J.: Foetal blood studies, Bull. Johns Hopkins Hosp. 47:221–230, 1930.

Haselhorst, G., and Stromberger, K.: Über den Gasgehalt des Nabelschnurblutes vor und nach der Geburt des Kindes und über den Gasaustausch in der Plazenta, Ztschr. Geburtsh. u. Gynäk. 10:49–78, 1931.

Huggett, A., St. G.: Foetal blood-gas tensions and gas transfusion through the placenta of the goat, J. Physiol. 62:373–384, 1927.

Huggett, A., St. G., and Hammond, J.: Physiology of the Placenta, in Parkes, A. S. (ed.): *Marshall's Physiology of Reproduction* (London: Longmans, Green & Co., Ltd., 1952), pp. 312–397.

Kaiser, I. H.; Cummings, J. N.; Reynolds, S. R. M., and Marbarger, J. P.: Acclimatization response of the pregnant ewe and fetal lamb to diminished ambient pressure, J. Appl. Physiol. 13:171–178, 1958.

Lamport, H.: The transport of oxygen in the sheep's placenta: The diffusion constant of the placenta, Yale J. Biol. & Med. 27:26–34, 1954.

Longo, L. D.; Power, G. G., and Forster, R. E.: Placental diffusion studies using carbon monoxide in sheep, J. Clin. Invest. 44:1070–1071, 1965.

Mott, J. C.: Haemorrhage as a test of the function of the cardiovascular system in rabbits of different ages, J. Physiol. 181:728–752, 1965.

Nechtman, C. M., and Huisman, T. H. J.: Comparative studies of oxygen equilibria of human adult and cord blood red cell hemolysates and suspensions, Clin. chim. Acta 10:165–174, 1964.

Nicholas, J. S.: The determination of the amount of hemoglobin present in rat fetuses during development, Am. J. Physiol. 83:499–501, 1928.

Noer, R.: A study of the effect of flow direction on the placental transmission, using artificial placentas, Anat. Rec. 96:383–389, 1946.

Power, G. G.; Longo, L. D.; Wagner, H. N.; Kuhl, D. E.,

and Forster, R. E.: Distribution of blood flow to the maternal and fetal portions of the sheep placenta using macro-aggregates, J. Clin. Invest. 45:1058, 1966.

Ross, B. B.: Comparative Properties of Lungs and Placenta: Graphical Analysis of Placental Gas Exchange, in A. V. S. de Reuck and R. Porter (ed.): *The Development of the Lung* (Ciba Foundation Symposium, 1967, pp. 238–254.

Tremblay, P. C.; Sybulski, S., and Maughan, G. B.: Role of the placenta in fetal malnutrition, Am. J. Obst. & Gynec. 91:597–605, 1965.

Wilkin, P.: Etude des facteurs physiques conditionnant les échanges transplacentaires, in Snoeck, J. (ed.): *Le Placenta Humain* (Paris: Masson & Cie, 1958), pp. 194–211. Les Theories explicatives du mechanisme des échanges transplacentaires, loc. cit., 248–279.

Williamson, C. S.: Influence of age and sex on hemoglobin, Arch. Int. Med. 18:505–528, 1916.

Wintrobe, M. M., and Schumacker, H. B.: Erythrocyte studies in the mammalian fetus and newborn, Am. J. Anat. 58:313–328, 1936.

Wulf, H.: Der Gasaustausch in der reifen Plazenta des Menschen, Ztschr. Geburtsh u. Gynak. 158:117–134, 269–319, 1962.

4

The Placenta and Foetal Growth

Foetal Growth

In 1906, Roberts pointed out that if growth in a lineal direction is uniform with time, one might expect that the cube root of the volume (or weight) also should bear a linear relation to time. He believed that the information then available on the growth of the human foetus from 3 months onward was consistent with this simple formulation. But his view received short shrift from the critics of the day because the data did not fit in the early embryonic period. By the time Needham (1931) wrote his three-volume book, *Chemical Embryology,* a good many theoretical and empirical approaches had been tried, but there was no common agreement on a general solution. However, MacDowell, Allen, and MacDowell (1927) had introduced a new idea, that the starting point from which growth was timed should not be insemination but some later date. For this they chose the appearance of the primitive streak (varying from 7.2 days for mice to 12 days for guinea pigs), and yet the results were still unsatisfactory.

In 1951, Huggett and Widdas achieved a general solution, by considering that growth at a linear rate began at some finite but undefined time after insemination (t_0). They were primarily concerned with growth during foetal life, that is to say, when the placental circulation was firmly established and the main phase of organogenesis was complete. They found that there was then a close linear relation between gestational age and the cube root of the weight in mice, rats, rabbits, guinea pigs, sheep, cows, and man, as weight$^{1/3} = a(t - t_0)$, where t is time and a is a constant. But the constants (a and t_0) which defined this relationship were different in different species, as can be seen from Figure 19 in which the slopes and the intercepts on the time axis are variable. The intercept on the time axis is, of course, always such that t_0 has a finite value.

In a recent paper, Spencer, Coulombe, and van Wagenen (1966) reported the results of calculations on foetal growth in rhesus monkeys as

$$\text{Weight}^{1/3} = 0.042t + 0.89.$$

In this case, when W is zero, t_0 is negative. They

Fig. 19.—The relation between the cube root of foetal weight and gestational age in different species. The upper end of each regression line indicates full term. Observations on the baboon and chimpanzee are given at full term only.

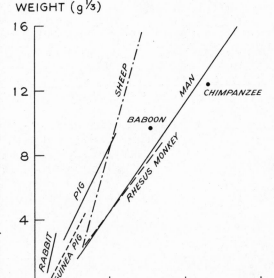

FOETAL WEIGHT ($g^{1/3}$)

used the figures of van Wagenen and Catchpole (1965) which included results on monkeys delivered vaginally or by caesarean section. But monkeys delivered vaginally are, on average, recorded as weighing less, probably because most deliveries take place at night and the infants are not weighed for several hours, by which time their fur is dry and they have passed urine and faeces but have not obtained much by suckling. The mean difference in weight is more than 40 Gm (i.e., nearly 10% of body weight at term; Fujikura and Niemann, personal communication), and van Wagenen and Catchpole's figures will thus have been biased downward toward the end of gestation where vaginal deliveries preponderate. I have calculated the relation between weight and gestational age in 381 deliveries by caesarean section in the rhesus monkey colony of the Laboratory of Perinatal Physiology, Puerto Rico, as

$$\text{Weight}^{1/3} = 0.0594t - 1.49$$
$$(\pm 0.00032, \text{ S.E.}).$$

This is a more reasonable result as the intercept on the time axis is finite (25 days); the slope of the relation between weight$^{1/3}$ and gestational age is greater than that of Spencer, Coulombe, and van Wagenen, as expected.

The result is also interesting because it shows that foetal growth rates are almost identical in the rhesus monkey and man. Comparable measurements on foetal growth in other old world primates are not available, but figures for the chimpanzee (Yerkes, 1943) and baboon (Lapin and Yakovleva, 1963) at term have been inserted as single points in Figure 19. It will be interesting to see whether the other Pongidae and Cercopithecidae also approximate to man, as more figures become available.

Huggett and Widdas were commendably cautious in their interpretation of the cube root relation and simply emphasized its practical use as a mathematical convenience for handling data which relate age to weight. No simple formula was found to be entirely satisfactory during the early days of gestation where there might be several rate-determining factors; delayed implantation was proposed as an extreme example. So, in a way, the wheel has turned full circle, and Roberts' contention has been justified in the context in which it was made, for he had considered development only after embryogenesis was complete. In retrospect, the rough treatment which his views received were due to a misrepresentation of his objective, because of the intense interest devoted to growth and form in the embryonic period in the first quarter of this century.

It is impossible to find fault with Huggett and Widdas' caution in their discussion of their observations. As they say, "it is not practical from the data to hazard any biochemical or physiological reason why, during this period of pregnancy, growth should follow a cube-root law—nor is it possible to assert from the data that a simple one-third power relationship is more accurate than some decimal power less than one-third." The body of the foetus is composed of different organs, growing at different rates, and the total rate of growth may depend on many factors operating separately. Yet the simplicity of the idea which led Roberts to write his brief article to the Lancet in 1906 is appealing, and perhaps there is a germ of truth in it.

This, at any rate, is the background against which we have to consider foetal growth. There is an empirical rule relating foetal weight to gestational age, whose biological foundation is unknown. It may be that in each of several species, continued growth is normally determined by a single variable of magnitude peculiar to that species, which gives it its *Specific Foetal Growth Velocity* (the slope of $W^{1/3}$ on age in Fig. 19). If this is so, we don't yet know what that variable is. During most of the last two-thirds of gestation, the growth of the foetus normally proceeds unimpaired. The principal deviation is related to differences in placental weight in late gestation.

The Effect of Placental Weight

In all the species in which the proposition has been examined toward term, the weight of the foetus increases with increasing weight of the placenta, in man (Adair and Thelander, 1925; Calkins, 1937; McKeown and Record, 1953), guinea pigs (Ibsen, 1928), rabbits (Rosahn and Greene, 1936), pigs (Waldorf, Foote, Self, Chapman, and Casida, 1957), sheep (Foote, Pope, Chapman, and Casida, 1959; Alexander, 1964,a), and mice (McLaren, 1965,a); only representative references are given to the large literature on the subject. Because of the large numbers involved the raw data are difficult to handle, but when examined in detail some interesting features emerge. This, and the fact that figures on the rhesus monkey have not been published, justifies the presentation of Figure 20, which shows observations on 147 monkeys delivered by caesarean section at 157 ± 2 days gestational age in the Laboratory of Perinatal Physiology in San Juan. The date of insemination was accurate to ± 1 day,

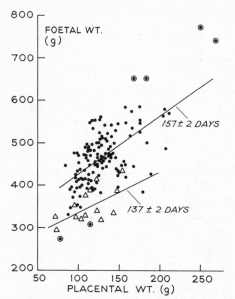

Fig. 20.—Observations on the relation between foetal and placental weights in the rhesus monkey at 157 ± 2 (●) and 137 ± 2 (△) days gestational age.

Fig. 21.—Observations on the distribution of placental and foetal weights in rhesus monkeys at 157 ± 2 days gestational age, plotted against a logarithmic weight scale.

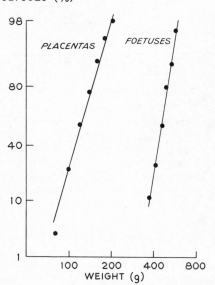

and all the foetuses were singletons. Twinning is rare in this species, probably only ~0.1%. Regression analysis gave the relation:

Foetal weight (Gm)
$$= 287 + 1.37 \text{ Placental weight (Gm)}$$
$$\pm 0.14 \text{ (S.E.)}$$

The correlation coefficient ($r = 0.63$) was highly significant ($P < 0.001$). In 14 monkeys at 137 ± 2 days gestation (0.82 of term) the correlation was still significant ($r = 0.59$; $P < 0.05$), but the slope and intercept of the regression line on the placental weight axis were different (Fig. 20). The numbers at earlier gestational ages were too few to warrant analysis. It is evident that there is a very strong correlation between foetal and placental weights near term.

In the group at 157 ± 2 days gestation, both placental and foetal weights showed a log-normal distribution (Fig. 21), behaving in this respect like other growth functions. Male monkeys tended to be a little heavier than females (but the difference was not statistically significant); the mean placental weights were identical (Table 11). Thus, although larger numbers would be needed to test the hypothesis exactly, the data do not suggest that the greater weight of males is due to their placentas.

Non-pregnant maternal weights, prior to insemination, were available for 92 of the monkeys at 157 ± 2 days gestation. Multiple regression analysis gave the result:

Foetal weight (Gm) = 300
+1.41 Placental weight (Gm)
$$\pm 0.20 \text{ (S.E.)}$$
$$- 2.72 \text{ Maternal weight (Gm)}$$
$$\pm 4.1 \text{ (S.E.)},$$

whence it was concluded that maternal weight was not a significant determinant of foetal weight, when placental weight was taken into account. The correlation between placental weight and maternal weight also was not significant ($0.1 > P > 0.05$) with the numbers available, but there was a significant relation between placental weight and parity

TABLE 11.—SEX DISTRIBUTION OF FOETAL AND PLACENTAL WEIGHTS IN RHESUS MONKEYS AT 157 ± 2 DAYS GESTATION (MEANS ± S.E.)

NORMAL	MALE	FEMALE
Number	80	67
Foetal weight (Gm)	474 ± 8	460 ± 8
Placental weight (Gm)	133 ± 11	132 ± 13

TABLE 12.—EFFECT OF MATERNAL PARITY ON PLACENTAL WEIGHT IN RHESUS MONKEYS AT 157 ± 2 DAYS GESTATION (MEANS $\pm$ S.E.)

PARITY	NUMBER	PLACENTAL WEIGHT (GM)
1	53	129 ± 4
2	33	136 ± 4
3	28	143 ± 8

(Table 12). Broadhurst and Jinks (1965) concluded that, apart from sex, parity was the most important determinant of foetal birth weight in the rhesus monkey. This observation could be accounted for if increasing parity provided a more favourable environment for placental and hence for foetal growth. It is evident that there are ample grounds for suspecting that there may be a causal relation between placental weight and foetal growth in this as in other species.

When this possibility was first considered (e.g., by Adair and Thelander, 1925; and Ibsen, 1928) it was pointed out that the placenta contains tissue of foetal origin, and it might, therefore, be expected that growth of both placenta and foetus should proceed hand-in-hand. Yet the idea of a causal connection was attractive to both the principal groups of workers who were concerned—the veterinary and agricultural professions on the one hand, and the physiologists and zoologists on the other hand. Placental size might limit foetal growth as a result of limitation of transfer of metabolic fuel (carbohydrate, fat, or oxygen) or materials built into the foetal structure, or by reason of insufficient hormone production. These ideas were found particularly attractive in the mid-1930s because of the evidence which then suggested that there might be quite simple haemodynamic factors involved, that the oxygen supply to the foetus might become critical toward term. It was, and still is, a fruitful field for speculation and one in which it has not been easy to design definitive experiments. Obviously, if a placenta is very small or, as sometimes in man, extensively infarcted, placental size may become the single most important factor in determining foetal growth. The only direct test of the hypothesis is the very interesting observation of Alexander (1964,b) who, in sheep, reduced the number of placental cotyledons by surgical removal of part of the uterine caruncles. This had the effect of reducing both total cotyledonary (placental) weight and foetal weight at term. It is strong evidence for a causal connection between the two. Alexander concluded

from these data that the suggestion of Barcroft and others that birth weight was restricted only if the placenta was very small was not justified. And, indeed, if this were so, one would hardly expect the relationship shown in Figure 20 for the rhesus monkey over such a large foetal and placental weight range. This conclusion is so important that its validity should be tested in species other than sheep, and the rhesus monkey seems an obvious candidate with its two placentas, of which the secondary one might be removed surgically early in gestation.

Alexander (1964,b) also made a suggestion of some practical interest. He pointed out that estimates of foetal age by weight or linear measurements were likely to be unreliable unless they were also correlated with placental weight. It is certainly true that a measurement of foetal weight alone is a poor guide to gestational age. For instance, B. B. Ross (unpublished) has calculated from measurements on 267 rhesus monkeys a predictive equation:

Gestational age (days)
± 6.8 (S.E.)
$$= 78.5 \log \text{weight (Gm)} - 50.4$$
± 5.9 (S.E.).

The age so estimated has a deviation of ± 15.8 days for 98% confidence, and is, therefore, not very useful. It remains to be seen whether inclusion of placental weight in the analysis will reduce the variance. It is not easy to make good use of the additional information, because the relation with placental weight changes with gestational age, as illustrated by the difference in the two regression lines of Figure 20.

There is a further point to consider. There is great variation in placental and foetal weight at one gestational age near term. To what extent does this imply a difference in physiological constitution? In the extreme case of a small-for-dates baby (e.g., with an infarcted placenta and weighing less than 2 standard deviations from the mean) there is no doubt now that we are dealing with a different physiological situation. Placental infarcts do occur in monkeys, but are uncommon and usually small. Two of the foetal monkeys at 157 ± 2 days gestation (ringed in Fig. 20) weighed less than 327 Gm and were, therefore, 2 S.D. below the mean; at the time they were delivered several years ago this fact was not known and the records tell us nothing of interest, save that one which was allowed to breathe spontaneously lived only a few hours. No note was made of pathological findings which could account for the low birth weight. Four foetal monkeys (also ringed in Fig. 20) weighed more than 607 Gm and were, therefore, 2 S.D. above the mean. We don't know whether these should be regarded as abnormal either; it might have been worth examining them and their placentas for pathological changes (e.g., oedema) had this information been available at the time. On the other hand, Figure 21 suggests that one might expect a few very small or very large placentas and foetuses. It may be difficult to distinguish the limits of normal and abnormal variation. Even in the group within 2 S.D. of the mean (467 ± 140 Gm) there is room for considerable physiological differences and these are worth exploring for their own sake. Until we know more, it may be wise for those who work with mature foetuses to make sure that experimental groups are matched for weight as well as age, and perhaps to exclude individuals which differ considerably from the mean.

Three further questions arise. What other factors may be operating to control foetal growth? And how great a reduction in placental mass is necessary to make this the principal determinant in species other than sheep, and is it of consequence in the normal population?

Much of the evidence to be considered has been observational rather than experimental in character. It has provided the background necessary to consider various means by which foetal growth may be limited. It is obvious, but worth noting, that serial measurements of growth have not been undertaken on a single foetus or placenta at different gestational ages. In animals, we are dependent on measurements of different members of a population (placentas and foetuses) whose uniformity is assumed, but which have rarely been examined closely for evidence of inhomogeneity. In man, we are restricted to the material which becomes available by natural means at different gestational ages. It is possible that the processes, natural or pathological, which have led to premature delivery may have affected or been determined by unusual changes in the placenta or foetus. Yet the fact that the relation between litter size and placental and foetal growth seems to be of a similar character in animals and man, suggests that, in the latter, premature delivery may not have caused gross distortion of the results.

The Evidence of Litter Size

Let us then return to the statistical relation between placental and foetal weight. We recognize that pla-

cental weight may be a misleading index of placental function, but in the absence of other more accurate measurements, and uncertain of which placental function is relevant (e.g., diffusion capacity for O_2, transfer function for amino-acids, or hormone production), we must make do with it for a time. Placental weight and foetal weight vary widely with gestation, so it is necessary to examine the effect of placental weight on foetal size at a fixed gestational age or ages. There is another factor involved, that of litter size. The weights of the placenta and of the foetus are both inversely related to the number of individuals in a litter of guinea pigs (Ibsen, 1928), rabbits (Hammond, 1935), sheep (Barcroft and Kennedy, 1939), man (McKeown and Record, 1953), and mice (McLaren, 1965,b). In rats the inverse correlation between litter size and foetal weight is uncertain, possibly because of sampling problems associated with rapid foetal growth (Campbell, Innes, and Kosterlitz, 1953), though Huggett and Widdas (1951) examined 120 litters and found no significant relation. The question arises whether litter size is a variable affecting foetal growth independently of placental weight and at different gestational ages. The observations of Ibsen (1928), who examined 415 foetuses from 113 litters of guinea pigs, suggested that this might be so toward the end of gestation but not before,

Fig. 22.—Human foetal and placental weights according to the duration of gestation. (Redrawn from McKeown and Record, 1953.)

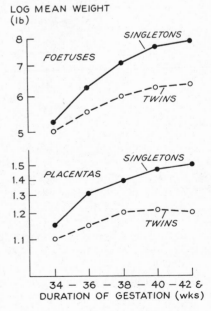

i.e., from the 55th day onward (0.82 of term), provided that there were more than 3 foetuses in the litter.

McKeown and Record (1953) examined the data on 4,931 single and 834 twin deliveries in man, using data from the Birmingham Maternity Hospital. Figure 22 shows that there was little difference between the weights in single and twin births, either of foetuses or placentas, at about 34 weeks gestation, but thereafter (from 0.9 of term onward) there was a large and steadily increasing difference in both. At first sight one might suppose that the difference in foetal weights was attributable to the difference in placental weights, but further analysis showed this not to be so. Figure 23 shows a comparison of the mean weights of twin and single births at corresponding placental weights. The number of placental weights below ¾ lb was small; at all other placental weights single babies were heavier than twins. This relation was due only partly to the difference in distribution by gestation, resulting from earlier onset of labour in twin pregnancies. Standardization of the results to allow for this effect reduced the difference by only a small amount (see Fig. 23). The observations of Ibsen in guinea pigs were also confirmed (Eckstein, McKeown, and Record, 1955). Observations were recorded at a fixed gestational age just before term (the 65th day from copulation) and showed that, at a given placental weight, foetal weight is greater

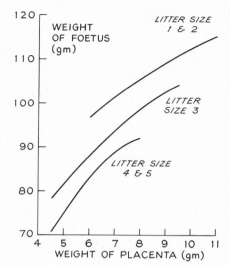

Fig. 24.—The relation between foetal and placental weights in guinea pigs, grouped according to litter size. (Redrawn from Eckstein, McKeown, and Record, 1955.)

in small than in large litters (Fig. 24). Thus Figures 23 and 24 suggest that in man and guinea pig both litter size and placental weight are independent variables, both of which affect foetal growth.

Site of Implantation

Ibsen (1928) also noticed in guinea pigs that the growth of a single foetus in one horn was influenced by the number of foetuses in the other horn. Eckstein and McKeown (1955), and Eckstein, McKeown, and Record (1955) have taken the matter a step further, also in guinea pigs, using a more rigorous analysis. In litters of less than 4, the association between foetal weight and litter size was independent of distribution between the 2 horns. But in litters of 4 or more there was evidence both of a local effect determined by contiguity of foetuses within the same horn and also of a general effect, determined by the number of foetuses in the other horn. That is to say, mean foetal weight was reduced both by an increase in numbers within the same uterine horn, and by an increase within the other horn. Placental weight was influenced in the same way. The results also suggested, but did not prove conclusively, that the local and general effects of litter size on foetal growth were not wholly explained by their influence on placental weight.

Two general hypotheses had been proposed to account for the effect of litter size on foetal growth, that of Hammond who had suggested that growth

Fig. 23.—The relation between human foetal and placental weights. (Redrawn from McKeown and Record, 1953.)

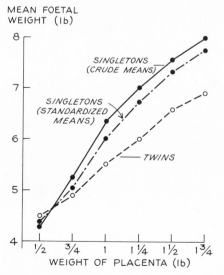

might be limited by the available amount of some maternal hormone or metabolic product, and that of Ibsen (1928), that crowding might limit growth of the placenta, and hence that of the foetus. Eckstein, McKeown, and Record's (1955) conclusions that there were both local and general effects of litter size were compatible with either hypothesis, but they also drew attention to the fact that both could be explained by limitation of blood flow to the uterus. They suggest that "blood pressure in the uterine artery may therefore be lower if there are several placentae in a horn than if there is only one," and ". . . such a decrease in arterial pressure would result in reduction of oxygen supply to at least the more distantly placed placentae." The presence of placentas in the opposite horn was expected to have a similar, though perhaps lesser, effect.

There is a further factor related to the position of implantation. Ibsen (1928), using guinea pigs, and Waldorf, Foote, Self, Chapman, and Casida (1957), using pigs, found that foetal and placental weights tended to decrease from the ovarian end of a horn to the middle, with an increase again near the cervical end. A similar trend was observed by Hashima (1956) and McLaren and Michie (1960) in mice. And, subsequently, McLaren and her colleagues undertook a thorough exploration of this and other variables in different strains of mice (e.g., McLaren, 1965,b). Birth weight, and foetal and placental weight at 17½ days gestation (0.92 of term), were all inversely related to the number of young in a litter. While many of the findings were similar to those of Eckstein, McKeown, and Record (1955) in guinea pigs, the effect of litter size on placental weight in mice appeared to be wholly general in character, i.e., irrespective of numbers in a given horn. There was a positive association between foetal and placental weight, suggesting a causal dependence of foetal growth on placental size. Foetal growth was not directly affected by position in the uterine horn, but only as a result of the gradient in placental growth. It was suggested that the effect of the position in the horn and of litter size on placental and foetal growth was likely to be due to haemodynamic factors. The blood supplies to the foetuses closest to the upper and lower origins of the vascular arcade from the aorta were likely to be greatest (Fig. 25), except for the uppermost foetus, which might share a single branch with the ovary. There were features which made this argument more plausible in mice, for it seemed unlikely that foetal growth was primarily deter-

mined by competition for a limited amount of maternal nutrient. When superfoetation was induced by gonadotrophin treatment in adolescent females, foetal weight was similar to that in normal adult pregnancies when allowance was made for factors such as litter size (Healy, McLaren, and Michie, 1960). Also foetuses dying in mid-pregnancy, when their nutritional demands would be small, exerted effects on the growth of survivors as if they themselves had survived. Presumably, their placentation affected the placentation and subsequent development of the remainder.

The haemodynamic hypothesis depends on the supposition that a short arterial arcade, albeit perhaps of small diameter, offers a sufficient resistance to blood flow to affect placental and foetal growth in late gestation. Now, it happens that little experimental work has been done on the haemodynamics of blood flow in arterial arcades, although these occur in many important places in the systemic circulation, in the mesentery, for instance, in the palm of the hand, or in a rabbit's ear as well as in the uterus of polytocous species. This is a field which merits some experimental study, although one would be surprised if the connecting vessels of an arcade should offer a resistance to flow in any way comparable to that of the more peripheral arterioles beyond the branches. It does not offer much resistance in the circle of Willis, judged by its ability in man to supply the arm with blood by retrograde flow through a vertebral artery when the normal supply is blocked. This may be a special case. The

Fig. 25.—Schematic diagram of the uterine blood supply to the placentas (P) in mice. (Redrawn from McLaren and Michie, 1960.)

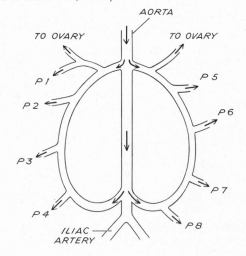

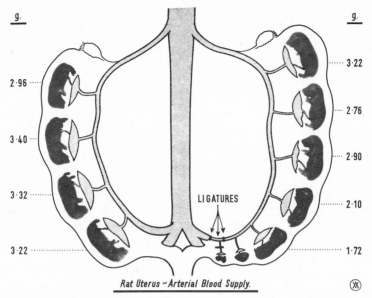

g.

g.

2·96

3·40

3·32

3·22

3·22

2·76

2·90

2·10

1·72

LIGATURES

Rat Uterus ~ Arterial Blood Supply.

Fig. 26.—Arterial blood supply of the rat uterus, showing the results observed on the 21st day of pregnancy, 5 days after the application of ligatures. The figures indicate the weights (Gm) of individual foetuses in a typical experiment (Wigglesworth, 1964).

hypothesis certainly could be put to experimental test. It might be possible to measure the pressures directly at different points in the arcade in the mouse or guinea pig uterus; it should be quite easy to do so in the pig in which a similar distribution of foetal and placental weight has been observed. It also should be possible to test this hypothesis in pregnant cats or dogs. Its least plausible feature is to explain the general effect of litter size, e.g., as when the growth of a single foetus in one horn is affected by the number of foetuses in the other horn. Notwithstanding the argument of Eckstein, McKeown, and Record (1955), it is unlikely that the systemic arterial pressure could be so reduced in a pregnant guinea pig by flow to placentas in one uterine horn as to affect significantly that to a placenta or placentas in the other horn.

The haemodynamic hypothesis has recently received support from some interesting experiments by Wigglesworth (1964). He tied the cervical end of the arterial arcade in the rat's uterus on one side on the 17th day of gestation and observed the effects on the 20–21st day. Retardation of foetal growth was observed and was greatest in those foetuses nearest the cervical end (Fig. 26). Ligatures were placed not only around the artery, but also at right angles in the tissue to prevent development of anastomotic channels. He records

that these ligatures had no effect on placental weight. At first sight, this evidence seemed to be an overwhelming vindication of the hypothesis. Yet there are snags. Why was placental weight not affected? Perhaps the numbers were too small to show an effect. The operation may have served autonomic nerves and lymphatic channels as well as blood vessels, and infarcts in the wall of the uterus were noticed. So it is not surprising that the foetuses closest to the site of interference grew less rapidly during the last few days of gestation. The retardation of foetal growth observed in these experiments may have been due to a gross reduction of blood flow to the maternal side of the placentas, but it does not follow that the differences in placental and foetal growth with site of implantation under normal conditions also is due to the same primary cause. There is an alternative explanation.

Ibsen (1928) explained his observations in guinea pigs by crowding. He measured the distances between placentas (from the centre of each decidua basalis) before the uterus was opened. Small placentas on average had a smaller distance on either side of them than did larger ones; at 65 days the correlation coefficient $r = 0.46 \pm 0.06$. The uppermost and lowermost implants can have only one adjacent placenta, and so they tended to be less crowded. They should have a larger area for development provided that they were not attached right at the very tip of a uterine horn. This idea may be susceptible to test. If the haemodynamic hypothesis were correct, one would expect that foetal and placental development in the centre of an arcade would be inversely related to the aggregate of all the placental masses on either side, whereas if crowding were the principal operative factor foetal and placental development should be related only to the distance between immediate neighbors.

Perhaps the real difficulty with the crowding hypothesis is to translate it into physiological terms. It is very easy to see how limitation of blood flow could affect placental development, but how might limitation of space act? It may involve two components, pressure from adjacent objects, and availability of internal uterine surface area, both of which act over a long period of time. Foetal deaths are common in polytocous animals early in gestation, and their incidence increases when superfoetation is induced by hormonal treatment or embryo transfer. The maximum number of living foetuses in rabbits at 29 days, after experimental overcrowding *in utero,* was 8 per uterine horn and 15 per litter, a large reduction from the number of implantations present at 9 days gestation (Hafez, 1964). The number of surviving foetuses in each horn was thus strictly limited, and this process of limitation had taken place shortly after implantation. Thus crowding is likely to have an effect on early placental development. Hafez concluded that none of the treatments used (including overcrowding) exerted any pronounced effect on foetal or placental weights, but noted that the number of surviving foetuses at term in his experiments was only slightly higher than those in naturally bred does of the strain used.

Congenital Runts

McLaren and Michie (1960) have also used the haemodynamic hypothesis as a possible explanation of the appearance of congenital runts in a population of mice. Runts are usually defined as animals whose growth is below that which is natural for their kind, and for which there is no other apparent cause, e.g., genetic dwarfism or congenital malformation of particular organs. McLaren and Michie used a more restricted definition of runts, namely, "any animal small below the natural growth of its litter," and used statistical methods to show that their mouse population was not homogeneous, but at 18½ days gestation contained a small number of unusually small foetuses—runts—in which some abnormal

growth-retarding factor had operated. This is an important conclusion, giving substance to the widespread belief that runts represent a discrete phenomenon, that they fall outside the normal range of variation in their species. The incidence of true runts was about 2%, and an extensive study of inbred and hybrid strains did not suggest that genetic factors were exercising an effect. There was no difference in incidence according to the environment in which the mother was kept, and there was no apparent association with litter size.

On the other hand, there did appear to be an association between runting and intra-uterine environment. In 96 uterine horns, 14 mouse runts were found, of which 5 might have been so defined by chance alone (for statistical reasons). Five runts were uppermost in the horn (next to the ovary) and 2 had placentas fused with those of another live embryo, a rather rare phenomenon. The placentas were not weighed. It was proposed that both these intra-uterine positions had a haemodynamic factor in common—the ovarian embryos because they shared their blood supply with the ovary, and the fused embryos because they shared with their partners. It was argued that the pressure at which maternal blood reached the placenta after passing down the uterine arteries might have been the determining factor, the diversion elsewhere (to the ovary or the fused placenta) reducing the effective pressure.

Here we are faced again with substantially the same problem as that considered in relation to normal arterial arcades. From experience of the circulation elsewhere the explanation suggested seems unlikely. There is the alternative possibility that the extreme ovarian position, and that close to another placenta, are unfavourable for placental development. Maternal blood flow through the placenta of a runt might be less than that through a normal foetus not because of a reduced pressure head, but because the placenta was smaller and its vascular resistance greater. Runts are not uncommon in litters of pigs, and it might be possible to obtain direct evidence in this species to settle the point in question. Also, some placental factor other than maternal blood flow could be limiting to foetal growth. This is clear from recent investigations in man.

It is only within the last 12 years that babies of abnormally small birth weight for their gestational age ("small-for-dates" or "dysmature" babies) have been recognized as a distinct entity, outside the normal range of variation in the human species. These infants have physical and biochemical character-istics in common with congenital or experimental runts of other species, which are considered else-where (p. 219). Here we are concerned only to rec-ognize that foetal growth retardation in man is sometimes associated with maternal hypertension and toxaemia of pregnancy, where there is indirect but substantial evidence that maternal blood flow to the uterus and placenta is reduced. For instance, the clearance of radioactive sodium injected into the intervillous space is less than in normal women (Browne and Veall, 1953; Dixon, Browne and Davey, 1963) and there are obliterative and degen-erative lesions in the spiral arteries (Dixon and Robertson, 1961) which are consistent with a large increase in vascular resistance on the maternal side. It was tempting to suppose that the consequent reduction in maternal blood flow was the immediate cause of foetal growth retardation.

In the human placenta, toxaemia of pregnancy is commonly associated with localized placental in-farction and degeneration of the foetal side of the area of exchange. Indeed, it has often been sug-gested that degeneration of the syncytiotrophoblast was the definitive placental lesion. So, although the primary defect may well be a reduction in maternal flow to the placenta, the secondary con-sequences are not circumscribed; they involve both physical reduction of the area of gas and nutrient exchange and destruction of placental tissues which are almost certainly involved in the elaboration of hormones. Aherne and Dunnill (1966) showed that in maternal hypertension the placental volume (363 ml) was less than in normal pregnancies (488 ml), and both the chorionic villous surface area and the foetal capillary surface area were reduced even more in proportion, even in placentas in which in-farction was negligible. With infarction, still greater reduction in the villous surface area occurred, from a normal value of ~12 M² to 4.5 M² or less. These are gross changes and it is hardly surprising that with lesions of this size some infants do not survive.

There was also a reduction in the volume of the placentas (350 ml) of human infants with nonspe-cific growth retardation at 39–40 weeks gestation, with a mean villous surface area of only 6.4 M² (Aherne and Dunnill, 1966). This is a particularly interesting observation because in these placentas, in which the incidence of infarction was small, the capillary surface area was only 1.9 M²/100 ml total placental volume, as compared with 4.00 M²/100 ml in normal placentas. One cannot help wondering whether this might also be true in multiple preg-nancies. Figures 22, 23, and 24 suggested that litter size and placental weight were independent vari-ables, both of which affected foetal growth. The results could be explained if foetal growth were normally dependent on some component within the placenta, such as villous capillary surface area or trophoblast volume, which formed a smaller pro-portion of total placental volume in large litters. This is a possibility which could be examined in multiple human and guinea pig pregnancies and in mouse runts.

The difference in interpretation, both as regards multiple pregnancies and runts, is an important one. It substitutes for the haemodynamic hypoth-esis that maternal blood flow is restricted by the vascular resistance of a maternal arterial arcade—the proposition that the primary effect is on some placental component, possibly on the exchange area. This might imply an increased vascular resist-ance on both sides of the placenta, maternal and foetal. No assumption is made about the nature of the growth-rate limiting substance or substances. Alternatively, the limiting factor might be hormone production in a placental component, e.g., the syn-cytiotrophoblast.

Growth During Late Foetal and Early Neonatal Life

In the rabbit and guinea pig, increase in foetal weight is almost linear with time toward the end of gestation, and then accelerates after birth (Fig. 27). This is also true of rhesus monkeys, in which growth rate increases by 31.5% once the immediate post-natal disturbance is over, whether they are de-

Fig. 27.—Prenatal and postnatal growth in the rab-bit and guinea pig, using data from Draper (1920), Rosahn and Greene (1936), and Altman and Dittmer (1962).

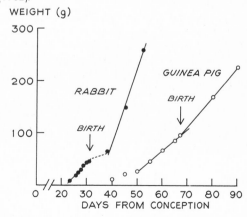

WEIGHT (g)

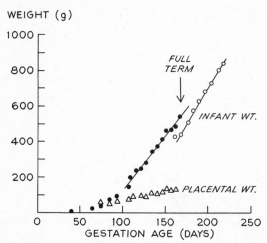

Fig. 28.—Prenatal (●) and postnatal (○) growth in the rhesus monkey.

of the prenatal and postnatal growth rate of singletons showed that the mean rate of growth declined during the last few weeks of gestation, but increased after birth (Fig. 29). The mean weekly increment in weight from birth to 3 months was almost identical with that from 30–36 weeks gestation. It was, therefore, suggested that the sigmoid character of the curve of prenatal growth in singletons was due to restrictions imposed by an intra-uterine environment, as with multiple births.

In using the mean birth weight of a population, McKeown and Record assumed that the births delivered were representative in respect of weight of all foetuses in the uterus at the same stage of gestation. The decrease in mean birth weight toward the end of gestation might have been due to contamination of the population with a small proportion of highly abnormal babies. This seems unlikely in view of the evidence of Lubchenco, Hausman, Dressler, and Boyd (1963), who constructed percentile curves of birth weights of liveborn infants from 24–42 weeks. So far as can be judged, there does not appear to be an abnormal distribution toward the end of gestation.

Naeye, Benirschke, Hagstrom, and Marcus (1966) compared the prenatal and postnatal growth of twins. They found that while most twins have a subnormal rate of growth during late gestation, they have an accelerated growth after birth, reaching median levels for singletons by 12 months of age. In twins who came to necropsy, the tissue abnormalities suggested that malnutrition was the main cause of their being underweight for their gestational age. Tissue components were measured by line sampling, i.e., by measuring each cell or cell component along measured lines onto which random microscopic fields were projected with a camera lucida. The weight deficit appeared to be due mainly to a subnormal cytoplasmic content of cells in the various organs, as in singletons for which there was evidence of malnutrition before birth. But in some twins, as for instance the smaller members

livered vaginally or by caesarean section (Table 13 and Fig. 28). After some weeks the growth rate declines in all these species. There appears at first sight to be no evidence of a retardation of foetal growth toward term as in man, even in the guinea pig with its large litter size (Table 3, p. 15). This conclusion must be regarded with some caution, for it could be argued for these three species that in a more favourable environment growth would have already accelerated before delivery.

Toward the end of human gestation the ratio between foetal and placental weight increases to a maximum (as in the monkey, Fig. 28), and then the rate of foetal growth begins to slow (Fig. 29). It is only as this stage is reached that a difference is perceptible between the mean weights of singletons and twins at equal placental weight (Fig. 23). McKeown and Record (1953) raised the question whether this was due to a change with increasing foetal age in the growth capacity of the foetus, or whether the apparent retardation of growth was due to the intra-uterine environment. Examination

TABLE 13.—Observations on Growth Rates of Rhesus Monkeys Before and After Delivery

Mode of Delivery	Age	Number	Regression of Body Weight (w, Gm) on Age (t, days)	For Regression Coefficients, P
Caesarean section	100–165 Days gestation	360	W = −508 + 6.24t (±0.31)	<0.001
Caesarean section	1–8 Weeks postnatal	20	W = −931 + 8.29t (±0.46)	
Vaginal delivery	145–179 Days gestation	124	W = −591 + 6.47t (±0.62)	<0.02
Vaginal delivery	1–8 Weeks postnatal	32	W = −920 + 8.32t (±0.29)	

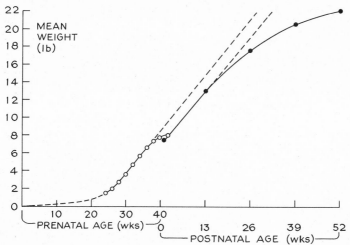

Fig. 29.—Prenatal and postnatal growth in human single births. (Redrawn from McKeown and Record, 1953.)

of monozygous pairs which were more than 25% below singleton standards, the organs had a deficit in cell numbers (Naeye, 1965). These facts could well explain the very rapid growth of such twins immediately after birth, while the cell deficit might restrict final growth potential. Of course, there are problems in the interpretation of these data, as the authors recognize, ranging from the assumption that fixation artifacts are of similar size in different babies, to the assumption that observations on twins which happen to die in the first few hours from birth (usually from cardiopulmonary difficulties) are relevant to those which survive and whose postnatal growth can, therefore, be measured. There are also special factors which can complicate human twin pregnancies; for instance, the greatest nutritional differences were seen most often in monozygous pairs in which blood could be exchanged through placental vascular anastomoses to the detriment of one partner. Yet the mean weight deficit at term was almost as great in dizygotic twins. The evidence is certainly consistent with and supports the view that failure to gain weight in twins late in gestation, as in singletons, is a consequence of the intra-uterine environment rather than an inherent decrease in foetal growth capacity.

These are important conclusions in relation to our general view of congenital runts and intra-uterine growth retardation. For we started with the expectation that this phenomenon was something outside the normal range of variation for the species, as McLaren's statistical observations in mice

had suggested. But the evidence in man suggests that intra-uterine growth retardation may have multiple causes. Some of these causes may be of a step-wise variation from normality, as in recognized congenital malformations (e.g., Down's syndrome, trisomy 18, microcephaly), haemolytic disease, or gross pathological changes in the placenta. Another may be a graded imperfection of placental function, such as might produce a graded imperfection of foetal growth, difficult to perceive except when large numbers are considered. So we must turn to a more detailed consideration of evidence for the ways in which such a result might be achieved.

Birth Weights at High Altitude

If O_2 supply were the limiting factor to foetal growth in late gestation, one might expect that birth weight might be less at high altitude. This could prove to be a rather naive view for several reasons. First, adults adapt to high altitude by increasing the O_2 carrying capacity of their blood and in other ways, and the maternal adaptations might go some way to maintaining an adequate O_2 supply to the foetus. Secondly, comparatively large changes in maternal arterial P_{O_2} cause only small changes in foetal arterial P_{O_2}, as described in the preceding chapter. And thirdly, populations which naturally live at high altitude may be genetically or socially selected, and also are often exposed to more extreme climatic variations (cold and low humidity). In the event the data available are difficult to assess partly for these reasons, but also because the other variables which we now know to affect birth weight (litter size, placental size, and so on), also must be considered.

In 1948, Moore and Price studied reproduction in several small laboratory species and concluded that there was no significant trend in mean birth weight with altitude. However, they had little quantitative information other than in rats, in which their figures suggest that litter size and birth weight were less at 14,200 feet than at three lower altitudes down to sea level. However, Krum (1957), and Fenton Kelly (personal communication), in a larger series, concluded that there was no significant difference in the birth weights of rats born at 12,470 feet and sea level. None of these authors measured placental weights. Krum made the interesting observation that the heart weights in rats born at altitude were greater, both absolutely and relatively, than in those born at sea level, suggesting that the hypoxia had affected the foetus sufficiently to cause myocardial hypertrophy (Table 14). It is interesting that the rat is the one species in which there is some doubt whether litter size affects foetal and placental development, a fact which makes one wonder whether it is the best species in which to study the effect of altitude on foetal weight, even though pure strains can be readily procured and it is cheap and easily handled.

The effect of altitude on foetal growth in sheep was examined by Metcalfe et al. (1962) at 14,900 feet in Morococha in the Peruvian Andes. They compared the growth of singletons in a local Merino flock with that in Welsh and Dorset ewes of a similar weight range at sea level. In contrast to rats, there was no difference in foetal heart weights. The weights of the placental cotyledons tended to be less at altitude; the foetal weights at sea level and altitude were similar, but the numbers over 130 days gestational age were small.

In man also, there is not a great deal of information. The median birth weight in 1955, in Lake County, Colorado, at 10,000 feet, and at 40 weeks gestational age, was 3.07 kg. This is rather less than that for 5,000 feet at Denver (3.29 kg), or near sea level in Baltimore (3.32 kg), or Birmingham, England (3.34 kg) (Lichty, Ting, Bruns, and Dyer, 1957; Lubchenco, Hansman, Dressler and Boyd, 1963). The Lake County statistics might be worth recalculating in relation to placental weights, for comparison with the data from Birmingham (as in Fig. 23).

This is an unsatisfactory state of affairs. The effect expected is likely to be small and only perceptible toward term and when full account is taken of all the possible variables, including gestational age, placental weight, litter size, and (in a polytocous species) site of implantation. The parity and weight of the mother also may influence foetal weight (see Cloete, 1939 for early references). No deliberate search for such an effect has been made using the large numbers required, toward term, in a single variety or pure strain. Until this is done we cannot decide whether O_2 supply is likely to be a limiting factor to foetal growth in late gestation under normal conditions.

Changes in Maternal Nutrition

The idea that foetal growth might be dependent on the limited availability of a normal maternal metabolic product or products (e.g., some form of carbohydrate, protein, or fat) is obviously true in the extreme case. There must be a minimum supply of these materials, just as there must be a minimum maternal blood flow to the placenta. What needs to be decided is whether this is likely to be a limiting factor under normal circumstances, in single or multiple pregnancies, in the species with which we are concerned on their normal diets, or as a result of limitation of food intake. As with limitation of maternal O_2 supply, the mother may be expected to react in such a way as to maintain the blood concentration of essential metabolic materials. Studies of this kind have so far been limited to a reduction in total food intake rather than reduction in specific constituents.

Attention was particularly directed to this ques-

TABLE 14.—HEART WEIGHTS IN NEWBORN RATS AT ALTITUDE
(12,470) AND SEA-LEVEL (250 FEET)

HEART WEIGHT	SEA-LEVEL	ALTITUDE	P
Mg	20.8 ± 0.63	29.8 ± 1.72	<.01
Mg/100 Gm body weight	0.40 ± 0.01	0.51 ± 0.02	<.01

The figures indicate the means ± S.E. (from Krum, 1957).

tion because of experience with farm animals in the late 1930s. It was noticed that in sheep up to about 90 days gestation (0.6 of term) the range of variation in weight about the mean was small; it was much greater at term. Restriction of maternal food intake was believed to have no effect on placental or foetal growth up to about 90 days. This is not quite true as subsequent investigations have shown (Foote, Pope, Chapman, and Cosida, 1959; Everitt, 1964), but the changes up to this age are certainly much smaller than those seen subsequently, when foetal weight can be affected very considerably. For instance, Wallace (1945) found that mature foetuses of ewes fed on a restricted diet for the last 8 weeks of gestation (0.38 of term) weighed only 57% of those from well fed ewes.

The interpretation of these findings is more difficult than at first appears. Although the litter weight is only about 11% of maternal weight in this species (Table 3, p. 15), an abrupt reduction of maternal food intake toward the end of gestation, and particularly in multiple pregnancies, readily leads to a complex series of metabolic changes with the development of a fatty liver in the mother and, ultimately, general somatic disturbances including convulsions, described as toxaemia of pregnancy (Parry and Shelley, 1961). This interesting condition has some similarities with the syndrome which bears the same name in man, but without maternal hypertension (even though renal malignant hypertension can be induced in sheep; Parker, Dungworth, and Galligan, 1966). For our present purpose its importance lies in the fact that the pregnant sheep seems peculiarly susceptible to sudden dietary disturbance, and even to a change in handling. This is such a prominent feature of the species that there should be some hesitation before concluding that the limitation of foetal growth by restriction of maternal food intake is solely by a direct action, i.e., by reducing the amount of circulating nutriment available. It could be by indirect means, e.g., hormonal, or as a result of a complex metabolic disturbance rather than a simple deficiency. Yet it must be said that Reid and Hinks (1962) found a tendency for maternal blood glucose concentration to fall in monotocous ewes fed suboptimally, particularly about 110 days gestation when foetal growth is most rapid. It is also interesting that maternal diet can affect cotyledonary weight in sheep (Foote *et al.,* 1959; Everitt, 1964) both at 90 days gestation and at term.

In other species, restriction of maternal food intake has to be extreme before foetal birth weight is decreased. Even in Holland, in 1945, there was only a very small reduction in human birth weight. In rats (in which the litter weight is nearly a quarter of maternal weight; Table 3, p. 15), a decrease in food intake to $\frac{1}{2}-\frac{1}{3}$ during the last 6 days of gestation (0.28 term) did not affect either foetal or placental weights (Campbell, Innes, and Kosterlitz, 1965). In rabbits, a decrease in food intake to one quarter of normal during the last 10 days of gestation (0.48 of term) also had little effect on foetal or placental weights (Harding and Shelley, unpublished). The view that foetal growth is normally dependent on maternal nutrition appears to have derived from the accidental first choice of an experimental species, the sheep, which is particularly susceptible. It is also, incidentally, difficult to judge from the accounts of these first experiments by how much maternal food intake was restricted. It seems fair to conclude that in normal circumstances maternal nutrition is not a limiting factor to foetal growth.

Hormones

Gross increase in foetal weight does not appear to be regulated by foetal production of the hormones which are necessary for normal development after birth. Destruction of the foetal hypophysis by irradiation in mice or by intra-uterine decapitation in rats and rabbits (Wells, 1947; Jost, 1947; 1954) did not greatly alter the progressive increase in body weight during gestation, even when the thyroid also was removed. Some foetal rabbits, decapitated at 19 days gestation, grew from a headless body weight of 2 Gm to 17–25 Gm by the 28th day, when control foetuses rarely weighed more than 30 Gm. Figure 30 shows the growth of a headless rat foetus in a hypophysectomized mother. A distinction is thus drawn between sexual differentiation and changes in the adrenals and some other organs (e.g., glycogen deposition in the liver) for which foetal hypophysial hormones are necessary in different species at variable stages of gestation, and the gross development of the main structure of the body.

These results are a little surprising, because morphological and biochemical data in several species, including the rat, rabbit, calf, sheep, monkey, and man show that the foetal thyroid is active before birth (Rall, Robbins, and Lewallen, 1964). Toward term the function of the foetal thyroid comes under the influence of foetal thyroid-stimulating hormone (TSH). And exposure to a cold environment (an ambient temperature of 23–29° C) during the first 36–48 hours from birth causes a rise in blood pro-

Fig. 30.—Rat foetuses of the same litter. The upper one was extracted from the uterus during the 17th day of pregnancy, and the next was decapitated at the same time. The decapitated foetus and two controls were removed 5 days later. The mother had been hypophysectomized on the 16th day of pregnancy. Maternal hypophysectomy and foetal decapitation did not alter foetal growth very much (Jost, 1962).

tein-bound iodine concentration and in thyroid-iodine clearance in normal human infants, suggesting a normal thyroid response to TSH secretion (Fisher, Oddie, and Makoski, 1966). Yet infants who are subsequently found to suffer from congenital hypothyroidism, even when this diagnosis is established as early as 5 months of age, are of normal weight at birth. The mean birth weight in one series of 49 cretins was 3.6 kg (Lowrey *et al.,* 1958).

So far as the foetal pituitary is concerned, the presence of human growth hormone has been detected by an immuno-assay method as early as 15 weeks gestation and in increasing quantities toward term. The human foetus also has a large serum level of growth hormone (Table 15). Human growth hormone in foetal blood does not seem to be derived from the mother, because isotopically labeled human growth hormone injected intravenously into pregnant women in labour did not cross to the foetus (Gitlin, Kumate, and Morales, 1965). Yet children who are subsequently found to be idiopathic hypopituitary dwarfs have a normal birth weight and grow at a normal rate for the first 2–3 months after birth at least (Root, 1965). And administration of human growth hormone to premature infants had no appreciable effect on fibula length, head circumference, or body weight (Chiumello, Vaccari, and Sereni, 1965), suggesting either that it was not a primary growth factor at this age or that there was already maximal stimulation by endogenous supply.

Yet when we turn from the development of gross body size to that of particular organs there is some very striking evidence of the action of growth hormone *in utero.* Zamenhof, Mosley, and Schuller (1966) have demonstrated that injection of purified bovine pituitary growth hormone into pregnant rats, while it did not alter foetal weight, caused in the offspring an increase in brain weight of 30%, an increase of total DNA per brain, and a rise in cerebral cortical cell density of 63%. The time chosen for administration, from the 7th to the 20th day of gestation, was that during which neurones are proliferating rapidly in this species. They quote evidence by other authors to suggest that such animals show a statistically better performance in behavioural tests. There are many further experiments which these findings suggest, to test the general proposition in other species (e.g., subhuman primates) and to determine whether the growth hormone passed the placenta (apparently unlike man). There is also the possibility that administration of growth hormone to premature infants may alter cortical development, even if not skeletal structure.

Maternal hypophysectomy has little effect on foetal or placental weight increase in rabbits (in which the foetus also was decapitated, Fig. 30), in

TABLE 15.—Concentrations of Hormones in Human Maternal and Foetal Blood at Term*

	Maternal Venous Blood Serum	Umbilical Venous Blood Serum
Chorionic growth hormone prolactin (μg/ml)	5.6 ± 0.39	0.019 ± 0.003
Human growth hormone (mμg/ml) Mean ± S.E.	5.0 ± 0.52	33.5 ± 4.6

* Kaplan and Grumbach, 1965,a.

rats (Campbell, Innes, and Kosterlitz, 1953; Knobil and Caton, 1953), or in other species including rhesus monkeys (Smith, 1954), goats (Cowie, Daniel, Prichard, and Tindal, 1963), and a woman who was hypophysectomized when 26 weeks pregnant for a metastatic carcinoma of the breast, and who delivered a normal 5 lb infant at 35 weeks (Little *et al.,* 1958). There may have been a small reduction in foetal weight at term after maternal hypophysectomy, but it was very small compared with the weight gain made over the latter part of gestation. Pregnancy continued after implantation of yttrium⁹⁰ into both the maternal and foetal hypophyses of 3 pregnant rhesus monkeys, but the details given are insufficient to judge whether destruction of the pituitaries was complete or whether foetal or placental growth was affected (Hutchinson, Westover, and Will, 1962). Nevertheless, taken as a whole, the evidence suggests that if gross foetal weight gain is under hormonal control it is not mainly through the pituitary growth hormones of either mother or foetus.

As Grumbach (1966) has pointed out, the recent evidence that the concentration of plasma growth hormone changes rapidly with changes in metabolic rate; that it rises during fasting, hypoglycaemia, and exercise; that it diminishes glucose utilization and raises plasma free fatty acid concentration by promoting the hydrolysis of triglycerides—this evidence of lability of secretion makes it difficult to appreciate the significance of changes in plasma concentration with age. The newborn infant has an elevated concentration of growth hormone, but this may be related to the metabolic changes which occur immediately after birth rather than to the normal control of growth rate during late foetal life.

A further possibility has arisen with the separate identification of a placental hormone, chorionic growth hormone prolactin (CGP) (Fukushima, 1961; Josimovich and McLaren, 1962). Using immunofluorescent methods, the specific fluorescence has been identified in the cytoplasm of the syncytiotrophoblast of the human placenta from the 12th week of gestation onward; it was not present in the underlying cytotrophoblast (Sciarra, Kaplan, and Grumbach, 1963). CGP is produced by human chorionic tissue grown *in vitro,* and as its concentration in maternal blood at term is very much greater than in foetal blood (Table 15), it is thought to be secreted from the placenta into the maternal blood. It disappears from maternal blood within 8 hours of delivery (Kaplan and Grumbach, 1965,b). It was present in large amounts in the plasma of a woman

delivered at 36 weeks, 12 weeks after hypophysectomy, and it was absent from the pituitary of a pregnant woman who died in the last trimester of cerebral haemorrhage, and from foetal pituitaries (Josimovich and Astwood, 1964). It appears to have many properties in common with human growth hormone, including that of mobilising free fatty acid *in vitro* and *in vivo.* Although in this respect it is less active than human growth hormone, it is present in maternal blood in a much higher concentration, and its daily production has been estimated (from measurements of half life) as 1.4–4.0 Gm/day at term in man (Kaplan and Grumbach, 1965,a).

There are many possible consequences of this very interesting development. For instance, the activity of CGP may be directly responsible for the increased rate of metabolism during pregnancy, and it may explain the rapid development of fatty livers in sheep showing signs of toxaemia of pregnancy. It has also been suggested by Grumbach that secretion of CGP into the maternal circulation may indirectly influence foetal growth. This may be so, but if CGP secretion is rate-limiting to foetal growth during the latter part of gestation, it is surprising that the rate of growth is identical soon after birth, as shown in Figure 29. There are many further investigations which suggest themselves before we can come to a considered view. One would like to know whether maternal plasma CGP concentration is reduced by placental infarction (e.g., identified by liberation of serum isocitric dehydrogenase activity from the infarcted area; Dawkins and Wigglesworth, 1961) or whether it is elevated in multiple pregnancies. This mechanism can also be regarded as a possible means of foetal homeostasis, as a means of communication between the foetus and its mother. CGP appears to be secreted by a foetal tissue, and if its secretion rate is modified by changes within the foetus it might influence the mother in such a way as to maintain the foetal internal environment. As the maternal half life of CGP appears to be quite short, it should be possible to study the effect of, say, foetal hypoglycaemia on maternal CGP plasma concentration even in an acute experiment (e.g., in the monkey).

Conclusion

Foetal growth is obviously determined by many factors, genetic and environmental. Of the latter in different species and under a variety of experimental conditions, statistical correlations have been established with maternal size, parity, nutrition and health, duration of pregnancy, litter size, position in the uterine horn, placental size, and environmental temperature. These correlations have suggested a variety of possible operative mechanisms. Of these, investigation of the effects of placental size, operating perhaps through hormone production or limitation of transfer capacity, and of the influence of the foetal pituitary seem most clearly indicated as fruitful lines for future research. Examination of the rate of increase of weight and cell count of individual organs, however laborious, is likely to give much more valuable information than measurement of total body weight alone. It would be surprising if this did not prove to be a most profitable field for investigation in the immediate future, and one that is likely to provide new information about the mechanisms of foetal metabolic homeostasis and, possibly, some further indication as to whether these normally determine the future growth potential of the individual.

REFERENCES

Adair, F. L., and Thelander, H.: A study of the weight and dimensions of the human placenta in its relation to the weight of the newborn infant, Am. J. Obst. & Gynec. 10:172–205, 1925.

Aherne, W., and Dunnill, M. S.: Morphometry of the human placenta, Brit. M. Bull. 22:5–8, 1966.

Alexander, G.: Studies on the placenta of the sheep (Ovis Aries L.) Placental size, J. Reprod. Fertil. 7:289–305, 1964,a.

Alexander, G.: Studies on the placenta of the sheep (Ovis Aries L.) Effect of surgical reduction in the number of caruncles, J. Reprod. Fertil. 7:307–322, 1964,b.

Altman, P. A., and Dittmer, A. S.: *Growth* (Washington, D. C.: Fed. Am. Soc. Biol., 1962).

Barcroft, J., and Kennedy, J. A.: The distribution of blood between the foetus and placenta in sheep, J. Physiol. 95:173–186, 1939.

Broadhurst, P. L., and Jinks, J. L.: Parity as a determinant of birth weight in the rhesus monkey, Folia. Primat. 3:201-210, 1965.

Browne, J. C., and Veall, N.: The maternal placental blood flow in normotensive and hypertensive women, J. Obst. & Gynaec. Brit. Emp. 60:141–147, 1953.

Calkins, L. A.: Placental variation, Am. J. Obst. & Gynec. 33:280–290, 1937.

Campbell, R. M.; Innes, I. R., and Kosterlitz, H. W.: Some dietary and hormonal effects on maternal, foetal and placental weights in the rat, J. Endocrinol. 9:68–75, 1953.

Chiumello, G.; Vaccari, A., and Sereni, F.: Bone growth and metabolic studies of premature infants treated with human growth hormone, Pediatrics 36:836–842, 1965.

Cloete, J. H. L.: Prenatal growth in the merino sheep. Onderstepoort J. Vet. Sc. 13:417–558, 1939.

Cowie, A. T.; Daniel, P. M.; Prichard, M. M. L., and Tindal, J. S.: Hypophysectomy in pregnant goats, and section of the pituitary stalk in pregnant goats and sheep, J. Endocrinol. 28:93–102, 1963.

Dawkins, M. J. R., and Wigglesworth, J. S.: Serum isocetric dehydrogenase in normal pregnancy and preeclamptic toxaemia, Path. Microbiol. 24:655–661, 1961.

Dixon, H. G.; Browne, J. C. M., and Davey, D. A.: Choriodecidual and myometrial blood-flow, Lancet 2:369–373, 1963.

Dixon, H. G., and Robertson, W. B.: Vascular changes in the placental bed, Path. et microbiol. 24:622–630, 1961.

Draper, R. L.: The prenatal growth of the guinea pig, Anat. Rec. 18:369–392, 1920.

Eckstein, P., and McKeown, T.: Effect of transection of one horn of the guinea pig's uterus on foetal growth in the other horn, J. Endocrinol. 12:97–107, 1955.

Eckstein, P.; McKeown, T., and Record, R. G.: Variation in placental weight according to litter size in the guinea pig, J. Endocrinol. 12:108–114, 1955.

Everitt, G. C.: Maternal undernutrition and retarded foetal development in merino sheep, Nature 201:1341–1342, 1964.

Fisher, D. A.; Oddie, T. H., and Makoski, E. J.: The influence of environmental temperature on thyroid, adrenal and water metabolism in the newborn human infant, Pediatrics 37:583–591, 1966.

Foote, W. C.; Pope, A. L.; Chapman, A. B., and Cosida, L. E.: Reproduction in the yearling ewe as affected by breed and sequence of feeding levels. II. Effects on foetal development, J. Anim. Sc. 18:463–474, 1959.

Fukushima, M.: Studies on somatotrophic hormone secretion in gynecology and obstetrics, Tohoku J. Exper. Med. 74:161–174, 1961.

Gitlin, D.; Kumate, J., and Morales, C.: Metabolism and maternofoetal transfer of human growth hormone in the pregnant woman at term, J. Clin. Endocrinol. 25:1599–1608, 1965.

Grumbach, M. M.: Growth hormone and growth, Pediatrics 37:245–248, 1966.

Hafez, E. S. E.: Effects of over-crowding *in utero* on implantation and fetal development in the rabbit, J. Exper. Zool. 156:269–288, 1964.

Hammond, J.: The changes in the reproductive organs of the rabbit during pregnancy. Trans. Dynam. Developm. 10:93–107, 1935.

Hashima, H.: Studies on the prenatal growth of the mouse with special reference to the site of implantation of the embryo, Tohoku, J. Agric. Res. 6:307–312, 1956.

Healy, M. J. R.; McLaren, A., and Michie, D.: Foetal growth in the mouse, Proc. Roy. Soc. (B) 153:367–379, 1960.

Huggett, A. St. G., and Widdas, W. F.: The relationship between mammalian foetal weight and conception age, J. Physiol. 114:306–317, 1951.

Hutchinson, D. L.; Westover, J. L., and Will, D. W.: The destruction of the maternal and foetal pituitary glands in subhuman primates, Am. J. Obst. & Gynec. 83:857–865, 1962.

Ibsen, H. L.: Prenatal growth in guinea pigs with special reference to environmental factors affecting weight at birth, J. Exper. Zool. 51:51–91, 1928.

Josimovich, J. B., and Astwood, B. L.: Human placental lactogen (HPL), a trophoblastic hormone synergising with chorionic gonadotrophin and potentiating the anabolic effects of pituitary growth hormone, Am. J. Obst. & Gynec. 88:867–879, 1964.

Josimovich, J. B., and McLaren, J. A.: Presence in the human placenta and term serum of a highly lactogenic substance immunologically related to pituitary growth hormone, Endocrinol. 71:209–220, 1962.

Jost, A.: Expériences de décapitation de l'embryon de lapin, C. R. Acad. Sc. Paris. 225:322–324, 1947.

Jost, A.: Hormones in the development of the foetus, Cold Spring Harb. Symp. Quant. Biol. 19:167–181, 1954.

Jost, A.: Endocrine factors in foetal development, Triangle. 5:189–193, 1962.

Kaplan, S. L., and Grumbach, M. M.: Immunoassay of human chorionic growth hormone-prolactin in serum and urine. Science. 147:751–753, 1965,a.

Kaplan, S. L., and Grumbach, M. M.: Serum chorionic "growth hormone-prolactin" and serum pituitary growth hormone in mother and foetus at term, J. Clin. Endocrinol. 25:1370–1374, 1965,b.

Knobil, E., and Caton, W. L.: The effect of hypophysectomy on foetal and placental growth in the rat, Endocrinol. 53:198–201, 1953.

Krum, A. A.: Reproduction and Growth of Laboratory Rats and Mice at Altitude. D. Phil. Thesis, Univ. Berkeley, California, 1957.

Lapin, B. A., and Yakovleva, L. A.: Comparative Pathology in Monkeys (Springfield, Ill.: Charles C Thomas, Publisher, 1963), p. 220.

Lichty, J. A.; Ting, R. Y.; Bruns, P. D., and Dyar, E.: Studies of babies born at high altitude, Am. J. Dis. Child. 93:666–678, 1957.

Little, B.; Smith, O. W.; Jessiman, A. G.; Selenkow, H. A.; Vant Hoff, W.; Eglin, J. M., and Moore, F. D.: Hypophysectomy during pregnancy in a patient with cancer of the breast, J. Clin. Endocrinol. 18:425–443, 1958.

Lowrey, G. H.; Aster, R. H.; Carr, E. A.; Ramon, G.; Beierwaltes, W., and Spafford, N. R.: Early diagnostic criteria of congenital hypothyroidism, Am. J. Dis. Child. 96:131–143, 1958.

Lubchenco, L. O.; Hausman, C.; Dressler, M., and Boyd, E.: Intrauterine growth as estimated from liveborn birth weight data at 24–42 weeks of gestation, Pediatrics 32:793–800, 1963.

MacDowell, E. C.; Allen, E., and MacDowell, C. G.: The prenatal growth of the mouse, J. Gen. Physiol. 11:57–70, 1927.

McKeown, T., and Record, R. G.: The influence of placental size on foetal growth in man, with special reference to multiple pregnancy, J. Endocrinol. 9:418–426, 1953.

McLaren, A.: Placental weight loss in late pregnancy, J. Reprod. Fertil. 9:343–346, 1956,a.

McLaren, A.: Genetic and environmental effects on foetal and placental growth in mice, J. Reprod. Fertil. 9:79–98, 1965,b.

McLaren, A., and Michie, D.: Congenital Runts, in Wolstenholme, G. E. W., and O'Connor, C. M. (eds.): Ciba Foundation Symposium on Congenital Malformations (London: J. & A. Churchill, Ltd., 1960), pp. 178–193.

Metcalfe, J.; Meschia, G.; Hellegers, A.; Prystowsky, H.; Huckabee, W., and Barron, D. H.: Observations on the growth rates and organ weights of foetal sheep at altitude and sea-level, Quart. J. Exper. Physiol. 47:305–313, 1962.

Moore, C. R., and Price, D.: A study at high altitudes of reproduction, growth, sexual maturity and organ weights, J. Exper. Zool. 108:171–216, 1948.

Naeye, R. L.: Organ abnormalities in a human parabiotic syndrome, Am. J. Path. 46:829–842, 1965.

Naeye, R. L.; Benirschke, K.; Hagstrom, J. W. C., and Marcus, C. C.: Intrauterine growth of twins as estimated from liveborn birth weight data, Pediatrics 37:409–416, 1966.

Needham, J.: Chemical Embryology (London: Cambridge University Press, 1931).

Parker, H. R.; Dungworth, D. L., and Galligan, S. J.: Renal hypertension in sheep, Am. J. Vet. Res. 27:430–443, 1966.

Parry, H. B., and Shelley, H. J.: Experimental induction and control of "toxaemia of pregnancy" in sheep, Path. Microbiol. 24:681, 1961.

Rall, J. E.; Robbins, J., and Lewallen, C. G.: The Thyroid, in Pincus, G.; Thimann, K. V., and Astwood, E. B. (ed.): The Hormones (New York: Academic Press, vol. 5, 1964), pp. 159–439.

Reid, R. L., and Hinks, N. T.: Studies on carbohydrate metabolism of sheep, Aust. J. Agric. Res. 13:1092–1098, 1962.

Roberts, R. C.: On the uniform lineal growth of the human foetus, Lancet 1:295–296, 1906.

Rosahn, P. D., and Greene, H. S. N.: The influence of intrauterine factors on the foetal weight of rabbits, J. Exper. Med. 63:901–921, 1936.

Root, A.: Growth hormone, Pediatrics, 36:940–950, 1965.

Sciarra, J. J.; Kaplan, S. L., and Grumbach, M. M.: Localization of antihuman growth hormone serum within the placenta: Evidence for a human chorionic growth hormone prolactin, Nature 199:1005–1006, 1963.

Smith, P. E.: Continuation of pregnancy in rhesus monkeys (macaca mulatta) following hypophysectomy, Endocrinol. 55:655–664, 1954.

Spencer, R. P.; Coulombe, M. J., and van Wagenen, G.: Intraspecies comparison of foetal growth, Growth 30: 1–7, 1966.

van Wagenen, G., and Catchpole, H. R.: Growth of the foetus and placenta of the monkey (macaca mulatta), Am. J. Phys. Anthropol. 23:23–34, 1965.

Waldorf, D. P.; Foote, W. C.; Self, H. L.; Chapman, A. B., and Casida, L. E.: Factors affecting foetal pig weight late in gestation, J. Anim. Sc. 16:976–985, 1957.

Wallace, L. R.: The effect of diet on foetal development, J. Physiol. 104:34–35P, 1945.

Wells, L. J.: Progress of studies designed to determine whether the foetal hypophysis produces hormones that influence development. Anat. Rec. 97:409, 1947.

Wigglesworth, J. S.: Experimental growth retardation in the foetal rat, J. Path. & Bact. 88:1–13, 1964.

Yerkes, R. M.: Chimpanzees (New Haven: Yale University Press, 1943).

Zamenhof, S.; Mosley, J., and Schuller, E.: Stimulation of the proliferation of cortical neurones by prenatal treatment with growth hormone, Science 152:1396–1397, 1966.

5

Maternal Placental and Myometrial Blood Flow

THERE ARE MANY interesting problems, both academic and practical, about the regulation of maternal blood flow to the uterus and placenta. We would like to know to what extent it is under autonomic nervous regulation; whether autonomic nervous stimulation may cause vasoconstriction or, perhaps under different conditions, vasodilatation; and if so, how this may affect the redistribution of cardiac output under changing physiological circumstances. We should like to know whether myometrial activity can cause an increase in myometrial blood flow, as muscular activity does elsewhere, and to what extent myometrial contraction influences maternal placental blood flow. We should consider whether flow to the uterus and placenta is maintained preferentially to that of other organs when the mother is placed in an unfavourable circumstance, as at altitude, during haemorrhage, or traumatic shock, and when her circulation is redistributed to preserve blood flow to her heart, brain, and muscles of respiration. The obstetricians and anaesthetists would like to know whether spinal anaesthesia or ganglion blockade is likely to affect maternal blood flow to the placenta. There are many such questions and singularly few answers, because the methods available are unsatisfactory.

There are two principal causes for this dissatisfaction. First, no method has yet been described which directly measures maternal placental blood flow independently of myometrial flow. And second, the accuracy of many of the methods which have been used for measuring total uterine flow (maternal placental + myometrial) is open to question. The uterus is supplied with uterine and ovarian

arteries and veins on both sides and by complex anastomoses of variable size with other vessels (e.g., rabbit, Barcroft and Rothschild, 1932; rhesus monkey, Ramsey, Corner, and Donner, 1963); therefore, measurement of flow through a single artery or vein may give an unrepresentative and misleading estimate of total flow. This also makes it more difficult to design a satisfactory way of checking the validity of indirect methods for measuring uterine blood flow.

Direct Methods

Two types of direct methods have been used for measuring uterine flow, by venous outflow or arterial inflow. Barcroft, Herkel, and Hill (1933) measured total venous outflow in rabbits under dial (diallyl-barbiturate) anaesthesia. The ovarian vessels were tied. The bladder, vagina, and rectum were removed to give access to the main venous drainage by the iliac veins. The peripheral end of one iliac vein was tied and that of the other was cannulated. Outflow from the latter was collected while the central end of the inferior vena cava was obstructed, over a period of 0.5–1.0 minute. The arterial pressure of the rabbit was maintained by transfusion with heparinised blood from a donor. The advantage of this method is that it is direct, and as accurate as the manipulation of a stop-watch and measuring cylinder allow. The disadvantage, as Huckabee (1962) has pointed out, is that anaesthesia and the fairly extensive surgery, in a species which is rather susceptible to manipulation, might have altered uterine flow. Uterine flow at term approached 30 ml/min, which was calculated as ~90 ml/kg total tissue weight (uterus, placentas, and foetuses) per minute; there is some reason to believe that, at least in larger species near term, it may be considerably higher. Uterine venous O_2 saturation was as low as 25% toward term, possibly because uterine flow was reduced as a result of the operation.

Robson and Schild (1938) removed the stomach, intestines, and spleen in cats under chloralose anaesthesia. They perfused one uterine artery at constant flow rate *in vivo,* using the cat's own blood from the upper end of the cannulated aorta, and measured the perfusion pressure as an index of uterine vascular resistance. In other experiments they measured the changes in volume of a single foetus, placenta, and the part of a uterine horn which contained them by an oncometer during uterine contractions. The methods were adequate for the authors' primary objective (to establish whether drug-induced uterine contractions impeded flow early in gestation), but the extensive surgery might have altered the physiological state of the mother and have interrupted some of the nerve supply to the uterus. This is always the problem with such direct methods, though their accuracy is unquestionable, and if a positive result is observed (e.g., vasoconstriction on drug injection or nerve stimulation) the observation establishes without doubt the existence of that mechanism.

Ahlquist (1950) used a somewhat similar method in pregnant dogs under general anaesthesia. The left uterine artery was cannulated peripherally and joined to the central end of a femoral artery via a Shipley optically recording rotameter. This was a better arrangement because it obviated the need for such an extensive dissection as that used by Robson and Schild.

Flow has also been measured in one or more uterine arteries using cuff electromagnetic flowmeters of different types, in acute studies on pregnant women at caesarean section for therapeutic abortion (Assali, Rauramo, and Peltonen, 1960), and in ewes (Wolkoff, McGee, Flowers, and Bawden, 1964), and after chronic implantation in pregnant dogs and sheep (Assali, Dasgupta, Kolin, and Holms, 1958; Greiss, 1965). There is some doubt as to the absolute values of these measurements because the instruments used required calibration (preferably *in vivo*) and were of types which are known to be subject to potentially large zero errors (see Appendix). Now that more accurate electromagnetic and ultrasonic types of cuff flowmeter are

becoming available, this problem can be minimized, but we are still left with the other difficulties of multiple arterial supply and of the distribution of flow to placenta and myometrium.

Indirect Methods

Kety and Schmidt (1948) showed that a reasonably accurate estimate of blood flow to the brain could be obtained by applying the Fick equation to the diffusion of an inert foreign gas (nitrous oxide) from the blood to the tissues, even though the blood concentration was varying with time, so long as sufficient measurements of concentration were made until equilibrium was obtained. There were two important features of this work. The brain is a relatively homogeneous organ so far as the solubility of nitrous oxide is concerned, and the accuracy of the method was established by simultaneous measurement of cerebral flow, using a bubble flowmeter in dogs and monkeys. The application of this principle of flow measurement to the uterus has not been satisfactory for several reasons. Nitrous oxide proved to be unsuitable because it took such a very long time for equilibrium to be attained (Assali, Douglass, Baird, Nicholson, and Suyemoto, 1953; Metcalfe, Romney, Ramsey, Reid, and Burwell, 1955). 4-aminoantipyrine appeared to come into equilibrium after 15–20 minutes (Huckabee and Walcott, 1960; Huckabee and Barron, 1961; Huckabee, Metcalfe, Prystowsky, and Barron, 1961; Huckabee, 1962), but its use as an indicator raised other problems. Analytical recovery of the substance from foetal blood and liver was not quantitative. There was good evidence for believing that there were some slowly equilibrating compartments within the uterus (e.g., allantoic and amniotic fluids). And although much effort was put into the development of the method, it was never checked by simultaneous measurement using direct flowmeters.

It is worth noting that the foetus, its fluids (allantoic, amniotic, gastrointestinal, and pulmonary), and circulations (blood and lymph) constitute a system of great complexity with many compartments. Equilibration of an inert material which enters into physical solution in the tissue fluids will not be attained for a long time, and the estimate of the total amount transferred from mother to uterus, placenta, and foetus (which is necessary for the Fick calculation) is likely to be inaccurate on these grounds alone. There is, in this respect, no great advantage to be gained by infusing the indicator material into the foetus and following its transfer to the mother; the situation will still be complicated by slow equilibration in the foetus. We may also consider the simpler case of O_2, as a model of a substance much of which is confined to the bloodstream. Equilibration of the foetal O_2 saturation after a stepwise change in the O_2 content of the gas breathed by a maternal ewe (e.g., from 21%–50%) is attained after 6–7 minutes, as compared with 1–2 minutes in the mother. This suggests that because of the complex character of the foetal circulation, equilibration of such a substance takes at least 5–6 minutes. [In the instance cited, foetal O_2 consumption would be unaltered and the distribution of O_2 within the bloodstream would not have been much affected by cardiovascular reactions.] The use of O_2 as an indicator substance would be unwise because the O_2 consumption of the foetus and placenta is high compared with the extra quantity accommodated in the foetal blood. It really seems unlikely that a satisfactory method will be found to adapt the Fick principle for measuring maternal myometrial and placental blood flow. The results with this method so far available can be regarded only as a very general indication of the size of flow to be expected.

The rate of clearance of radioactive sodium injected either into the myometrium or into the intervillous space has been used as an index of human maternal myometrial or placental flow, respectively (Browne and Veall, 1953; Dixon, Browne, and Davey, 1963). The results are impossible to interpret directly and quantitatively in terms of blood flow, though they may indeed give a fair indication as to when flow is very much reduced in particular circumstances, as for instance when there are occlusive lesions on the maternal side of the placental vascular bed (Dixon and Robertson, 1961). These are qualitative methods, but nonetheless valuable when there is nothing else available.

Results

With the reservations about methods already expressed, Table 16 suggests that total uterine blood flow may be 100–300 ml/min per kg tissue (uterus, placenta, and foetus) near term in several species. This seems about right as can be seen from a rough calculation using data from anaesthetized sheep. Let us suppose that in its passage through the placenta the maternal blood O_2 saturation is reduced from 85% to about 45%, as unpublished measurements *in vivo* suggest. With a maternal O_2 carrying capacity of $\sim$11 ml/100 ml this would give an extraction of 4.4 ml O_2/100 ml maternal placental blood flow. The combined O_2 consumption of placenta and foetus near term under these conditions is a mean of 22 ml/min for a combined tissue weight of 4.5 kg (Campbell, Dawes, Fishman, Hyman, and James, 1966), or 4.9 ml/kg tissue per minute. This then could be supplied by a maternal flow of 110 ml/min per kg tissue. This calculation does not take into account myometrial O_2 consumption, which might be greater or less than 4.9 ml/kg min; Sir Joseph Barcroft would, therefore, have probably described it as a rather rugged calculation. The estimate of 110 ml/min per kg tissue is consistent with the observed flow in a *single* uterine artery of 186–262 ml/min in unanaesthetized sheep at term (Assali, Dasgupta, Kolin, and Holms, 1958; Greiss, 1963). In unanaesthetized animals one might expect O_2 consumption, and therefore minimal calculated uterine flow, to be rather greater.

TABLE 16.—MEASUREMENTS OF UTERINE BLOOD FLOW IN DIFFERENT SPECIES

METHOD	SPECIES	AGE	MEAN UTERINE FLOW/KG TISSUE*	AUTHORS
Collection of venous effluent	Rabbit	Near term	$\sim$90	Barcroft, Herkel, and Hill (1932)
Cuff electromagnetic flowmeter	Man	10–28 Weeks gestation	94–127	Assali, Rauramo, and Peltonen (1960)
N_2O equilibration	Man	Term	124	Metcalfe, Romney, Ramsey, Reid, and Burwell (1955)
N_2O equilibration	Man	Term	150	Assali, Douglass, Baird, Nicholson, and Suyemoto (1953)
4-Aminoantipyrine equilibration	Goat	0.5–1.0 of term	280	Huckabee, Metcalfe, Prystowsky, and Barron (1961)

* Uterus, placenta(s), and foetus(es).

It is interesting that Huckabee and Barron's (1961) estimate of uterine blood flow (in the goat) is so very much greater than that of other authors on other species (Table 16). This is a matter of considerable consequence because, using this estimate of flow obtained by the indirect 4-aminoantipyrine method, they have deduced from the arteriovenous O_2 difference a measure of O_2 consumption for the uterus and its contents (~ 10 ml/kg min) which also is high compared with other measurements made of O_2 consumption in the foetal goat (Barcroft, 1946) or lamb (Dawes and Mott, 1959). Is this difference due to variation in physiological conditions, e.g., in anaesthesia, or does the 4-aminoantipyrine method of measuring uterine flow give an overestimate?

When we come to consider evidence for the mechanisms which influence uterine and maternal placental flow, the information available is very limited. As one might reasonably expect, uterine contractions reduce uterine flow whether they are due to spontaneous labour or to the administration of oxytocic drugs, in pregnant dogs and sheep (Ahlquist, 1950; Assali, Dasgupta, Kolin, and Holms, 1958; Greiss, 1965,a; using flowmeters). In dogs, uterine contractions sufficient to cause a rise in uterine pressure of 20–30 mm Hg caused a decrease in uterine blood flow of 10–50%, limited to that horn which was contracting at the time (Ahlquist, 1950). Evidence for a reduction in uterine flow during uterine contraction was also obtained as a result of cineangiographic studies in monkeys (Martin, McGaughey, Kaiser, Donner, and Ramsey, 1964) and in three women with malformed foetuses (Borell, Fernström, Ohlson, and Wiqvist, 1965). The slowing of flow was attributed mainly to local compression of the arterioles by the myometrium. It seems much more likely that the principal effect of uterine contraction would be to reduce the transuterine arteriovenous pressure difference by arresting venous outflow, and hence causing a very large and rapid rise in venous pressure. Both mechanisms could contribute, but the difference between them might be important. If uterine flow were reduced solely as a result of venous stasis there would be a large pool of maternal blood sequestered in the placenta with which gas exchange, albeit at a lesser rate, could continue. The effect of maternal placental venous congestion on umbilical flow is unknown. If uterine flow were reduced solely as a result of arterial compression, the volume of blood on the maternal side of the placenta would be reduced, and the immediate physiological conse-

quences for the foetus might be different.

The effect of stimulation of sympathetic efferent nerves on blood flow to the pregnant uterus does not appear to have been reported in detail, though Greiss (1965) refers to unpublished observations in which lumbar sympathetic nerve stimulation caused uterine vasoconstriction. Ramsey (1963) states that there are no sympathetic nerves in the endometrial portion of the spiral arterioles. Much the largest systematic investigation of the effect of drugs is that of Ahlquist (1950) who found that single intra-arterial injections of 0.2–2.0 µg adrenaline and noradrenaline into the uterine artery of dogs caused vasoconstriction (not attributable to increased myometrial activity). Dibenamine caused a small (10–15%) increase in flow. Histamine, and priscoline and heparin (which probably release histamine locally) caused vasodilatation, as did acetylcholine. Pentobarbitone also caused uterine vasodilatation, as it does in other peripheral vascular beds. Pitressin and pitocin both caused a decrease in uterine flow, the latter mainly if not entirely as a result of increased myometrial activity.

Subsequent investigations confirmed the vasoconstrictor effect of adrenaline and noradrenaline (single injections of 1–2 µg/kg or infusions of 0.1–1.0 µg/kg min intravenously) on the uterine vessels of sheep (Adams, Assali, Cushman, and Westersten, 1961; Greiss, 1963). Administration of angiotensin caused a rise in maternal arterial pressure and in uterine flow; presumably the latter was passive.

These investigations make it clear that the uterine vascular bed reacts independently of myometrial activity. Qualitatively, the nature of the reactions are similar to those in peripheral vascular beds such as those of skeletal muscle and the abdominal viscera, rather than those in the heart, lungs, or perhaps brain. Greiss (1965,b), in a brief note, states that during maternal haemorrhage in pregnant sheep, uterine flow falls more in proportion than arterial pressure. As he says, this could be due to the shape and position of the pressure-flow curve in the uterine bed, rather than to uterine vasoconstriction. Obviously, much more extensive and quantitative investigations are needed, including a study of the acute and chronic effects of changes in maternal gas tensions and pH, and an examination of the possibility of reflex control of uterine blood flow.

The effect of hormones also should be worth pursuing further. In 1939, Holden recorded that injection of 0.1 µg estradiol subcutaneously into an immature mouse causes a large increase in the vascularity of the uterus, beginning within 2 hours. Greiss and Marston (1965) found that conjugated equine estrogens caused a mean 36% increase in uterine blood flow, accompanied by a small fall in arterial pressure, in pregnant ewes within 2 hours.

Conclusion

I feel bound to conclude that this is a field in which, though perhaps no great discoveries of general physiological importance are likely to be made, there are urgent practical reasons for obtaining a much better quantitative understanding of its basic physiology and pharmacology. It is also a field in which studies on subhuman primates, as well as dogs and sheep, might be justified in view of the very different anatomical arrangements of the maternal blood supply to the placenta. But this would be conditional on the development of more accurate and reliable methods of measuring uterine flow without gross physiological disturbance, and of distinguishing between flow to the myometrium and to the maternal side of the placenta. These are formidable technical problems, but they certainly should not be impossible. It is unsatisfactory that we know little more about the control of uterine blood flow than that it increases when arterial pressure rises.

There are certain clinical and experimental observations which are most readily explained by a reduction of maternal placental blood flow. The best authenticated is that in pre-eclampsia, in which the combination of the radioactive sodium clearance method and histological study of the maternal side of the placenta, already referred to, leave little doubt that flow has been decreased by a pathological reduction in arteriolar calibre of some duration. What is less certain is the proposition that in some individuals maternal placental flow is decreased acutely by anxiety, pain, or excitement, or chronically by a mechanism involving the autonomic nervous system. This is a possible, perhaps the most probable, explanation of evidence of transient partial foetal asphyxia and metabolic acidosis in experimental preparations in animals. It is an attractive, plausible, but unsubstantiated hypothesis which needs further investigation.

REFERENCES

Adams, F. H.; Assali, N.; Cushman, M., and Westersten, A.: Interrelationships of maternal and fetal circulations. I. Flow-pressure responses to vasoactive drugs in sheep, Pediatrics 27:627–635, 1961.

Ahlquist, R. P.: The action of various drugs on the arterial blood flow of the pregnant canine uterus, J. Am. Pharm. A. (Scient. Ed.) 39:370–373, 1950.

Assali, N. S.; Dasgupta, K.; Kolin, A., and Holms, L.: Measurement of uterine blood flow and uterine metabolism, Am. J. Physiol. 195:614–620, 1958.

Assali, N. S.; Douglass, R. A.; Baird, W. W.; Nicholson, D. B., and Suyemoto, R.: Measurement of uterine blood flow and uterine metabolism, Am. J. Obst. & Gynec. 66:248–253, 1953.

Assali, N. S.; Rauramo, L., and Peltonen, T.: Measurement of uterine blood flow and uterine metabolism, Am. J. Obst. & Gynec. 79:86–98, 1960.

Barcroft, J.: Researches on Prenatal Life (Oxford: Blackwell Scientific Publications, 1946).

Barcroft, J.; Herkel, W., and Hill, S.: The rate of blood flow and gaseous metabolism of the uterus during pregnancy, J. Physiol. 77:194–206, 1933.

Barcroft, J., and Rothschild, P.: The volume of blood in the uterus during pregnancy, J. Physiol. 76:447–459, 1932.

Borrell, V.; Fernström, I.; Ohlson, L., and Wiqvist, N.: Influence of uterine contractions on the uteroplacental circulation at term, Am. J. Obst. & Gynec. 93:44–57, 1965.

Browne, J. C., and Veall, N.: The maternal placental blood flow in normotensive and hypertensive women, J. Obst. & Gynec. Brit. Emp. 60:141–147, 1953.

Campbell, A. G. M.; Dawes, G. S.; Fishman, A. P.; Hyman, A. I., and James, G. B.: The oxygen consumption of the placental and foetal membranes in the sheep, J. Physiol. 182:439–464, 1966.

Dawes, G. S., and Mott, J. C.: The increase in oxygen consumption of the lamb after birth, J. Physiol. 146: 295–315, 1959.

Dixon, H. G.; Browne, J. C. M., and Davey, D. A.: Choriodecidual and myometrial blood-flow, Lancet 2:369–373, 1963.

Dixon, H. G., and Robertson, W. B.: Vascular changes in the placental bed, Path. Microbiol. 24:622–630, 1961.

Greiss, F. C.: The uterine vascular bed: Effect of adrenergic stimulation, Obst. & Gynec. 21:295–301, 1963.

Greiss, F. C.: Effect of labor on uterine blood flow. Am. J. Obst. & Gynec. 93:917–923, 1965,a.

Greiss, F. C.: Uterine vascular responses to hemorrhage during ovine pregnancy, Obst. & Gynec. 25:411–412, 1965,b.

Greiss, F. C., and Marston, E. L.: The uterine vascular bed: Effect of estrogens during ovine pregnancy, Am. J. Obst. & Gynec. 93:720–722, 1965.

Holden, R. B.: Vascular reactions of the uterus of the immature rat, Endocrinol. 25:593–596, 1939.

Huckabee, W. E.: Uterine blood flow, Am. J. Obst. & Gynec. 84:1623–1633, 1962.

Huckabee, W. E., and Barron, D. H.: Factors affecting the determination of uterine blood flow in vivo, Circ. Res. 9:312–318, 1961.

Huckabee, W. E.; Metcalfe, J.; Prystowsky, H., and Barron, D. H.: Blood flow and oxygen consumption of the pregnant uterus, Am. J. Physiol. 200:274–278, 1961.

Huckabee, W. E., and Walcott, G.: Determination of organ blood flow using 4-aminoantipyrine, J. Appl. Physiol. 15:1139–1143, 1960.

Kety, S., and Schmidt, C. F.: The nitrous oxide method

for the quantitative determination of cerebral blood flow in man: Theory, procedure and normal values, J. Clin. Invest. 27:476–483, 1948.

Martin, C. B.; McGaughey, H. S.; Kaiser, I. H.; Donner, M. W., and Ramsey, E. M.: Intermittent functioning of the uteroplacental arteries, Am. J. Obst. & Gynec. 90:819–823, 1964.

Metcalfe, J.; Romney, S. L.; Ramsey, L. H.; Reid, D. E., and Burwell, C. S.: Estimation of uterine blood flow in normal human pregnancies at term, J. Clin. Invest. 34:1632–1638, 1955.

Ramsey, E. M., in Oliver, T. K. (ed.): *Neonatal Respira-tory Adaptation* (Washington, D. C.: U. S. Public Health Service Publication No. 1432, 1963), p. 19.

Ramsey, E. M.; Corner, G. W., and Donner, M. W.: Serial and cineangiographic visualization of maternal circulation in the primate (hemochorial) placenta, Am. J. Obst. & Gynec. 86:213–225, 1963.

Robson, J. M., and Schild, H. O.: Effect of drugs on the blood flow and activity of the uterus, J. Physiol. 92:9–19, 1938.

Wolkoff, A. S.; McGee, J. A.; Flowers, C. E., and Bawden, J. W.: Alterations in uterine blood flow in the pregnant ewe, Obst. & Gynec. 23:636–637, 1964.

6

The Umbilical Circulation

Methods for Measuring Umbilical Flow

It is surprising that direct measurements of umbilical blood flow have been made only comparatively recently, in preparations which bear some reasonable relation to physiological conditions. It is surprising because umbilical flow is self-evidently necessary to foetal survival, and comprises more than half the combined output of the ventricles, and one might have supposed that it would, therefore, have been the subject of intensive investigation. In fact, as long ago as 1884, Cohnstein and Zuntz placed a stromuhr in an umbilical artery of a few foetal lambs. The volume of blood flow which they recorded was low by present-day standards, which is hardly to be wondered at in view of the methods which were available to them. What is amazing is that none followed their lead until 1949, when Cooper and Greenfield devised an ingenious adaptation of the venous occlusion plethysmograph to fit the foetus. A foetal lamb was wholly immersed in a bath of warm saline arranged as a plethysmograph; it was still attached to its mother by an intact umbilical cord. When the cord was compressed to occlude the veins (but not the arteries) the foetus bled into its placenta. The immediate rate of decrease of foetal volume was taken as a measure of umbilical flow. Using this method, Cooper, Greenfield, and Huggett (1949) made the first systematic measurements of umbilical blood flow at different gestational ages in the sheep, and showed that flow increased very considerably with increasing foetal weight toward term. The same results were obtained using either Welsh mountain sheep (a small breed, in which the ewes usually weigh 30–45 kg) delivered under spinal anaesthesia (Cooper, Greenfield, and Huggett, 1949) or Clun-Hampshire sheep (in which the ewes weigh 60–100 kg) delivered un-

der pentobarbitone anaesthesia (Acheson, Dawes, and Mott, 1957). These results have been combined and are shown as open circles (O) in Figure 31.

The venous occlusion plethysmograph method for measuring umbilical flow was good, because it involved little interference with the foetus, but unfortunately it was liable to unsuspected and systematic sources of error. Umbilical blood flow is normally such a large fraction of the venous return to both ventricles that, when the umbilical vein is occluded, arterial pressure begins to fall within a few heart beats and pressure in the placental end of the umbilical vein rises rapidly. Thus it becomes

Fig. 31.—Umbilical blood flow has been plotted against gestational age in foetal lambs, using results obtained with an electromagnetic flowmeter under chloralose anaesthesia (●) for comparison with those using venous occlusion plethysmography (O). (Redrawn from Dawes, 1962.)

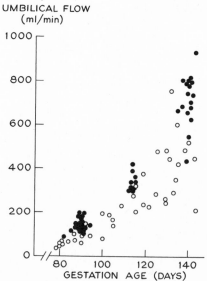

particularly necessary to obtain a true measure of the rate of change of foetal volume within the first 1–2 seconds after venous occlusion. But this is the period which is most liable to distortion because of the inertia of the volume recorder and because of the difficulty in occluding the umbilical veins exactly at the point at which they enter the plethysmograph. The effect is to cause the venous occlusion plethysmograph to give an underestimate of flow (often large) (Dawes and Mott, 1959).

The next method which was used for measuring total umbilical flow in foetal lambs was to insert a flowmeter between the divided ends of the abdominal portion of the umbilical vein. A small incision is made curving around the left side of the umbilicus and running thence in the midline to the lower end of the sternum. The exposure is much improved by emptying the stomach. The abdominal part of the umbilical vein is usually 3–5 cm long at term and this gives ample room for cannulating both ends; also, this vessel does not readily go into extreme spasm, unlike the umbilical arteries. When this method was first used, arrangements were made to ensure that the foetus was rendered hypoxaemic for as short a time as possible. The ewe was given 100% O_2 to breathe. The right external jugular vein of the foetus was cannulated and, when all was ready, was rapidly joined to the placental end of the umbilical vein in the abdomen (Dawes, Mott, and Rennick, 1956). Finally, the hepatic end of the umbilical vein was cannulated and joined to the placental end. Subsequent experience showed that this rather clumsy and elaborate arrangement was unnecessary. Both ends of the cut umbilical vein can be cannulated while the umbilical cord is occluded within less than 2 minutes in a mature foetal lamb with complete and rapid recovery of heart rate, blood pressure, arterial pH, and blood gas tensions when the cord is released. Usually 10 minutes is sufficient for umbilical flow (measured with a cuff flowmeter, see below) to return to its initial value. The advantage of cannulating the umbilical vein is that flow can be measured with precision, with more accuracy than is possible by indirect methods, and that once the flowmeter head is installed, it requires little attention. The disadvantages, the time required for the preparation, surgical interference, and the brief period of asphyxia while the cord is occluded, can be minimized with practice.

Several types of flowmeter have been used in the common (i.e., abdominal) umbilical vein of the foetal lamb. The density flowmeter (Dawes, Mott, and Vane, 1953) was an accurate and fairly reliable instrument, but offered a rather high resistance to flow. It was abandoned in favour of the velodyne flowmeter (Dawes and Mott, 1959) which offered no resistance to blood flow at any flow rate, because it used a pump whose speed was adjusted by a negative feed-back circuit to reduce the pressure drop across it to zero. It was, however, a bulky piece of apparatus and clumsy to use. It, in turn, was abandoned after a year's experience in favour of a cannulated type of electromagnetic flowmeter (Wyatt, 1961). The gauge heads used in umbilical veins of mature foetal lambs have an internal diameter of 5 mm and are short, so that they offer a negligible resistance to flow. They have proved extremely reliable over the last 7 years and are very accurate. The deviation between the zero reading observed when the magnet current is switched off and when the vessel is occluded is $< 1\%$ of full scale. The maximum error observed in flow measurement over 5-hour trial periods was $< 2\%$ of scale, and the average error was considerably less (full scale reading with this type of gauge head could be adjusted from 250–1,000 ml/min). These errors compare favourably with those observed in the measurement of arterial pressures.

It has always struck me as strange that investigators have apparently been prepared to accept methods of blood flow measurement which are grossly inaccurate as compared with methods of pressure measurement. The regulation of arterial pressure is really only a means to an end, which is the proportional distribution of cardiac output according to the need of the various tissues. So I believe that accuracy in the measurement of flow is at least as important, probably more important, than accuracy in the measurement of pressure. We may have accepted the situation hitherto, perhaps with reluctance, because accurate instruments have not been available, or because it was thought that less accurate measurement was all that was needed. It is also often assumed that the simplest and most obvious methods of flow measurement do not need to have their accuracy tested. But trials of the collection of effluent blood in a measuring cylinder over measured periods of time show how difficult it is to achieve an accuracy of even 2%. A more accurate method of calibration is to use a motor-driven piston.

Cuff electromagnetic flowmeters are inherently less accurate than the cannulated type. The decision to use one or the other on the umbilical vein must depend on the experimental design. So far as the foetal lamb is concerned, the abdomen must be opened to expose the common umbilical vein, because one cannot assume that the flow is equal in the two cord veins which exist in this species. Leaving aside the variation in accuracy between different types of cuff electromagnetic flowmeter, which is discussed elsewhere (Appendix), the application of a cuff flowmeter to this particular vessel presents problems. The vessel is thin and is not supported by surrounding tissue, so that the cuff tends to twist and sag upon it and usually needs to be held by a clamp. Although the vessel does not normally constrict rapidly, it usually does constrict slowly, over a period of 10–20 minutes, and may thus detach itself from close contact with the flowmeter head. This can give rise to an error if the flowmeter has no warning device to draw attention to this phenomenon. Electromagnetic flowmeters give a faithful record only if flow is axially symmetrical. When a cannulated flowmeter is placed in the umbilical vein, end-pieces can be used which ensure sufficient distance so that flow from the two veins which meet just within the umbilicus has become homogeneous. But when a cuff flowmeter is placed too near the umbilicus an error has been observed due to axial asymmetry of flow. The error of measurement using a cuff electromagnetic flowmeter can be as little as $\pm 3\%$ but may be very much more, according to the precautions which are taken and the instrument which is used. It is also important to realize that some errors can be in one direction, giving a systematic under- or over-estimate of flow.

The use of a cuff electromagnetic flowmeter to measure flow in a single umbilical artery is more likely to give a misleading measure of flow than its use on the common abdominal umbilical vein. Not only are these instruments less reliable on thicker-walled vessels, but the umbilical arteries are particularly liable to spasm, in which case flow may decrease in the artery surrounded by the cuff. If the decrease is sufficient, arterial pressure may rise sufficiently to increase flow in the other umbilical artery. Also as there is little or no anastomosis between cotyledonary arteries supplied from either umbilical artery, measurement of umbilical flow in a single artery can give a grossly misleading estimate of total umbilical blood flow.

Only one indirect method for computing umbilical blood flow has been described so far.* Barron,

* Another has appeared since, described by Meschia, G., Cotter, J. R., Makowski, E. L., and Barron, D. H.: Simultaneous measurement of uterine and umbilical blood flows and oxygen uptakes, Quart. J. Exper. Physiol. 52:1–18, 1967.

Meschia, Cotter, and Breathnach (1965) infused urea into pregnant sheep and measured the umbilical arteriovenous differences at intervals during the next half hour. They calculated the quantity of urea transferred to the foetus by grinding it up, analysing an extract, and making allowance for production and excretion during the half hour period. They then calculated mean umbilical flow by the Fick principle. No estimate of the accuracy of the final measurement was given. It is probable that, as in so many other situations, indicator-dilution methods will be used to measure umbilical flow on a large scale within the next few years. The fact that one of these methods has been checked in another vascular bed does not necessarily mean that its reliability will be identical in the umbilical circulation. One can only hope that investigators will check one method against another.

UMBILICAL BLOOD FLOW AND VASCULAR RESISTANCE: CHANGES WITH AGE

There is more information about the volume of umbilical blood flow and its regulation in sheep than there is in other species. As Figure 31 shows, umbilical flow increases with gestational age and, therefore, with foetal weight, whether measured with a venous occlusion plethysmograph under spinal or pentobarbitone anaesthesia (o) or with a more accurate cannulated electromagnetic flowmeter under light chloralose anaethesia (•). The increase in flow is not, however, in proportion to foetal weight. Umbilical flow falls from 231 ml/kg min at 87–95 days gestation to 170 ml/kg min at 137–141 days gestation (Table 17; term is ~147 days). So far as O_2 transport is concerned this fall is offset by a rise in the O_2 carrying capacity of the blood from 10.5 ± 0.9 to 16.4 ± 0.5 ml/100 ml (Dawes and Mott, 1964). Hence the net O_2 transport capacity of the umbilical circulation (flow $\times$ O_2 capacity of the blood) was increased under these experimental conditions from 23–27 ml O_2/kg min. The O_2 consumption of foetal lambs falls slightly, from 5.4 ± 0.5 to 4.6 ± 0.3 ml/kg min over the same period of time. At first sight it would appear that the lamb has a larger margin of safety near term. However, this is probably not so in practice; first, because not all of the umbilical blood passes through the area of gas exchange in the placental cotyledons, and secondly because of the large variations in O_2 saturation observed in the umbilical vessels.

TABLE 17.—OBSERVATIONS ON UMBILICAL VASCULAR RESISTANCE IN FOETAL LAMBS AT DIFFERENT GESTATIONAL AGES

	GESTATIONAL AGE IN DAYS		
	86–95	114–116	134–143
Number of lambs	14	9	10
Weight, kg	0.62	1.83	3.96
* Time for cannulation, mins	2.9	2.3	1.9
Placental cotyledonary weight, Gm	532 ± 30	399 ± 24	487 ± 11
Arterial pressure, mm Hg	36 ± 0.2	43 ± 1.7	62 ± 3.4
Common umbilical vein pressure, mm Hg	5.9	8.1	10.5
Umbilical vein flow, ml/min	144 ± 9	341 ± 15	692 ± 45
ml/kg/min	231 ± 17	186 ± 5	170 ± 7
For umbilical flow vs. femoral arterial-umbilical vein pressure			
Intercept of regression line on pressure axis, mm Hg	11.4 ± 0.8	9.3 ± 0.8	7.1 ± 1.2
Slope of regression line ml/min per mm Hg	7.7 ± 0.6	13.9 ± 1.2	17.0 ± 1.1
Slope/kg cotyledonary weight	15.6 ± 1.3	34.7 ± 2.3	40.1 ± 3.9

The figures indicate the means ± S.E.

Anaesthetic, chloralose 30–40 mg/kg; cannulated electromagnetic flowmeter (Wyatt, 1961); rectal temperature maintained at 38–39°C.

* Calculated as the time from occlusion to release of the umbilical cord.

The data on pressure-flow regression lines were obtained during brief periods of aortic compression.

Umbilical flow is dependent on the pressure gradient which drives the blood from the end of the descending aorta through the cord to the placenta and foetal membranes, and thence back again to the inferior vena cava (Fig. 32). At term this pressure gradient is ~65 mm Hg in the foetal lamb, and measurement of the pressure at different points shows that the greatest drop in pressure (~40 mm Hg, Fig. 33) occurs between the cotyledonary arteries and veins, that is to say, across the capillary beds of the foetal villi and of the extra-cotyledonary chorionic membrane, which are in parallel (Fig. 32).

Fig. 32.—Plan of the umbilical circulation in the sheep.

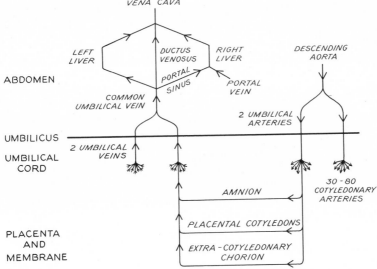

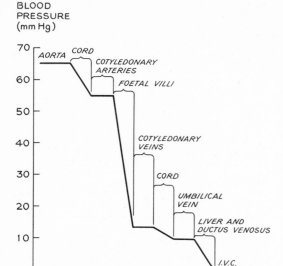

Fig. 33.—The pressure drop across the umbilical circulation in lambs at term. (Redrawn from Dawes, 1962.)

The drop in pressure across the umbilical cord is less (~10 mm Hg along the arteries and ~5 mm Hg along the veins), as also is that across the liver sinusoids and ductus venosus (~10 mm Hg). By the time blood reaches the common umbilical vein, flow is almost entirely non-pulsatile. We are now in a position to consider the relative changes in the vascular resistance of the component parts of the umbilical circulation with increasing gestational age, from ~90 gestational days, when the placental cotyledons have already reached their maximal weight but the foetus is not viable, until ~140 days (i.e., within a few days of term).

Three groups of lambs were studied, at 86–95, 114–116, and 134–143 days gestational age. The cannulation of the common umbilical vein was more difficult and took a little longer in the smaller lambs (Table 17), but these are better able to withstand a short period of asphyxia. There was no relation, within any age group, between the duration of asphyxia during cannulation and subsequent measurements of flow or pressure, made after a recovery period of 10–15 minutes.

The pressure drop down the arterial side of the umbilical cord, between the aorta (measured from a catheter introduced through a femoral artery) and a cotyledonary artery, increased from 2–10 mm Hg during the latter half of gestation (r = 0.90; for flow $\dot{Q}$ and pressure p, $\dot{Q} = 21 + 62.8$ p). No measurements were made of the length of the um-

bilical arteries, within or without the abdomen, or of their internal diameter or tortuosity, so we are not in a position to say whether the relation between pressure and flow shown in Figure 34 is simply a result of haemodynamic change or partly due to anatomical development of the arteries. This is a problem which might be worth closer study as providing an interesting example of flow down a long length of curving blood vessel without branches. It is interesting to note that the pressure drop across the umbilical arteries, expressed in terms of the total pressure gradient from aorta to inferior vena cava, increased from a mean of $\frac{2}{36}$ (5.5%) at ~90 days to $\frac{10}{62}$ (16%) at term. During the same period of time the pressure in the common umbilical vein rose from 5.9 to 10.5 mm Hg (Table 17) and contributed a steady 16–17% of the total pressure gradient.

Attention was particularly concentrated on that part of the umbilical circulation between the descending aorta and the common umbilical vein, because not only was that evidently the part which contributed most resistance to blood flow through the foetal side of the placenta, but it also seemed to change the most with age. Pressure-flow diagrams were constructed *in vivo* (using a method which derives from the work of Burton and his colleagues; Nichol *et al.*, 1951), either by raising venous pressure or by reducing arterial pressure. When venous pressure was raised by partial constriction of the umbilical vein, the slopes of the linear pressure-flow regression lines passed close to the origin of the pressure and flow axes (Fig. 35, O). But when arterial pressure was reduced by compression of the descending aorta of the foetus, the pressure-flow regression line cut the pressure

Fig. 34.—The drop in pressure down the umbilical arteries at 90 days (◖), 115 days (○), and 140 days (●) gestation in sheep.

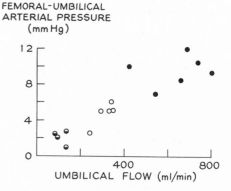

axis at a finite pressure. The same phenomenon has been seen in other vascular beds, in the lung for instance, and may be due to the fact that when transmural pressure is reduced, vessels tend to collapse. When flow was reduced by aortic compression, the pressure-flow regression lines cut the pressure axis at a mean pressure of 11 mm Hg at ∼90 days gestation and at 7 mm Hg at ∼140 days (Table 17). The difference between these values is small but statistically significant, suggesting that vascular collapse, perhaps in the cotyledons, may occur at a higher transmural pressure at the lower gestational age. It would be interesting to know whether this was related to a structural change in the smaller blood vessels with time, such as the development of a stronger parenchymatous support to offset the natural tendency to collapse afforded by elastic and muscular tissue in the wall.

A number of observations on umbilical vascular resistance were made at different gestational ages, using aortic compression to produce pressure-flow diagrams. This was thought to give a more realistic picture than venous compression because, as will be seen, umbilical flow more often changes as a result of changes in arterial than in venous pressure. The observations are summarized in Table 17 and Figure 36. Between 90 and 115 days gestation umbilical vascular resistance decreased very considerably, as shown both by the change in slope and pressure-intercept. Arterial pressure increased, but only by a small amount, from a mean of 36 to 43 mm Hg. Mean umbilical flow rose from 144 to

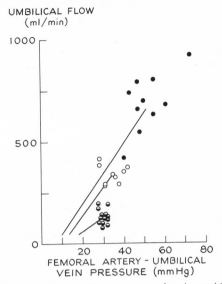

Fig. 36.—Pressure-flow diagrams for the umbilical circulation in foetal lambs of 90 (⊙), 115 (○), and 140 (●) days gestation. The lines are the mean regression lines of all observations at the three ages, obtained by aortic compression; the points indicate the mean femoral arterial pressure of each lamb. (Redrawn and modified from Dawes, 1962.)

341 ml/min (137%); if there had been no increase in pressure it would still have risen to 278 ml/min (93%). Between 115 and 140 days gestation the decrease in umbilical vascular resistance, though statistically significant, was less than that observed over the preceding 25 days. If there had been no further increase in arterial pressure, flow would have risen only from 341 to 410 ml/min (20%). But arterial pressure rose from 43 to 62 mm Hg and so flow increased to 692 ml/min (106%). These results suggested that the increase in umbilical flow required to maintain foetal life and growth is achieved at first mainly by a fall in umbilical vascular resistance, but that during the last 3–4 weeks of gestation (about 0.16 of term in the sheep), any further increase is achieved mainly by a rise in arterial pressure.

It is worth while looking back at this evidence, which was obtained in 1961–2 and published only in a rather brief summary (Dawes, 1962), a little more critically. There are two points to be considered. First, as has already been mentioned, in sheep the weight of the placental cotyledons reaches its maximum at about 90 days gestation (which was one of the reasons for choosing this as the starting date), and then declines a little toward term. By

Fig. 35.—Pressure-flow diagrams in the umbilical circulation of foetal lambs at 92 and 139 days gestation obtained by aortic compression (●) or abdominal umbilical vein compression (○).

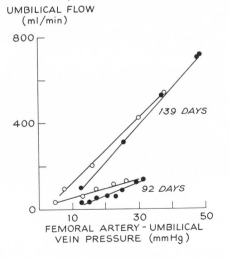

chance, I picked a group of lambs at 115 days gestation whose placental cotyledonary mass was significantly less than that of the other two groups. We do not know whether there is a direct relation between cotyledonary weight and the mass of foetal vessels, though this seems a reasonable assumption in normal lambs. Unfortunately, the numbers in each age group are too few to determine a quantitative correlation between cotyledonary mass and umbilical vascular resistance. I have recalculated the slope of the pressure-flow regression lines at the three gestational ages in terms of cotyledonary weight (last line of Table 17), and this reduced neither the variance about the means nor the significance of the difference between the slopes of the regression lines at 115 and 140 days gestational age. So it is unlikely that the results were much distorted by the arbitrary selection of these particular groups of lambs. The second point is a more difficult one. During the latter half of gestation in the sheep the weight of the foetal membranes increases considerably, and these structures are supplied by the umbilical vessels in parallel with the cotyledons (Fig. 32). We do not know whether the proportion of total umbilical flow which passes through the cotyledons changes with gestational age. We cannot assume that total umbilical blood flow gives anything more than a rough indication of flow through the area of gas exchange within the placenta in this species.

THE REGULATION OF UMBILICAL BLOOD FLOW IN SHEEP

It might have been thought that the method used to obtain the data for umbilical pressure-flow diagrams would itself distort the results, as it was necessary to reduce umbilical flow for a short period of time. In fact, there was no evidence of distortion unless flow was reduced very considerably for 2 or more minutes. This suggested that even large changes in foetal blood gas tensions must have relatively small effects on umbilical vascular resistance. This was so.

Administration of low oxygen mixtures (7.5–10%) to the ewe, even sufficient to cause abrupt foetal bradycardia, had no demonstrable effect on umbilical vascular resistance in 5 foetal lambs at ~90 days gestational age. In 4 lambs at 114–115 days gestation, extreme hypoxaemia (in one instance the ewe stopped breathing) caused a minor degree of umbilical vasoconstriction (Fig. 37). In some instances no vasoconstriction was

seen during a 5-minute period of hypoxaemia, but appeared during recovery. In 7 lambs of 134–140 days gestation administration of 10% O_2 to the ewe regularly caused vasoconstriction in the umbilical circulation. The first effect of hypoxaemia at this age was to cause a rise of systemic arterial pressure and thus an increase in umbilical flow. In some instances the arterial pressure rise was quite considerable (e.g., from 64–84 mm Hg, while common umbilical vein pressure rose from 10.5–14.5 mm Hg and inferior vena caval pressure by 1.8 mm Hg) with a consequent increase in umbilical flow (from 705–915 ml/min). Thereafter, arterial pressure usually remained steady or fell by a few mm Hg while flow decreased during the next few minutes. Inspection of the pressure-flow diagram showed that there was umbilical vasoconstriction, but even after 10 minutes hypoxaemia, when femoral arterial Po_2 had fallen from 25 to 8 mm Hg, the change was small. Foetal hypercapnia was induced by giving the ewe gas mixtures containing 3–10% CO_2 to breathe, the tendency for the foetal arterial Po_2 to rise (as a result of maternal hyperventilation and the Bohr effect) being offset by reducing the O_2 content of the gas mixture to 17–18%. There was only a trivial increase in umbilical vascular resistance, even when foetal arterial Pco_2 was raised to 80 mm Hg.

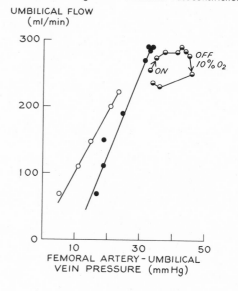

Fig. 37.—Pressure-flow diagrams in a foetal lamb of 115 days gestation obtained by aortic (●) or abdominal umbilical vein (○) compression. The ewe was given 10% O_2, in place of air, to breathe for 10 minutes and the changes in pressure and flow (◖) indicated a minor degree of umbilical vasoconstriction.

The interpretation of these results depends on whether the umbilical vessels are innervated. The abdominal parts of the umbilical arteries and the umbilical vein are certainly innervated, and vasoconstriction in these parts of the umbilical circulation might occur as a direct result of efferent sympathetic nervous activity, though this has not yet been demonstrated by direct experiment. The evidence for innervation of the cord vessels and the foetal side of the placenta is controversial. Spivack (1943) reviewed the literature critically and, using methylene blue, concluded that there was little evidence of innervation of the extra-abdominal vasculature in man and the guinea pig as compared with the intra-abdominal portion. Yet she described a network on human foetal membranes which took up the dye "and whose nature was hard to establish." A search has been made for nerve bundles in the umbilical cord, generally without success, but Barclay, Franklin, and Prichard (1944) show a microscopic section of the umbilical cord of a calf in which a nerve bundle was identified by Amoroso. Zaitev (1959) has described the presence of neural elements in human cords for 10 cm beyond the umbilicus but no further. Recently, Jacobson (personal communication, 1966) has found elements on the foetal side of the human placenta which take up methylene blue and have the appearance of nerve bundles and, in other areas, of terminal fibres. The umbilical arteries from human cord 10 cm or more from the umbilicus contain very little noradrenaline (<0.005 μg/Gm) as compared with the femoral artery of the dog (0.03 μg/Gm) (Davignon, Lorenz, and Shepherd, 1965; Eltherington, personal communication) so it seems unlikely that they would respond to sympathetic nerve stimulation. It is interesting that, nevertheless, they responded to an increase in transmural pressure by vasoconstriction in a manner which reminded Davignon *et al.* of the myogenic reflex of Bayliss (1902), presumably by a direct effect on the smooth muscle.

We conclude that the vasoconstrictor effect of hypoxaemia on the umbilical circulation might be due in part to reflex vasoconstriction on the intra-abdominal portion, but on the extra-abdominal portion must have been either direct or as a result of substances which reached the vessels through the blood stream. It may have been due to the release of catecholamines from the foetal adrenals. Comline and Silver (1961) had shown that more catecholamines (mainly noradrenaline) were released by foetal asphyxia at term than at 90 days

gestation, and subsequent observations showed that this was due to hypoxaemia rather than to hypercapnia (Comline, Silver, and Silver, 1965). Experiments were therefore done to determine the effect of intravenous infusions of noradrenaline, or in some instances adrenaline into the foetus on the umbilical circulation.

Previous observations had shown that the effect of injections of drugs like acetylcholine or catecholamines on the foetal circulation was different according to which vein was used (Dawes, Mott, and Rennick, 1956). In this instance, infusions were given into a catheter introduced through a femoral vein, so that the drug would reach the inferior vena cava, and hence mimic the effect of release via the adrenal veins. Intravenous infusions of relatively large doses of noradrenaline or adrenaline, up to and including 0.5 μg/kg min, had no effect on umbilical vascular resistance at any age, though they caused a considerable increase in arterial pressure and umbilical flow. At both 86–91 days gestation (11 lambs) and 131–143 days (6 lambs) infusion of 1–2 μg/kg min noradrenaline or adrenaline caused umbilical vasoconstriction, often of rather abrupt onset. In the mature lambs this was as large, sometimes a little larger, than that observed during severe hypoxaemia for 12 minutes. Pressures were measured at several points in the circulation, in the inferior vena cava, common umbilical vein, and in a cotyledonary and femoral artery. When noradrenaline was infused in an amount sufficient to cause an easily perceptible degree of umbilical vasoconstriction, there was little change in inferior vena caval pressure. There was usually a small rise in common umbilical vein pressure, but the combined vascular resistance of the liver sinusoids and ductus venosus (in parallel) did not rise significantly. On the other hand, there was a substantial rise in vascular resistance in each of the three other parts of the umbilical circulation, i.e., in the umbilical arteries (between aorta and cotyledonary arteries), in the placental cotyledons, and in the umbilical veins (between the cotyledonary veins and the umbilical vein in the abdomen). There was often an easily perceptible local reduction in external diameter in one or more parts of the cord vessels.

Hence the umbilical vasoconstriction observed during hypoxaemia in foetal lambs near term, and less readily at ~115 days gestation, can well be explained by liberation of catecholamines. The failure to observe vasoconstriction during hypoxaemia at ~90 days gestation is not due to insensitivity of the blood vessels, but may be attributed to the fact that less catecholamines are secreted. But the most outstanding feature of these observations is that the umbilical vessels *in vivo* are so unreactive. This was not wholly expected because they have the reputation of going into spasm with very slight provocation, a story that is not entirely true. It is true that they do react vigorously to longitudinal stretch, but they may be compressed with impunity, and without causing severe spasm, providing pressure is applied with a soft edge and that the smaller vessels are not damaged.

A second feature of these observations was that, with increasing doses of noradrenaline, there was already a large change in foetal arterial pressure and heart rate before umbilical vascular resistance was altered, confirming the hypothesis proposed on rather less secure evidence (Dawes, Mott, and Rennick, 1956) that the principal effect of adrenaline and noradrenaline is to cause changes in the foetus rather than the placenta. A striking result of this was seen in experiments on 3 lambs of ∼90 days gestational age, which were placed in a plethysmograph filled with warm saline, but still attached to the ewe by an intact umbilical cord. Infusion of adrenaline or noradrenaline (0.5–1.0 μg/kg min) caused a fall of foetal volume of up to 8 ml within 2 minutes due to transfer of blood to the foetal side of the placenta (the urachus was tied).

It is tempting to speculate that this redistribution of blood volume and of blood flow serves a useful purpose. It may well do so, but we cannot yet prove it beyond reasonable doubt. The extra blood derived from the foetus may distend the larger umbilical vessels and the extra-cotyledonary chorionic membrane as well as increasing the volume of blood in the area of gas exchange. Increased velocity or volume of blood flow within the area of gas exchange will not necessarily be advantageous to the foetus; that must depend on whether this results in a more favourable state of affairs, particularly taking into account the perfusion:perfusion ratio. An increase in the rate of blood flow may mean that more foetal blood is exposed within the exchange area, but for a shorter period of time. An increase in umbilical flow may be advantageous in increasing O_2 uptake from the placenta, but that advantage could be offset by an increase in foetal O_2 consumption as the result of catecholamine secretion, e.g., in brown adipose tissue (see Chapter 14). The physiological problem is a good deal more complex than it appears at first sight. As one so often finds in foetal physiology, only the first few steps have yet been taken.

So far, we have considered the effect of acute hypoxaemia and hypercapnia on umbilical vascular resistance, such as is likely to occur sometime before or during birth. Under natural conditions it is unlikely that umbilical arterial Po_2 will exceed, say, 40 mm Hg at the outside, or that arterial Pco_2 will decrease below 30 mm Hg. However, such changes can be induced artificially, by ventilating the lungs of a foetal lamb while it is still attached to the placenta with an intact umbilical cord. If the mother is simultaneously given O_2 to breathe, the umbilical arterial and venous Po_2 can be raised to ∼90 mm Hg while the Pco_2 is reduced to ∼25 mm Hg. This had remarkably little immediate effect on umbilical blood flow (Campbell, Dawes, Fishman, Hyman, and James, 1966). Umbilical flow usually decreased gradually over a period of 2 hours or so after delivery of the lamb, whether or not the lungs were ventilated, and irrespective of large rapid changes in foetal arterial Po_2 and Pco_2. Hence, taking into consideration both the effects of foetal asphyxia and foetal ventilation, one is forced to the conclusion that there is almost no direct local effect of changes in blood gas tensions on the umbilical vascular bed *in vivo* in this species.

It is unusual to come across a vascular bed in which hypoxaemia and hypercapnia have so little effect. One might have expected either vasodilatation as in the brain, or vasoconstriction as in the lung. Even the foetal lung, as with other tissues, shows reactive hyperaemia after a period of ischaemia, despite the consequent asphyxia (Dawes and Mott, 1962). It would be interesting to know whether reactive hyperaemia also can be demonstrated in the placenta. Of course, it would be necessary to render it ischaemic on both sides, by simultaneous occlusion of the umbilical cord and of the uterine arteries, while the foetus is ventilated in order to prevent catecholamine release by asphyxia. This is certainly a practicable experiment, and one that is not too difficult to carry out. If reactive hyperaemia should occur on both sides of the placenta, as would be reasonable to suppose, this might provide some basis for a local regulation of the perfusion:perfusion ratio.

We may consider the changes in umbilical vascular resistance with age (Fig. 36). The results show that umbilical flow depends mainly on two factors:

1. The transumbilical arteriovenous pressure gradient, of which much the most important variable, with age or at any given age, is the mean arterial pressure.

2. The development of the foetal vessels within the placenta and membranes.

Although there are good qualitative descriptions of the development of these vessels in the sheep (Wimsatt, 1950), there is no quantitative information from which one can judge whether the changes in vascular resistance observed are related to anatomical alterations in the placental cotyledons or membranes. The cotyledons have already reached their maximal weight by ~90 days gestation, but the membranes continue to grow until term and this may contribute to the fall in vascular resistance. It is also probable that within the cotyledons the vessels of the foetal villi continue to develop as in the human placenta (Crawford, 1962). There is an interesting complication here, since an increase in the area of gas exchange could be achieved either by multiplication of vessels in parallel (with a consequent fall in vascular resistance) or by elongation of the vascular network (with a rise in resistance). More information is clearly needed.

Within the three groups of normal lambs which were studied (Table 17) the vascular resistance did not show a clear significant relation to cotyledonary weight, probably because the variation in weight was not great. But there were 2 twin lambs of 114 days gestational age, not included in Table 17, each of whose placental cotyledons weighed much less than those of any other lamb (185 and 210 Gm). The umbilical vascular resistances and the arterial pressures (53 and 56 mm Hg) of these twins were abnormally high, although their body weights (1.9 and 1.5 kg) were within the normal range; there was no ambiguity about their gestational age. Neither macroscopic nor microscopic examination of the cotyledons showed any gross abnormality. One may suppose that these were examples of lambs which might well have perished before birth or on delivery, and perhaps it might be worth while looking for more of them.

THE CONTROL OF UMBILICAL BLOOD FLOW IN MAN

In man we are on more difficult ground because although it is widely believed that hypoxaemia causes umbilical vasodilatation and vice versa, the only evidence is derived from experiments in which the umbilical cord and/or the placenta has been perfused *in vitro* after delivery under conditions which are demonstrably highly unnatural. The perfusion fluid has usually been a salt solution; sometimes with plasma or dextran; homologous blood has been used only occasionally. It is evident both from published evidence and from unpublished work in our laboratory (J. Goodwin and G. B.

James) that such preparations are usually very vasoconstricted. Thus Panigel (1962) shows a record from work on a full-term isolated human cord in which the pressure gradient down an umbilical artery was ~50 mm Hg for a flow of 130 ml/min human plasma. He used the full arterial pressure of a term foetus (which *in vivo* drives the blood from aorta to inferior vena cava) for perfusion of one cord artery (from umbilicus to placenta) at a volume of blood flow which would barely sustain life in a 3 kg infant, assuming that total umbilical flow was 260 ml/min (see Table 18). In the intact foetus *in utero* the pressure drop down the cord arteries, between umbilicus and placenta, cannot be more than ~5 mm Hg. So the vascular resistance of Panigel's cord artery must have been 15–20 times greater than *in vivo* (assuming that the pressure-flow diagram is linear and passes through the origin). Similarly, Nyberg and Westin (1957) illustrated the effects of oxygen upon the isolated human placenta perfused with whole blood at normal arterial pressures (for the infant at birth) but at a flow of only about 10 ml/min.

Nyberg and Westin (1957) and Panigel (1962) observed that when the perfusion fluid was equilibrated with 100% O_2 the umbilical vessels constricted, while with 5% CO_2 they dilated. There are two points here. First, the P_{O_2} of the perfusion fluid could have risen to ~700 mm Hg (on exposure to 100% O_2), and the P_{CO_2} could have fallen to ~0 mm Hg (on exposure to air); these are values far outside the normal foetal ranges. Secondly, it could well be that as the artery was already tightly constricted its reactions to changes in blood gas tensions were unusual. Davignon, Lorenz, and Shepherd (1965) noted that the vasoconstriction caused by bradykinin, 5-hydroxytryptamine, and angiotensin in the isolated human cord artery was most easily elicited when the tone was high; the flow rate was only ~5 ml/min at a normal foetal arterial pressure. The fact that umbilical arteries can react under such circumstances to oxygen or drugs is very interesting, but has no relation to normal behaviour *in utero*. Panigel also found that the umbilical vein and the placental cotyledons behaved in qualitatively the same way, but much less vigorously. The same reservations apply with equal force.

It could be that there is a true species difference, that the umbilical vessels react to changes in blood gas tensions in man but not in sheep. I have not found any account of similar isolated perfusion experiments on sheep cords or placentas for comparison with those in man. Such an experiment might

TABLE 18.—SPECIMEN CALCULATION ON HUMAN FOETAL O_2 CONSUMPTION AND
UMBILICAL FLOW

Foetal O_2 consumption at, say, 4.5 ml/kg min.
  Total O_2 consumption for infant weighing 3 kg = 13.5 ml/min.
  O_2 carrying of foetal blood ~20 ml/100 ml.
  * Probable umbilical arteriovenous O_2 difference ~25% of full saturation = 5 ml/100 ml.
  Minimum umbilical flow needed = 270 ml/min. or 90 ml/kg min.

* Assuming umbilical vein saturation of, say, 75%: Umbilical artery 50%; inferior vena cava (below liver) ~25% to give a very small margin of safety.

help to decide whether the difference was in the species or in the experimental method.*

Various authors since von Euler (1938) have observed that the isolated perfused human cord vessels and placenta constrict vigorously to adrenaline, and also to noradrenaline and other drugs (e.g., Panigel, 1962). Here there is an additional reason to be cautious in interpreting the results, because at the flow rates used for perfusion a single rapid injection of adrenaline would give a high local concentration, far higher than that which results from an infusion into the inferior vena cava of an intact foetal lamb. There is no doubt that in both species noradrenaline and adrenaline can, if administered in large quantities, cause umbilical vasoconstriction. That is not the issue. The question is whether sufficient is liberated, even in exceptional circumstances, to achieve the relatively large concentrations required to produce a significant physiological effect. In man we do not yet have the necessary information.

VALUES FOR UMBILICAL BLOOD FLOW

Now that we have considered the various methods for measuring umbilical flow, its variation with gestational age and some of the physiological factors involved (so far as they are known), we are in a position to compare the values obtained. I think it is important at this stage not to label any of these as normal values, because this may tend to give the reader a false view of an author's omniscience. The values recorded are those found under a variety of experimental conditions. It is interesting to compare them because this may suggest further experiments.

The values for umbilical flow in sheep at term

* B. V. Lewis has since shown that the isolated perfused umbilical arteries of sheep react to oxygen in a similar fashion to those of man. The difference is therefore not due to species.

have tended to rise with better methods to a mean figure of about 175 ml/kg min (Table 19) at a mean femoral arterial pressure of 60–65 mm Hg, and an arterial P_{O_2} ~25 mm Hg and P_{CO_2} ~40 mm Hg. Providing maternal ventilation is unimpaired, delivery under light chloralose anaesthesia, local or spinal anaesthesia does not appear to affect the outcome. However, I have just a little suspicion about this happy coincidence. It could be the result of instrumental artifacts, anaesthesia, and variations in breed of sheep or size of placenta operating in different directions. It would be interesting to see the effect of inducing general anaesthesia in a sheep in which umbilical flow was already being measured, after delivery by caesarean section under local or spinal anaesthesia. For instance, administration of pentobarbitone might cause systemic vasodilatation in the foetus (as it so often does in adult animals) and a redistribution of cardiac output. It might also alter umbilical vascular resistance; the net effect on umbilical flow is impossible to predict.

Finally, there is some information on umbilical flow in man. The venous occlusion plethysmograph (Greenfield, Shepherd, and Whelan, 1951) and one form of electromagnetic flowmeter (Odelblad, 1950) evidently proved too difficult to use, as the authors have reported only one successful observation each. So we are left with two sets of results, one in early foetuses at therapeutic abortion, and the other 1–2 minutes after normal delivery. The calculation of Table 18 suggests that the minimum umbilical flow in man would be expected to be 90 ml/kg/min. The observations in Table 19 are consistent with this estimate, taking into account the fact that flow might be expected to fall rapidly after delivery. But the usual experience of those who have measured blood flows, in the foetus and elsewhere, has been that with more experience the flows observed increase. It is often difficult to say exactly why this happens, except that with more speed and skill several small items add up to make a perceptible difference. So I would not be very surprised if umbilical flows in man crept up to 150 ml/kg/min in the next few years.

It is also interesting to speculate what umbilical blood flow is likely to be in some species which are smaller at birth than lambs or human infants, which have a higher rate of O_2 consumption and a lower O_2 carrying capacity. For instance, a newborn rabbit of 50 Gm has a minimal O_2 consumption of $\sim$20 ml/kg/min; but let us suppose it is only half that before delivery. The O_2 carrying capacity of its blood at birth is 16 ml/100 ml. So, if the umbilical arteriovenous O_2 difference is 25% of full saturation (as in Table 18), umbilical blood flow must be at least 250 ml/kg/min. In the rat, which has a lower haemoglobin concentration at birth than the rabbit (Table 10, p. 30), it might have to be even more. These species are used so extensively for experimental work that it would be worth finding out whether these speculations have any justification in fact.

References

Acheson, G. H.; Dawes, G. S., and Mott, J. C.: Oxygen consumption and the arterial oxygen saturation in foetal and newborn lambs, J. Physiol. 135:623–642, 1957.

Assali, N. S., and Morris, J. A.: Circulatory and metabolic adjustments of the foetus at birth, Biol. Neonat. 7:141–159, 1964.

Assali, N. S.; Rauramo, L., and Peltonen, T.: Measurement of uterine blood flow and uterine metabolism, Am. J. Obst. & Gynec. 79:86–98, 1960.

Barclay, A. E.; Franklin, K. J., and Prichard, M. M. L.: *The Foetal Circulation* (Oxford: Blackwell Scientific Publications, 1944).

Barron, D. H.; Meschia, G.; Cotter, J. R., and Breathnach, C. S.: The haemoglobin, oxygen, carbon dioxide, and hydrogen ion concentrations in the umbilical bloods of sheep and goats as sampled via indwelling plastic catheters, Quart. J. Exper. Physiol. 50:185–195, 1965.

Bayliss, W. M.: On the local reactions of the arterial wall

TABLE 19.—MEASUREMENTS OF UMBILICAL BLOOD FLOW

Species	Authors	Gestational Age	Anaesthetic	Method	Mean Umbilical Flow (ml/kg min)	
Sheep	Cooper, Greenfield, and Huggett (1949)	>129 days	Spinal to ewe	Venous occlusion plethysmograph	(6)	138 ± 31
	Dawes, Mott, and Widdicombe (1954)	>129 days	Pentobarbitone	* Density flowmeter	(9)	98 ± 6
	Dawes and Mott (1959)	135–146 days	Chloralose 40–70 mg/kg	* Velodyne flowmeter	(10)	104
	Dawes and Mott (1964)	87–95 days	Chloralose 40 mg/kg	* Cannulated electromagnetic flowmeter	(22)	217 ± 12
		137–141 days	Chloralose 30 mg/kg	* Cannulated electromagnetic flowmeter	(10)	170 ± 14
	Assali and Morris (1964)	Near term	Spinal to ewe	* Cuff electromagnetic flowmeter		132 ± 43 (S.D.)
	Assali (1966, personal communication)	Near term	Spinal to ewe	* Cuff electromagnetic flowmeter		183 ± 20 (S.D.)
	Meschia, Cotter, Breathnach, and Barron (1965)	81–94 days	Spinal to ewe	Fick principle	(5)	183
		123–136 days	Spinal to ewe	Urea infusion to ewe	(10)	164
Man	Assali, Rauramo, and Peltonen (1960)	10–28 weeks		† Cuff electromagnetic flowmeter	(10)	110
	Štembera, Hodra, and Janda (1965)	35–42 weeks (<100 secs. from normal delivery)		† Local thermodilution	(17)	75 ± 7

* In or on abdominal common umbilical vein.   † Cord vein.
The figures in brackets indicate the number of individual observations, where recorded. Flow is given as mean ± S.E., except where otherwise indicated.

to changes of internal pressure, J. Physiol. 28:220–231, 1902.

Campbell, A. G. M.; Dawes, G. S.; Fishman, A. P.; Hyman, A. I., and James, G. B.: The oxygen consumption of the placenta and foetal membranes in the sheep, J. Physiol. 182:439–464, 1966.

Cohnstein, J., and Zuntz, N.: Untersuchungen über das Blut, den Kreislauf und die Athmung beim Säugethier-Fötus, Pflüger's Arch. ges. Physiol. 34:173–233, 1884.

Comline, R. S., and Silver, M.: The release of adrenaline and noradrenaline from the adrenal glands of the foetal sheep, J. Physiol. 156:424–444, 1961.

Comline, R. S.; Silver, I. A., and Silver, M.: Factors responsible for the stimulation of the adrenal medulla during asphyxia in the foetal lamb, J. Physiol. 178:211–238, 1965.

Cooper, K. E., and Greenfield, A. D. M.: A method for measuring the blood flow in the umbilical vessels, J. Physiol. 108:167–176, 1949.

Cooper, K. E.; Greenfield, A. D. M., and Huggett, A., St. G.: The umbilical blood flow in the foetal sheep, J. Physiol. 108:160–166, 1949.

Crawford, J. M.: Vascular anatomy of the human placenta, Am. J. Obst. & Gynec. 84:1543–1567, 1962.

Davignon, J.; Lorenz, R. R., and Shepherd, J. T.: Response of human umbilical artery to changes in transmural pressure, Am. J. Physiol. 209:51–59, 1965.

Dawes, G. S.: The umbilical circulation, Am. J. Obst. & Gynec. 84:1634–1648, 1962.

Dawes, G. S., and Mott, J. C.: The increase in O_2 consumption of the lamb after birth, J. Physiol. 146:295–315, 1959.

Dawes, G. S., and Mott, J. C.: The vascular tone of the foetal lung, J. Physiol. 164:465–477, 1962.

Dawes, G. S., and Mott, J. C.: Changes in O_2 distribution and consumption in foetal lambs with variations in umbilical blood flow, J. Physiol. 170:524–540, 1964.

Dawes, G. S.; Mott, J. C., and Rennick, B. B.: Some effects of adrenaline, noradrenaline and acetylcholine on the foetal circulation in the lamb, 134:139–148, 1956.

Dawes, G. S.; Mott, J. C., and Vane, J. R.: The density flow meter, a direct method for the measurement of the rate of blood flow, J. Physiol. 121:72–79, 1953.

Dawes, G. S.; Mott, J. C., and Widdicombe, J. G.: The foetal circulation in the lamb, J. Physiol. 126:563–587, 1954.

von Euler, U. S.: Action of adrenaline, acetylcholine and other substances on nerve-free vessels (human placenta), J. Physiol. 93:129–143, 1938.

Greenfield, A. D. M.; Shepherd, J. T., and Whelan, R. F.: The rate of blood flow in the umbilical cord, Lancet. 2:422–424, 1951.

Meschia, G.; Cotter, J. R.; Breathnach, C. S., and Barron, D. H.: The diffusibility of oxygen across the sheep placenta, Quart. J. Exper. Physiol. 50:466–480, 1965.

Nichol, J.; Girling, F.; Jerrard, W.; Claxton, E. B., and Burton, A. C.: Fundamental instability of the small blood vessels and critical closing pressures in vascular beds, Am. J. Physiol. 164:330–344, 1951.

Nyberg, G., and Westin, B.: The influence of oxygen tension and some drugs on human placental vessels, Acta physiol. scandinav. 39:216–227, 1957.

Odelblad, E.: Strömningshastighetsmätning i navel—artärerna efter partus, Nord. med. 43:221, 1950.

Panigel, M.: Placental perfusion experiments, Am. J. Obst. & Gynec. 84:1664–1683, 1962.

Spivack, M.: On the presence or absence of nerves in the umbilical vessels of man and guinea pigs, Anat. Rec. 85:85–109, 1943.

Štembera, Z. K.; Hodr, J., and Janda, J.: Umbilical blood flow in healthy newborn infants during the first minutes after birth, Am. J. Obst. & Gynec. 91:568–574, 1965.

Wimsatt, W. A.: New histological observations on the placenta of the sheep, Am. J. Anat. 87:391–458, 1950.

Wyatt, D. G.: A 50 C/S cannulated electromagnetic flowmeter, Electron. Eng. 33:650–655, 1961.

Zaitev, N. D.: Development of neural elements in the umbilical cord, Arkh. Anat. Gistol. i Embriol. 37(10):81–88, 1959.

7

The Pulmonary Circulation in the Foetus and Newborn

IN THE FOETUS the two sides of the heart work in parallel to pump blood from the great veins to the aorta (Fig. 38). In this flow system the circulation through the lungs occupies a central position. If its resistance to blood flow should be low, a large portion of the output of the right heart would enter the left atrium, a diversion which would seem to have little purpose and which could increase the work of the left heart. No doubt it was teleological considerations of this kind which led William Harvey to propose that the volume of blood flow through the foetal lung must be small. But if this is so, at birth a remarkable change must occur in the pulmonary circulation. The course of the circulation through the two sides of the heart must then alter toward the adult system in which the ventricles work in series and the lung becomes for the first time the organ of gaseous exchange.

Fig. 38.—Plan of the foetal circulation, to show that the two sides of the heart pump blood from the great veins to the aorta in parallel by way of the foramen ovale (F.O.) and ductus arteriosus (D.A.). (Redrawn from Born, Dawes, Mott, and Widdicombe, 1954.)

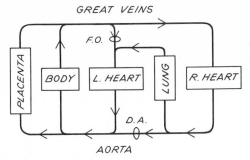

These ideas have led to much detailed work upon the control of blood flow through the lungs in the foetus and newborn. Indeed, we now know as much or more about the vascular regulation in the foetal lungs as in any other foetal organ. This fact, and the crucial position which the lungs occupy in the circulation, make it sensible to consider this evidence in some detail before trying to build up a picture of the foetal circulation as a whole.

Before doing so it is as well to recall some of the physiological background. During the past 20 years a revolution has taken place in our views about the control of the circulation in the adult lung. Up until 1946, and even for some years afterward, it was generally believed that the lungs were a toneless vascular structure which accepted passively the output of the right heart. Perhaps that is partly true of the normal adult lung at sea level, but it certainly is not true of the normal lung at altitude, nor of the lung which is affected by pathological changes. The crucial observation was made by von Euler and Liljestrand (1946) that hypoxia causes a rise in pulmonary arterial pressure in the cat, a rise which they correctly attributed to pulmonary vasoconstriction. And at about the same time it was noticed that some patients with congenital cardiac anomalies had a considerable and apparently permanent rise in pulmonary arterial pressure, an observation which the then new technique of cardiac catheterisation greatly facilitated. Within the next 10 years many papers appeared which established without doubt that the vascular bed of the lungs in the adult normally constricted in response to local reduction of O_2 partial pressure, even in isolated perfused preparations in which the participation of the central nervous system was excluded. The effect of hypercapnia in causing vasoconstriction was less certain. Evidence was also presented by Daly and Daly (1959) that changes in arterial blood gas tensions can have a reflex effect on the pulmonary vascular bed through the aortic and carotid chemoreceptors in adult dogs.

Early Observations in Foetal Lungs

The first direct measurements on the pulmonary vascular bed in the foetus were designed to discover what happened to pulmonary arterial pressure when the lungs were first ventilated at birth. Foetal lambs were delivered under general anaesthesia, and were kept warm and with an intact umbilical cord. The foetal chest was opened and it was found that lateral pressure in the main pulmonary artery was greater than that in the descending aorta (just beyond the distal end of the ductus arteriosus) throughout the cardiac cycle. On ventilation of the lungs pulmonary arterial pressure fell rapidly, and this was accompanied by an increase in pulmonary flow from sixfold to tenfold (Fig. 39; Dawes, Mott, Widdicombe, and Wyatt, 1953). There was a small increase in left atrial pressure. The flowmeter used (the "density flowmeter") was inserted between the cut ends of the left pulmonary artery and was clumsy by present standards. But it measured flow directly, as the time taken for a fixed volume of fluid to pass through the instrument, and the pressure drop across it was small in comparison with pulmonary arterial pressure in the foetus. It was concluded that there was a very large decrease in pulmonary vascular resistance on first ventilation of the lungs.

During the course of the same series of experiments it was observed that expansion of the unventilated lungs with warm saline either had no effect or reduced pulmonary blood flow. Rhythmic positive pressure ventilation with air, O_2, or N_2 caused a large increase in pulmonary flow with a fall in pulmonary arterial pressure, and even a single full inflation with N_2 had the same effect. Therefore, it was thought that the principal increase in pulmonary flow at birth was due to gaseous expansion of the lungs; the experiments did not suggest that the composition of the gas was important, but on this point the number of observations was small. Much more attention was directed to the fact that the fall in pulmonary arterial pressure was so large that the direction of blood flow through the ductus arteriosus was reversed.

In the foetus, pulmonary arterial pressure is

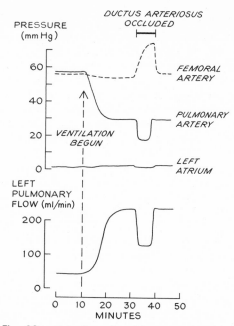

Fig. 39.—The effect of positive pressure ventilation on pulmonary blood flow and pressures in a mature foetal lamb. (Redrawn from the data of Dawes, Mott, Widdicombe, and Wyatt, 1953.)

greater than aortic pressure, and most of the output from the right heart passes through the ductus arteriosus to the aorta (right-to-left). Within a few minutes of ventilation in the lamb the direction of flow reverses (left-to-right), as can be shown most dramatically by brief occlusion of the ductus arteriosus (Fig. 39). Before ventilation this causes a rise in pulmonary arterial pressure, whereas afterward it causes a fall. This reversal of flow, its dependence on the continued patency of the ductus arteriosus and foramen ovale, and the physiological consequences of these vascular rearrangements in the newborn diverted attention during the next 5 years from a further investigation of the mechanisms by which gaseous expansion of the lungs caused pulmonary vasodilatation. But several incidental observations were made which suggested that this was a subject which needed more detailed study.

First it was noticed that, on ventilation of the isolated perfused lungs of foetal lambs, while gaseous expansion with N_2 caused pulmonary vasodilatation, substitution of air caused yet further vasodilatation (Born, Dawes, and Mott, 1955). It was concluded that while the initial pulmonary vasodilatation did not depend on the presence of O_2 in the ventilating gas mixture, yet the composition of the latter was important; an analogy was drawn with similar observations on the isolated perfused lungs of adult cats (Nisell, 1948, 1950; Duke, 1951, 1954). It was also noticed that small doses of 5-hydroxytryptamine caused pulmonary vasoconstriction as in adults. Secondly, Paul Wood became curious about the effect of acetylcholine in causing pulmonary vasodilatation in children with pulmonary hypertension associated with cardio-vascular congenital anomalies. He suggested that the effect of acetylcholine might be worth further exploration in foetal lungs, and a few preliminary experiments in isolated perfused unventilated foetal lungs showed that it caused a profound vaso-dilatation (Dawes, 1959). Thirdly, during the course of unpublished experiments on unventilated foetal lambs *in vivo*, it was noticed that the circulation time between the right atrium and left carotid artery, read from indicator dilution curves using I^{131} labeled serum albumen, was subject to wide fluctuations under different physiological circumstances. Among other possible causes, this might have been due to changes in pulmonary circulation time. It was recalled that left pulmonary blood flow in un-ventilated lungs varied from 2.8–25.4 ml/kg body weight in different lambs (Dawes, Mott, Widdi-combe, and Wyatt, 1953). The circulation in the foetal lungs might be more labile than was hitherto supposed, a proposition which soon received ample confirmation.

Two approaches were used. In the experiments reported by Dawes and Mott (1962) the main emphasis was on the unventilated foetal lung *in vivo* which was shown to vasodilate very greatly in response to injections of small doses of acetylcholine or histamine, or as a result of raising the O_2 saturation (and hence the Po_2) of foetal arterial blood by giving the mother high O_2 mixtures to breathe. Conversely, asphyxia caused an extreme degree of pulmonary vasoconstriction. In experiments carried out independently and concurrently, Cook, Drinker, Jacobson, Levison, and Strang (1963) set out to examine the effect of hypoventilation in the newborn lamb. They showed that changes in the gaseous composition of the blood were associated with a profound alteration in the vascular tone in newly ventilated lungs. What was especially interesting was the fact that addition of 10% CO_2 to the ventilating gas mixture caused a very large pulmonary vasoconstriction. Nothing of this magnitude had been seen in adult lungs.

There were some points of difference in interpretation of the results obtained by the two groups which needed resolving. Thus Cook *et al.* were inclined to attribute the increase in pulmonary flow on first ventilation of the lungs mainly, if not entirely, to the (probably local) effect of changes in alveolar gas tensions, while Dawes and Mott believed that gaseous expansion of itself was an important factor, irrespective of gas composition. In order to resolve the difference of opinion, Leonard Strang and Dawes and Mott joined forces and spent an agreeable spring working together, at the end of which everyone was contented, because they were all partly right. From this point on the results may be discussed rather more systematically, but something must first be said about pressure-flow relations in the foetal and newborn lung.

PRESSURE-FLOW RELATIONS IN THE FOETAL LUNG

It is common practice to describe the vascular resistance of an organ in terms of the quotient of pressure and flow, e.g.:

Pulmonary vascular resistance

$$= \frac{\text{pulmonary arterial-left atrial pressure}}{\text{flow}}$$

There is nothing wrong with this practice, providing its limitations are recognized. In the special case of the foetal lung the limitations are such as to make the practice of doubtful value. A hint of the difficulty was given earlier (Dawes, Mott, Widdicombe, and Wyatt, 1953) when it was pointed out that it was not known whether the relation between pressure and flow in the neonatal lung was linear. When the ductus arteriosus was briefly occluded, pulmonary arterial flow rose relatively more than pulmonary arterial pressure, and pulmonary vascular resistance (as calculated on the basis described above) fell by up to 35% within a few seconds.

Fig. 40.—Schematic diagram of method for drawing pulmonary pressure-flow curves *in vivo*, by flow from a vertical tube, as used by Cassin, Dawes, Mott, Ross, and Strang (1964).

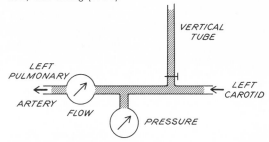

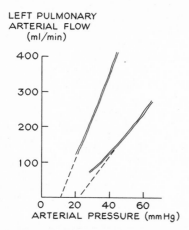

Fig. 41.—Examples of *in vivo* pulmonary pressure-flow curves from a mature foetal lamb. (From Cassin, Dawes, Mott, Ross, and Strang, 1964.)

Pressure-flow curves were constructed before and after ventilation of foetal lungs in anaesthetized lambs in the following manner (Cassin, Dawes, Mott, Ross, and Strang, 1964). The central end of the left carotid was connected to the peripheral end of the left pulmonary artery via a cannulated type of electromagnetic flowmeter. A vertical tube was attached to the connection (Fig. 40); the lamb was heparinised. The transpulmonary (arterial-atrial) pressure and flow were displayed on the X and Y axes, respectively, of an oscilloscope or rapid response X-Y recorder to give an instantaneous pressure-flow curve as blood ran in from the vertical tube, the connection to the left carotid being temporarily occluded. The curves so produced, of which some examples are shown in Figure 41, agreed exactly with those described by progressive step-wise reduction in flow by tightening a screwclip on the connection with the left carotid artery, provided flow was not thereby reduced too much or for too long (i.e., provided asphyxia was avoided). These curves are not linear through the origin; an increase in pressure causes a disproportionate increase in flow. Physiological changes (such as ventilation of the lung) cause an alteration in both slope and position of the curve. Yet it is possible to handle the data simply and for statistical purposes by determining the slope and intercept on the pressure axis of the steep linear part of the curve (as indicated by the dotted lines in Fig. 41), before it begins to bend toward the origin. These measurements define its shape and position. Allowance can then be made for the resistance to blood flow of the external circuit and of the weight of the animal (or its lungs).

This procedure gives a more accurate picture of the changes in the pulmonary vascular bed on ventilation of the lungs. It is particularly valuable in premature lambs, where administration of a vasodilator agent may cause only a small rise in flow and fall in arterial pressure (and so little apparent change in vascular resistance as calculated in the conventional manner) but a large shift in the position of the upper part of the pressure-flow curve.

THE EFFECT OF GASEOUS EXPANSION OF THE LUNGS

Gaseous expansion of the lungs caused pulmonary vasodilatation irrespective of any change in arterial blood gas composition and by a direct action. This conclusion is now supported by several lines of evidence. When the lungs of foetal lambs are rebreathed with a gas mixture containing 3% O_2 and 7% CO_2 in N_2 (i.e., approximately in equilibrium with the foetal arterial Po_2 and Pco_2) there is either no change in the composition of the ventilating gas mixture or a slight increase in O_2 content; there is an insignificant change in arterial blood gas tensions. Yet there is a considerable pulmonary vasodilatation (Cassin, Dawes, Mott, Ross, and Strang, 1964). These results have been substantiated by Lauer, Evans, Aoki, and Kittle (1965), also in foetal lambs, but using a cuff electromagnetic flowmeter applied to the right pulmonary artery. Similarly, expansion of the foetal lungs by introducing 25 ml/kg of the same gas mixture into the tracheal cannula (to give a peak intratracheal pressure of

Fig. 42.—Effect of gaseous expansion of the lungs (indicated by the arrows) with 3% O_2 and 7% CO_2 in N_2 in mature foetal lambs, either with or without bilateral thoracic sympathectomy and vagotomy. (Redrawn from Colebatch, Dawes, Goodwin, and Nadeau, 1965.)

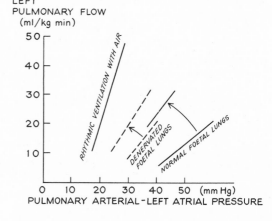

34–51 mm Hg, released after 5 secs) caused a prolonged pulmonary vasodilatation which reached its maximum over 5–10 minutes (Colebatch, Dawes, Goodwin, and Nadeau, 1965). As Figure 42 shows, the effect persists after denervation of the lungs (bilateral sympathectomy T 1–8 and section of the cervical vago-sympathetic trunks), although sympathectomy itself led to pulmonary vasodilatation. Figure 42 also demonstrates that the vasodilatation caused by gaseous expansion of the lungs, irrespective of gas composition, is a substantial part (one third, at least) of the acute pulmonary vasodilatation caused by rhythmic positive pressure ventilation with room air.

This latter conclusion has been reinforced recently in another way. The unventilated lungs of mature foetal lambs were perfused *in vivo* with arterial blood derived from well-ventilated twins (i.e., with blood which had a Po_2 ~80 mm Hg and a Pco_2 <30 mm Hg) in cross-circulation experiments (Campbell, Cockburn, Dawes, and Milligan, 1966). Subsequent rhythmic ventilation with air of the previously unexpanded lungs caused a considerable pulmonary vasodilatation. Thus gaseous expansion of foetal lungs causes pulmonary vasodilatation whether the gas composition of the blood which perfuses them is foetal arterial (Po_2 ~25, Pco_2 ~45 mm Hg) or adult in character.

The mechanism responsible for this pulmonary vasodilatation is evidently local, within the parenchyma of the lung. It was shown by Macklin (1946) that expansion of the adult lung dilates some blood vessels, probably by radial traction. Although this is an oversimplification of the situation, because of evidence first that expansion compresses other pulmonary vessels (probably capillaries; Riley, 1962) and second that brief lung expansion can cause a transient pulmonary vasoconstriction by a different mechanism (Colebatch and Nadeau, 1965), yet Macklin's observations provide a possible analogue to the pulmonary vasodilatation on gaseous expansion of the foetal lung. Fluid expansion of the foetal lung causes an alteration in lung geometry only so long as the fluid is retained, and at an increased tracheobronchial pressure which must compress the pulmonary capillaries. When the trachea is opened after fluid expansion of the foetal lung, the fluid drains away over the next minute or two, and pulmonary blood flow, which was reduced by fluid expansion, returns to its initial level. But gaseous expansion of the lung introduces a gas-fluid interface, and causes a prolonged change in the geometry of the alveoli even when the tracheobronchial tree is opened to the atmosphere. The physical effect of gaseous expansion is, therefore, very different from that of fluid expansion.

There is another point to be considered. The fact that fluid expansion of the lung reduces pulmonary flow has been mentioned. The foetal lung continuously forms fluid, a phenomenon which will be considered in more detail in Chapter 11. This fluid is probably normally swallowed, rather than allowed to pass through the nose and mouth. In anaesthetised foetal lambs it accumulates in the tracheobronchial tree in such amounts that, unless the trachea is cannulated and allowed to drain continuously, pulmonary blood flow is reduced and arterial pressure begins to fall (presumably by reduction of venous return as the lungs expand in the chest) within an hour. Thus it is always necessary to drain the tracheobronchial tree if the foetus is to be maintained in good physiological condition. Recently, Forrest Adams (personal communication) has observed that tracheobronchial fluid pressure is elevated even in unanaesthetised foetal lambs newly delivered by caesarean section from ewes under spinal anaesthesia. This raises the possibility that pulmonary vascular resistance *in utero* is even greater than that observed in the experiments described above. It is possible that the normal expression of fluid from the foetal lungs as the chest passes through the birth canal may reduce the tracheobronchial pressure, and thus contribute to pulmonary vasodilatation on delivery.

The Effect of Changes in Gas Composition on Pulmonary Vascular Resistance

Changes in gas composition, either of the arterial blood supplying the unventilated foetal lungs, or of the mixture used to ventilate the lungs, caused large alterations in vascular resistance. These are illustrated in Figure 43. Increasing the O_2 content of the gas mixture used to ventilate the lungs of lambs, which were still attached by an intact umbilical cord to the placenta, caused only a small rise in foetal arterial Po_2 (because of continuing umbilical flow) but a large pulmonary vasodilatation. Subsequent removal of 7% CO_2 from the ventilating gas mixture caused a yet further pulmonary vasodilatation of about the same size. Qualitatively, the same results were obtained when the left lung, through which flow was measured, was not ventilated, but the gas composition of the arterial blood was altered by ventilating the right lung only. Thus

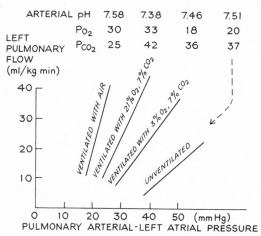

ARTERIAL pH	7.58	7.38	7.46	7.51
LEFT PULMONARY FLOW (ml/kg min)	P_{O_2} 30	33	18	20
	P_{CO_2} 25	42	36	37

Fig. 43.—The effect of ventilation with different gas mixtures upon the mean arterial blood gases and pH and pulmonary arterial pressure: flow curves in mature foetal lambs. (From the data of Cassin, Dawes, Mott, Ross, and Strang, 1964.)

either a rise in arterial P_{O_2} or a reduction in P_{CO_2} led to a highly significant and substantial pulmonary vasodilatation, independently of one another.

Over the range P_{O_2} 16–34, P_{CO_2} 25–42 mm Hg, either a 10 mm Hg rise in P_{O_2} or a 10 mm Hg fall in P_{CO_2} caused the same degree of pulmonary vasodilatation. But it was by no means certain that the relation between arterial or alveolar P_{O_2} or P_{CO_2} and pulmonary vascular resistance was linear, rather than curvilinear, even over this narrow range. Certainly, the relation did not necessarily hold outside this range, because raising the arterial P_{O_2} from 50 to 150 mm Hg, by ventilation with 100% O_2 in place of air, had little effect on pulmonary vascular resistance at a fixed P_{CO_2} (Dawes, 1966). These facts are reminiscent of the situation in adult lungs, in which also hypoxia does not cause an increase in pulmonary vascular resistance until the alveolar P_{O_2} is reduced below about 50 mm Hg.

Recently, Lauer, Evans, Aoki, and Kittle (1965) had the ingenious idea of expanding the lungs of mature foetal lambs with dextran-saline solution or blood of differing oxygen content. Expansion of the foetal lungs with a deoxygenated solution of low P_{CO_2} caused a small transient rise in pulmonary flow with little change in arterial pressure. But when the lungs were flushed with a solution of high O_2 content, there was a large rise in pulmonary flow and a small fall in arterial pressure. They did not record the effect on foetal arterial blood gas tensions, but it is likely that the pulmonary vasodila-

tation was entirely due to a local effect of the increase in bronchopulmonary P_{O_2}.

There is no doubt that in adult lungs hypoxia can cause pulmonary vasoconstriction by a direct action in isolated perfused lungs. Conversely, as already mentioned, in the isolated perfused lungs of mature foetal lambs substitution of air for nitrogen as the ventilating gas caused pulmonary vasodilatation (Born, Dawes, and Mott, 1955). Also the effects of acute asphyxia in causing pulmonary vasoconstriction in unventilated lungs *in vivo*, and of changes in gas tensions after ventilation, both persisted undiminished after denervation of the lungs in foetal lambs (Colebatch, Dawes, Goodwin, and Nadeau, 1965). It was concluded that, if hypoxaemia or hypercapnia did cause pulmonary vasoconstriction in the foetus by an indirect reflex action, it was probably small in comparison with the local direct effect.

Yet there were two considerations which made it necessary to investigate the possibility more thoroughly. First it was noticed that sympathectomy caused pulmonary vasodilatation in the mature foetal lamb (Fig. 42). Stimulation of the sympathetic nerves to the lung (which in the lamb arise from T 3–5) at term also caused a remarkable degree of pulmonary vasoconstriction. Even at 80–90 days gestation (~0.6 of term, when the lungs cannot be expanded and the foetus is not viable) sympathetic stimulation can reduce pulmonary flow by 75%. The blood vessels of the foetal lungs also constrict very readily on injection of small doses of adrenaline or noradrenaline into the pulmonary artery, in a manner different from adult lungs, which are relatively insensitive to catecholamines. Secondly, there was the consideration that if the lungs were unusually susceptible to reflex vasoconstriction in the immediate neonatal period, this might be disadvantageous to their use as an efficient organ of gaseous exchange. For instance, perfusion of alveoli might be dictated in part by general physiological responses (e.g., of systemic arterial chemoreceptors or baroreceptors) rather than by local ventilation. This could exaggerate maldistribution of blood flow and ventilation and perhaps contribute in part to the development of the respiratory distress syndrome.

Two series of experiments were undertaken. In the first the left carotid was joined to the peripheral end of the left pulmonary artery as in Figure 40, in immature lambs of 80–90 days gestation. When the vertical tube was filled with foetal arterial blood withdrawn before the onset of asphyxia (P_{O_2} 13–29,

$PCO_2 < 44$ mm Hg) the pulmonary vasoconstriction caused by 2–4 minutes acute asphyxia (on occlusion of the cord) was *wholly* relieved within a few seconds of the blood from the vertical tube entering the left pulmonary artery. When the vertical tube was filled with blood withdrawn during asphyxia ($PO_2 < 2$, $PCO_2 > 40$ mm Hg) the vasoconstriction was not relieved (Campbell, Dawes, Fishman, and Hyman, 1965). The possibility of a reflex mechanism was excluded by the use of hexamethonium, which blocked the pulmonary vasoconstrictor effect of stimulation of the sympathetic chain, but did not abolish the response to asphyxia or its immediate relief on introduction of normal arterial blood. Circulating catecholamines could not account for the effect, since injection of a dose sufficient to cause this degree of vasoconstriction had an effect lasting 10 minutes. It was concluded that asphyxia caused pulmonary vasoconstriction wholly by a direct local action, already at this comparatively early gestational age.

This conclusion was reinforced by experiments in which the lungs of a foetal lamb were perfused from its twin in cross-circulation experiments (Campbell, Cockburn, Dawes, and Milligan, 1966). The arrangement used is illustrated diagrammatically in Figure 44. In lambs ~90 days gestational age, asphyxia of the lungs of the recipient (by perfusion with asphyxiated blood from the donor, whose umbilical cord was temporarily occluded) caused intense pulmonary vasoconstriction. But asphyxia of the body of the recipient (by cord occlusion, its lungs being supplied with normal blood from the donor) caused no vasoconstriction. However, in older, more mature foetal lambs, asphyxia

of the body of the recipient alone caused a small degree of pulmonary vasoconstriction, which could be demonstrated repeatedly, and which was abolished either by administration of hexamethonium or by cutting the sympathetic supply to the lung. This demonstrates that a mechanism for the reflex control of the pulmonary vascular bed exists in the mature foetal lamb, from ~100 days gestation onward. Possible sensory pathways have not been explored.

In assessing the value of this evidence it is important to remember that the stimulus used was acute total asphyxia, induced by temporary occlusion of the umbilical cord. This reduces the arterial PO_2 in the foetus to < 5 mm Hg within 2 minutes and raises the PCO_2 by 15–30 mm Hg; the arterial pressure rises considerably at the same time. This stimulus was chosen as being likely to result in a reflex response in a preliminary search. It may well not be the most effective stimulus. The rise of arterial pressure may act, reflexly, in an opposite sense to chemoreceptor stimulation, and the direct effect of asphyxia on the immature foetal nervous system may be to cut short cardiovascular reflex discharges abruptly. There was even, in 2 mature lambs, a hint of reflex pulmonary vasodilatation during asphyxia after the sympathetic nerves to the lung had been cut. We may, therefore, be dealing with a very complex phenomenon. It would be unwise to regard it as insignificant on the evidence so far available. The demonstration of a reflex mechanism also makes interpretation of the effects of changes in blood gas concentrations peculiarly difficult, as we now have to consider the possibility of several sites of action, locally in the lungs, reflexly via the arterial chemoreceptors, or centrally on the nervous system. There is evidence, summarized in Chapter 11, that the carotid chemoreceptors are not normally active in the foetus, though they become activated a minute or so after the umbilical cord is occluded. The aortic chemoreceptors have not been investigated in this respect.

THE EFFECTS OF ASPHYXIA AND ISCHAEMIA

We may next consider the nature of the effective stimulus to pulmonary vasoconstriction during hypoxia or hypercapnia, while recognizing the difficulties introduced by possible multiple sites of action. In 1958, Liljestrand suggested that the pulmonary vascular response to hypoxia in the adult might be related to the local production of H^+ ions

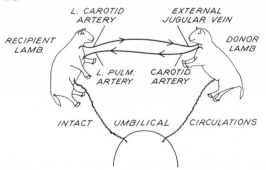

Fig. 44.—Schematic diagram of the arrangement used for cross-perfusion between twin lambs. Flow between the two lambs was continuously measured by electromagnetic flowmeters and that from the recipient to the donor was continuously adjusted to be equal to that in the reverse direction.

L. CAROTID ARTERY

EXTERNAL JUGULAR VEIN

RECIPIENT LAMB

DONOR LAMB

L. PULM. ARTERY

CAROTID ARTERY

INTACT   UMBILICAL   CIRCULATIONS

in the lungs. A direct test of this hypothesis in isolated perfused adult cat lungs proved negative (Duke, Killick and Marchant, 1960). The vasoconstrictor response to hypoxia was independent of arterial pH. In newborn calves, Rudolph and Yuan (1966) found that the change in pulmonary vascular resistance on exposure to hypoxia was dependent on arterial pH (Fig. 45). In these experiments pulmonary vascular resistance was calculated as the quotient of pressure and flow, and flow was measured with an electromagnetic flowmeter calibrated *in vivo* from indicator dilution curves; both these procedures reduce the accuracy of the estimate and yet the relation illustrated is clear. The flowmeter probe was applied to the main pulmonary artery and the ductus arteriosus was tied; it is difficult to guess at the possible effects on sensory nerves from the great vessels or motor nerves to the lungs.

Rudolph and Yuan state that in their experiments there was no relation between pulmonary vascular resistance and P_{CO_2}. In this there is a discrepancy with the observations on the unventilated or ventilated lungs of foetal lambs (Cook, Drinker, Jacobson, Levison, and Strang, 1963; Cassin, Dawes, Mott, Ross, and Strang, 1964), in which a statistically highly significant relation was demonstrated. But there are many differences between the two sets of experiments, as to age, species, anaesthetic, experimental preparation, and procedure; in Rudolph and Yuan's experiments the chest was closed and the calves were breathing spontaneously, whereas in the others the lambs were rhythmically ventilated by positive pressure. It would, therefore, be unwise to conclude that the apparent difference results from more than an accidental choice of experimental conditions. Figure 43 shows that when CO_2 was removed from the ventilating gas mixture in lambs, when arterial P_{CO_2} fell and there was a consequential pulmonary vasodilatation, there was also a rise in arterial pH (hardly surprising, considering the Henderson-Hasselbalch relation). The question of whether it is pH or P_{CO_2} which is the immediate local determinant of pulmonary vascular resistance recalls the debate, some 30 years ago, as to whether it was a local change in pH or P_{CO_2} which controlled the activity of the respiratory centre.

The most important and the common finding in all these investigations has been that in the foetus and newborn the pulmonary vascular bed is very sensitive to changes in alveolar or arterial P_{O_2}, P_{CO_2} and/or acidosis. The adult lung also normally vasoconstricts in response to local hypoxia, a local

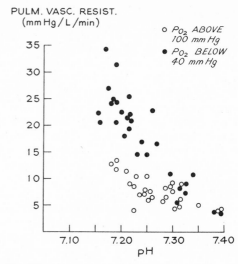

Fig. 45.—Response of the pulmonary vascular resistance in four newborn calves to changes in arterial pH when the arterial $P_{O_2} > 100$ mm Hg (o) or below 40 mm Hg (●). (Redrawn from Rudolph and Yuan, 1966.)

response which appears to be characteristic of the lung alone, but one which can be modified by circumstances. For instance, the vasoconstriction can be abolished by sodium azide (Duke and Killick, 1952). It is absent in some forms of experimental preparation using dogs' lungs, when the preparation has been ischaemic or at a lower temperature (Daly, Ramsay, and Waaler, 1962), or when small volumes of blood are continuously recirculated (Cropp, 1965). The aberration from normality which determines failure to vasoconstrict during hypoxia is not known with certainty, but the fact that it can occur is very interesting. It is possible that hypoxia causes pulmonary vasoconstriction by a direct action on the smooth muscle of the vessel walls, or by the local release of a vasoconstrictor agent (such as noradrenaline). Barer (1966,a,b) has observed in adult cats that the pulmonary vasoconstriction of hypoxia is blocked by dibenamine, phentolamine, phenoxybenzamine, and guanethidine, and is often absent after administration of reserpine; the vasoconstrictor responses to hypercapnia were unaffected, suggesting that it may act by a different mechanism. In the immature foetal lamb also dibenamine blocks both the pulmonary vasoconstriction due to asphyxia and that caused by injection of noradrenaline (Cassin, Dawes, and Ross, 1964); however, there has always been some suspicion that the action of dibenamine may be unspecific.

There is another fact which is relevant. In the unventilated foetal lung ischaemia is followed by a brief period of pulmonary vasodilatation (Fig. 46), i.e., of reactive hyperaemia such as can be readily demonstrated in such peripheral vascular beds as that of the hindlimb. This phenomenon was not seen after ventilation of the lung, even when it was ventilated with nitrogen (Dawes and Mott, 1962), but the effect of ischaemia has not been examined during ventilation with 3% O_2 and 7% CO_2 in nitrogen. The demonstration of reactive hyperaemia in the foetal lung suggests that the mechanisms which control pulmonary vascular tone are even more complex than at first appeared. For 2 minutes asphyxia causes intense pulmonary vasoconstriction which lasts 5–10 minutes after release of the umbilical cord. Yet here is a stimulus, ischaemia, in which asphyxia must be a large component part, and yet it is at once followed by pulmonary vasodilatation.

The difference between the two experimental situations is that during asphyxia pulmonary flow continues, although at a diminished rate, and the transmural pressure to which the pulmonary arteries are subjected is increased. During ischaemia, flow is arrested and pulmonary arterial pressure falls from 50–65 to 3–4 mm Hg. The metabolic activity of the foetal lung is far from negligible (Dawes, Mott, and Widdicombe, 1954); it consumes about 0.75 ml O_2/100 Gm wet weight per minute, which is 5% of the O_2 consumption of the whole foetus (Campbell, Cockburn, Dawes, and Milligan, 1966). In the ischaemic lung metabolic activity must continue, without blood flow to remove excess H^+ ions and provide glucose. It is reasonable to expect that in some pathological situations the normal response of the foetal lung, of vasoconstriction to asphyxia, may be modified. This may account for some otherwise puzzling occasional observations, unpublished, in which at the end of long experiments on the lungs of foetal lambs there has been progressive vasodilatation, although the arterial pH was steadily falling below 7.0.

There is, perhaps, a moral to be drawn from this. We are still in a relatively early stage of trying to elucidate all the various mechanisms which control the pulmonary circulation in the foetus and newborn. Attention has been mainly directed to the dramatic effects of acute experiments in animals in good condition. When it comes to applying the knowledge gained to sick human infants or animals, it may be that the behaviour of physiologically "bad" preparations is more appropriate.

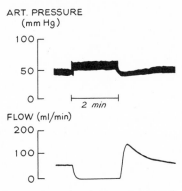

Fig. 46.—Arrest of pulmonary arterial flow for 2 minutes (during the signal mark) in the unventilated lung of a lamb was followed by reactive hyperaemia. (Redrawn from Dawes and Mott, 1962.)

THE EFFECTS OF DRUGS

The action of drugs upon the pulmonary circulation in the foetus is comparatively easy to study, and very dramatic. Some actions, the vasoconstrictor effect of adrenaline and noradrenaline (0.1–0.5 $\mu g/kg$ intra-arterially) and the vasodilator action of acetylcholine (~ 1 $\mu g/kg$) have already been mentioned. Small doses of histamine (~ 1 $\mu g/kg$) and isoprenaline (~ 0.5 $\mu g/kg$) also cause profound pulmonary vasodilatation.

During the course of experiments over a number of years (Dawes and Mott, 1962; Cassin, Dawes, Mott, Ross, and Strang, 1964; Colebatch, Dawes, Goodwin, and Nadeau, 1965), many incidents of unexplained and very sizeable "spontaneous" pulmonary vasodilatation were observed in foetal lambs. Some of these, perhaps most, can now be attributed to the generation of a substance, which has the properties of bradykinin, in the flow path which connected the left carotid to the left pulmonary artery (Fig. 40); for the unexpanded foetal lung is exquisitely sensitive to the pulmonary vasodilator properties of small doses (of the order of 1 ng = 10^{-9} Gm) of bradykinin injected close-arterially (Campbell, Dawes, Fishman, and Hyman, 1966). This vasodilator substance does not appear to be generated so much from foetal plasma, on glass contact, as from some non-erythrocyte cellular component, either platelets or more probably white cells. In this respect, there appears to be a difference from adult plasma (including the plasma of adult sheep) in which bradykinin is readily generated by glass contact. This difference needs further investigation.

There are several features of drug action in the foetal lung which deserve particular consideration. The effects of acetylcholine, histamine, and iso-prenaline (in causing vasodilatation), and of adren-aline, noradrenaline, and 5-hydroxytryptamine (in causing vasoconstriction) are very similar in lambs of 75–90 days gestation (300–600 Gm weight and previable, in which the lungs cannot be expanded), and in lambs of 140 days gestation (within a week of term; 3–6 kg), when doses are calculated per kg. It is possible, but not certain, that the vasodilator effect of bradykinin is less in the younger lambs; the situation is complicated by the fact that this drug is very rapidly destroyed in the blood stream, even in very immature foetal lambs. The general similarity of the results in the immature and mature foetal lambs is interesting, because it supports the hypothesis that the basic control of pulmonary vascular tone (though not perhaps the nervous con-trol) is already established at an early stage of foe-tal life. The pulmonary and systemic arterial pres-sures rise in the foetal lamb from 30–35 mm Hg at 80–90 days gestation to 55–70 mm Hg at 140 days. But the slope and position of the pressure-flow curves at the two ages are not very different when allowance is made for the variation in foetal weight (Table 20). The slope of the pressure : flow curve (per kg foetal weight) is identical; only the pressure intercept is greater in older lambs.

In both immature and mature foetal lambs vaso-dilator agents (acetylcholine, histamine, bradyki-nin) cause a very large increase in pulmonary blood flow. In mature lambs this can amount to six- to tenfold, that is, as much as on subsequent ventila-tion with air. But when these drugs are injected into the lungs of foetal lambs which have been re-cently ventilated, and in which pulmonary blood flow has, therefore, already increased, they have little or no action. This is to say, they cause vaso-dilatation in a vasoconstricted lung, but not in one which is already vasodilated. The same is true of sheep which are 2–3 months old (i.e., after birth) which are well on the way to maturity and weigh

15–25 kg. In such lambs in a normal physiological condition acetylcholine causes, if anything, a small vasoconstriction (perhaps by release of catechol-amines locally), and bradykinin has little action. But when left pulmonary vascular resistance is in-creased by lung collapse, hypoxaemia, and hyper-capnia, both drugs cause a clear pulmonary vaso-dilatation. Similar results were obtained with acetylcholine in adult dogs. This may go some way to explaining the variable results obtained by other authors in dogs, and also suggests that the obser-vations in lambs and sheep were not due to a spe-cies difference. The observations of Chu *et al.* (1965) show that acetylcholine causes pulmonary vasodi-latation in the newborn human infant also.

The view has been widely expressed that the special characteristics of the pulmonary circulation in the foetus, its high vascular resistance, and great lability, are dependent on the development of a thick arteriolar muscular coat as a result of the high pulmonary arterial pressure which obtains at term. There are excellent histological observations which show that the smooth muscle mass of the pulmo-nary arterioles, like those of other organs, increases greatly toward the end of gestation and normally regresses shortly after birth, within a few weeks in man (Wagenvoort, Neufeld, and Edwards, 1961; Naeye, 1961), as pulmonary arterial pressure pro-gressively falls. Yet the pulmonary blood vessels of the foetal lamb are already intensely reactive at 75–90 days gestational age, when arterial pressure is still relatively low. And normal ventilation of the lungs at term, by causing pulmonary vasodilata-tion, of itself creates a situation in which they are liable to be less reactive. So the situation may be more complicated than at first appeared, and would repay further investigation.

EVIDENCE IN DIFFERENT SPECIES

Finally, we should consider evidence as to whether the mechanisms which operate in acute experi-ments on anaesthetized foetal lambs, where a more

TABLE 20.—PULMONARY VASCULAR RESISTANCE IN FOETAL LAMBS OF DIFFERENT GESTATIONAL AGES (TERM IS ~147 DAYS)

	DAYS GESTATION	NUMBER	PRESSURE INTERCEPT (mm Hg)	SLOPE OF STEEP PART OF PRESSURE-FLOW CURVE (ml/min per mm Hg per kg Foetal Weight)
Mature	135–143	23	36 ± 1.7	0.89 ± 0.17
Immature	84–94	18	25 ± 1.1	0.86 ± 0.22

The figures indicate the means ± S.E. Unpublished data by Campbell, Dawes, Fishman, and Hyman.

rigorous analysis is possible, also obtain in intact unanaesthetized animals and in other species. On these points the evidence is incomplete. Stahlman, Shepard, Gray, and Young (1964) found that hypoxia caused strong pulmonary vasoconstriction in intact unanaesthetized newborn lambs, using indicator dilution methods. Reeves and Leathers (1964) found that hypoxia caused a large rise in pulmonary arterial pressure in anaesthetized young calves, which persisted after denervation of the lungs. Rudolph and Yuan (1966), as already described, (Fig. 45) analysed some of the component factors in greater detail in anaesthetized newborn calves. But adult cattle seem particularly susceptible to pulmonary hypertension, causing a syndrome known as brisket disease, on chronic exposure to altitudes over 8,000 feet, that is to say at a not particularly great height (Hecht *et al.,* 1959, 1962). It is still not clear whether the remarkably vigorous responses of the pulmonary circulation in the newborn calf are to some extent a characteristic of the species.

In the newborn human infant also there is evidence that the pulmonary circulation is very labile. Moderate hypoxia causes a large rise in pulmonary arterial pressure in mongols in whom there was no evidence of congenital heart disease (James and Rowe, 1957). Observations in normal infants on the bi-directional character of the shunt across the ductus arteriosus during the first day or two from birth also are most readily explained in this way. And Chu *et al.* (1965) invoke this phenomenon as an explanation for their observations on infants suffering from the respiratory distress syndrome. The evidence in man is restricted to the period after birth, is less direct than that in animals, but quite consistent with the latter.

The consequences and clinical implications of the extreme lability of the pulmonary circulation at birth will be discussed in Chapter 13. First we must consider the organization of the foetal circulation as a whole.

References

Ardran, G. M.; Dawes, G. S.; Prichard, M. M. L.; Reynolds, S. R. M., and Wyatt, D. G.: The effect of ventilation of the foetal lungs upon the pulmonary circulation, J. Physiol. 118:12–22, 1952.

Barer, G. R.: Reactivity of the vessels of collapsed and ventilated lungs to drugs and hypoxia, Circulation Res. 18:366–378, 1966,a.

Barer, G. R.: The effect of catecholamine blocking and releasing agents on the changes in the pulmonary circulation caused by hypoxia and hypercapnia, J. Physiol. 186:97P, 1966.

Born, G. V. R.; Dawes, G. S., and Mott, J. C. The viability of premature lambs, J. Physiol. 130:191–212, 1955.

Born, G. V. R.; Dawes, G. S.; Mott, J. C., and Widdicombe, J. G.: Changes in the heart and lungs at birth, Cold Spring Harb. Symp. Quant. Biol. 19:102–108, 1954.

Campbell, A. G. M.; Cockburn, F.; Dawes, G. S., and Milligan, J. E.: Pulmonary blood flow and cross-circulation between twin foetal lambs, J. Physiol. 186:96P, 1966.

Campbell, A. G. M.; Dawes, G. S.; Fishman, A. P., and Hyman, A. I.: Pulmonary vasoconstriction during asphyxia in immature foetal lambs, J. Physiol. 181:47–48P, 1965.

Campbell, A. G. M.; Dawes, G. S.; Fishman, A. P., and Hyman, A. I.: Bradykinin and pulmonary blood flow in the foetal lung, J. Physiol. 184:80P, 1966.

Cassin, S.; Dawes, G. S., and Ross, B. B.: Pulmonary blood flow and vascular resistance in immature foetal lambs, J. Physiol. 171:80–89, 1964.

Cassin, S.; Dawes, G. S.; Mott, J. C.; Ross, B. B., and Strang, L. B.: The vascular resistance of the foetal and newly ventilated lung of the lamb, J. Physiol. 171:61–79, 1964.

Chu, J.; Clements, J. A.; Cotton, E.; Klaus, M.; Sweet, A. Y.; Thomas, M. A., and Tooley, W. H.: The pulmonary hypoperfusion syndrome, Pediatrics 35:733–742, 1965.

Colebatch, H. J. H.: Dawes, G. S.; Goodwin, J. W., and Nadeau, R. A.: The nervous control of the circulation in the foetal and newly expanded lungs of the lamb, J. Physiol. 178:544–562, 1965.

Colebatch, H. J. H., and Nadeau, R. A.: Pulmonary vasoconstriction provoked by brief lung inflation, J. Physiol. 179:385–401, 1965.

Cook, C. D.; Drinker, P. A.; Jacobson, H. N.; Levison, H., and Strang, L. B.: Control of pulmonary blood flow in the foetal and newly born lamb, J. Physiol. 169:10–29, 1963.

Cropp, G. J. A.: Effect of high intra-alveolar O_2 tensions on pulmonary circulation in perfused lungs of dogs, Am. J. Physiol. 208:130–138, 1965.

Daly, I., de B., and Daly, M., de B.: Effects of stimulation of the carotid body chemoreceptors on the pulmonary vascular bed in the dog: The "vasosensory controlled perfused living animal" preparation, J. Physiol. 148: 201–219, 1959.

Daly, I., de B.; Ramsay, D. J., and Waaler, B. A.: Conditions governing the pulmonary vascular response to ventilation hypoxia in isolated perfused lungs of the dog, J. Physiol. 163:46P, 1962.

Dawes, G. S.: In *Pulmonary Circulation* (ed.) Adams, W., and Veith, I. (New York: Grune and Stratton, Inc., 1959), p. 300.

Dawes, G. S.: Vasodilatation in the unexpanded foetal lung, Med. Thorac. 19:345–353, 1962.

Dawes, G. S.: Pulmonary circulation in the foetus and new-born, Brit. M. Bull. 22:61–65, 1966.

Dawes, G. S., and Mott, J. C.: The vascular tone of the foetal lung, J. Physiol. 164:465–477, 1962.

Dawes, G. S.; Mott, J. C., and Widdicombe, J. G.: The foetal circulation in the lamb, J. Physiol. 126:563–587, 1954.

Dawes, G. S.; Mott, J. C.; Widdicombe, J. G., and Wyatt, D. G.: Changes in the lungs of the newborn lamb, J. Physiol. 121:141–162, 1953.

Duke, H. N.: Pulmonary vasomotor responses of isolated perfused cat lungs to anoxia and hypercapnia, Quart. J. Exper. Physiol. 36:75–88, 1951.

Duke, H. N.: The site of action of anoxia on the pulmonary blood vessels of the cat, J. Physiol. 125:373–382, 1954.

Duke, H. N., and Killick, E. M.: Pulmonary vasomotor responses of isolated perfused lungs to anoxia, J. Physiol. 117:303–316, 1952.

Duke, H. N.; Killick, E. M., and Marchant, J. V.: Changes in pH of the perfusate during hypoxia in isolated perfused cat lungs, J. Physiol. 153:413–422, 1960.

von Euler, U. S., and Liljestrand, G.: Observations on the pulmonary arterial blood pressure in the cat, Acta physiol. scandinav. 12:301–320, 1946.

Hecht, H. H.; Lange, R. L.; Carnes, W. H.; Kuida, H., and Blake, J. T.: Brisket disease, Tr. A. Am. Physicians 72:157–171, 1959.

Hecht, H. H.; Kuida, H.; Lange, R. L.; Thorne, J. L., and Brown, A. M.: Brisket disease, Am. J. Med. 32:171–183, 1962.

James, L. S., and Rowe, R. D.: The pattern of response of pulmonary and systemic arterial pressures in newborn and older infants to short periods of hypoxia, J. Pediat. 51:5–11, 1957.

Lauer, R. M.; Evans, J. A.; Aoki, H., and Kittle, C. F.: Factors controlling pulmonary vascular resistance in fetal lambs, J. Pediat. 67:568–577, 1965.

Liljestrand, G.: Chemical control of the distribution of the pulmonary blood flow, Acta physiol. scandinav. 44:216–240, 1958.

Macklin, C. C.: Evidences of increase in the capacity of the pulmonary arteries and veins of dogs, cats and rabbits during inflation of the freshly excised lung, Rev. Canad. Biol. 5:199–232, 1946.

Naeye, R. L.: Arterial changes during the perinatal period, Arch. Path. 71:121–128, 1961.

Nisell, O. I.: Effects of oxygen and carbon dioxide on the circulation of isolated and perfused lungs of the cat, Acta physiol. scandinav. 16:121–127, 1948.

Nisell, O. I.: The action of oxygen and carbon dioxide on the bronchioles and vessels of the isolated perfused lungs, Acta physiol. scandinav. 21:Suppl. 73, 1950.

Reeves, J. T., and Leathers, J. E.: Hypoxic pulmonary hypertension of the calf with denervation of the lungs, J. Appl. Physiol. 19:976–980, 1964.

Riley, R. L.: In *Ciba Symposium on Pulmonary Structure and Function* (ed.) Reuck, R. V. S., and O'Connor, M. (London: J. & A. Churchill, Ltd., 1962).

Rudolph, A. M., and Yuan, S.: Response of the pulmonary vasculature to hypoxia and H^+ ion concentration changes, J. Clin. Invest. 45:399–411, 1966.

Stahlman, M.; Shepard, F.; Gray, J., and Young, W.: The effects of hypoxia and hypercapnia on the circulation in newborn lambs, J. Pediat. 65:1091–1092, 1964.

Wagenvoort, C. A.; Neufeld, H. N., and Edwards, J. E.: The structure of the pulmonary arterial tree in fetal and early postnatal life, Lab. Invest. 10:751–762, 1961.

The Foetal Circulation

THE COURSE OF the circulation in the foetus has been extensively studied and there are few uncertainties left. Figure 47 is a diagram of the circulation in the foetal lamb, in which the figures indicate the mean $O_2\%$ saturation in each vessel. Early anatomical investigations (summarised elsewhere; Dawes, 1964) were concerned mainly with the problem as to whether well oxygenated blood returning from the placenta was thoroughly mixed within the heart and great vessels with poorly oxygenated blood returning from the foetal tissues or whether, as Sabatier (1778) had suggested, the well oxygenated blood was directed preferentially to the ascending aorta to supply the heart and brain, while the rest was returned to the placenta. The fact that the blood in the descending aorta supplied not only the placenta but the abdominal viscera, lower trunk, and legs was not taken account of in the interesting debate which ensued over the next 150 years. We now know, thanks primarily to the work of Huggett (1927) in goats, that carotid arterial blood contains more oxygen than does that in the descending aorta of the foetus. Observations by Barcroft (1946) in foetal lambs confirmed this conclusion, but he also found that the difference in O_2 content between the two vessels was variable, a point which will be discussed in more detail below.

The most interesting fact established by these and subsequent investigators was that the blood was quite thoroughly mixed in the two sides of the heart, so that inferior and superior vena caval blood streams which entered with an O_2 saturation of 67% and 31%, respectively, emerged (after mixing with azygos, coronary, pulmonary, bronchial, and Thebesian venous blood) with O_2 saturations which averaged 62% from the left heart, 52% from the right heart, and 58% in the descending aorta (Fig. 47). Thus mixing of the blood streams is in-

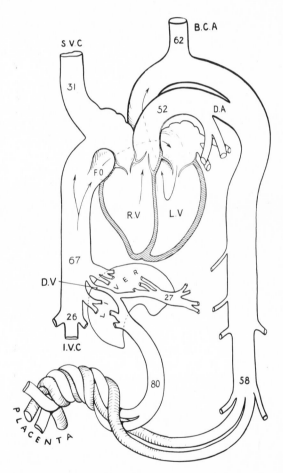

Fig. 47.—Diagram of the circulation in the mature foetal lamb. The numerals indicate the mean O_2 saturation (%) in the great vessels of 6 lambs; *R.V.* right ventricle, *L.V.* left ventricle, *S.V.C.* superior vena cava, *B.C.A.* brachiocephalic artery, *F.O.* foramen ovale, *D.A.* ductus arteriosus, *D.V.* ductus venosus. (From Born, Dawes, Mott, and Widdicombe, 1954.)

complete, but much more complete than Sabatier supposed.

In mature foetal lambs and rhesus monkeys under comparable experimental conditions the difference between the O_2 saturation of blood from branches of the ascending aorta (brachial or carotid) and descending aorta (femoral artery) averaged 4–9% in different series of experiments (Dawes, Mott and Widdicombe, 1954; Dawes, Jacobson, Mott, and Shelley, 1960; Dawes and Mott, 1964). This gives a measure of the difference to be expected under good physiological conditions and general anaesthesia. The weight of the brain in the sheep is 1.3% of body weight at birth, while in the rhesus monkey it is 12% (Table 4, p. 16), a fact which would suggest that carotid and vertebral flow might be greater in the latter. Yet there was no evidence of a difference in the relative O_2 contents of ascending and descending aortic blood in the two species. No observations are available on unanaesthetized foetuses *in utero*, a situation which might be worth examination if cerebral O_2 consumption and flow were greater than under general anaesthesia.

The reasons for the partial but incomplete mixing of inferior and superior caval blood in the foetal heart were elucidated by the cineangiographic observations of Barclay, Barcroft, Franklin and Prichard (Barclay, Franklin and Prichard, 1944; Barcroft, 1946). They showed that in mature foetal lambs a large part of thoracic inferior vena caval blood enters the left atrium directly through the foramen ovale, the remainder continuing onward to enter the right atrium (Fig. 48). Normally, superior vena caval blood entered only the right atrium. These conclusions have been verified subsequently in other ways and species, by withdrawing blood

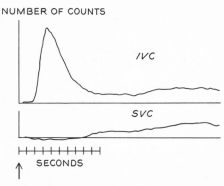

NUMBER OF COUNTS

IVC

SVC

SECONDS

Fig. 49.—Foetal lamb of 127 days gestation. Injection at the arrow of I^{131}-labelled serum albumen into the inferior vena cava (*ivc*) caused a rapid and large increase in counting rate from a scintillation counter on a carotid loop, whereas injection of the same quantity into the superior vena cava (*svc*) caused no immediate change. (From unpublished observations by Dawes, Groom, Mott, Rowlands, and Thomas.)

samples for O_2 analysis as in Figure 47, by injection of radio-iodinated serum albumen I^{131} into the inferior or superior vena cavae of mature foetal lambs while recording activity from a scintillation counter on a carotid loop (Fig. 49), and by cineangiographic studies in the immature foetal lamb (Dawes and Mott, unpublished), human infant (Lind and Wegelius, 1954), and puppy (Handler, 1956).

Although the cineangiographic evidence is visual and persuasive, when we come to consider why we believe that no superior vena caval blood normally passes the tubercle of Lower and the crista dividens to enter the left atrium by the foramen ovale (Fig. 48), cineangiography is a clumsy and insensitive tool. If, after a superior vena caval injection, small quantities of contrast medium were to enter the left atrium in this way they would be diluted by large quantities of inferior vena caval blood and might well be imperceptible. In an intact foetal lamb, a 5:1 dilution of contrast medium is difficult to detect against the variable radio-opacity of thoracic structures. In order to obtain sufficient differential radio-opacity relatively large amounts of the contrast medium must be injected, and the rise in superior vena caval pressures can be large enough to distort the normal distribution of blood flow. The use of other indicators which can be injected in small amounts (say 0.5 ml in a mature foetal lamb), such as radio-iodinated serum albumen or dyes, provides a much more sensitive measure of distribution of flow. It is evident from Figure 49 that the quantity of indicator entering the left atrium from the superior vena cava must be very small indeed.

Fig. 48.—The entry of the great veins into the foetal heart, to illustrate the fact that the foramen ovale lies between the inferior vena cava and left atrium.

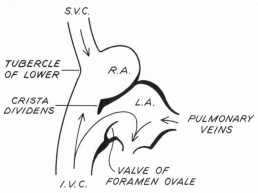

S.V.C.

TUBERCLE OF LOWER

CRISTA DIVIDENS

R.A.

L.A.

PULMONARY VEINS

VALVE OF FORAMEN OVALE

I.V.C.

The anatomical arrangement which makes it possible for blood to enter the left atrium directly from the inferior vena cava is shown in Figure 48. In the foetus the left atrium extends dorsally beneath the rest of the heart to join the inferior vena cava at the foramen ovale. Blood flowing up the inferior vena cava divides into two streams at the crista dividens to enter the right or left atrium directly. This anatomical arrangement is best seen by cutting the inferior vena cava across at the level of the diaphragm and looking up it toward the heart; an excellent picture of this view of the entry of the inferior vena cava into the heart was given by Barclay, Franklin, and Prichard (1944). The history of this anatomical feature is curious. The illustrations of early anatomists (Fabricius, ca. 1533–1619; Lower, 1669; Drake, 1728) show quite clearly that they had the facts right, i.e., that the foramen ovale opened directly off the inferior vena cava. But in the late 18th century this work was forgotten and from then until 1938 it was generally believed that the foramen ovale lay between the two atria, despite the occasional publication of evidence to the contrary. It seems probable that this misconception arose because examination of the heart by standard autopsy methods in the newborn infant can distort the natural position of the atria and venae cavae so as to give a false impression of their relative positions. Although the correct facts were established without ambiguity by Barclay, Barcroft, Barron, Franklin, and Prichard, and were made widely available in their original papers, reviews, and 2 books, articles still appear in which the old misconception is retained and illustrated. For instance, in a recent review Assali and Morris (1964) say that "from the inferior vena cava, the column of blood flows toward the right side of the heart where it is met *in the right atrium* by the crista dividens of the foramen ovale" (my italics). In this and another paper (Morris, Bekey, Assali, and Beck, 1965) and reviews by Patten (1963) and by Rudolph (1965), the diagrams give the impression that the foramen ovale connects the two atria and is far removed from the inferior vena cava. The design of these illustrations may have been determined by considerations of draughtsmanship, but they are misleading in an important feature of the foetal circulation and it would be sad if the error were perpetuated.

Alterations in the Distribution of Blood Flow Through the Foetal Heart

There are other lines of evidence which suggest that, though the foregoing account of the distribution of blood flow within the great vessels and heart of the foetus is normally correct, there are circumstances in which it is altered. It was to be expected that changes in the momentum, as well as the lateral pressures, of the two caval blood streams which meet at the heart might alter the outcome. This might well result during asphyxia. Pohlman (1907, 1909) injected cornstarch granules into the jugular veins of foetal pigs which were separated from the mother and, as they were not breathing, asphyxiated. He observed that they were equally distributed between the two ventricles.

In 1959, some further observations were made by cineangiography on the course of the foetal circulation in asphyxiated lambs (Adamsons, Dawes, and Mott, unpublished). These showed that when the heart rate had dropped from ~200/min to 85–110/min, a large quantity of contrast medium passed from the superior vena cava into the upper end of the inferior vena cava, and thence through the left heart to reach the brachiocephalic and carotid arteries, at the same time as the rest of the contrast medium passed through the right heart to reach the lungs and descending aorta (via the ductus arteriosus, Fig. 47). In 2 of the 8 lambs (of 82–86 days gestation) the contrast medium (thorotrast) was introduced into the superior vena cava from a side-arm of a polyethylene loop joining the cut ends of an external jugular vein, so that venous pressure was not raised by a sudden injection; the result was the same. Similar results were also obtained in 5 mature foetal lambs either when the umbilical cord was tied to cause complete asphyxia, or on producing foetal hypoxaemia by giving the ewe 10–6% O_2 to breathe in place of air (the umbilical cord being intact). On each occasion contrast medium, introduced into a jugular vein as described above, was observed to enter the upper end of the inferior vena cava at each heart beat in large quantities.

There was a common factor in these experiments apart from asphyxia and hypoxaemia, in that heart rate was reduced. It seemed possible that a similar change might be produced if the heart was slowed in the absence of hypoxaemia. The peripheral end of the right vagus was stimulated to slow the heart from an initial rate of 190–205 beats/min. When the rate was reduced to less than 100 beats/min large quantities of contrast medium passed from the superior vena cava to the upper end of the inferior vena cava during each cardiac cycle. When the rate was reduced to 120–135 beats/min less contrast medium appeared in the inferior vena cava. In many experiments the time of each x-ray exposure was recorded with the electrocardiogram on moving

TABLE 21.—EFFECT OF CHANGING UMBILICAL BLOOD FLOW ON THE DIFFERENCE IN O_2 CONTENT (EXPRESSED AS A % OF O_2 CARRYING CAPACITY) IN SIMULTANEOUS CAROTID AND FEMORAL ARTERIAL BLOOD SAMPLES IN FOETAL LAMBS OF 87–95 DAYS GESTATION AGE

UMBILICAL BLOOD FLOW (ML/KG MIN)	NUMBER OF OBSERVATIONS	CAROTID-FEMORAL ARTERIAL O_2 DIFFERENCE (%)
>150 (Control)	12	8.4 ± 0.86
<120 (Umbilical vein constriction)	29	13.8 ± 1.43
>150 (Control)	12	6.1 ± 1.29
<120 (Bleeding)	28	11.1 ± 0.87

paper. During cardiac slowing, thorotrast first appeared in the upper end of the inferior vena cava shortly after the P wave, either just before or simultaneously with the QRS complex. The shadow increased in size and density and disappeared after the T wave, to reappear again in subsequent cardiac cycles.

These results appear to suggest that the maintenance of a relatively high heart rate, which is common to foetuses of different species in good physiological condition (man ~140, lamb ~180 beats/min), is a prerequisite to the normal distribution of foetal venous blood entering the heart. But there is another point which deserves consideration. In the foetus the superior and inferior vena caval blood streams are moving, with a certain momentum, in opposite directions, and very small differences in lateral venous pressure or flow velocity may affect their confluence at the entry of the right atrium. This may concern not merely changes of heart rate, acting locally, but changes in peripheral vascular resistance which, by altering the distribution of cardiac output, could alter the distribution of venous return to the inferior and superior vena cava. To take a case in point, stimulation of the peripheral vagus not only slows the heart but also causes a fall in arterial pressure. This could result in a greater decrease in inferior vena caval return than in superior vena caval return; the proposition has not yet been tested. Occlusion of the umbilical cord to cause acute asphyxia in mature foetal lambs causes a fall in inferior vena caval pressure and a rise in superior vena caval and right atrial pressure (Dawes, Mott, and Widdicombe, 1955).

We conclude that, though they are still poorly understood, the factors which determine the distribution of the venous return to the two sides of the foetal heart are dynamic, not static. They are liable to change with the physiological condition of the foetus. They are dependent not so much on the gross anatomy of the great vessels as on the interplay of physiological forces which may be more complex than at first appeared.

There is supporting evidence for this view from other experiments. Barcroft, Barron, Cowie, and Forsham (1938) found wide variations in the difference between the O_2 contents of carotid and umbilical (or femoral) arterial blood in foetal lambs. It seemed unlikely that the variation could be due entirely to differences in anaesthesia, handling, or sampling times, but Barcroft made particular mention of vascular spasm in the umbilical cord. So experiments were undertaken in which umbilical blood flow was deliberately reduced (Dawes and Mott, 1964). The mean carotid-femoral arterial O_2 difference was significantly increased in immature foetal lambs by umbilical vein constriction or bleeding (but not by constriction of the descending aorta) sufficient to reduce umbilical flow quite substantially, to below 120 ml/kg min (Table 21). In foetal lambs near term the mean carotid-femoral arterial O_2 difference was less, and was less affected by these procedures.

The Outputs of the Two Sides of the Foetal Heart

The two sides of the foetal heart are of much the same shape and size, like the twin kernels of a nut as Harvey put it, and thus very different from the adult. They work in parallel to pump the blood from the great veins to the pulmonary artery and aorta, and these are joined by a widely patent ductus arteriosus. So the right and left sides of the heart have about the same capacity (as Pohlman showed in the foetal piglet, 1909), are filled at approximately the same pressure, eject blood against the same arterial pressure, and so might reasonably be expected to have about the same output. It was obviously necessary to make measurements to find out whether the outputs were indeed equal.

The problem was first examined by an indirect

method (Dawes, Mott and Widdicombe, 1954). In certain of the great vessels two streams of blood of differing O_2 content meet. For instance, superior vena caval blood (31% saturated) joins inferior vena caval blood (67% saturated) in the right heart, and these streams mix to give a pulmonary arterial effluent which is 52% saturated (Fig. 47). From this one may calculate the proportion of superior and inferior vena caval bloods which enter the right atrium. A similar analysis was applied to the other three points in the foetal circulation where streams of blood of different O_2 content mix, in the upper part of the inferior vena cava, in the left atrium, and at the junction of the ductus arteriosus and descending aorta. It was then possible, with certain assumptions, to calculate the volume of blood flow in all the principal vessels as a fraction of the combined output of both ventricles, from determinations of the O_2 content of blood samples withdrawn simultaneously from 8 different vessels. Such measurements were made in duplicate on 6 mature foetal lambs under pentobarbitone anaesthesia; points of special interest were examined in more detail on other lambs. The results are shown in Table 22 as a fraction of the output of both ventricles and, assuming an umbilical blood flow of 180 ml/kg min as the most likely estimate in the anaesthetized mature foetal lamb (Chapter 6), as ml/kg foetus per min. The output of the left ventricle was calculated as a little greater than that of

the right ventricle; the difference was statistically significant.

Of course, this method has limitations. Variations in flow pattern and mixing could introduce artifacts; yet duplicate estimates of O_2 content in different vessels agreed well. It was, nevertheless, desirable to check the results by an independent method. The first attempt to do this was by Dawes, Groom, Mott, Rowlands, and Thomas (unpublished) using an I^{131} labeled serum albumen indicator dilution method in 1959–60. This was adapted from the method which Groom, Rowlands, and Thomas (1965) had successfully developed in adult cats. Left cardiac output was measured by injection into the left atrium with a scintillation counter on a carotid loop; right heart output was measured by injection into the superior vena cava or right atrium, while pulmonary arterial blood was withdrawn through a counter from a catheter introduced through a femoral artery and the ductus arteriosus. In mature foetal lambs under chloralose anaesthesia there was no significant difference between right and left heart outputs. However, the scatter in the observations was large, ranging from 110–260 ml/kg min, and when this method was checked against the direct Fick method in lambs up to 3 weeks old (when the foetal vascular channels were closed) there was a systematic discrepancy such that the indicator dilution method gave a measurement which on average was 22% low. The

TABLE 22.—BLOOD FLOW THROUGH THE MAJOR VESSELS OF THE FOETAL LAMB (ADAPTED FROM DAWES, MOTT AND WIDDICOMBE, 1954)

	% OF COMBINED OUTPUT OF BOTH VENTRICLES ($\pm$S.E.)	FLOW* (ML/KG MIN)
R + L ventricle	100	315
R ventricle	45 $\pm$ 1.2	142
L ventricle	55 $\pm$ 1.2	174
Thoracic inferior vena cava	76 $\pm$ 1.5	240
I.V.C. flow to R heart	29 $\pm$ 1.6	92
I.V.C. flow through foramen ovale	46 $\pm$ 1.6	145
Superior cava + coronary veins	15 $\pm$ 0.9	47
Lungs	10 $\pm$ 1.6	31
Ductus arteriosus	35 $\pm$ 2.4	110
Aortic isthmus†	38 $\pm$ 2.5	120
Hinderpart of body	19 $\pm$ 2.6	60
Umbilical flow	57 $\pm$ 2.0	180

* Assuming an umbilical blood flow of 180 ml/kg min.

† That part of the aortic arch between the origin of the brachiocephalic vessels and the junction with the ductus arteriosus.

Note: The sum of blood flow through the foramen ovale ($\sim$45%) and ductus arteriosus (35%) is less than the combined output of both ventricles by a figure which is *double* pulmonary blood flow (10%) because this blood alone passes through both ventricles in series.

TABLE 23.—ESTIMATES OF BLOOD FLOW IN MATURE FOETAL LAMBS

BLOOD FLOW (ML/KG MIN)	DAWES, MOTT, AND WIDDICOMBE (1954)*	MAHON, GOODWIN, AND PAUL (1966)	ASSALI, MORRIS, AND BECK (1965)
Right heart output	142	180	138
Left heart output	174	182	97 (less coronary)
Foramen ovale	175		60
Ductus arteriosus	110		101
Pulmonary	31		37

* See Table 22, p. 95.

results were, therefore, not published, in the expectation that it might soon be possible to make a further independent check when accurate cuff electromagnetic flowmeters of suitable size were available. These can be made absolute instruments, not requiring independent calibration (Appendix), but their development has proven more difficult than was anticipated 6 years ago.

Mahon, Goodwin, and Paul (1966) have recently published the results of a similar study in mature foetal lambs also under chloralose anaesthesia, but using a dye dilution method in place of a radio-isotope. They used almost the same injection and sampling technique; the method of blood flow measurement was not compared with the Fick or other methods. They obtained a roughly similar measure of right and left heart output. Their figures agree with those of Dawes, Groom, Mott, Rowlands, and Thomas both in their mean value and large standard deviation (left heart 180 ± 56; right heart 182 ± 50 ml/kg min).

There are several questions which arise from these observations. First, we may wonder whether the small difference between the right and left cardiac outputs calculated by Dawes, Mott and Widdicombe (1954) was due to the fact that pento-barbitone was used as an anaesthetic. In adults, this is known to cause vasodilatation in some peripheral vascular beds as compared with chloralose. The difference could also have been due to an erroneous assumption in the method used, but no indication of this has emerged during the last 12 years. The difference could also have been due to chance; although it was statistically significant the number of animals used was small. There is another point. It would hardly be surprising if the cardiac output did not vary from lamb to lamb from time to time and under different physiological conditions. A difficulty in interpreting all these results

is that we do not know enough either about the conditions under which the observations were made (e.g., umbilical flow, arterial pH, P_{CO_2} and P_{O_2}) or the effect which variations in these conditions have upon cardiac output and its distribution in the foetal circulation. The wide variations in cardiac output have already been mentioned. Mahon, Goodwin, and Paul (1966) recorded that the heart rate in their foetal lambs was 252 ± 31 (S.D.) beats/min. This is high (the normal heart rate of a foetal lamb is 180–200/min). So it may be that under different conditions or at different heart rates the outputs of the right and left heart may be equal or unequal in the foetus. We certainly don't yet have enough evidence to show that one view is right and the other wrong. And such measurements have as yet been made only in the mature foetal lamb near term. The results might be quantitatively different in other species or at an earlier age.

Assali, Morris, and Beck, (1965) measured flow in the ascending aorta, pulmonary artery, and ductus arteriosus of mature unanaesthetized foetal lambs (whose mothers were under spinal anaesthesia) by applying a cuff type of electromagnetic flowmeter (which required calibration and was estimated to have an error of ±10%). There are several differences in the experimental method from those already described, the absence of anaesthesia, the wide thoracotomy required to place the flowmeter gauge heads, and the probability of damage to nerves (afferent and efferent) as they cross the great vessels. Comparison with other results (Table 23) is also complicated by the fact that part of the output of the left heart enters the coronary arteries before it reaches the ascending aorta, and is compounded by uncertainty as to the absolute values of any of these measurements. All that we are justified in concluding is that they support the view that mean blood flow through both sides of the heart is rather higher in the foetus than in adult sheep (115–123 ml/kg min; Cross, Dawes, and Mott, 1959; Metcalfe and Parer, 1966), and they give additional confirmation of the conclusion that pulmonary blood flow is relatively low. The differences between the measurements are of uncertain significance.

The Distribution of Cardiac Output in the Foetus

The normal distribution of cardiac output in the foetus can be gauged in a general way from the data presented in Table 22, while recognizing that these were obtained under one particular set of experimental conditions. The two most important features of the foetal circulation (of which Barcroft and his colleagues were well aware from their cineangiographic and other studies) are the relatively large proportion of the combined output of both ventricles which passes through the umbilical cord to supply the placenta and foetal membranes (57%), and the small proportion which flows through the foetal lungs (10%). Thus it is no exaggeration to say that the foetal circulation is, to a large extent, dominated by the high blood flow, low vascular resistance, and relatively unreactive nature of the umbilical circulation. In contrast, blood flow through the foreparts and hindparts (i.e., all the other foetal tissues excluding the lungs) was only 15% and 18%, respectively.

Blood flow through the special foetal vascular channels also is high (foramen ovale, 46%; ductus arteriosus, 35% of the combined output of both ventricles), which may be regarded as a natural corollary of the large umbilical flow. Yet it is interesting that human infants with gross malformations of the heart, with premature closure of the foramen ovale, or with aortic or pulmonary atresia, can survive to term. Although the anatomical arrangement of these special vascular channels permits the normal, almost equal development of the two sides of the heart, which is necessary for normal growth after birth, it is not essential to have more than one normal ventricle for foetal survival. This is a further illustration of the fact that separation of the confluent bloodstreams within the heart is probably of limited biological significance during foetal life.

There are a few measurements only of blood flow through other major blood vessels or individual organs, other than the lungs, in mature foetal lambs. Femoral and left circumflex coronary arterial flows are ~3 ml/kg foetal weight per min and carotid and superior sagittal sinus venous flows are ~5 ml/kg min. The rather small carotid and sagittal sinus flows are related to the small proportion of brain: body weight in the lamb at birth (Table 4, p. 16; 1.3%). One might well expect these flows to be a much larger proportion of cardiac output in foetuses of species with a relatively heavier brain. The skin represents a high proportion of foetal body weight in many species (Table 4, p. 16), but no measurements of skin flow are available. The immature foetal lamb has a surprisingly high rate of urine formation (Alexander and Nixon, 1961), and might, therefore, have a high renal blood flow. The observations of Rudolph, Heymann, and Hait (1965) on the distribution of radioactive 50 μ glass spheres after intravenous injection in foetal lambs suggest that renal flow is not a large fraction of cardiac output.

Even though the large blood flow through the umbilical circulation must have the effect of damping out acute haemodynamic alterations in the foetus, there is no doubt that cardiac output is redistributed under particular circumstances in the mature foetal lamb. Moderate hypoxaemia causes a rise in heart rate and blood pressure (Born, Dawes, and Mott, 1956). Measurements using the I[131] labeled serum albumen indicator dilution method suggested that cardiac output increased with the increase in heart rate, but the wide scatter in serial measurements under steady state conditions (and the large possible error which is to be expected with any indicator dilution method, about ±15%, make it desirable to confirm this by a more reliable method. Moderate hypoxaemia, hypercapnia, or a combination of both cause a rise in arterial pressure with little change in umbilical vascular resistance, so that umbilical blood flow is increased (Born, Dawes, and Mott, 1956; and Chapter 6). This is accompanied by a relatively large reduction in foetal pulmonary and femoral arterial flow, and an increase in coronary, carotid and superior sagittal sinus flow. Thus, as in the adult, blood flow is redistributed to maintain the circulation through the heart, brain, and organs of gaseous exchange at the expense of blood supply to those tissues which are, in the short term, more expendable.

Arterial Blood Pressure and Cardiovascular Control in the Foetus

The mean arterial blood pressures vary widely at birth in different species (Table 24). One cannot conclude that they are necessarily higher in those which are more active or "mature," because arterial pressure in the rhesus monkey, which is well-

TABLE 24.—MEAN ARTERIAL PRESSURES AT BIRTH IN DIFFERENT SPECIES

SPECIES	ARTERIAL PRESSURE (MM HG)	SOURCE
Man	53	Dittmer and Grebe (1959)
Sheep	66	Dawes and Mott (1964)
Dog	35	Clark (1932); Handler (1956)
Rhesus monkey	45	Dawes, Jacobson, Mott, and Shelley (1960)
Cat	30	Clark (1932); Handler (1956)
Rabbit	30	Mott (1965)
Rat	14	Adolph (1957)

developed at birth and clings to its mother as she swings about, is less than that in the human infant. Arterial pressure rises during foetal life at different rates in different species (Fig. 50). There is some evidence to suggest, in the foetal lamb, that the more rapid rise toward the end of gestation is associated with the development of autonomic nervous control. A good deal more evidence has accumulated since this hypothesis was proposed and is worth a brief summary.

In the lamb exposure to moderate hypoxaemia causes a rise in foetal heart rate from 75–80 days gestation onward, but there is little increase in arterial pressure before 100 days (Born, Dawes, and Mott, 1956). Yet moderate or severe asphyxia causes a progressive rise in arterial pressure as early as 75 days gestation (Cassin, Dawes, and Ross, 1964). This latter is probably due both to a direct vasoconstrictor effect of asphyxia on the lungs (Chapter 7) and to liberation of noradrenaline

from the adrenals by the direct effect of hypoxia (Comline and Silver, 1961; 1965). Reflex control of the pulmonary circulation is present by ~100 days gestation and of the adrenal medulla by 130 days (term is 147 days). Injection of hexamethonium causes a fall in foetal arterial pressure and heart rate after 100 days gestation, and thoracic sympathectomy at term causes a fall in heart rate. Maximal stimulation of the peripheral ends of the vagi causes a barely perceptible bradycardia at 60 days gestation, a fall of ~30% at 90 days, and of ~80% at term. Autonomic efferent nerves are fragile and easily damaged in very young foetuses, and their size, stimulation characteristics, and conduction velocities have not been systematically explored; negative results of electrical excitation, therefore, should be interpreted with caution.

The baroreceptor reflexes may be developed quite early in the foetal lamb. Barcroft and Barron (1945) observed that a rise of arterial pressure

Fig. 50.—Mean arterial blood pressure in the rat, rabbit, dog, lamb, and rhesus monkey before (– – –) and after (———) birth, indicated by the arrow.
(Redrawn with additions from Dawes, 1961.)

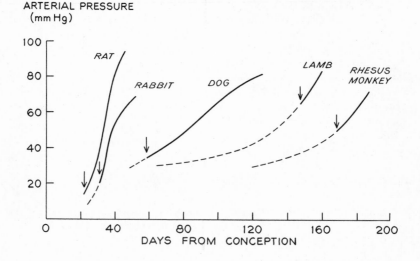

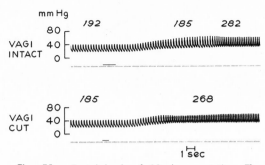

mm Hg

| VAGI INTACT | *192* | *185* | *282* |

| VAGI CUT | *185* | *268* |

1 sec

Fig. 51.—Foetal lamb of 90 days gestation. The slowing of the heart, when the femoral arterial pressure rose after injection of 2 μg adrenaline into a femoral vein **(above)**, was abolished by cutting the vagi **(below)**. (From Dawes, Mott, and Rennick, 1956.)

caused by injection of adrenaline or noradrenaline is often associated with acute bradycardia, which is abolished by cutting the vagi; this phenomenon can be seen as early as 90 days gestation (Fig. 51: Dawes, Mott, and Rennick, 1956). Conversely, haemorrhage at this age causes a sustained tachycardia (Dawes and Mott, 1964); this evidence is indirect and there are alternate (though less likely) explanations. Near term carotid occlusion causes a rise of arterial pressure and there is baroreceptor activity in the afferent nerves from the carotid sinus (Cross and Malcolm, 1952; Purves and Biscoe, 1966).

So far as the systemic arterial chemoreceptors are concerned, only those of the carotid body have yet been investigated in the foetus. Cross and Malcolm (1952) found that these were functional in the sense that hypoxia caused an increase in discharge activity in-between bursts of baroreceptor spikes. Purves and Biscoe (1966) reported that the tonic activity of carotid chemoreceptors was very low in the foetal lamb, even at an arterial Po_2 of 20–25 mm Hg. So far as control of the circulation is concerned, if we may judge by the adult, the chemoreceptors of the aortic body are likely to be more important than those of the carotid body (Comroe, 1964). There is evidence that in the foetus the former are supplied from the pulmonary trunk rather than the aorta (Boyd, 1961; Coleridge, Coleridge, and Howe, 1966), and hence with blood containing less O_2 (Fig. 47) and more CO_2. This would provide a more sensitive index of foetal physiological condition, and there may be some logic in this. During foetal life it is the maintenance of a proper distribution of blood flow which is important. The foetus does not normally make respiratory movements *in utero,* so control by the carotid

chemoreceptors, whose principal effect is on breathing, is of less moment. A direct attack on the function of the aortic chemoreceptors in the foetus might well repay the formidable technical difficulties which are involved in their isolation and study.*

Certainly, there are reasons for believing that there is a tonic control of the distribution of blood flow in the anaesthetized mature foetal lamb. For instance, when the arterial Po_2 is raised and the Pco_2 is lowered by ventilation with room air (in place of 3% O_2 and 7% CO_2 in nitrogen) femoral arterial flow increases and coronary, carotid, and sagittal sinus flow are reduced. The mechanisms which are involved have not been studied; in the heart and brain they might involve a local effect of Po_2 and Pco_2.

In species other than the lamb we have to depend, for evidence of the development of reflex regulation of the circulation, almost entirely on observations made after birth. These will be considered elsewhere (Chapter 14); all that need be said here is that this evidence supports the view that a considerable degree of nervous control is normally established by the end of gestation. It does not otherwise help in understanding the special characteristics of the foetal circulation.

Next there is the question as to whether nervous control of the foetal circulation is necessary to survival during foetal life and after birth. This requires chronic experiments which so far as I know have not yet been done on sheep. There is evidence on foetal rats and rabbits which, although decapitated *in utero* at 0.7–0.8 of term, continued to survive and to grow at almost the same rate as littermate controls until they were deliberately killed for examination near term (Jost, 1947; 1954). Obviously, in these species central nervous control of the foetal circulation is not essential. The human infant also can survive until term with gross abnormalities of the brain stem and spinal cord. Altogether, this evidence suggests that, as in the adult, provided the individual is not subjected to gross disturbances, the local mechanisms which regulate heart rate, force of contraction, and peripheral

---

* Since this was written, it has been shown that injection of small doses of cyanide into the left atrium of foetal lambs causes a rise of arterial pressure, femoral vasoconstriction and a complex change in heart rate. These are abolished or greatly reduced by cervical vagotomy, and are attributed to functional aortic chemoreceptors. In the lamb, the latter receive their blood supply from the left heart only, and seem to be the primary line of foetal defence in blood gas homeostasis (Dawes, Lewis, Milligan, Roach and Talner, unpublished).

vasomotor tone are sufficient to ensure survival without central control. The foetus is in a particularly favoured position in this respect, as it is bathed in amniotic fluid, warmed by its mother, and protected from the chances of extra-uterine life. This should not be taken to imply that nervous control of the foetal circulation, and particularly at birth, may not have some biological advantage; we have no experimental evidence. It is possible that a further study of the foetus early in gestation, before central control has developed, may help us to understand better some of the local peripheral mechanisms by which vasomotor tone is regulated, and on which nervous control is superimposed.

Foetal Blood Volume

The volume of blood in the foetal circulation requires special mention because of the observation that the proportion in the placenta, membranes, and umbilical cord exceed that in the body of the foetal lamb up to about 100 days gestation. Presumably, the same is true in all other species up until the time at which the weight of the foetus begins to exceed that of the placenta, but this has not been studied. At term, the quantity of blood in the foetal lamb is 5–6 times that in the placenta (Barcroft, 1946).

These observations have some interesting consequences. When arterial pressure is raised, particularly in immature foetal lambs, either as a result of hypoxaemia and hypercapnia, or on injection or infusion of adrenaline or noradrenaline, part of the foetal blood volume is transferred to the placenta and cord. When the umbilical vein is partially compressed as much as 15 ml/kg, blood (about 12% of the volume of blood in the foetus) can be shifted to the placenta within a minute (Dawes and Mott, 1964). This phenomenon is interesting for two reasons. First, it goes some way to explaining why the blood pressure responses to hypoxaemia or hypercapnia are relatively less in immature foetal lambs of 80–100 days gestation. The effects of vasoconstriction in the foetus on arterial pressure will be minimized by the large and distensible vascular bed of the placenta which is supplied in parallel. This fact should make us cautious about drawing inferences, based only on arterial pressure measurements in immature foetuses, as to the development of vascular reflexes. Secondly, it is important clinically in that compression of the cord during labour and delivery, sufficient to obstruct the vein but not the arteries, leads to displacement of foetal blood

to the placenta, particularly in infants which are small in relation to their placenta, i.e., immature.

The Ductus Venosus and Hepatic Blood Flow

The abdominal portion of the umbilical vein enters the liver to join the portal vein, and from the trunk which unites them (the portal sinus) there arises the ductus venosus. The ductus venosus runs, surrounded or almost surrounded by the substance of the liver, and on its under surface, to the junction of the main hepatic veins with the inferior vena cava (Fig. 47). In man, it is about half as wide as the umbilical vein and, unlike the hepatic branches of the umbilical and portal veins, it usually gives no branches to the substance of the liver. Although the ductus venosus is normally present until birth in the human, lamb, and many other species, it disappears at an early stage of gestation in the horse and pig. In the latter all umbilical and portal venous blood passes through the liver substance in late foetal life. We must suppose, though no measurements are available, that the vascular resistance of the liver is low.

Cineangiography in the foetal lamb (Barclay, Franklin, and Prichard, 1944; Barcroft, 1946; Peltonen and Hirvonen, 1965) and human infant (Lind and Wegelius, 1954) has shown that substantial quantities of contrast medium, injected into the umbilical vein, pass through the ductus venosus, by-passing the substance of the liver to appear rapidly in the inferior vena cava. The oxygen content of blood in the ductus venosus was identical with that in the umbilical vein, and much greater than that in the portal vein, so it is unlikely that portal venous blood normally enters the ductus venosus (Amoroso, Dawes, Mott, and Rennick, 1955). Barclay, Franklin, and Prichard (1944) suggested on the basis of their cineangiograms that at least a ninth, and probably more, of umbilical venous blood reached the inferior vena cava via the ductus venosus in the lamb. No direct measurements of ductus venosus flow have been made; it is a problem which presents formidable difficulties. Direct surgical access is possible, and occlusion of the vessel caused no significant change of heart rate, blood pressure, or carotid arterial O_2 saturation. These observations were made in 1955, at a time when measurement of umbilical venous flow was only possible by clumsy and difficult methods. It would be interesting to study the effect of occlusion of the ductus venosus on umbilical venous flow and pressure, which would be a more sensitive index of a disturbance in the normal transhepatic circulation. Even so, it seems that the ductus venosus is of limited biological significance toward term.

Barron (1942), and Barclay, Franklin, and Prichard (1944) described a sphincter at the junction of the portal sinus and the ductus venosus which was innervated by branches of the vagus, possibly postganglionic sympathetic fibers. The separate identity of the sphincter as a distinct anatomical structure has been challenged recently by Lind (1966) and others who have interpreted the histological appearance of the upper end of the ductus venosus as a diffuse unorganized collection of smooth muscle and elastic tissue of doubtful functional significance. Reynolds and Mackie (1962) had suggested that the sphincter might act as a regulator of umbilical venous pressure in foetal life, but the observation which led to this proposal (a rise in umbilical vein pressure on injection of adrenaline) can be explained in other ways (e.g., by vasoconstriction in liver sinusoids).

Finally, there is an unsolved problem about the venous blood supply to the right side of the liver. The left side receives well oxygenated blood from the umbilical vein. The right side receives portal venous blood which is mixed with an unknown quantity of umbilical venous blood. The degree of admixture is of some interest because, as Figure 47 shows, the O_2 saturation of portal venous blood was only 27% in lambs near term. There are more haemopoietic foci on the right side (Emery, 1956), which also shows more degenerative changes in stillbirths or early neonatal deaths attributed to intra-uterine anoxia (Gruenwald, 1949). So there are good reasons for further investigation of hepatic blood flow under different physiological conditions. Hepatic arterial blood flow in the foetus has received little attention; the observations of Rudolph, Heymann, and Hait (1965) suggest that it is very low indeed compared with umbilical flow.

The Effect of Drugs on the Foetal Circulation

There are several features of the foetal circulation which affect the action of drugs (such as catecholamines or acetylcholine) which have a transient effect on the heart and vessels on intravenous injection. For instance, a substance injected into a femoral vein will be carried up the inferior vena cava and diluted with a large quantity of blood returning from the placenta. If it is completely mixed, Table 22 shows that about 60% of the injected material will enter the left heart through the foramen ovale, where it will be further diluted with pulmonary venous blood before ejection into the ascending aorta and reaching the coronary arteries. The remainder will enter the right side of the heart to be diluted with superior vena caval blood; it will then be ejected into the pulmonary trunk and so reach the lungs and the descending aorta (via the ductus arteriosus). A substance injected into the superior vena cava will not reach the coronary arteries until it has passed through the lungs, placenta, or the lower part of the foetus. As was to be expected, therefore, injections of adrenaline, noradrenaline, or acetylcholine into foetal lambs caused a larger change of heart rate when given by a femoral vein than by a jugular vein, even though inferior vena caval flow is about 5 times greater than that in the superior cava (Dawes, Mott, and Rennick, 1956). This was true both at term and half-way through gestation in foetal lambs.

In adult animals, injections of adrenaline into the portal vein cause a smaller rise of systemic arterial pressure than do injections of the same quantity into a jugular or femoral vein (Carnot and Josserand, 1902). This is due to removal of 0.6–0.8 of the injected material during its passage through the liver, the proportion removed falling as the quantity injected is increased. The same is true of noradrenaline (for references to the large literature, see Dawes, 1946). It was, therefore, not surprising that alternate injections into the umbilical vein of small quantities of adrenaline or noradrenaline caused a smaller mean rise in arterial pressure than on injection into a femoral vein in mature foetal lambs (unpublished). The difference was less than in adult cats, probably because of the hepatic short-circuit through the ductus venosus. This may help to explain why injections of equal doses per kg body weight of sympathetic amines into the umbilical vein have been recorded as causing less effect than in adults of the same species (Adams, Assali, Cushman, and Westersten, 1961; Assali, Holm, and Sehgal, 1962; Reynolds and Mackie, 1962).

Injections of adrenaline and noradrenaline caused a larger rise of systemic arterial blood pressure in mature foetal lambs when the umbilical cord was tied and ventilation was begun than in the same lambs under foetal conditions (Dawes, Mott, and Rennick, 1956). There are several reasons for this. There is the increase in peripheral vascular resistance due to removal of the placenta and the difference in dilution and distribution of the injected material to the heart and blood vessels. The situation is complicated by the rise in arterial Po_2 and fall in Pco_2 on ventilation, and by the haemodynamic consequences of constriction of the ductus arteriosus by sympathetic amines. Probably the most important single factor is the removal of the umbilical circulation, which appears less sensitive to injected catecholamines than other parts of the foetal circulation. Thus the smaller pressure response to such drugs in the foetus is not due to relative insensitivity of the heart or the blood vessels in the foetus itself, but to the course of the foetal circulation and its other special features. Comparisons have also been made between the arterial pressure responses of foetal and adult animals of other species (rat, cat, and rabbit) to intravenous injections of adrenaline. When the small size and normal low arterial pressures of these foetuses are taken into account, together with the experimental conditions and site of injection, the difference between the per cent rise of pressure in the foetus and adult is small (Dawes, Handler, and Mott, 1957). It can be explained, as in the lamb, by the special characteristics of the foetal circulation.

Most of these observations have been made near term and it does not follow that the same conclusions hold earlier in gestation. In lambs halfway through gestation injections of adrenaline cause a greater increase in heart rate for a given rise of blood pressure. This could be due to the progressive development of a depressor reflex in older foetal lambs, or to a smaller shift of foetal blood volume to the placenta, or to a change in the sensitivity of some foetal vascular bed or beds with increasing gestational age. Measurements of arterial pressure are difficult to interpret unless they are accompanied by measurements of blood flow, particularly in the foetal circulation.

There are other problems encountered in interpretation even when flow is measured. Born, Dawes, Mott, and Rennick (1956) observed that infusion of adrenaline or noradrenaline caused a decrease in the external diameter of the ductus arteriosus while arterial pressure was raised, i.e., the muscle wall of the ductus constricted against an increased transmural pressure. Smith, Morris, Assali, and Beck (1964) concluded from measurements of ductus arteriosus flow that catecholamines do not exert any specific action upon the ductus circulation in foetal lambs. They applied a cuff electromagnetic flowmeter to the vessel, which

must have precluded direct observation of changes in diameter and already compressed the vessel to get a good fit; if it then had constricted, their measurements of flow would have been unreliable. The same authors also concluded that intravenous infusions or injections of adrenaline or acetylcholine had no effect on pulmonary vascular resistance because the respective increases and decreases in flow were paralleled by proportional changes in arterial pressure. But the relationship between flow and pressure in the pulmonary vascular bed is not linear through the origin (Chapter 7). When this fact is taken into account, their observations must indicate that adrenaline had caused pulmonary vasoconstriction and acetylcholine vasodilatation, in agreement with the results of previous workers.

Congenital Malformations of the Heart and Great Vessels

The organization of the foetal circulation explains many features of congenital cardiac lesions which would otherwise be difficult to understand. For instance, it is evident that, provided cardiac output (and hence umbilical flow) is high, a single ventricle is quite compatible with survival. Using the data of Figure 47 and Table 22 for $O_2\%$ saturation and blood flow, complete mixture in a single ventricle would result in the output of blood having an O_2 saturation of 60%. This contrasts with carotid blood of 62% and pulmonary arterial blood of 52% saturation in Figure 47, but is conditional on the output of the hypothetical single ventricle being 315 ml/kg min (i.e., the sum of the two normal ventricles). In acute experiments on mature foetal lambs umbilical blood flow was reduced from a mean of ~180 to ~100 ml/kg min before foetal O_2 consumption decreased (Dawes and Mott, 1964). So, evidently the normal lamb has a moderate reserve and one may suppose that survival with a single ventricle is not necessarily contingent on a cardiac output of ~300 ml/kg min; 200 ml/kg min might suffice. It should surely be enough if the O_2 carrying capacity were increased. Right heart outputs in excess of 300 ml/kg min have been recorded in newborn lambs (Cross, Dawes, and Mott, 1959), though these were well ventilated and oxygenated.

Transposition of the great vessels should reverse the normal distribution of better oxygenated blood to the ascending aorta and less well oxygenated blood to the descending aorta. But as we have already seen, the normal difference between the O_2 contents of these bloods is small. Otherwise the effect of transposition on the foetal circulation is likely to be of little immediate consequence. The abnormal blood supply to and from the lungs in this condition and in other malformations, which is so often fatal after birth, is unimportant so long as the placenta is the organ of gaseous exchange. Also, because right and left ventricular pressures are almost identical, the presence of interventricular septal defects are of trivial importance in foetal life.

It is evident that one may take great liberties with the foetal circulation and, as a foetus, still survive. It is as yet impossible to estimate what advantage, if any, there is in having an anatomically normal circulation or brain for survival until birth, because we do not have the statistical information on which to base a judgment. But, on present evidence, it looks as if the exact course of the circulation is less important than a high cardiac output, provided that any change introduced is gradual.

There are probably some congenital anomalies whose ultimate appearance at birth includes not only a primary defect but also a secondary physiologically dependent abnormality. For instance, premature closure of the foramen ovale is usually associated with left ventricular hypoplasia, and such infants may die within a short while of birth from left ventricular failure. One may speculate that the normal development of the left ventricle is conditional upon an adequate venous return. If, at some early period in foetal life the valve of the foramen ovale becomes adherent to the foramen, left atrial inflow will be reduced to the volume of pulmonary venous return, and the left ventricle will fail to grow at the normal rate.

This type of reasoning may be pursued further, and more speculatively. Certain types of teratogenic agents cause cardiac malformations only if applied at the particular time of gestation when the heart is undergoing anatomical transformation (organogenesis; say ~10–17 days in the rat). Others cause malformations when applied at an earlier stage of development (e.g., hypercapnia; Haring, 1960). It is possible that the latter agents may act not simply by disturbing the metabolism of the growing cardiac tissue but, indirectly, as a result of haemodynamic alterations. This takes us back, beyond the foetal period of life, to an embryonic stage whose physiology is wholly unexplored. Let us suppose that a drug should cause vasoconstriction in peripheral vessels at one stage of development. If the principal effect were in the blood supply to a vital organ (the heart or placenta), the embryo would die; if

it were on less vital organs (the limbs) the embryo would live but be deformed. It would be surprising if many teratogenic agents acted in this way, but some may. At the present moment we have neither the basic knowledge nor the technical expertise in working with embryos *in vivo* to pursue these possibilities.

Finally, there are another group of cardiovascular anomalies which are closely related to the changes which occur at birth, which appear to be the result of defects of function rather than of anatomical structure (though these are often hard to separate). They include anomalies related to the ductus arteriosus and aorta (including coarctation) and the pulmonary vascular bed. They will be considered in Chapter 12 with the changes in the circulation at birth.

Conclusion

This account of the foetal circulation has been built on the evidence accumulated by a small number of investigators, mainly using sheep and mainly toward the end of gestation. The general picture seems to make sense, to fit with what is known or guessed at in other species, and to provide a reasonably satisfactory basis for understanding what happens at birth. But it does not compare for wealth of detail and accuracy with what is known of the adult. There are many features which deserve further study, and particularly in other species and at other stages of gestation. The facts at present suggest that the normal foetus is ruggedly constructed, with a fair safety margin based on a relatively high cardiac output which distributes well-mixed blood to the placenta and foetal tissues in roughly equal quantities. Yet some infants die before birth or during labour. There is no inconsistency here. The animal experiments on which much of our knowledge of the foetal circulation is based have usually been designed to establish the course of blood flow and the mechanisms which control it, rather than to provide the statistical information on which we might form a rational appreciation of normal variation.

Most experiments have been acute and have involved extensive surgical interference under general anaesthesia. Of the normal foetus *in utero* we still know comparatively little. It has been assumed that as the intra-uterine environment is constant in respect of temperature and the support afforded by amniotic fluid, the foetus is thereby insulated from sensory stimuli. But we do not know by experiment how effective this insulation is, or whether the foetal heart rate, blood pressure, cardiac output, and its distribution alter by day and night, as the mother eats, walks, or sleeps. The intra-uterine insulation may be of more importance to some other aspects of foetal physiology (e.g., temperature control) than to the circulation.

REFERENCES

Adams, F. H.; Assali, N.; Cushman, M., and Westersten, A.: Interrelationships of maternal and foetal circulations. I. Flow-pressure responses to vasoactive drugs in sheep, Pediatrics 27:627–635, 1961.

Adolph, E. F.: Ontogeny of physiological regulations in the rat, Quart. Rev. Biol. 32:89–137, 1957.

Alexander, D. P., and Nixon, D. A.: The foetal kidney, Brit. M. Bull. 17:112–117, 1961.

Amoroso, E. C.; Dawes, G. S.; Mott, J. C., and Rennick, B. R.: Occlusion of the ductus venosus in the mature foetal lamb, J. Physiol. 129:64–65, P, 1955.

Assali, N. S.; Holm, L. W., and Sehgal, N.: Regional blood flow and vascular resistance of the foetus in utero. Action of vasoactive drugs, Am. J. Obst. & Gynec. 83: 809–817, 1962.

Assali, N. S., and Morris, J. A.: Maternal and fetal circulations and their interrelationships, Obst. & Gynec. Surv. 19:923–948, 1964.

Assali, N. S.; Morris, J. A., and Beck, R.: Cardiovascular haemodynamics in the fetal lamb before and after lung expansion, Am. J. Physiol. 208:122–129, 1965.

Barclay, A. E.; Franklin, K. J., and Prichard, M. M. L.: *The Foetal Circulation and Cardiovascular System, and the Changes That They Undergo at Birth* (Oxford: Blackwell Scientific Publications, 1944).

Barcroft, J.: *Researches on Prenatal Life* (Oxford: Blackwell Scientific Publications, 1946).

Barcroft, J., and Barron, D. H.: Blood pressure and pulse rate in the foetal sheep, J. Exper. Biol. 22:63–74, 1945.

Barcroft, J.; Barron, D. H.; Cowie, A. T., and Forsham, P. H.: The oxygen supply of the foetal brain of the sheep and the effect of asphyxia on foetal respiratory movement, J. Physiol. 97:338–346, 1938.

Barron, D. H.: The "sphincter" of the ductus venosus, Anat. Rec. 82:398, 1942.

Born, G. V. R.; Dawes, G. S., and Mott, J. C.: Oxygen lack and autonomic nervous control of the foetal circulation in the lamb, J. Physiol. 134:149–166, 1956.

Born, G. V. R.; Dawes, G. S.; Mott, J. C., and Rennick, B. R.: The constriction of the ductus arteriosus caused by oxygen and by asphyxia in newborn lambs, J. Physiol. 132:304–342, 1956.

Born, G. V. R.; Dawes, G. S.; Mott, J. C., and Widdicombe, J. G.: Changes in the heart and lungs at birth, Cold Spring Harb. Symp. Quant. Biol. 19:102–108, 1954.

Boyd, J. D.: The inferior aortico-pulmonary glomus, Brit. M. Bull. 17:127–131, 1961.

Carnot, P., and Josserand, P.: Des différences d'action de l'adrénaline sur la pression sanguine suivant les voies de pénétration, C.R. Soc. Biol., Paris 54:1472–1474, 1902.

Cassin, S.; Dawes, G. S., and Ross, B. B.: Pulmonary blood flow and vascular resistance in immature foetal lambs, J. Physiol. 171:80–89, 1964.

Clark, J. A.: Some foetal blood-pressure reactions, J. Physiol. 74:391–400, 1932.

Coleridge, H.; Coleridge, J. C. G., and Howe, A.: A search for pulmonary arterial chemoreceptors in the new-born kitten and adult cat, Physiol. 184:15–16, P, 1966.

Comline, R. S., and Silver, M.: The release of adrenaline and noradrenaline from the adrenal glands of the foetal sheep, J. Physiol. 156:424–444, 1961.

Comline, R. S.; Silver, I. A., and Silver, M.: Factors responsible for the stimulation of the adrenal medulla during asphyxia in the foetal lamb, J. Physiol. 178: 211–238, 1965.

Comroe, J. H.: The peripheral chemoreceptors, in Fenn, W. O., and Rahn, H. (eds.): *Handbook of Physiology: Sect. 3-Respiration* (Washington, D.C.: American Physiological Society, 1964), Vol. 1, pp. 557–584.

Cross, K. W.; Dawes, G. S., and Mott, J. C.: Anoxia, oxygen consumption and cardiac output in new-born lambs and adult sheep, J. Physiol. 146:316–343, 1959.

Cross, K. W., and Malcolm, J. L.: Evidence of carotid body and sinus activity in new-born and foetal animals, J. Physiol. 118:10, P, 1952.

Dawes, G. S.: Amidines, guanidines and adrenaline inactivation in the liver, Brit. J. Pharmacol. 1:21–37, 1946.

Dawes, G. S.: Changes in the circulation at birth, Brit. M. Bull. 17:148–153, 1961.

Dawes, G. S.: Physiological changes in the circulation after birth, in Fishman, A. P., and Richards, D. W.: *Circulation of the Blood, Men and Ideas* (New York: Oxford University Press, 1964), pp. 743–816.

Dawes, G. S.; Handler, J. J., and Mott, J. C.: Some cardiovascular responses in foetal, new-born and adult rabbits, J. Physiol. 139:123–136, 1957.

Dawes, G. S.; Jacobson, H. N.; Mott, J. C., and Shelley, H. J.: Some observations on foetal and new-born rhesus monkeys, J. Physiol. 152:271–298, 1960.

Dawes, G. S., and Mott, J. C.: Changes in O_2 distribution and consumption in foetal lambs with variations in umbilical blood flow, J. Physiol. 170:524–540, 1964.

Dawes, G. S.; Mott, J. C., and Rennick, B. R.: Some effects of adrenaline, noradrenaline and acetylcholine on the foetal circulation in the lamb, J. Physiol. 134: 139–148, 1956.

Dawes, G. S.; Mott, J. C., and Widdicombe, J. G.: The foetal circulation in the lamb, J. Physiol. 126:563–587, 1954.

Dawes, G. S.; Mott, J. C., and Widdicombe, J. G.: Closure of the foramen ovale in newborn lambs, J. Physiol. 128: 384–395, 1955.

Dittmer, D. S., and Grebe, R. M.: *Handbook of Circulation* (Philadelphia: W. B. Saunders Company, 1959).

Drake, J.: *Anthropologia Nova, or, a New System of Anatomy. The Appendix* (London: W. and J. Innys, 1728).

Emery, J. L.: The distribution of haemopoietic foci in the infantile human liver, J. Anat. 90:293–297, 1956.

Fabricius, H.: *The Embryological Treatises.* Tr. by H. B. Adelmann. (Ithaca, New York: Cornell University Press, 1942).

Groom, A. C.; Rowlands, S., and Thomas, H. W.: Some circulatory responses to haemorrhage in the cat: A critical level of blood volume for the onset of hypotension, Quart, J. Exper. Physiol. 50:385–405, 1965.

Gruenwald, P.: Degenerative changes in the right half of the liver resulting from intra-uterine anoxia, Am. J. Clin. Path. 19:801–813, 1949.

Haring, O. M.: Cardiac malformations in rats induced by exposure of the mother to carbon dioxide during pregnancy, Circulation Res. 8:1218–1227, 1960.

Handler, J. J.: The foetal circulation and its changes at birth in some small laboratory animals, J. Physiol. 133: 202–212, 1956.

Huggett, A. St. G.: Foetal blood-gas tensions and gas transfusion through the placenta of the goat, J. Physiol. 62:373–384, 1927.

Jost, A.: Expériences de décapitation de l'embryon de lapin, C.R. Acad. Sc., Paris 225:322–324, 1947.

Jost, A.: Hormonal factors in the development of the fetus, Cold Spring Harb. Symp. Quant. Biol. 19:167–181, 1954.

Lind, J.: In Cassels, D. (ed.): *The Heart and Circulation in the Newborn and Infant* (New York: Grune & Stratton, Inc., 1966), pp. 130–132.

Lind, J., and Wegelius, C.: Human fetal circulation: Changes in the cardiovascular system at birth and disturbances in the post-natal closure of the foramen ovale and ductus arteriosus, Cold Spring Harb. Symp. Quant. Biol. 19:109–125, 1954.

Lower, B.: *Tractatus de Corde. Item de motu et colore sanguinis et chyli in eum transitu* (London: Jacobi Allestry, 1669).

Mahon, W. A.; Goodwin, J. W., and Paul, W. M.: Measurement of individual ventricular outputs in the fetal lamb by an indicator dilution technique, Circulation Res. 19:191–198, 1966.

Metcalfe, J., and Parer, J. T.: Cardiovascular changes during pregnancy in ewes, Am. J. Physiol. 210:821–825, 1966.

Morris, J. A.; Bekey, G. A.; Assali, N. S., and Beck, R.: Dynamics of blood flow in the ductus arteriosus, Am. J. Physiol. 208:471–476, 1965.

Mott, J. C.: Haemorrhage as a test of the function of the cardiovascular system in rabbits of different ages, J. Physiol. 181:728–752, 1965.

Patten, B. M.: From fetus to newborn baby, in Fishbein, M. (ed.): *Birth Defects* (Philadelphia: J. B. Lippincott Company, 1963), pp. 125–135.

Peltonen, T., and Hirvonen, L.: Experimental studies on fetal and neonatal circulation, Acta paediat. Suppl. 161, 1965.

Pohlman, A. G.: The fetal circulation through the heart, Bull. Johns Hopkins Hosp. 18:409–412, 1907.

Pohlman, A. G.: The course of the blood through the heart of the fetal mammal, with a note on the reptilian and amphibian circulations, Anat. Rec. 3:75–109, 1909.

Purves, M. J., and Biscoe, T. J.: Development of chemoreceptor activity, Brit. M. Bull. 22:56–60, 1966.

Reynolds, S. R. M., and Mackie, J. D.: Umbilical venous pressure and other cardiovascular responses of fetal lambs to epinephrine, Am. J. Physiol. 203:955–960, 1962.

Rudolph, A. M.: The effects of postnatal circulatory adjustments in congenital heart disease. Pediatrics 36: 763–772, 1965.

Rudolph, A. M.; Heymann, M., and Hait, G.: Distribution of the circulation in the fetus in utero, Circulation 32:II, 183, 1965.

Sabatier, R. B.: Mémoire sur les organes de la circulation du sang du foetus, Mém. Acad. Roy. Sc., Paris 198: 778, 1778.

Smith, R. W.; Morris, J. A.; Assali, N. S., and Beck, R.: Effects of chemical mediators on the pulmonary and ductus arteriosus circulation in the fetal lamb, Am. J. Obst. & Gynec, 89:252–260, 1964.

9

Foetal Blood Gas Tensions and pH

IN ADULTS, changes in O_2 consumption have little effect on arterial Po_2. But in the foetus, O_2 supply is dependent on maternal placental blood flow. If this is constant, then an increase in the O_2 uptake by the placenta or foetus must lead to a lower foetal arterial Po_2 (because the mean Po_2 on the maternal side of the placenta falls as O_2 is removed). So far there is no evidence that maternal blood flow to the placenta is increased to compensate for increased O_2 utilization, from moment to moment; it is a point that needs investigating. In the absence of such evidence we would expect that with changing foetal activity and different experimental conditions the foetal blood gas tensions might be more variable than in adults.

There are two further elements which add to the variability. The first is due to changes in umbilical blood flow. Other things (e.g., maternal placental flow and foetal O_2 uptake) being equal, a fall in umbilical flow leads to a fall in umbilical arterial Po_2. A fall in foetal haemoglobin concentration will have the same effect as a reduction in umbilical blood flow; both may reduce the total quantity of O_2 carried from the placenta in the umbilical vein

to mix in the heart and great vessels with venous blood from the foetal tissues. Secondly, the difficulties in studying the respiratory physiology of the foetus are exaggerated not only by the fact that we have to deal with two individuals, linked by a complex organ of gaseous exchange, but also because the foetus is relatively inaccessible. There are good reasons to suppose that both changes in the mother and the acute interference of operative surgery can induce alterations in foetal blood gas tensions and pH which are not always easy to explain.

These generalisations apply with more force to O_2 than to CO_2, mainly because CO_2 is more diffusible. As Table 25 shows, the Pco_2 gradient across the placenta is much less than that for O_2. Small changes in maternal arterial Pco_2 are quickly followed by changes in the same direction, and of almost identical size, in foetal blood. Only in abnormal conditions (e.g., during labour, in abruptio placenta, or other instances of foetal asphyxia and metabolic acidosis) does the foetal arterial Pco_2 exceed that of the mother by more than about 10 mm Hg. During human pregnancy at term (and also in sheep, Chapter 11, Table 34, p. 133) there

TABLE 25.—MEAN VALUES OF BLOOD GAS TENSIONS† AND pH IN 9 MATURE FOETAL LAMBS UNDER CHLORALOSE ANAESTHESIA

	Po_2 (MM HG)	Pco_2 (MM HG)	pH
Maternal artery	82	36	7.44
Maternal placental cotyledonary vein	43	40	7.40
Foetal placental cotyledonary vein	32	43	7.36
Foetal femoral artery*	24	45	7.33

Unpublished observations: Cockburn, Campbell, Dawes, Milligan, and Ross.

† Measured by blood gas electrodes (Radiometer) and corrected for differences in blood and electrode temperature.

* This is equivalent to an umbilical arterial sample as both are branches of the descending aorta.

is a reduction in maternal arterial P_{CO_2} to about 32 mm Hg (Doring and Loeschke, 1947), so that normal foetal arterial P_{CO_2} is not very much greater than in the nonpregnant adult. Saling (1964,a) gives a mean figure of 44.5 mm Hg for arterialized scalp blood P_{CO_2} at the onset of delivery. The cause of the decrease in maternal P_{CO_2} during pregnancy is uncertain. It has been attributed to increased progesterone blood levels in man, but this is unlikely to be the reason in sheep (Edgar and Ronaldson, 1958).

Before we discuss the respiratory physiology of the foetus in detail there are some technical points to consider. Until the introduction of P_{O_2} and P_{CO_2} polarographic electrodes a few years ago, computation of blood gas tensions was a laborious affair. It was dependent on measurement of O_2 and CO_2 contents and capacities and reference to a dissociation curve, variable from one animal to another, and so the tensions were calculated from multiple measurements. With recent technical improvements in blood gas electrodes they are now probably more accurate and very much simpler. In the past, results were much more often expressed in terms of O_2 saturation of foetal arterial blood rather than P_{O_2}, and this has some sense. For when a foetus becomes severely hypoxaemic it also becomes acidaemic. The consequent Bohr shift of the HbO_2 dissociation curve to the right reduces the change in arterial P_{O_2} in such conditions. Thus during labour foetal scalp blood O_2 saturation falls from 42 to 30%, but P_{O_2} falls only from 20 to 17 mm Hg (Saling, 1964,a). So, though most of the older results are expressed in terms of O_2 saturation, this does give a slightly more sensitive measure of foetal oxygenation than does P_{O_2}.

The computation of P_{O_2} from HbO_2 dissociation curves in ruminants presents a special problem. In 1955, Harris and Warren observed the occurrence of two electrophoretically distinct types of haemoglobin in adult sheep and goats. Subsequent investigations showed that there were as many as 4 types of haemoglobin in various breeds of sheep, which differed in their electrophoretic and chromatographic behaviour, their resistance to alkali denaturation, were of different amino-acid composition and possessed different O_2 affinities (Fig. 52; Huisman, van Vliet, and Sebens, 1958). The differences in O_2 affinity were also seen in haemoglobin solutions (Fig. 52), and must, therefore, be due to differences in the haemoglobin molecule rather than in the red cell internal environment. Even in the pure bred Dorset sheep there were two types of

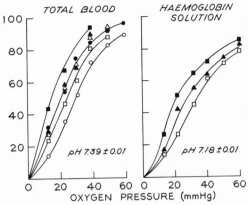

SATURATION OF HAEMOGLOBIN WITH OXYGEN (%)

Fig. 52.—HbO_2 dissociation curves of blood samples from adult sheep (o, Dutch Texel, homozygous for Hb 1; ●, Dutch Texel, homozygous for Hb 11; □, *Ammotragus lervia*, North Africa; ■, Argali, *Ovis ammon*, North and Central Asia; △, Heidschnucken, native of the Lüneberger Heide, Germany; ▲, European Mouflon, (*Ovis musimon*, originating in South and Central Europe). (Redrawn from Huisman, van Vliet, and Sebens, 1958.)

haemoglobin with different O_2 affinities (Naughton, Meschia, Battaglia, Hellegers, Hagopian, and Barron, 1963). The presence of these haemoglobins appears to be genetically determined, but mixtures of two haemoglobins have been found in some breeds. Huisman, van Vliet, and Sebens (1958) pointed out that the Argali sheep, with the highest O_2 affinity, (Fig. 52. ■) live above the timber-line in the mountains of northern and central Asia, but A. lervia which lives in the mountains of North Africa has a much lower O_2 affinity (Fig. 52, □). Hence if there once were a teleological association between high O_2 affinity and high altitude, it is no longer clear. These observations must cast doubt on the accuracy of many of the earlier estimates of P_{O_2} from HbO_2 dissociation curves in sheep, where the measurement of O_2 content and the dissociation curve were not made on the same blood. Van Vliet and Huisman (1964) have also made the interesting observation that during anaemia due to repeated bleeding a new haemoglobin variant may appear in the blood of Texel sheep, chemically different but having the same O_2 affinity as that of the two haemoglobins normally present.

It is comparatively easy to obtain umbilical arterial blood, and as the O_2 content of this is normally intermediate between that of the carotid and pulmonary arteries, (whose differences are small, Fig. 47, p. 91) it provides a reasonable measure of the arterial O_2 supply to the foetus. But there are some unusual circumstances in which this may be misleading, such as when the difference in the O_2 content of carotid and descending aortic blood is much increased (e.g., by reducing umbilical flow in immature lambs, Chapter 8). Or if a foetal lamb is subjected to haemorrhage, its O_2 uptake from the placenta may fall while umbilical arterial, venous and carotid O_2 saturation may rise by as much as 20% (Dawes and Mott, 1964). So it should not be assumed too readily that umbilical arterial O_2 saturation or Po_2 is an infallible guide to the state of the foetus.

In the past few years there have also been two important technical developments which have made it possible to obtain information about foetal blood gas tensions and pH in utero under relatively natural conditions. First, Saling (1964,b) described a method for obtaining capillary blood from the scalp of the human foetus during labour. This has proved of considerable practical value in obstetric management as well as giving much other information. Secondly, Meschia, Cotter, Breathnach, and Barron (1965) reported preliminary results using catheters inserted into the umbilical vessels of foetal sheep and goats, and maintained in position *in utero* for periods up to several weeks while the mother was free from obvious stress. The full potentialities of these new methods need further development. Together they should provide the necessary statistical information for a much better evaluation of the internal environment of the foetus than has hitherto been possible. Earlier work had produced a good deal of confusion which it may now be possible to straighten out.

The Adequacy of Foetal O_2 Supply Near Term

The analogy drawn between the behaviour of the infant after birth and that of the acclimatized mountaineer returning to sea level has already been mentioned (Chapter 3). This suggested that the high O_2 capacity of the baby at birth was the result of prolonged hypoxaemia toward the end of gestation and the work of Barcroft (1946) and his colleagues supported this hypothesis. They observed in rabbits that prolongation of gestation led to a progressive fall in the O_2 content of uterine venous blood and to foetal hypoxia; if delivery did not

take place by about 34 days from conception (term is normally $\sim$31 days) most of the foetuses died. There was a progressive rise in the O_2 carrying capacity of the blood in their foetal lambs, continuing toward the end of gestation (Fig. 53, $\bigcirc$). The observations were made in acute experiments on lambs delivered by caesarean section, under maternal spinal anaesthesia, into a warm saline bath; the mother was supine. In the same preparations there was a fall in foetal arterial and umbilical venous O_2 saturation toward term. The data appeared to support the idea that the normal foetus of this species outgrew its placenta, that is to say that foetal O_2 consumption increased at a rate which was greater than the increase in the capacity of the placenta to supply it. These observations in animals also provided indirect support for the concept of the ageing placenta as likely to be a phenomenon of pathological significance in man. It was proposed that progressive deterioration in the placenta as an organ of gaseous exchange (e.g., by fibrin deposition and infarcts) might exaggerate the problem faced by the growing foetus near term. And evidence was adduced (Walker, 1953) to support the proposition that larger babies of greater gestational age had a higher O_2 carrying capacity. This evidence was challenged on various grounds and need not concern us now except as an illustration of the very wide consideration which the general hypothesis received.

Finally, a large literature accumulated (well summarized by Wulf, 1962) on the O_2 contents and partial pressures of maternal and umbilical blood on delivery in man. The mean figures for umbilical blood quoted are misleading unless one also takes

Fig. 53.—Changes in O_2 carrying capacity of the blood (means $\pm$S.D.) with gestational age in sheep according to Barcroft ($\bigcirc$, 1946) and Born, Dawes, and Mott ($\bullet$, 1956).

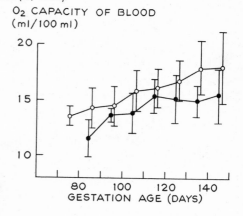

O_2 CAPACITY OF BLOOD (ml/100 ml)

GESTATION AGE (DAYS)

account of the very wide variations observed in individual observations. Even the mean figures for umbilical arterial O_2 saturation varied from 13–42% (in 19 investigations) while those for Po_2 varied from 8–16 mm Hg (in 9 investigations). Wulf's own figures for umbilical arterial Po_2 on delivery ranged from 1–25 mm Hg, and for umbilical venous Po_2 from 11–47 mm Hg. The simplest explanation for these large variations was that many babies were asphyxiated during delivery. The low figures quoted by Wulf and many others must have resulted from partial interruption of uterine or umbilical blood flow on delivery. This conclusion was supported by the observation that the consequent metabolic acidosis is gradually corrected, and the blood pH and buffer base rises progressively during the 24 hours after birth (James, Weisbrot, Prince, Holaday, and Apgar, 1958). It was, therefore, evident that measurements on delivery were unlikely to give reliable information about the conditions of intra-uterine life in man, and the spate of papers on the measurement of cord blood oxygen fell to a trickle.

Meanwhile there was evidence which suggested another explanation for the high O_2 carrying capacity recorded by Barcroft in foetal lambs near term. Born, Dawes, and Mott (1956) observed that a brief period of hypoxaemia caused an abrupt rise in O_2 capacity within a few minutes. Their figures for O_2 carrying capacity in lambs which were not hypoxaemic (Fig. 53, ●) were substantially less than those of Barcroft, and showed a much smaller increase after 100 days gestational age. In both series, the range of variation about the mean was large, also suggesting that the value observed was readily altered by changes in the experimental conditions. Thus the rise in O_2 capacity was not contingent upon a prolonged period of hypoxaemia (as at altitude) but might result from any one of a variety of abrupt disturbances to the foetus.

Finally, and more convincingly, Barron, Meschia, Cotter, and Breathnach (1965), using indwelling catheters in unanaesthetised lambs *in utero,* found no tendency for the O_2 capacity of the blood to increase after 100 days gestation, and no evidence of a systematic fall in arterial O_2 saturation. Although the numbers of lambs used was not stated, and may have been small, it is evident that the original hypothesis of a progressively more deficient O_2 supply toward term in normal lamb foetuses is hardly tenable any longer.

The difference between these observations and those of Barcroft and his colleagues, and of Barron

(1951), Kaiser and Cummings (1957), and Metcalfe, Meschia, Hellegers, Prystowsky, Huckabee, and Barron (1962) gives rise to some concern. They all had observed a rise in foetal O_2 capacity and a fall in arterial O_2 saturation toward term. The common factor was that the mother was conscious, under spinal or local anaesthesia, and subjected in an unaccustomed and disturbed state to acute experimental interference. It may be the last factor which is of crucial importance. The difficulties of interpretation have not been underrated by any of these workers, who have appreciated and explicitly stated that they were not working with a "natural" preparation. The mechanism by which these changes are effected is uncertain. One might speculate that they resulted from a decrease in maternal placental blood flow, which induced foetal hypoxaemia and hence a rise in O_2 carrying capacity. This is possible, yet the umbilical arterial O_2 saturation of unanaesthetised lambs *in utero,* examined by indwelling catheters in unstressed docile mothers by Barron *et al.* (1965), was relatively low (36–53%, pH 7.22–7.37); and in these lambs the O_2 capacity was not high (about 10–14 ml O_2/100 ml blood). So, evidently this level of umbilical arterial O_2 saturation was not associated with an elevation of haemoglobin concentration in normal lambs *in utero.*

It is evident that a better index of chronic foetal hypoxia is needed. No one appears to have studied foetal red cell mass in this connection. Yet measurements of foetal blood erythropoietin concentrations may be a more practical and useful measure. Thus Finne (1966) found that the concentration (estimated from the rate of Fe^{59} incorporation into the erythrocytes of polycythaemic mice) was lower in the cord blood of normal premature human infants than on delivery at term. It was raised in some infants which were postmature, or in association with pre-eclamptic toxaemia; it was raised considerably in erythroblastosis foetalis when the haemoglobin was less than 12 Gm%. So this may turn out to be the tool we need to solve this problem.

Foetal O_2 Consumption and General Anaesthesia

It was suggested in the opening paragraph of this chapter that changes in foetal (or placental) O_2 consumption might be one of the variables that could alter the oxygenation of foetal arterial blood. Foetal O_2 consumption has been measured under a variety of conditions and at different ages in foetal lambs as the product of umbilical arteriovenous O_2

difference and umbilical blood flow. There is bound to be a large variation in such calculations, as they depend on the subtraction of two O_2 contents sampled at a particular moment in time, and on measurements of blood flow which also may vary. The presentation of such calculations in foetal lambs to 4 significant figures (Meschia *et al.*, 1965) gives a misleading impression of the accuracy attainable. Repeated measurements in the same anaesthetised lamb, using a high fidelity cannulated electromagnetic flowmeter, indicated a time-to-time variation of $\pm 15\%$.

Table 26 summarizes observations of O_2 consumption in foetal lambs at different ages. All the authors kept the lambs warm, by a variety of methods, so we are probably safe in assuming that they were in a neutral thermal environment (i.e., that cold exposure was not acting as a stimulant to O_2 consumption). This is a practical point of some importance because foetal lambs (still connected to the mother by an intact cord and not breathing) will shiver on exposure to cold. The observations show a good measure of agreement considering the wide variety of methods used. Those in anaesthetised mature foetal lambs agree well with the O_2 uptake of 12 anaesthetised lambs of 136–144 days gestation, separated from the mother and artificially ventilated for 1–2 hours (4.5 ± 1.2 ml/kg min; Acheson, Dawes and Mott, 1957). This is reassuring in view of the much greater technical difficulties in handling foetuses.

Barcroft (1946) suggested that O_2 consumption per kg body weight probably fell during the last half of gestation in sheep. The evidence for this conclusion came from indirect estimates of O_2 consumption, but is substantiated by the last 4 pairs of observations in Table 26. Under anaesthesia the difference between immature and mature lambs is small and significant statistically in only one series (Dawes and Mott, 1964), but this series contained more animals, used a better method of measuring umbilical flow, and less anaesthetic. The difference was larger in unanaesthetised lambs (Meschia *et al.*, 1965). This does not help to explain why the arterial O_2 saturation of more mature lambs is often less.

There are no measurements of O_2 consumption in foetal lambs with and without general anaesthesia using the same method of measurement. One would suppose that general anaesthesia might cause a small reduction in foetal O_2 uptake, as in the adult, by abolishing skeletal muscle tone, reducing cerebral O_2 consumption, and in other ways. The difference between the observations (Table 26) of Dawes and Mott, (1964) and of Meschia *et al.* (1965) could be explained in this way. If O_2 uptake is less in anaesthetised lambs, this might also help to explain the low umbilical arterial O_2 saturation sometimes seen in unanaesthetised as compared with anaesthetised foetal lambs (Table 27).

There is another feature of the O_2 consumption of the foetus which deserves mention. In adult animals exposed to progressively increasing hypoxae-

TABLE 26.—MEASUREMENTS OF THE O_2 CONSUMPTION OF FOETAL LAMBS

AUTHORS	GESTATIONAL AGE (DAYS)	NUMBER OF LAMBS	FOETAL ANAESTHESIA	METHOD OF UMBILICAL FLOW MEASUREMENT	CALCULATED FOETAL O_2 UPTAKE (ML/KG MIN $\pm$ S.E.)
Barcroft, Kennedy, and Mason (1939)	111–152	7	None	None*	4.8 ± 0.6
Barcroft and Torrens (1946) Barcroft and Elsden (1946)		3	None	None†	5.3
Dawes, Mott, and Widdicombe (1954)	136–143	5	Pentobarbitone	Density flowmeter	4.6 ± 0.8
Acheson, Dawes, and Mott (1957)	79–87 117–138	7 14	Pentobarbitone	Venous occlusion plethysmograph‡	4.0 ± 0.9 3.7 ± 1.0
Dawes and Mott (1959)	85–90 135–146	5 10	Chloralose 50–70 mg/kg	Velodyne flowmeter	4.8 ± 0.7 4.2 ± 0.5
Dawes and Mott (1964)	87–95 137–141	22 10	Chloralose 40 mg/kg Chloralose 30 mg/kg	Cannulated electromagnetic flowmeter	5.4 ± 0.5 (P <0.02) 4.6 ± 0.3
Meschia, Cotter, Breathnach, and Barron (1965)	81–94 123–136	5 10	None	Application of Fick principle using urea	8.8 ± 0.3 (P <0.01) 5.9 ± 0.4

Note: The mother was given either general anaesthesia by intravenous injection or infusion, or spinal anaesthesia.
* Method based on rate of decline of carotid O_2 saturation after umbilical cord occlusion.
† Assumed as 50% of cardiac output, which was measured by cardiometer $+15\%$ for coronary flow.
‡ Now known to give an underestimate of flow and hence of O_2 consumption.

TABLE 27.—MEASUREMENTS OF UMBILICAL BLOOD O_2 SATURATION IN FOETAL LAMBS NEAR TERM

	FOETAL ANAESTHESIA	O_2 SATURATION (%) IN	
		UMBILICAL ARTERY	UMBILICAL VEIN
Dawes, Mott, and Widdicombe (1954)	Pentobarbitone	58	80
Dawes and Mott (1964)	Chloralose	52	69
Kaiser and Cummings (1957)	None*	23	65
Barron, Meschia, Cotter, and Breathnach (1965)	None	36–53 (range)	65–84 (range)

* A small dose of pentobarbitone had been given to the ewe before local anaesthesia.
The figures are means except where otherwise noted.

mia, O_2 uptake is maintained, or even increased, to provide the extra energy for hyperventilation, until a point is reached when abrupt collapse of the circulation occurs. But in foetuses, O_2 consumption falls during severe hypoxaemia, and can be supported at a much reduced level (Acheson, Dawes, and Mott, 1957; Dawes and Mott, 1959) for as much as an hour. There is redistribution of flow within the circulation (to maintain the blood supply to the heart, placenta, and brain) and progressive development of metabolic acidosis. The point to be made here is that as a temporary expedient in the face of hypoxaemia this process is efficient; as O_2 uptake is reduced the arterial P_{O_2} is relatively greater than it would otherwise be. But you get "nothing for nothing and damn little for sixpence." In this case the cost that is paid is a progressively falling tissue and blood pH, which may ultimately prove fatal.

General anaesthesia affects both the mother and the foetus, and it is important to realize the consequences. The most obvious result is to induce hypoventilation of the mother. This is illustrated in Table 28, which shows that pentobarbitone anaesthesia in pregnant rhesus monkeys caused a fall in maternal arterial P_{O_2} of 20 mm Hg, a rise in P_{CO_2} of 6 mm Hg, and a small rise in pH and decrease in

excess acid (i.e., negative base excess) attributed to absence of muscular movements during caesarean section and delivery. All these changes were statistically significant, but they were reflected only to a limited extent in the foetus. There was a trifling reduction in umbilical arterial P_{O_2} (for the reasons already discussed in Chapter 3), a mean rise in P_{CO_2} of 6 mm Hg, and no significant change in pH or excess acid. In this instance, the differences observed in the foetus could be wholly passive and dependent on those in the mother. The mean alterations in the partial pressure of CO_2 were identical in the arterial bloods of mother and foetus. Deeper anaesthesia will reduce maternal arterial P_{O_2} more and raise the P_{CO_2} yet further, in both mother and foetus. But the changes in foetal P_{CO_2} will be greater than in P_{O_2}. As the foetus becomes more hypoxaemic and develops a metabolic acidosis, this increases the rate of fall of arterial pH and rise in P_{CO_2}. The latter are, therefore, a more sensitive index of foetal condition than changes in P_{O_2} in the early stages of hypoxia.

In the previous paragraph no account has been taken of the possible effects of general anaesthesia on maternal placental or umbilical blood flow, on the distribution of maternal and foetal flows in the placenta, or on placental metabolism. This does

TABLE 28.—OBSERVATIONS ON MATERNAL AND UMBILICAL ARTERIAL BLOOD FROM RHESUS MONKEYS DELIVERED NEAR TERM UNDER LOCAL OR PENTOBARBITONE (24–43 MG/KG) ANAESTHESIA* (MEANS ± S.E.), FROM COCKBURN, DANIEL, DAWES, JAMES, MYERS, DE CURET AND ROSS (UNPUBLISHED)

		P_{O_2} (MM HG)	P_{CO_2} (MM HG)	pH	EXCESS ACID (MEQ/L)
Mother	Local	100 ± 3	30.5 ± 1.3	7.30 ± 0.03	9.3 ± 1.3
	pentobarbitone	80 ± 3	36.3 ± 1.6	7.36 ± 0.07	4.7 ± 0.7
Foetus	Local	19.3 ± 1.9	46.3 ± 2.6	7.26 ± 0.02	8.8 ± 0.7
	pentobarbitone	17.5 ± 1.4	52.3 ± 2.5	7.24 ± 0.02	8.5 ± 0.9

* This is sufficient to cause deep surgical anaesthesia on delivery 30 minutes after induction.

not mean these are not important considerations but only that we have no information about them.

The use of general anaesthetics in man (e.g., pentobarbitone, cyclopropane, or nitrous oxide and ether) has been regarded by some in the past as causing a small degree of foetal hypoxaemia. Where this conclusion was based on cord blood samples on delivery, it was not convincing because of the great variability already described. The use of Saling's method for obtaining foetal scalp blood samples during labour will help here. The reactivity of the infant delivered under a general anaesthetic may be affected by partial asphyxia, by anaesthesia, or by the conditions of delivery, and, therefore, provides a very uncertain measure of foetal oxygenation *in utero*.

Maternal Ventilation

The effect of changes in maternal ventilation are more complex than might at first appear. Forced ventilation of pregnant guinea pigs caused a profound foetal metabolic acidosis (Morishima, Moya, Bossers, and Daniel, 1964). At first it looked as if this was due wholly to the associated maternal hypotension and hypocapnia. But subsequent experiments showed that mechanical hyperventilation still caused the development of some degree of foetal acidosis in the absence of maternal hypotension and when hypocapnia was prevented by adding 5% CO_2 to the ventilating gas mixture (Morishima, Daniel, Adamsons, and James, 1965). Spontaneous hyperventilation induced by administration of 5% CO_2 or lobeline caused only small changes in the foetus. The mechanism proposed for the effect of mechanical hyperventilation of the mother in causing foetal acidosis was a reduction in maternal placental flow as a result of hypocapnia or, when this was prevented, indirectly by impairment of maternal venous return. These hypotheses have not been tested experimentally.

In anaesthetised pregnant ewes, Motoyama, Rivard, Acheson, and Cook (1966) also found that maternal hyperventilation had an adverse effect on the foetus, causing a fall in umbilical venous and carotid arterial Po_2, and, when prolonged, leading to metabolic acidosis and foetal distress. In contrast to the experiments on guinea pigs described above, hyperventilation without hypocapnia (i.e., with 3–5% CO_2) did not cause a fall in arterial Po_2 in 3 foetal lambs. The fact that, in the presence of hypocapnia, umbilical vein Po_2 fell suggested that transplacental O_2 transport was impaired. This could

have been due to a decrease in maternal placental flow as had been proposed for the guinea pig experiments. Measurements with a cuff electromagnetic flowmeter on one umbilical artery suggested that umbilical flow was reduced (by 7–37%) during maternal hyperventilation with hypocapnia. This observation must be treated with reservation because of the unreliability of the instrument used, particularly when applied to a single umbilical artery as a measure of total umbilical blood flow.

I have made some unpublished observations, which are relevant, during the course of other investigations on spontaneously breathing anaesthetised pregnant ewes. They were given gas mixtures containing 5–10% CO_2 to breathe; the O_2 content of the mixture was reduced from 21% to 18–19%, so that maternal arterial Po_2 remained unchanged despite hyperventilation. Nevertheless, umbilical arterial Po_2 rose by 6–8 mm Hg. This could be accounted for neither by a shift in the HbO_2 dissociation curve, nor by an alteration in total umbilical venous blood flow which remained unchanged.

This is the converse situation to that observed by Motoyama *et al.* (1966). In their experiments, maternal hypocapnia caused a fall in foetal arterial Po_2, while in mine hypercapnia caused a rise. The simplest explanation for all these observations is that a rise in maternal Pco_2 causes maternal placental vasodilatation, as in other peripheral vascular beds. Here we come back to the difficulty discussed in Chapter 5, that there is as yet no good method of making the measurements needed to test this hypothesis. But it would be possible and interesting to determine whether the phenomenon is dependent on the integrity of the autonomic nerve supply to the uterus. There are alternative possibilities. For instance, it could be due to an alteration in placental metabolism, or to a change in the placental perfusion: perfusion ratio (i.e., to an improvement in the distribution of flows in the area of gas exchange), or to a decrease in umbilical flow through the foetal membranes, or to a decrease in foetal O_2 uptake. This is a fairly formidable list to sort out. It illustrates vividly the difficulty, in our present state of knowledge, in coming to any firm conclusion as to the actual mechanisms which determine foetal blood gas tensions in particular experimental circumstances. Much of the basic work in this field has yet to be done.

It was pointed out by Moya, Morishima, Shnider, and James (1965) that these findings may have some clinical application in man. During caesarean section moderate controlled hyperventilation somewhat reduced foetal acidosis, but maternal hyperventilation with gross alkalosis (arterial $P_{CO_2} <$ 19 mm Hg) was associated with a low foetal arterial pH on delivery. The numbers were small (only 2 in the latter group) but the findings suggestive. It should be emphasized that the bulk of the experimental evidence suggests that it is hypocapnia, rather than hyperventilation of itself, which is the operative agent in causing deterioration of the foetus.

And perhaps the converse also is worth experimental study. It has been known for a long while that giving a mother 100% O_2 to breathe (e.g., in foetal distress) has only a small effect on foetal arterial P_{O_2}, and Figure 16 (p. 36) showed that this was also true in the foetal lamb. But it might be worth investigating the effect of giving the mother 95% O_2 and 5% CO_2 to gain, simultaneously, the small effects of both hypercapnia and a high maternal P_{O_2}.

Gas Tensions in the Amniotic Fluid

Because the amniotic fluid can be regarded as forming a fairly large part of foetal extracellular space, and is more readily available for investigation than foetal blood, some consideration has been given to it as a means of deriving information about the foetus. It is probable that most amniotic fluid, once the urethra becomes patent, is derived from foetal urine. Certainly foetal lambs (Alexander, Nixon, Widdas, and Wohlzogen, 1958) and pigs (Perry and Stanier, 1962) secrete large quantities of hypotonic urine in mid-gestation. Conversely, in human cases of renal agenesis there is little amniotic fluid. So there may be a moderately rapid circulation of urine to amniotic fluid, eventually swallowed and reabsorbed by the foetus *in utero*. Gas equilibration of amniotic fluid could also occur through the amnion and foetal skin.

Measurements of amniotic fluid P_{O_2} in man cover a wide range, 0–40 mm Hg, usually intermediate between umbilical vein and umbilical arterial P_{O_2} (Romney, Kaneoka, and Gabel, 1962), and tending to fall toward term (according to Sjöstedt, Rooth, and Caligara, 1958). Observations on the pH and P_{CO_2} also showed wide variations. However, Quilligan (1962) found that the mean gas tensions of the amniotic fluid surrounding 9 dead foetuses *in utero* was within the normal range. So it is not surprising that, as an indication of foetal condition, such measurements have not proved very useful. There is probably some temporal relation between foetal asphyxia and metabolic acidosis in the amniotic fluid, but it has not been established. It might be complex, and variable with different conditions. For instance, acute asphyxia caused an abrupt cessation of urinary secretion in foetal lambs despite a rise in arterial pressure (Dawes, Mott, and Shelley, 1959). At best, studies of the amniotic fluid can provide only a rough index of what happened to the foetus some time before.

Yet there is little doubt that the foetal tissues are, indirectly, in dynamic equilibrium with this large volume of fluid. Its existence cannot be ignored when considering foetal gas and acid-base changes, even though we know little about it yet. It can contain quite large quantities of fixed acids (e.g., in conditions of partial asphyxia and acidaemia), although whether these are derived entirely from foetal urine remains to be seen.

The Placenta and Acid-Base Balance

For a short period of time, under asphyxial conditions, the foetus can obtain some energy for survival by anaerobic glycolysis, at the expense of converting relatively large amounts of carbohydrate into lactic acid. There is no good evidence that this is a normal continuing process *in utero*. If it were, large quantities of carbohydrate would need to be supplied and large quantities of lactic acid removed for the provision of a small proportion of the energy normally provided by aerobic metabolism. Measurements of umbilical arteriovenous differences show that there is normally no significant transfer of lactate from the foetus into or across the placenta.

However, during foetal metabolic acidaemia, as a result of partial asphyxia, the foetal lactate concentration is raised above that in the mother and lactate is transferred from the umbilical blood into the placenta (i.e., the concentration in umbilical venous blood becomes less than that in umbilical arterial; Barker and Britton, 1958). Isotopically labeled lactate is rapidly transferred into the placenta in foetal monkeys and the label (but not necessarily the lactate) appears in the mother's blood (Friedman, Gray, Grynfogel, Hutchinson, Kelly, and Plentl, 1960). It is uncertain how much lactate is metabolised during transit within the placenta and how much is transferred to maternal blood during partial foetal asphyxia, in part because of the difficulty of obtaining maternal placental blood uncontaminated with myometrial blood.

Most observations so far have been made in an unsteady state and are, therefore, difficult to interpret. There are indications that equilibration of foetal with maternal blood after an episode of foetal asphyxia is slow, occupying a period of 30–60 minutes in lambs (Dawes, Mott, and Shelley, 1959). But this may be due more to slow recovery of the foetus and slow transfer of hydrogen ions and lactate from the foetal tissues to the circulating blood than to delays in transplacental passage. Also during recovery some lactate is passed into the foetal urine and hence to the amniotic and allantoic sacs, which also may delay final equilibration.

We must consider the alternative situation in which maternal acidaemia (e.g., due to strong physical efforts during exercise or labour) may affect the acid-base status of the foetus. It has even been suggested that under such circumstances lactate ions might be transferred to the foetus. The CO_2 tensions in maternal and foetal blood certainly will equilibrate rapidly, but changes in Na^+, K^+, Ca^{++} or Cl^- are likely to be slower (Widdas, 1961; Dancis, 1965). For instance, when ammonium chloride was given by stomach tube to produce acidosis in pregnant rabbits, it was 3 hours before the foetal plasma chloride concentration reached the maternal level (Dancis, Worth, and Schneidau, 1957). In this respect, transplacental equilibration may be slow, but there is a dearth of evidence in other species. The rabbit is not a good subject for this type of experiment, because it is so susceptible to disturbances in its environment. The osmolarity of foetal plasma is normally equal to or slightly less than that of maternal plasma, and movement of water across the placenta is rapid. But the normal transplacental osmolar relation can be readily disturbed, e.g., by transient asphyxia which causes a rapid rise in plasma osmolarity (Meschia, Battaglia, and Barron, 1957). All these factors, the mechanisms which regulate transplacental transfer of base and chloride and osmolarity, combine to complicate the analysis. At the present moment we do not have enough information from which to construct a satisfactory model of the dynamics of transplacental acid-base exchange.

Conclusion

It is evident that the normal foetus *in utero* can make do with an arterial Po_2 which by adult standards is very low. This is possible mainly because of a high cardiac output which ensures a large blood flow both to the placenta and to the foetal tissues. It is true that in some individuals of some species toward the end of gestation the O_2 carrying capacity of foetal blood is high and the HbO_2 dissociation curve is shifted well to the left of the maternal; the blood can then carry more O_2 at the same Po_2. But this is not always so.

Adults of most species will not tolerate an arterial Po_2 as low as that which is normal in foetal life. There is no inherent biochemical difficulty in explaining this difference, since most isolated enzyme systems require the supply of O_2 at a partial pressure less than 1 mm Hg. But one must suppose either that foetal tissues have an unusually rich supply of capillaries or that the diffusion of O_2 is more rapid or utilization is less. Our knowledge here is incomplete. In the human foetal brain (Niemineva and Tervillä, 1953; Diemer and Henn, 1964), as in other organs and species, the capillary density increases rapidly with age (e.g., Table 29). Immature foetal tissues contain less solid matter and the concentration of mitochondrial protein increases with age (e.g., Samson, Balfour and Dahl, 1960). At an early embryonic age utilization of oxygen per Gm wet weight of tissue is presumably less than that later in foetal life, but no quantitative analysis of the changes in vascularization with O_2 consumption or tissue tension has been undertaken.

We need, for various purposes, some indication of what may be reasonable values of foetal Po_2,

TABLE 29.—CHANGES IN CAPILLARY DENSITY IN THE HUMAN
CEREBELLUM WITH AGE*

Conceptual Age (months)	Length of Capillary Net (cm/mm³)	Average Distance Between Capillaries (μ)	Number of Capillaries (per mm²)
3–4	0.2	707	2
5	2.6–3.9	196–160	26–39
6–7	5.3–8.7	137–107	53–85
10	12.8–16.7	92–77	128–167

* Niemineva and Tervilä, 1953.

P_{CO_2}, and pH. They are needed both for what may be called the natural history of foetal physiology, a description of normal values in different species at different periods of gestation, and for experimental purposes. We have too little information in either respect. All that I can presume to do is to give some indication of the limits of reasonable values encountered in the anaesthetised foetal sheep (under chloralose) and monkey (under pentobarbitone). In these species, in reasonable conditions, one may find a range of umbilical arterial P_{O_2} 20–35 mm Hg, P_{CO_2} 35–55, and pH 7.2–7.5, depending on maternal ventilation, and, presumably, placental perfusion. One may, and should, ask the question whether a particular or each particular experiment represents such a gross deviation from normality as to make the results inconclusive. There are some obvious tests which may be applied. If a physiological mechanism is repeatedly demonstrated to exist under a variety of experimental conditions, the conclusions stand. In each experiment it is easy to determine whether a foetus is deteriorating by serial measurements of arterial pH (anaesthetised foetal lambs usually deteriorate rapidly when umbilical arterial $P_{O_2} < 18$ mm Hg). But it does not follow that an animal is normal simply because it is not deteriorating. Its margin of safety may already be reduced and the mechanisms which readjust blood supply to the different organs and tissues may already be brought into play. Caution is needed in interpreting results. Much of our knowledge of foetal physiology is based on observations made under abnormal conditions, and although I hope and expect that most of them will stand the test of time, the past history of physiology has rightly been one of continual reappraisal.

REFERENCES

Acheson, G. H.; Dawes, G. S., and Mott, J. C.: Oxygen consumption and the arterial oxygen saturation in foetal and new-born lambs, J. Physiol. 135:623–642, 1957.

Alexander, D. P.; Nixon, D. A.; Widdas, W. F., and Wohlzogen, F. X.: Gestational variations in the composition of the foetal fluids and foetal urine in the sheep, J. Physiol. 140:1–13, 1958. Renal function in the sheep foetus, J. Physiol. 140:14–22, 1958.

Barcroft, J.: *Researches on Prenatal Life* (Oxford: Blackwell Scientific Publications, 1946).

Barcroft, J., and Elsden, S. R.: The oxygen consumption of the sheep foetus, J. Physiol. 105:25, P, 1946.

Barcroft, J.; Kennedy, J. A., and Mason, M. F.: The direct determination of the oxygen consumption of the foetal sheep, J. Physiol. 95:269–275, 1939.

Barcroft, J., and Torrens, D. S.: The output of the heart of the foetal sheep, J. Physiol. 105:22, P, 1946.

Barker, J. N., and Britton, H. G.: Lactate and pyruvate metabolism in the sheep, J. Physiol. 143:50, P, 1958.

Barron, D. H.: Some aspects of the transfer of oxygen across the syndesmochorial placenta of the sheep, Yale J. Biol. & Med. 24:169–190, 1951.

Barron, D. H.: A comparative study of the alkali reserve of normal, pregnant and fetal sheep, Yale J. Biol. & Med. 26:119–125, 1953.

Barron, D. H.; Meschia, G.; Cotter, J. R., and Breathnach, C. S.: The hemoglobin, oxygen, carbon dioxide and hydrogen ion concentrations in the umbilical bloods of sheep and goats as sampled via indwelling plastic catheters, Quart. J. Exper. Physiol. 50:185–195, 1965.

Born, G. V. R.; Dawes, G. S., and Mott, J. C.: Oxygen lack and autonomic nervous control of the foetal circulation in the lamb, J. Physiol. 134:149–166, 1956.

Dancis, J.: The role of the placenta in fetal survival, Pediat. Clin. North America 12:477–492, 1965.

Dancis, J.; Worth, M., and Schneidau, P. B.: Effect of electrolyte disturbances in the pregnant rabbit on the fetus, Am. J. Physiol. 188:535–537, 1957.

Dawes, G. S., and Mott, J. C.: The increase in oxygen consumption of the lamb after birth, J. Physiol. 146:295–315, 1959.

Dawes, G. S., and Mott, J. C.: Changes in O_2 distribution and consumption in foetal lambs with variations in umbilical blood flow, J. Physiol. 170:524–540, 1964.

Dawes, G. S.; Mott, J. C., and Shelley, H. J.: The importance of cardiac glycogen for the maintenance of life in foetal lambs and new-born animals during anoxia, J. Physiol. 146:516–538, 1959.

Dawes, G. S.; Mott, J. C., and Widdicombe, J. G.: The foetal circulation in the lamb, J. Physiol. 126:563–587, 1954.

Diemer, K., and Henn, R.: The capillary density in the frontal lobe of mature and premature infants, Biol. Neonat. 7:270–279, 1964.

Doring, G. K., and Loeschke, H. H.: Atmung und Säure-Basen-gleichgewicht in der Schwangerschaft, Arch. ges. Physiol. 249:437–451, 1947.

Edgar, D. G., and Ronaldson J. W.: Blood levels of progesterone in the ewe, J. Endocrinol. 16:378–384, 1958.

Finne, P. H.: Erythropoietin levels in cord blood as an indicator of intrauterine hypoxia, Acta paediat. 55:478–489, 1966.

Friedman, E. A.; Gray, M. J.; Grynfogel, M.; Hutchinson, D. L.; Kelly, W. T., and Plentl, A. A.: The distribution and metabolism of C[14] labeled lactic acid and bicarbonate in pregnant primates, J. Clin. Invest. 39:227–235, 1960.

Harris, H., and Warren, F. L.: Occurrence of electrophoretically distinct hemoglobins in ruminants, Biochem. J. 60:xxix, 1955.

Hasselbalch, K. A.: Ein Beitrag zur Respirationsphysiologie der Gravidität, Skand. Arch. Physiol. 27:1–12, 1912.

Huisman, T. H.: van Vliet, G., and Sebens, T.: Sheep haemoglobins, Nature. 182:171–174, 1958.

James, L. S.; Weisbrot, I. M.; Prince, C. E.; Holaday, D. A., and Apgar, V.: The acid-base status of human infants in relation to birth asphyxia and the onset of respiration, J. Pediat. 52:379–394, 1958.

Kaiser, I. H., and Cummings, J. N.: Hydrogen ion and hemoglobin concentration, carbon dioxide and oxygen content of blood of the pregnant ewe and fetal lamb, J. Appl. Physiol. 10:484–492, 1957.

Meschia, G.; Battaglia, F. C., and Barron, D. H.: A comparison of the freezing points of fetal and maternal plasmas of sheep and goat, Quart. J. Exper. Physiol.. 42:163–170, 1957.

Meschia, G.; Cotter, J. R.; Breathnach, C. S., and Barron, D. H.: The diffusibility of oxygen across the sheep placenta, Quart. J. Exper. Physiol. 50:466–480, 1965.

Metcalfe, J.; Meschia, G.; Hellegers, A.; Prystowsky, H.; Huckabee, W., and Barron, D. H.: Observations on the placental exchange of the respiratory gases in pregnant ewes at high altitude, Quart. J. Exper. Physiol. 47: 74–92, 1962.

Morishima, H. O.; Daniel, S. S.; Adamsons, K., and James, L. S.: Effects of positive pressure ventilation of the mother upon the acid-base state of the fetus, Am. J. Obst. & Gynec. 93:269–273, 1965.

Morishima, H. O.; Moya, F.; Bossers, A. C., and Daniel, S. S.: Adverse effects of maternal hypocapnea on the newborn guinea-pig, Am. J. Obst. & Gynec. 88:524–529, 1964.

Motoyama, E. K.; Rivard, G.; Acheson, F., and Cook, C. D.: Adverse effect of maternal hyperventilation on the foetus, Lancet 1:286–288, 1966.

Moya, F.; Morishima, H. O.; Shnider, S. M., and James, L. S.: Influence of maternal hyperventilation on the newborn infant, Am. J. Obst. & Gynec. 91:76–84, 1965.

Naughton, M. A.; Meschia, G.; Battaglia, F. C.; Hellegers, A.; Hagopian, H., and Barron, D. H.: Hemoglobin characteristics and the oxygen affinity of Dorset sheep, Quart. J. Exper. Physiol. 48:313–323, 1963.

Niemineva, K., and Tervilä, L.: On the capillary bed of the human fetal cerebellar hemispheres, Acta anat. 19: 204–209, 1953.

Perry, J. S., and Stanier, M. W.: The rate of flow of urine of foetal pigs, J. Physiol. 161:344–350, 1962.

Quilligan, E. J.: Amniotic fluid gas tensions, Am. J. Obst. & Gynec. 84:20–24, 1962.

Romney, S.; Kaneoka, T., and Gabel, P. V.: Perinatal oxygen environment, Am. J. Obst. & Gynec. 84:25–31, 1962.

Saling, E.: Die Blutgasverhältnisse und der Säure-Basen-Haushalt des Feten bei ungestörtem Geburtsablauf, Ztschr. Geburtsh. u. Gynäk. 161:262–292, 1964,a.

Saling, E.: Technik der endoskopischen Microblutentnahme am Feten, Geburtsh, u. Frauenh. 24:464–469, 1964,b.

Samson, F. E.; Balfour, W. M., and Dahl, N. A.: Rate of cerebral ATP metabolism in rats, Am. J. Physiol. 198: 213–216, 1960.

Sjöstedt, S.; Rooth, G., and Caligara, F.: The oxygen tension of the amniotic fluid, Am. J. Obst. & Gynec. 76:1226–1230, 1958.

Van Vliet, G., and Huisman, T. H. J.: Changes in the haemoglobin types of sheep as a response to anaemia, Biochem. J. 93:401–409, 1964.

Walker, J.: Oxygen Levels in Human Umbilical Cord Blood, in Anoxia of the new-born infant (Springfield, Ill.: Charles C Thomas, Publisher, 1953), pp. 158–170.

Widdas, W. F.: Transport mechanisms in the foetus, Brit. M. Bull. 17:107–111, 1961.

Wulf, H.: Der Gasaustausch in der reifen Plazenta des Menschen, Ztschr. Geburtsh. u. Gynäk. 158:117–134; 269–319, 1962.

10

Labour and Delivery

THERE IS GREAT VARIATION in the duration of gestation in animals of different species. On the whole, larger animals, which in a favourable environment live longer, usually have a longer gestational period (Fig. 54). The marsupials are an obvious exception. The young opossum are delivered from a mother weighing about 1 kg less than 13 days from conception. There must be a mechanism which regulates the duration of gestation and which starts labour at the time, appropriate to each species, when the young can survive in the environment provided for them. This is one of the interesting and only partly solved problems of biology. As the proceedings of a recent conference showed, the factors which normally determine the start of labour are still obscure (Marshall and Burnett, 1963). Yet there are a number of observations which suggest various ways of tackling the problem experimentally.

Increased uterine activity, seemingly identical with that observed in normal labour, often occurs in extra-uterine pregnancy at the expected time. Similarly, after removal of the foetus early in gestation, when the placenta is left *in situ,* it often remains there until about the normal time from conception in the rabbit (Hammond, 1914), rat (Kirsch, 1938), mouse, and rhesus monkey (van Wagenen and Newton, 1943). Hence change in uterine size with gestation is unlikely to be an important element in determining the onset of labour. Of course, in any hollow viscus lined with muscle,

MATERNAL
WEIGHT (g)

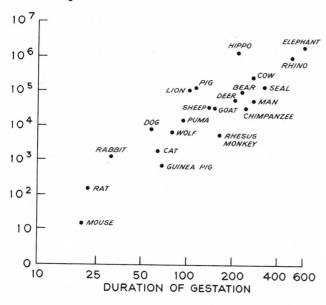

Fig. 54.—Normal duration of gestation (days) in relation to body size in different species.

a sudden reduction in volume will alter the relation between transmural pressure and circumferential tension, in such a way that if the muscle tension is maintained, transmural pressure will increase. (This is a consequence of the law of Laplace, $P = t/r$; where P is pressure, t is tension, and r, radius.) This may help to explain why removal or loss of amniotic fluid may precipitate labour. But normally labour starts without an apparent change in uterine volume.

There is much evidence to show that oxytocin is released during labour. For instance, in the pregnant woman the progressive increase in the frequency and intensity of uterine contractions is accompanied by similar changes in the smooth muscle of the mammary gland; both can be mimicked by oxytocin infusion (Caldeyro-Barcia, 1960). Measurements of oxytocin-like activity in the maternal blood of many species, including man, show that its concentration increases greatly, particularly toward the end of the first stage of labour. The concentration is greater in samples from the jugular vein than from peripheral veins. Yet labour can occur after maternal hypophysectomy in rhesus monkeys and in women (in which the operation was performed for treatment of advanced carcinoma of the breast), and in sheep after section of the pituitary stalk (Cowie, Daniel, Prichard, and Tindal, 1963). The descriptions given of labour in hypophysectomised women suggest that it is slower and less forceful. This would agree with the proposition that, while not essential to the initiation of normal labour, the release of oxytocin from the maternal pituitary accelerates the process and forces it to a successful conclusion. We then have to look further afield for the initial stimulus. If this is ultimately dependent for its effect on a change in reactivity of uterine muscle, perhaps through changing levels of progesterone, it is evidently not implemented through the maternal hypophysis. And although blood progesterone levels fall shortly before the end of pregnancy in man, in sheep progesterone was not detectable for 2–3 weeks before term. So in this species parturition does not at once follow its disappearance from the blood (Edgar and Ronaldson, 1958).

There are at least two ways in which a system might be devised in order to ensure that labour and delivery did not occur too early, at a time when the foetus was not viable. First, the growth of the foetus might, at some particular stage of development, initiate labour. For instance, the foetal lung, on whose maturity at birth survival is unquestionably

dependent, or the pituitary may have built into it the key factor whose production on maturation might permit labour to start. Secondly, some other tissue of foetal origin (e.g., in the placenta) might have a natural life which, adjusted to the species, would result after a fixed period of time in the release of the necessary stimulus. Evidence has already been given that something resembling labour may occur in the absence of the foetus, and lead to the expulsion of the placenta. This would favour the second type of hypothesis. But there are some observations which suggest that the foetus influences the outcome.

Holm (1958) described the effects of a recessive autosomal gene in dairy cows, whose presence in the foetus resulted in a prolongation of pregnancy 90 days past term in Holstein-Friesians. Among Guernseys, a similar effect was observed with prolongation of gestation from the normal 280 days to 510 days. In both instances, the foetuses remained alive, and the maternal mammary gland remained virginal in appearance. In the Holstein-Friesian the foetal pituitary gland was two-thirds of the normal size at term; the Guernsey invariably had a foetus with cranial anomalies ranging from moderate hydrocephalus to anencephalus with absence of anterior pituitary tissue, and often of posterior pituitary tissue also. Attempts to induce labour by oxytocin infusion were unsuccessful. In cattle, the progesterone concentration in peripheral blood normally declines 10 days to 2 weeks before term (Short, 1958), but did not decline in Holstein-Friesians or Guernseys with prolonged gestation. In sheep also there is a syndrome of prolonged gestation associated with grazing on Veratrum californicum in the high altitude ranges of Idaho (Binns, Thacker, James, and Huffman, 1959). Genetic factors were discounted, and it was proposed that nutritional or toxic factors had caused the associated aplasia of the foetal pituitary gland. These observations strongly suggest that in cattle and sheep the foetal pituitary influences the duration of gestation; Holm (in Marshall and Burnett, 1963) was inclined to emphasize the role which the foetal adrenals might play in this. In the previous work by Jost and others on the effects of foetal decapitation in utero, the foetuses always appear to have been delivered by caesarean section or examined postmortem before natural term, so that the effect of foetal hypophysectomy on the initiation of labour has not been systematically examined.

We must still, for the moment, regard the problem of what initiates labour as uncertain. There is a good deal of circumstantial evidence that delivery can be postponed or even that labour may be temporarily arrested after it has begun. Most animals (e.g., mice, rabbits, sheep, rhesus monkeys) usually deliver during the hours of darkness, natural or artificial, as does man. Of 63 spontaneous vaginal deliveries in rhesus monkeys in the Perinatal Physiology Colony in San Juan, Puerto Rico (during a 3-year period, and in which the times were recorded), only 8 took place between 8 a.m. (when the normal laboratory staff came on duty) and 5 p.m. (when they left). It is a common experience with everyone who has worked with animals that the overt presence of an observer delays delivery; this occurs only too often shortly after he has left the room, perhaps for only a few minutes. We might also wonder how it is that a woman who has become exhausted, and in whom the progress of labour appears to have ceased, may rapidly complete delivery after a period of sleep and rest. Is there a common mechanism which explains both phenomena? Does apprehension, anxiety, or exhaustion prevent liberation of the oxytocin which is needed to bring labour to delivery? Does it happen in hypophysectomised animals? Or is it dependent exclusively on the sympathetic nervous system?

The Effects of Labour and Delivery upon the Foetus

In man, the effects of labour and delivery upon the foetus are now fairly well documented. Saling (1964) has shown during normal human labour that there is a progressive fall in scalp blood Po_2 and O_2 content, with a rise in Pco_2 and pH (Table 30). The blood samples obtained are arterialized but may contain some venous blood and tissue fluid. The methods which have to be used are not strictly anaerobic, and there may have been a small gas exchange with the air, especially of CO_2. However, great care has obviously been taken in collection and analysis, and on delivery the values are intermediate between those of umbilical arterial and venous samples (nearer to the former than the latter), as they should be. This is an important contribution, for it demonstrates clearly the dangers, reiterated by many during the past 10 years, of relying on cord blood samples on delivery as a guide to the intra-uterine environment.

The fall in the O_2 content of foetal blood during normal labour is probably mainly the result of a decrease in maternal placental flow during uterine contractions. Saling (1964) noted that the O_2 saturation of scalp blood varied with uterine activity when labour was well established. Surprisingly, he found that the saturation was greater during a contraction than during relaxation. In mature foetal monkeys *in utero,* blood samples taken from a femoral artery at or just after the peak of a contraction (of up to 35 mm Hg) consistently contained less O_2 than samples withdrawn during a quiescent period between contractions (Dawes, Jacobson, Mott, and Shelley, 1960). The difference may be due to the effect of changes in cephalic pressure on scalp samples. The monkey observations are interesting because the mean maternal arterial pressure is about 120 mm Hg; so it seems likely that a reduction in maternal placental flow during uterine contractions must be mainly the result of restriction of venous outflow, thereby reducing the net pressure gradient driving maternal blood through the placenta. There are other factors which may contribute to the changes in foetal blood during normal labour without general anaesthesia, including the effects of maternal hyperventilation and acidaemia and, possibly, the indirect effects of painful sensations and anxiety. It is interesting and reassuring that the gross results of all these are usually as small as Table 30 indicates.

The abnormal complications of labour may take many forms, and I am certainly not competent nor would I wish to discuss all these in detail. Yet, so far as the foetus is concerned, there are some distinctions which should be made. First, there are complications in which the primary defect is a deficiency of maternal O_2 supply or blood flow to the uterus. This may occur as a result of maternal hypoxaemia when it can usually be corrected quickly. Maternal inhalation of nitrous oxide mixed with less than 21% O_2 is a special case which is wholly inexcusable. A decrease in maternal placental flow may be remediable (as in maternal hypotension associated with a supine position or in haemorrhagic shock) or not (as in premature separation of the placenta). Caldeyro-Barcia (1963) has reported that in some women in a supine (but not in a lateral)

TABLE 30.—MEAN CHANGES IN SCALP BLOOD VALUES DURING NORMAL HUMAN LABOUR (SALING, 1964)

	AT ONSET OF LABOUR	AT END OF LABOUR
O_2 saturation (%)	42	30
Po_2 (mm Hg)	20	17
Pco_2 (mm Hg)	44	51
pH	7.31	7.28

position, strong uterine contractions are associated with twisting or compression of the descending aorta to such an extent as to obliterate the femoral pulse and to reduce uterine perfusion as shown by angiography. The result in the foetus of any one of these abnormalities is to cause a fall in umbilical venous and, hence, in foetal arterial O_2 content. Foetal arterial pressure, heart rate, and umbilical blood flow may rise or fall; the result will depend on the duration and extent of foetal hypoxaemia.

Secondly, labour may affect the foetus by compression of the umbilical cord around the neck or limbs, against the rim of the pelvis, or by prolapse. The pressure in the umbilical vein is much less than that in the umbilical arteries, so the immediate effect of cord compression is to reduce umbilical flow by partial or complete occlusion of the vein. In foetal lambs this causes little immediate change in arterial pressure; transfer of some blood from the foetus to the cord and placenta; a rise in heart rate if the occlusion is incomplete or brief, and a fall if it is complete and prolonged; little change in the O_2 content of umbilical venous blood, but a fall in foetal O_2 consumption, and the development of metabolic acidaemia if occlusion is prolonged or repeated. Both reduction in maternal O_2 supply to the placenta and cord compression ultimately cause foetal hypoxaemia and acidaemia, but they achieve this in different ways. Unfortunately, from the obstetrician's point of view, these are rarely clearly distinguishable.

Changes in Foetal Heart Rate

The effect of labour in causing foetal asphyxia has, until the development of blood sampling from the presenting scalp, had to be judged almost entirely from changes in foetal heart rate and the absence or presence of meconium. In all but the few hospitals in the major cities of the world where facilities for scalp sampling and analysis are available in the delivery room, these traditional methods are still all that is available.

In foetal lambs, even at a relatively early gestational age (0.6 of term) the primary effect of mild hypoxaemia or partial asphyxia is to cause an increase of heart rate (Born, Dawes, and Mott, 1956). Sympathetic tone to the heart is developed early in gestation, and the cardioacceleration is reflex (rather than due to direct hypoxic release of noradrenaline into the circulation from the adrenals) because it is blocked by hexamethonium. Even on complete cord occlusion, and hence complete asphyxia, this primary cardioacceleration is

often perceptible. If the hypoxaemia or asphyxia is mild and transient, when it is relieved foetal heart rate gradually returns to its initial value over a period of 5–15 minutes. The recovery is more prolonged the greater the duration of partial asphyxia. It is strange to have to record that the physiological reasons for the reflex tachycardia during foetal hypoxaemia have not been systematically studied. It is most likely to be due to a central effect on the medullary centres.

With progressively increasing hypoxaemia or asphyxia the heart rate ultimately begins to slow, but this slowing does not become apparent until the carotid arterial O_2 saturation is reduced, on the average, to about 15% (the normal value is more than 50%), i.e., not until the asphyxia is profound and when foetal O_2 consumption has already begun to decline. As with the tachycardia, recovery is slow largely because the two sides of the heart work in parallel rather than in series, and, therefore, equilibration of blood gas contents and tensions in the foetal circulation is gradual. The causes of the bradycardia are complex. As in adults, there may be reflex cardiac slowing by excitation of the systemic arterial chemoreceptors of the aortic and carotid bodies and, if the arterial pressure rises, as a result of the depressor reflex. Bauer (1938, 1939), using newborn rabbits, and Barcroft (1946), using foetal sheep, showed that the immediate fall in heart rate on abrupt anoxia or asphyxia was reflex, as its appearance was delayed by giving atropine or by bilateral section of the cervical vagosympathetic trunks. (The latter cuts the afferent nerves from the aortic bodies and other cardiopulmonary sensory receptors, as well as the efferent vagal nerves to the heart.) There is, in addition, a direct effect of hypoxaemia and hypercapnia on cardiac muscle, which causes slowing in foetal lambs even when autonomic ganglionic transmission is blocked by hexamethonium.

A short period of acute severe asphyxia, which has caused a fall in heart rate, is always succeeded by a "rebound" tachycardia. The causes of this are complex because they involve not only a reflex increase in heart rate, but also the possibility of a direct effect of hypoxia in releasing catecholamines from the adrenals. Early in gestation hypoxia appears to cause release of (principally) noradrenaline by a direct action; this is replaced by a reflex mechanism before term in the lamb, but not in the calf (Comline and Silver, 1966). For those who seek a teleological explanation of every biological variant, this seems to be a singularly pointless instance of species specificity.

In the human infant, Caldeyro-Barcia and his colleagues (1966) have made a thorough study of the temporal course of the heart rate changes during labour. There is a small semantic problem. Caldeyro-Barcia takes the view that the word bradycardia implies a continued reduction of heart rate over a prolonged period of time. Transient falls in heart rate, in his nomenclature, are, therefore described as dips (in heart rate). In English medical usage and to physiologists, the word bradycardia means no more than slowing of the heart, which may be either transient or prolonged, and this distinction, therefore, seems unnecessary.

It now seems generally agreed that the first effect of abnormal human labour, resulting in the delivery of a depressed infant (Apgar score 6 or less), is to cause a persistent rise in the basal level of foetal heart rate (mean 143 ± 2 (S.E.) beats/min normally) to above 155 beats/min. In 15 abnormal labours the basal rate rose to 165 ± 3 beats/min (Caldeyro-Barcia et al., 1966). Small, brief fluctuations of heart rate, either upward or downward, seemed to be of little prognostic significance.

Two types of transient falls of heart rate which do have some significance have been distinguished. Type 1 (Fig. 55) is brief and is closely associated in time with a uterine contraction; the delay from the peak intra-uterine pressure to the nadir (maximal point of fall) of heart rate is 3.15 ± 7.5 (S.D.) seconds. There was no significant difference in Type 1 incidence in infants who on delivery were vigorous or depressed. The frequency of Type 1 falls in heart rate increased with progressive cervical dilatation. The phenomenon was attributed to compression of the head which when effected experimentally *in utero* causes a transient fall in heart rate of similar character (Méndez-Bauer et al., 1963).

In Type 2 the fall in heart rate is of slower onset and longer duration (Fig. 55). The delay from peak intra-uterine pressure to the nadir of heart rate is 41 ± 23 (S.D.) seconds. The incidence was significantly greater in infants who were depressed on delivery. It was also greater when the cord was around the neck and in toxaemia of pregnancy, maternal hypoxaemia or hypotension, and after strong bearing-down efforts or uterine contractions, all of which are often associated with partial foetal asphyxia. The conclusion that this type of fall in heart rate is associated with (and perhaps due to) foetal hypoxaemia was confirmed by measurements on scalp blood samples (Caldeyro-Barcia et al., 1966). But there is an odd fact about the values recorded. It was concluded that the critical level below which a fall in heart rate of this type (2) was

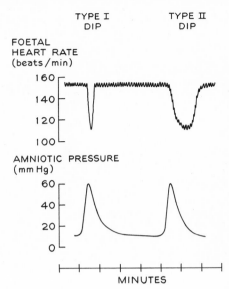

Fig. 55.—Illustration of the two types of fall in heart rate observed during labour. (After Caldeyro-Barcia et al., 1966.)

expected "corresponded approximately to a Po_2 of 20 mm Hg (oxygen saturation 30% for pH 7.20) in the capillary blood from the foetal scalp." This value for Po_2 is identical with that found by Saling at the onset of labour, though the values for O_2 saturation and pH differ (Table 30). If the analytical methods were identical this would mean that all of Saling's babies would have falls of heart rate of this type during normal labour, when the mean Po_2 falls to 17 mm Hg. They obviously didn't. The most likely explanation of the discrepancy is a difference in analytical methods or standards. It is less likely to be due to a difference between the scalp blood of babies in Berlin and Montevideo. The point is of some importance in drawing attention to the variation to be expected in Po_2 measurements, which even with the same operator rarely have a reproducibility better than ± 1.5 mm Hg over the range under discussion. There is not much point in arguing about the possible physiological significance of variations in Po_2 of a few mm Hg, observed in different laboratories, unless identical standards and methods have been used in calibration.

In clinical practice, of course, many variations on these patterns of heart rate changes occur, and have been well described by Caldeyro-Barcia et al. (1966). A combination of persistent elevation of basal heart rate with an increasing incidence of brief falls of Type 2 is of sinister significance. If the cause of asphyxia is not relieved, ultimately the falls in heart rate of Type 2 become prolonged and overlap to produce a persistent decrease.

The administration of a small dose of atropine (0.03–0.10 mg/kg foetus) into the human foetal buttock *in utero* during labour (Méndez-Bauer *et al.*, 1963) caused a rise in basal foetal heart rate of 10–35 beats/min, lasting for about 2 hours, and almost complete elimination of falls in heart rate of Type 1 or on manual compression of the foetal head or fontanelles. Falls in heart rate of Type 2 were reduced in 60–70%. The results are consistent with the attribution of transient falls in heart rate of Type 1 to head compression, and of Type 2 to foetal hypoxaemia. The latter agrees well with the results of the animal experiments already described.

The effects upon the capacity of the foetus to survive labour, delivery, or asphyxia of drugs (such as atropine and hexamethonium) which interfere with the normal autonomic regulation of the foetal circulation have not been studied directly in experimental animals. Maternal administration of reserpine, which depletes maternal and foetal catecholamine stores and has other actions as well, caused an increase in the stillbirth and neonatal mortality rates of guinea pigs (Towell *et al.*, 1965). But this is not comparable to administration of a small dose of atropine to the foetus, which has not been shown to do any harm. It would not be expected to do any good either. The purpose of raising the question at all is to advocate caution in the use of drugs, given to mother or foetus, which disturb the autonomic nervous system, because the normal response of the foetal circulation to asphyxia depends in part on this. For instance, if the foetal heart rate rises too high, cardiac filling and hence cardiac output will be impaired. I have occasionally seen signs suggestive of this in mature foetal lambs during infusions of catecholamines and in other circumstances. I would not discount the possibility that there might be drugs with a beneficial action to the foetus in labour, but there is as yet no clear physiological prescription for this.

Maternal Administration of 100% O_2

The possible beneficial effects of maternal administration of 100% O_2, in place of room air, during abnormal labour in which evidence of foetal asphyxia has developed, has often been debated. There are two views on this, the first that the beneficial effects, if any, are so marginal as to be worth-less, and the second that any benefit, however small, is worthwhile (e.g., while preparations are made for caesarean section). Perhaps the results of O_2 administration have been disappointing to those who supposed that this might cause a large change in the foetus. As already discussed (Chapter 3), the effect can only be expected to be small, but not negligible (see Fig. 16, p. 36).

Towell (1966) has recently taken a rather pessimistic view of the matter, and quoted observations on 2 monkeys in which (for reasons unknown) raising the maternal arterial Po_2 had only a little effect on foetal arterial Po_2. This anecdotal report has to be set against the volume of evidence in sheep, in which maternal inhalation of O_2 in place of air has unquestionably and repeatedly caused a moderate increase in umbilical venous and arterial O_2 saturation and Po_2 (e.g., Born, Dawes, Mott, and Rennick, 1956; Dawes and Mott, 1962; Comline, Silver, and Silver, 1965; Purves and Biscoe, 1966). Towell suggests that the effects of O_2 administration may be less certain "when foetal distress is due to interference with gaseous exchange across the placenta." But it is difficult to understand her reasoning. Whether this interference occurs (as she suggests) as a result of a reduction in maternal placental blood flow, in the size of the gas exchange area (by placental separation or infarction), or in umbilical flow (by cord compression), an increase in the O_2 content and Po_2 of maternal arterial blood should cause an increase in umbilical venous O_2 content unless the extra O_2 is removed by the placenta. This is a matter which could readily be put to experimental test. In doing so, it is important to recognize that moderate hypoxaemia may reduce foetal O_2 uptake; if O_2 uptake increases as a result of giving the mother O_2 to breathe, and umbilical flow does not change, there should be a rise in umbilical venous O_2 content, but there may be little change in umbilical arterial Po_2.

So far as clinical evidence is concerned, James (1958) found that administration of O_2 to mothers did not appreciably alter the O_2 saturation in cord blood obtained after delivery. But the natural variation in values, due to delivery, is large compared with the effect to be anticipated. Others have come to the conclusion that maternal O_2 administration increased the O_2 content of cord blood on delivery (Prystowsky, 1959; Quilligan *et al.*, 1960; Vasicka *et al.*, 1960). What is more relevant is the observation by Caldeyro-Barcia *et al.* (1966) that administration of O_2 reduced or abolished the brief falls in heart rate (of Type 2) observed in abnormal labour. This is fairly direct evidence of a beneficial effect, and to my mind sufficient to justify administration of O_2 in practice.

While we are on the point, it is worthwhile to make a rough guess at how much extra O_2 might usefully be required or provided. The total minimal O_2 consumption (in a neutral thermal environment) of a newborn human infant is about 14 ml/min. During foetal hypoxaemia this is reduced by redistribution of the cardiac output to supply the heart and brain in preference to other organs. We do not know the normal apportionment of O_2 consumption to the various organs, although the brain (13% of body weight) might take a share greater than its proportionate weight. Still less do we know the minimal O_2 consumption of the foetus needed to avoid brain damage in conditions of partial asphyxia maintained, say, for an hour. It may well be much less than the normal O_2 uptake of a newborn infant at rest. We also must take into account the fact that even during abnormal labour with severe slowing of the foetal heart, it is unlikely that foetal O_2 supply is wholly arrested. So, taking all these arguments into consideration, even 10% of normal O_2 consumption, that is to say, 1.4 ml/min, might prove valuable. Theoretically, this could be provided by raising maternal arterial Po_2 to 700 mm Hg even if maternal placental blood flow were reduced to 100 ml/min. This is the most favourable view.

Other Effects of Labour and Delivery

Labour and delivery may sometimes have other effects upon the foetus. The principal result of abnormal labour is to cause successive brief episodes of partial asphyxia, and we must take into account not only the immediate but also the cumulative effects. Very little attention has been given to this experimentally, and for the most part we can only guess at the result. Partial asphyxia causes mobilization of reserves of glycogen and free fatty acids which are not readily replaced. In newborn rats it takes a long while to recover after a period of anoxia which is just short of fatal. It is 3–4 hours before the cardiac glycogen concentration returns to normal and the rat recoups its usual ability to endure a succeeding period of anoxia (Stafford and Weatherall, 1960).

The mother becomes tired after several hours of labour. It is a condition which is hard to define in strict physiological and biochemical terms. We have no evidence to prove that maternal exhaustion has an effect on the foetus, but it would be hardly surprising. The foetus also is squeezed intermittently to an extent to which it has not been accustomed. In the human, the head, and presumably its contents, is moulded into a new and unnatural shape. But how these processes affect the physiology of the foetus is not known, other than that normal reactions are so distorted for the first 48 hours after delivery that neurological examination for the purpose of determining gestational age is of little value until later. One may guess that the results are similar to the effect of prolonged acute experiments on foetuses *in vivo*, a gradual and insidious deterioration, with a fall of arterial pressure so slow as to be imperceptible over a period of 10–15 minutes. In clinical terms, prolonged labour may result in the birth of a "flat" baby, one which, while not unresponsive to stimuli, lies quiet and motionless for many hours, no different from normal so far as its blood constituents have been measured, but so different in behaviour as to raise the suspicion that it is exhausted. It is not surprising that if labour exceeds 16 hours or the second stage more than half an hour, the Apgar score is less on delivery, particularly in primiparae (e.g., Krokfors, Wist, and Hirvensalo, 1963).

References

Barcroft, J.: *Researches on Prenatal Life* (Oxford: Blackwell Scientific Publications, 1946).

Bauer, D. J.: The effect of asphyxia upon the heart rate of rabbits at different ages, J. Physiol. 93:90–103, 1938.

Bauer, D. J.: Vagal reflexes appearing in asphyxia in rabbits at different ages, J. Physiol. 95:187–202, 1939.

Binns, W.; Thacker, E. J.; James, L. F., and Huffman, W. T.: A congenital cyclopian-type malformation in lambs, J. Am. Vet. M. A. 134:180–183, 1959.

Born, G. V. R.; Dawes, G. S., and Mott, J. C.: Oxygen lack and autonomic nervous control of the foetal circulation in the lamb, J. Physiol. 134:149–166, 1956.

Born, G. V. R.; Dawes, G. S.; Mott, J. C., and Rennick, B. R.: The constriction of the ductus arteriosus caused by oxygen and by asphyxia in newborn lambs, J. Physiol., 132:304–342, 1956.

Caldeyro-Barcia, R.: Factors controlling the actions of the pregnant human uterus, in Knowlessar, M. (ed.): *Physiology of Prematurity, Transactions of the Fifth Conference* (New York: Josiah Macy, Jr., Foundation, 1960), pp. 11–117.

Caldeyro-Barcia, R.: In Oliver, T. K. (ed.): *Neonatal Respiratory Adaptation* (Washington, D.C.: U.S. Public Health Service Publication No. 1432, 1963).

Caldeyro-Barcia, R.; Méndez-Bauer, C.; Poseiro, J. J.; Escarcena, L. A.; Posé, S. V.; Bieniarz, J.; Arnt, I.; Gulin, L., and Althabe, O.: Control of human fetal heart rate during labor, in Cassels, D. E. (ed.): *The Heart and Circulation in the Newborn and Infant* (New York: Grune & Stratton, Inc., 1966), pp. 7–36.

Comline, R. S., and Silver, M.: Development of activity in the adrenal medulla of the foetus and new-born animal, Brit. M. Bull. 22:16–20, 1966.

Comline, R. S.; Silver, I. A., and Silver, M.: Factors responsible for the stimulation of the adrenal medulla during asphyxia in the foetal lamb, J. Physiol. 178: 211–238, 1965.

Cowie, A. T.; Daniel, P. M.; Prichard, M. M. L., and Tindal, J. S.: Hypophysectomy in pregnant goats, and section of the pituitary stalk in pregnant goats and sheep, J. Endocrinol. 28:93–102, 1963.

Dawes, G. S.; Jacobson, H. N.; Mott, J. C., and Shelley, H. J.: Some observations in foetal and new-born rhesus monkeys, J. Physiol. 152:271–298, 1960.

Dawes, G. S., and Mott, J. C.: The vascular tone of the foetal lung, J. Physiol. 164:465–477, 1962.

Edgar, D. G., and Ronaldson, J. W.: Blood levels of progesterone in the ewe, J. Endocrinol. 16:378–384, 1958.

Hammond, J.: On some factors controlling fertility in domestic animals, J. Agric. Sc. 6:263–277, 1914.

Holm, L. W.: Genetic factors in prolonged gestation in Holstein-Friesian cattle, in Villee, C. A. (ed.): *Gestation, Transactions of the Fifth Conference* (New York: Josiah Macy, Jr., Foundation, 1958), pp. 131–162.

James, L. S.: Biochemical Aspects of Asphyxia, in *Adaptation to Extra-Uterine Life,* 31st Ross Conference on Pediatric Research (Columbus, Ohio: Ross Laboratories, 1958.

Kirsch, R. E.: A study on the control of length of gestation in the rat with notes on maintenance and termination of gestation, Am. J. Physiol. 122:86–93, 1938.

Krokfors, E.; Wist, A., and Hirvensalo, M.: Effect of duration of labour, age and parity on the Apgar score of the newborn infant, Ann. chir. et Gynaec. Fenniae Suppl. 118:1–14, 1963.

Marshall, J. M., and Burnett, W. M. (ed.): *Initiation of Labor* (Washington, D.C.: U.S. Public Health Service Publication No. 1390, 1963).

Méndez-Bauer, C.; Poseiro, J. J.; Arellano-Hernández, Q.; Zambrana, M. A., and Caldeyro-Barcia, R.: Effects of atropine on the heart rate of the human fetus during labor, Am. J. Obst. & Gynec. 85:1033–1053, 1963.

Prystowsky, H.: Fetal blood studies. XI. The effect of prophylactic oxygen on the oxygen pressure gradient between the maternal and fetal bloods of the human in normal and abnormal pregnancy, Am. J. Obst. & Gynec. 78:483–488, 1959.

Purves, M. J., and Biscoe, T. J.: Development of chemoreceptor activity, Brit. M. Bull. 22:56–60, 1966.

Quilligan, E. J.; Vasicka, A.; Aznar, R.; Lipsitz, P. J.; Moore, T., and Bloor, B. M.: Partial pressure of oxygen in the intervillous space and the umbilical vessels, Am. J. Obst. & Gynec. 79:1048–1052, 1960.

Saling, E.: Die Blutgasverhältnisse und der Säure-Basen-Haushalt des Feten bei ungestörtem Geburtsablauf, Ztschr. Geburtsh. u. Gynäk. 161:262–292, 1964.

Short, R. V.: Progesterone in blood. II. Progesterone in the peripheral blood of pregnant cows, J. Endocrinol. 16:426–428, 1958.

Stafford, A., and Weatherall, J. A. C.: The survival of young rats in nitrogen, J. Physiol. 153:457–472, 1960.

Towell, M. E.: The influence of labor on the fetus and newborn, Pediat. Clin. North America 13:575–598, 1966.

Towell, M. E.; Hyman, A. I.; James, L. S.; Steinsland, O. S.; Gerst, E. S., and Adamsons, K.: Reserpine administration during pregnancy, Am. J. Obst. & Gynec. 92:711–716, 1965.

van Wagenen, G., and Newton, W. H.: Pregnancy in the monkey after removal of the fetus, Surg. Gynec. & Obst. 77:539–543, 1943.

Vasicka, A.; Quilligan, E. J.; Aznar, R.; Lipsitz, P. J., and Bloor, B. M.: Oxygen tension in maternal and fetal blood, amniotic fluid, and cerebrospinal blood of the mother and baby, Am. J. Obst. & Gynec. 79:1041–1047, 1960.

11

The Establishment of Pulmonary Respiration

Surface Active Material

BEFORE EFFECTIVE VENTILATION can be established after birth the lung must be developed to a stage such that the alveoli can be inflated and the forces which oppose this must be overcome.

At an early stage of gestation the alveoli are solid and the lung is inexpansible. For instance, in lambs at 94–104 days gestation, rhythmic positive-pressure ventilation causes the appearance, as seen from the outside, of silvery tubes within the lung; these are bronchi made visible by the gas within them and not concealed from view by superficial alveoli. After ventilation, for a while the superficial alveoli begin to expand in patches, raised from the surface of the lung. Often, after ventilation for 10–20 minutes, although the peak inflation pressure is less than that used initially, emphysematous bullae develop over these patches and expand until they rupture. In lambs of 110–120 days gestation, the silvery appearance of the bronchioles is not seen on beginning ventilation (using the same inflation pressures), the surface of the lungs is more even, and the superficial alveoli fill well but patchily. With increasing age toward term there is little difference in the external appearance of the lungs during inflation, but the tidal air per unit body weight (or lung weight) increases with age in lambs ventilated at the same pressure (Fig. 56). There is no difference in the result whether the chest is open (●) or intact (○). When oxygen is used for ventilation, the uptake is adequate to maintain or to increase arterial O_2 saturation, after tying the umbilical cord, from 110–115 days onward.

Even at term, the peak intratracheal pressure required to expand the lung for the first time is high, often more than 30 mm Hg. There is also another change in the lung with age. At 110–120 days gestation, the lungs collapse completely on expiration, whereas near term the alveoli remain distended after the first inflation. To understand these phenomena we have to consider the factors which determine alveolar surface tension. More than 35 years ago, it was found that when excised adult dogs' lungs, which had been rendered airless,

Fig. 56.—Tidal air at peak positive inflating pressure of 30 mm Hg in foetal lambs of different gestational ages, with closed (○) or open (●) chests, 10–60 minutes after beginning ventilation. (From the data of Born, Dawes, and Mott, 1955.)

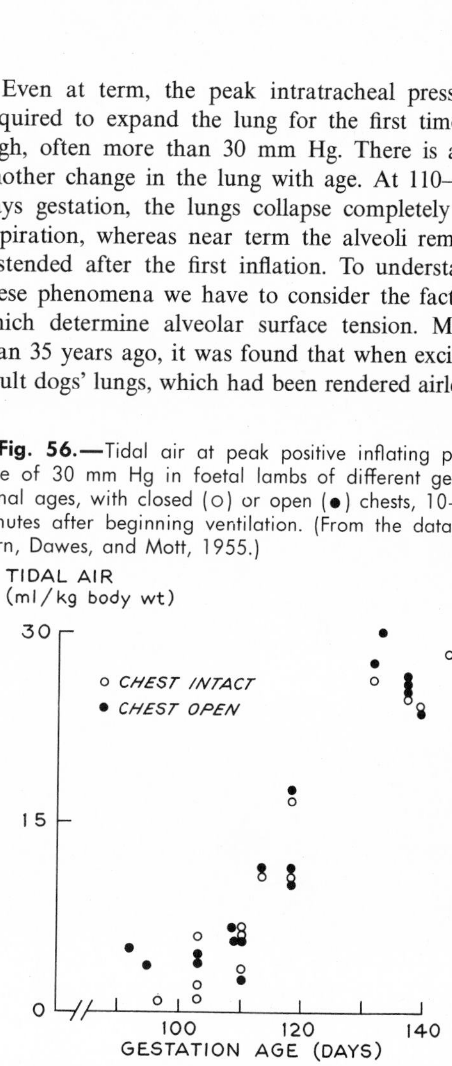

125

were distended with saline, the pressure required was considerably less than that required for distention with air. In the latter case, there is an air-liquid interface in the alveoli, and it was concluded that more than two-thirds of the elastic recoil of the lungs was due to surface tension forces (von Neergaard, 1929). In these circumstances, then, surface tension forces are high. The remarkable implications of this observation were not appreciated at the time.

In 1954, Radford pointed out that, having regard to the calculated internal surface area of the lungs and the known surface tensions of body fluids, the surface tension forces should be sufficient to cause total collapse of the lungs. During the next two years, Pattle began to study the effect of antifoaming agents in the treatment of pulmonary oedema, and noticed that small bubbles found in the airways during acute lung oedema, or expressed from excised lungs, did not collapse. They formed a stable foam, which implied that their surface tension must be very low indeed (Pattle 1958, 1963). As Mead (1961) has remarked in his admirable and lucid review of the subject, this is a classic example of a result of far broader significance than that to be expected from the original question asked. It demonstrated that there must be some substance within the lungs with remarkable surface-active properties. There was an apparent paradox, for surface tension had been shown to be high in the lungs during distention but was negligible in the small bubbles expressed from the lungs. The explanation of this paradox was given by Clements, Brown, and Johnson (1958). They proposed that there might be within the alveoli an internal lining layer whose surface tension altered with changes in surface area, a property which was known to be possessed by thin monomolecular films of complex molecules. When lung washings were spread on a trough and the surface area was gradually reduced there was a fall in surface tension as the film was compressed and the molecules packed more tightly. And within a short while evidence was published to justify the conclusion that some surface-active material was produced in the normal adult or mature newborn lung, but which was absent from the lungs of human infants dying from the respiratory distress syndrome (hyaline membrane disease; Avery and Mead, 1959). This material is a complex of protein and lipids, particularly dipalmitoyl lecithin. The lipid fraction is present in normal lungs in a concentration of about 5 mg/Gm, about one-eighth of the total lung lipids (Clements, 1963).

The production of surface-active material is related to the pulmonary alveolar cells, called pneumonocytes by Macklin (1954), who suggested that they discharged granules which somehow controlled alveolar surface tension. In the adult the alveolar cells contain osmiophilic lamellar inclusion bodies such as normally appear in the cells of no other tissues, and which may be discharged into the alveolar spaces (Campiche, 1960; Sorokin, 1963). It is probable that these bodies are the source of the material (Klaus, Reiss, Tooley, Piel, and Clements, 1962). Pattle (1961) argued, from observations in rats, mice, and guinea pigs, that the first appearance of surfactant was related to the time at which the cuboidal epithelium disappeared from the alveoli. Yet in species with a longer gestational age (sheep, man) there is an interval of some weeks between these two events (Howatt et al., 1965; Reynolds and Strang, 1966). In the foetal lamb, the lamellar inclusion bodies appear in alveolar cells about 5 days before surface-active material is first detected. Even this small apparent discrepancy is explicable since, though its presence may be detected qualitatively, it cannot yet be measured quantitatively. Howatt et al. (1965) have also shown that the upper parts of the lung, in lambs, develop their surface-active properties earlier than the lower parts, a difference which may be related to the larger number of bronchial subdivisions which must be completed in the lower parts before development of the terminal air spaces. In human infants, the material is present from the 23rd week of gestation onward, and in increasing amounts until term. Its mere presence does not imply that sufficient is available to form an adequate lining layer and there is inadequate information about its rate of turnover. It is probably normally available in sufficient quantity from the 30th week onward, although enough must be present in a proportion of infants even earlier.

The importance of surface-active material in the lung at birth has been neatly illustrated by Reynolds and Strang (1966). Figure 57, a shows pressure-volume curves obtained on inflating the lungs of a mature foetal lamb within a week of full term. The continuous line shows that a pressure of 18 cm H_2O (the opening pressure) was required before any significant volume of air entered the lung; full inflation was achieved at about 40 cm H_2O. On deflation about a quarter of the maximum lung volume was retained. No opening pressure was needed for the second breath (interrupted line), and the lung could then be inflated to three-quarters of its full volume with a pressure of only about 15 cm

PERCENTAGE OF
LUNG VOLUMES

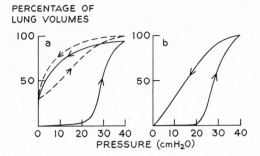

PERCENTAGE OF
SURFACE AREA

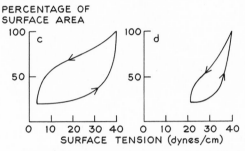

SURFACE TENSION (dynes/cm)

140 DAYS' GESTATION   122 DAYS' GESTATION

Fig. 57.—Observations on a mature foetal lamb (140 days gestation, **a**) to show the pressure-volume curves of the first (*solid line*) and subsequent (*interrupted line*) pulmonary inflations. In an immature lamb (122 days gestation, **b**) the effects of subsequent inflations superimpose on that of the first. The lower figures **(c, d)** show the corresponding surface tension-area diagrams of lung extracts spread as a film on the surface of liquid in a trough. During compression of the film, the surface tension falls much more in the extract from the mature lung, indicating the presence of surface active material. (From Reynolds and Strang, 1966.)

H_2O. Figure 57, *b* shows the pressure-volume curve of an immature foetal lamb of about 122 days gestation. The inflation curve was similar to that at 140 days gestation, but on deflation the lung collapsed completely. On a second inflation the lungs would need to be opened again, and the opening pressure would be as great as that for the first breath. This would greatly increase the work of breathing.

The surface tension-area curves of lung extracts from these 2 lambs are shown in Figures 57, *c* and *d*. The lung extracts were used to form a film on a Wilhelmy surface-tension balance, which was then stretched and compressed by a moveable barrier.

On compression, the extract from the mature lung reached a much lower surface tension. Thus, *in vivo* the lungs of the immature lamb collapsed on deflation because a high surface tension persisted as the alveolar surface area declined.

In summary then, the lungs need to develop both air spaces and surface active material before they can be adequately ventilated. Table 31 shows that these functional capabilities develop at relatively different gestational ages in different species.

The physical characteristics of the tracheobronchial tree also influence the minimum pressure required to expand the lung at birth. At any given surface tension the pressure required for opening is

TABLE 31.—SOME ASPECTS OF LUNG DEVELOPMENT IN DIFFERENT SPECIES

		GESTATION AGE AT WHICH			
SPECIES	LUNGS BECOME EXPANSIBLE	PROPORTION OF TERM	LUNGS CONTAIN SURFACE-ACTIVE MATERIAL	PROPORTION OF TERM	SOURCES
Mouse			17–18 days	0.9	Buckingham and Avery (1962)
Rabbit	27 days	0.87	29 days	0.94	Pattle (1958); Reynolds and Strang (1966)
Sheep	110 days	0.75	125 days	0.85	Fauré-Fremiet and Dragoiu (1923); Born, Dawes, and Mott (1955); Howatt *et al.* (1965)
Man	16 weeks	0.40	30 weeks	0.75	Loosli and Potter (1959); Avery and Mead (1959); Reynolds and Strang (1966)

TABLE 32.—COMPARISON OF LUNG MEASUREMENTS IN INFANT AND
ADULT MAN

	INFANT	ADULT	ADULT/INFANT
Body weight (kg)	3	70	23
Lung weight (Gm)	50	800	16
Alveolar diameter (mm)	0.05	0.20	4
	0.07	0.13	2
Bronchiole diameter (mm)	0.1	0.2	2
Bronchial diameter (mm)	3.8–4.4	11.1–14.0	
Tracheal diameter (mm)	5.7–6.0	14.4–16.5	

Sources: Clements (1961); Engel (1962).

inversely related to the radius of the opening unit, and airway resistance is related to the fourth power of the diameter. As the negative intrapleural pressure, which can be generated during the first few breaths in any species, is limited (though it may be as low as −50 mm Hg), so the minimum size of the bronchioles and alveoli at birth in all mammalian species is limited. In man, as Table 32 shows, the diameters of the bronchioles only double from infancy to adulthood; those of the bronchi and trachea increase about threefold, while alveolar diameter increases about fourfold (as estimated from histological measurements) or twofold (calculated from the difference between the pressures required to expand saline-filled or gas-filled lungs; Clements, 1961). Thus with increasing body size in newborn and adult man and animals, the mean radius of individual spaces remains within narrow limits and the number of terminal air spaces increases. Lung growth after birth proceeds by the elaboration of new units. The number of bronchial generations continues to rise somewhat after birth in mice and men (Willson, 1928), even though in man 65–75% of the bronchial formations are completed between 10–14 weeks gestation (Bucher and Reid, 1961).

Breathing Movements *In Utero*

Before we consider the mechanisms for the initiation of breathing after birth, it seems reasonable to review what is known about respiratory movements *in utero*. In 1946, Barcroft gave a very interesting description of the development of respiratory movements in response to tactile stimuli in early foetal life in the sheep. The foetal sheep was a more favourable object of study in this, as in many other respects, because "unlike the rat, the sheep does not run through the gamut of its intrauterine development in 21 days, and as the phases of development do not crowd upon one another, they are more easily discerned." The development of movement generally, and of respiratory movement in particular, was divided into 4 phases.

First, at 35–40 days gestation the foetus reacts to a sharp tap on the face by a brief single spasm which at first involves the head and neck alone, but spreads to other muscles, including the diaphragm, in a few days. The sensory area from which the response can be elicited also increases in size. Secondly, by 40 days gestation the spasm becomes rhythmic, and the frequency of the rhythm increases from 40–60 per minute. Thirdly, between 38–45 days the character of the response alters so that the rhythmic movements of the respiratory muscles succeed a brief initial writhing movement of the torso and limbs. Fourthly, comes the stage of inhibition. At 50 days gestation the slightest touch evokes a response, but by 60 days the foetus has become inert and unreactive, save to the strongest stimulus. In Barcroft's words, "If the cord of a healthy but inert foetus of, say, 65 days be occluded, the foetus will throw off its inertia. The demonstration is dramatic if the foetus be one of twins. The control will present all the appearance of being asleep, while that with the cord occluded will wake to activity. In essence it reverts to the condition at which we left it at 50 days, though the detail of its movement has changed somewhat, being less crude than formerly. No further development in kind occurs before the birth of the foetus. The stage is, in fact, set for the first breath, though only half the gestation period has elapsed."

The period of gestation at which respiratory behaviour can first be elicited varies in different species. Becker, King, Marsh, and Wyrick, (1964) explored it in rats by clamping the uterine vessels. The results showed that respiratory activity on asphyxia was barely perceptible on the 17th day of

TABLE 33.—FIRST DEVELOPMENT OF RESPIRATORY BEHAVIOUR IN RESPONSE TO
STIMULI IN DIFFERENT SPECIES

SPECIES	FIRST RESPONSE AT	PROPORTION OF TERM	SOURCE
Rat	17 days	0.78	Becker, King, Marsh, and Wyrick (1964)
Guinea pig	40 days	0.60	Bergström (1962)
Sheep	40 days	0.27	Barcroft (1946)
Man	112 days	0.40	Bergström and Bergström (1963)

gestation, but thereafter increased rapidly until term (22 days). As with so many other mechanisms, development is relatively later (as a proportion of full term) in species with a short gestational period (Table 33).

In 1937, Snyder and Rosenfeld had observed regular breathing movements in mature foetal rabbits, cats, and guinea pigs, usually still *in utero* but with the uterus delivered into Ringer's solution at 37°C, or observed through the intact abdominal wall. They remarked "the clue to the disagreement" (with earlier observations of foetal apnoea) "lies in the condition under which observations were carried out. In animals prepared by our method, respiration is revealed during foetal life. In contrast, in animals otherwise prepared, the foetus is usually in a state of apnea." It was recognized that either hypoxaemia or hypercapnia might induce respiratory movements in otherwise apnoeic foetuses, or modify them if they were already present. During the next few years this was repeatedly shown to be true (Windle, Monnier, and Steele, 1938; Barcroft, 1946), and it was concluded by Windle, Becker, Barth, and Schulz (1939) that even in small animals such as rabbits and guinea pigs there were normally no foetal breathing movements near term in the absence of asphyxia. The observations of Snyder and Rosenfeld were attributed to the disturbances induced by the methods of observation. These conclusions have been confirmed by a more recent critical re-evaluation of the data, both by direct observation (Becker, King, Marsh, and Wyrick, 1964) and after injection of radiopaque contrast medium or dye into the amniotic fluid in rats or guinea pigs (Carter, Becker, King, and Barry, 1964; King and Becker, 1964).

In 1946, Davis and Potter concluded from observations on human infants, that "during the intra-uterine period respiratory movements are intermittent, irregular and shallow but they result in the free circulation of amniotic fluid through the lungs." This conclusion, of shallow movements leading to free circulation of fluid, is incompatible with the physical characteristics of fluid breathing, which will be described later in this chapter. Davis and Potter introduced radiopaque contrast medium into the amniotic fluid and x-rayed the lungs after delivery and tying the cord. The presence of contrast medium in the airways could well have been accounted for by the conditions of delivery by caesarean section under local or spinal anaesthesia, and its wide distribution throughout the lung by the subsequent respiratory efforts of the infants. McLain (1964) introduced radiopaque contrast medium into the amniotic fluid of 75 pregnant women and was unable to detect it within the lungs *in utero* in a single foetus.

Thus, in all species, the weight of the evidence suggests that the mature foetus normally does not make rhythmic respiratory movements *in utero*, provided it is not disturbed by physical stimuli or by partial asphyxia. The transpleural pressure in a mature lamb near term is negligible, suggesting that there is little tone in the respiratory muscles. Nevertheless, it would be interesting to study the changes in transpleural pressure during gestation, for instance, using a transducer implanted in a lamb or monkey foetus early in development (with continuous 24-hour recording), to determine whether from time to time it flexed its respiratory muscles. These are evidently well prepared to sustain continuous activity after delivery, and do not readily fatigue. It is hard to believe that they are wholly inactive *in utero;* brief periods of activity might well pass undetected or be dismissed as a reaction to an abnormal stimulus.

The Onset of Breathing After Birth

When a baby is born it is removed from a warm moist environment to a cool one where its weight is not supported by surrounding fluid; it is already a little asphyxiated on delivery and its umbilical cord is tied; it is squashed and squeezed during labour and it is handled maybe gently but in an unaccus-

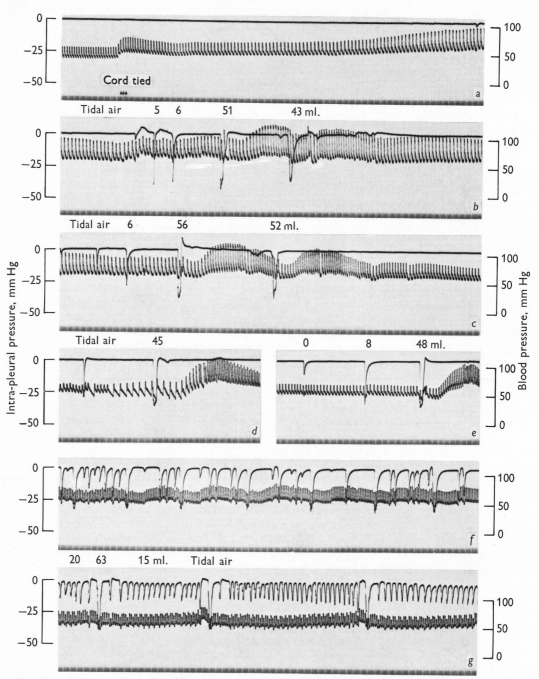

Fig. 58.—Records of intrapleural **(above)** and systemic arterial pressure **(below)** in a mature lamb delivered by caesarean section under local anaesthesia. Records a–c are continuous and each is 68 seconds long. Record d is taken 4 minutes, e, 5 minutes, f, 9 minutes after tying the umbilical cord. (From Born, Dawes, and Rennick, 1956.)

tomed manner after birth. It then begins to breathe. In face of so many violent changes, it is a nice matter to decide which, if any, is the essential stimulus to normal rhythmic respiration, and it is not surprising that the mechanisms involved have long been a matter of debate.

The initial respiratory efforts must be considerable to achieve expansion of the lungs with air, but once this has been achieved adequate ventilation usually can be maintained by respiratory efforts which are little different from those in the adult. We can thus distinguish two phases, of which the first is signalled by strong gasping efforts, usually preceded by some degree of asphyxia, and the second is the establishment of normal rhythmic breathing movements accompanied by a rise in arterial Po_2 well above the foetal arterial level and a fall in Pco_2 down to the foetal level. Now it is an astonishing fact that quite extensive manipulations, and surgery under local anaesthesia, may be undertaken on lamb or monkey foetuses without arousing respiratory efforts. In such animals the arterial Po_2 is often about 25 mm Hg and the Pco_2 35–45 mm Hg. A few hours after separation from the placenta the systemic arterial Po_2 exceeds 60 mm Hg and the Pco_2 is unchanged; yet the newborn lamb or monkey is breathing quietly and rhythmically. So, at first sight, the cause of this transformation is evidently neither tactile manipulation nor changes in blood gas tension or pH. It is necessary to proceed to more elaborate experiments to separate and identify the possible mechanisms.

When mature foetal lambs are delivered by caesarean section under spinal or local anaesthesia, and laid alongside their mother on a warmed table with an intact umbilical cord, they make no respiratory movement and lie inert with the eyes closed. When the umbilical cord is tied there is a brief small rise in arterial pressure (Fig. 58, a), followed by a small decline with some slowing of the heart. Then the pressure begins to rise more steeply and eventually, after two brief relatively ineffectual gasps, the lamb takes a deep breath (Fig. 58, b: intrapleural pressure -42 mm Hg, tidal volume 51 ml) sufficient to cause the absorption of some oxygen, as shown by the subsequent brief increase in heart rate. During this period of nearly a minute since the cord was tied there is always a considerable fall in arterial Po_2 and a small rise in Pco_2; at the time when respiratory efforts begin the foetus also makes other signs of arousal, squirming, shaking its head, and sometimes opening its eyes. After a further breath the arterial pressure begins to fall and the heart slows until another pair of respiratory efforts causes the same response as before (Fig. 58, c). The same cycle of events is repeated again and again during the next few minutes until the intervals between breaths gradually decrease, and although breathing is still periodic, the fluctuations in blood pressure and heart rate gradually subside (Fig. 58, f, g). In this experiment (representative of many such observations) normal rhythmic breathing is established solely as a result of tying the umbilical cord, and without tactile or thermal stimulation.

In other experiments, cold alone was used as a stimulus to breathing (Dawes, 1965, 1966). Cold is, of course, well known as a respiratory stimulus both at birth (e.g., Barcroft, 1946) and in the adult, but

ARTERIAL PRESSURE
(mm Hg)

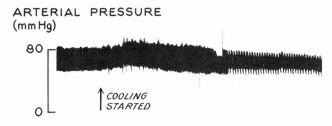

OESOPHAGEAL PRESSURE
(mm Hg)

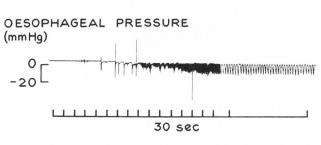

30 sec

Fig. 59.—Records of femoral arterial pressure **(above)** and intra-oesophageal pressure **(below)** in a mature lamb delivered by caesarean section under local anaesthesia, with intact umbilical cord and liquid-filled lungs. Cooling by application of ice-cold water was begun at the arrow and initiated quiet rhythmic respiratory movements.

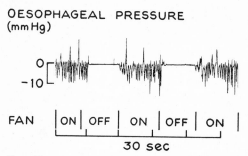

OESOPHAGEAL PRESSURE
(mm Hg)

Fig. 60.—Record of intra-oesophageal pressure in a mature foetal lamb with intact umbilical circulation to the placenta and liquid-filled lungs. Cooling the wet fleece by fan-initiated breathing movements.

systematic experiments were needed to distinguish the effects of cold and partial asphyxia at birth. Mature foetal lambs were delivered by caesarean section under light chloralose or local anaesthesia. A liquid-filled tracheal cannula was inserted and they were cooled by the application of ice cubes and the use of a fan. When the rectal temperature dropped from the normal value (in sheep) of about 39.5–40°C by 3–4°, the lambs began to shiver and to make respiratory movements (Fig. 59). After a few initial small gasps rhythmic liquid breathing was established, at a rate ~60/min, with intrapleural (or intra-oesophageal) pressure changes of 12–15 mm Hg and a tidal volume of 2–4 ml liquid.

The application of cold caused a transient rise of arterial pressure, but no significant change in arterial pH, P_{CO_2}, or O_2 saturation. The respiratory movements caused relatively large variations in arterial pressure presumably because, unlike the adult, the thorax contains no gas, so that respiratory movements are transmitted undamped to the circulation.

When the lamb is cooled so that it is shivering, but respiratory movements have not yet begun, they can usually be elicited at once on application of an ice cube or ice-cold water, particularly to the face or mouth. Warm blocks of metal or warm water are without effect. Often, switching a fan on or off will start or stop breathing movements (Fig. 60). This is due to the cooling rather than the tactile effect of the increased air movement, because the stimulus is effective only as long as the lamb's coat is wet. When regular movements have been initiated by cooling in a foetal lamb breathing liquid, the Hering-Breuer reflexes can be demonstrated. Lowering the intratracheal pressure, by lowering a saline reservoir attached to the liquid-filled tracheal tube, accelerates breathing movements, while raising the pressure arrests them (Fig. 61). Both the liquid deflation and inflation reflexes are abolished by cutting both vagi in the neck. This is further evidence that the movements are truly those of rhythmic respiration.

Fig. 61.—Records as in Figure 59. Lowering intratracheal pressure (during the signal mark, **A**) caused an acceleration of respiratory movements, while raising pressure (**B**) arrested them.

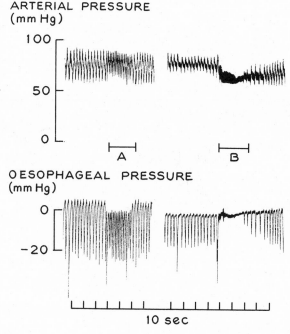

These experiments demonstrate that it is possible to elicit, by an appropriate stimulus, normal quiet regular liquid breathing in a foetus without any change in the blood gas tensions or pH. Thus, the maintenance of rhythmic breathing in the normal infant after birth need not be due to the rise in arterial PO_2 (even though neonatal hypoxaemia may cause respiratory arrest). It is also interesting that even very strong and repeated tactile stimuli, such as might be expected to cause pain, elicited a gasp but did not cause sustained respiratory movements in unanaesthetized lambs with an intact cord and no other impediment to breathing (i.e., nothing over the head or face; Harned, Wolkoff, Pickrell, and MacKinney, 1961). This is contrary to general belief. It is evident that neither exposure alone (unaccompanied by cooling) nor painful stimuli are of themselves an adequate stimulus to rhythmic respiration.

The Role of the Systemic Arterial Chemoreceptors

In early work on the foetuses of small animals *in utero* near term (rabbits, cats, and guinea pigs), foetal hypoxaemia or hypercapnia induced by giving the mother low O_2 or high Co_2 mixtures to breathe either had no effect (Windle, Monnier, and Steele, 1938) or depressed pre-existing respiratory activity (Snyder and Rosenfeld, 1937). Rosenfeld and Snyder (1938) found that newborn rabbits, even those delivered at 29 days (the limit of viability; term is normally 31 days), reacted vigorously by hyperpnoea to hypercapnia, hypoxia, or to administration of cyanide. They concluded that the respiratory activity of the foetus in the intra-uterine environment closely resembled that of an adult animal after denervation of the carotid body area, and questioned whether failure of functional activ-

ity in the foetus was related to lack of structural differentiation or to lack of activity in an organ already capable of functioning. Although their observation of pre-existing foetal respiratory activity now makes us wonder whether their foetuses were not already mildly asphyxiated (in which case further asphyxia would naturally be depressant), the ideas which they expressed have proved stimulating and puzzling.

At an early period of gestation, corresponding roughly to Barcroft's third stage of the development of respiratory function, the foetus responds by increased respiratory activity to hypoxia or hypercapnia (in cats at rather less than 40 days; Windle, Monnier, and Steele, 1938: in sheep at 58–69 days; Barcroft and Karvonen, 1948). Thereafter, the stage of inhibition supervenes and the foetus becomes remarkably unresponsive. The effect of administration of a large range of doses of cyanide, usually given into the umbilical vein (whence most would reach the left side of the heart) or occasionally to a carotid artery, was examined in sheep (Barcroft and Karvonen, 1948; Reynolds and Mackie, 1961). This had a trivial effect in causing foetal respiratory movements even though foetal arterial pressure rose or fell and the heart slowed, and although on some occasions the doses were sufficient to cause stimulation of maternal ventilation, after a short delay, presumably after some cyanide had crossed the placenta.

In 1964, Harned, Rowshan, MacKinney, and Sugioka produced a moderate degree of hypercapnia and hypoxaemia (separately) in mature foetal lambs, delivered under spinal anaesthesia, measured the changes in foetal arterial blood gas compositions, and found that these did not initiate rhythmic breathing. Tying the umbilical cord invariably did start breathing. Their results, summarized in Table 34, show some points of wider interest.

TABLE 34.—Changes in Mean Arterial Blood Gas Concentration in Maternal Sheep and Mature Foetal Lambs*

	Mother (Arterial)			Foetus (Right Brachial Artery)		
Condition of Mother	PO_2 (Mm Hg)	PCO_2 (Mm Hg)	pH	PO_2 (Mm Hg)	PCO_2 (Mm Hg)	pH
Standing, unanaesthetized	89	26	7.47			
Supine, spinal anaesthesia						
Breathing air	69	23	7.49	19	39	7.31
Breathing 6.5% CO_2, 21% O_2 in N_2	90	46	7.32	25	53	7.22
Breathing 10% O_2 in N_2	41	23		11	14	7.37

* The observations were recorded after a 10-minute period of breathing each new gas mixture. (After Harned, Rowshan, MacKinney, and Sugioka, 1964.)

Spinal anaesthesia and the adoption of the supine position caused a considerable fall in maternal arterial Po_2; the Pco_2 was already low as in pregnant women. Administration of 6.5% CO_2 to the mother caused hyperventilation and an increase in arterial Po_2 so that the foetal Po_2 rose passively at the same time as the Pco_2. Contrariwise, when the mother was given 10% O_2 in N_2 to breathe, she also hyperventilated, and her arterial Pco_2 and Po_2 (and those of the foetus) fell simultaneously. Thus when foetal Pco_2 was raised, Po_2 also was raised and vice versa. Now Purves and Biscoe (1966) showed in newborn lambs that hypoxia potentiates the effect of hypercapnia in increasing ventilation. Thus the conditions under which Harned *et al.* originally studied their effects upon the foetal lamb were the least favourable to observe a positive effect. Subsequently, they have shown that perfusion of the right common carotid artery with blood having a low Po_2 and pH can result in the initiation of sustained respiratory movements (Harned, MacKinney, Berryhill, and Holmes, 1966). They also noticed that in such lambs, breathing vigorously, the vessels of the umbilical cord became constricted. In the newborn rabbit (Dawes and Mott, 1959; Blatteis, 1964) and lamb (Purves and Biscoe, 1966), the respiratory response to hypoxia or to administration of cyanide was almost entirely abolished by bilateral section of the carotid sinus/body nerves, suggesting that the carotid bodies were the principal site of action. So it remains to be seen whether the relative insensitivity of the foetus to hypoxaemia was due to a peripheral or central phenomenon, or to both.

In 1952, Cross and Malcolm observed the activity in the carotid sinus nerves of 2 foetal lambs. Maternal hypoxia caused the foetal heart to slow and increased the activity in the nerve between the bursts of baroreceptor spikes; conversely, this diastolic activity was reduced by giving the mother 100% O_2 to breathe. They concluded that the carotid chemoreceptors were probably functional in the foetus. However, reconsideration of this evidence, and particularly of the illustrative tracing published by Cross (1961), suggests that the increase in activity in this multifibre preparation might have been due to recruitment of pressoreceptor fibers firing throughout the cardiac cycle, as a result of a rise in arterial pressure. Indeed, Cross implied as much in 1961, and emphasized the need for a study of single fibre preparations, Purves and Biscoe (1966), also using multifibre preparations, concluded that the activity of the carotid chemoreceptors was very low in the mature sheep foetus even at a Po_2 of 20–25 mm Hg. The principal difficulty in using single fibre preparations is to identify them as chemoreceptor afferents in the foetal condition. Yet so far the results do suggest that chemoreceptor activity in the foetus is less than after birth, i.e., that the chemoreceptors of the carotid body are influenced other than by the arterial blood gas tensions. We, therefore, have two problems. Why are the carotid chemoreceptors relatively inactive in the foetal lamb? and will this alone explain the lack of respiratory activity in the foetus?

Purves and Biscoe (1966) have recently made the interesting observation that when the umbilical cord is tied in a foetal lamb there is a great increase in efferent postganglionic activity in the cervical sympathetic nerves before the first breath. The activity is rhythmic in character and the rhythm is not cardiac, which may suggest that some central rhythmic process is building up which ultimately becomes apparent in respiratory movements. At the same time the arterial pressure is rising (Fig. 58), and if the vagi are previously cut, the heart accelerates, and peripheral vasoconstriction begins to develop in the limbs; so this is probably one special instance of a generalized sympathetic discharge. It was suggested that if, in the foetus, cervical sympathetic tone is low, flow through the carotid body may be very high, so that the receptors will be relatively insensitive to small changes in O_2 content. When sympathetic tone is increased, flow will be reduced as a result of vasoconstriction, as shown in adult cats by Daly, Lambertsen, and Schweitzer (1954), and the sensitivity of the receptors will thus be increased. This is a somewhat heretical view, as it is widely believed that the adequate stimulus to the carotid body is O_2 tension rather than content, but it is one that deserves study. There is a possible complication, as Joels and Neil (1963) have pointed out, that the carotid body is alleged to contain many arteriovenous anastomoses; this also needs further investigation. Alternatively, the sympathetic efferents may influence the chemoreceptor cells by a direct effect. The carotid body used to be included among the "paraganglia" or extra-medullary chromaffin tissues. Its staining reactions indicated the presence of some catecholamines associated with membrane-bound granules, which suggested to Boyd (1961) the hypothesis that "there is included in the mechanism underlying the chemoreceptor function of the carotid body a local humoral factor, which may well be noradrenaline; when released from the cells this, or a related catecholamine, may induce the discharge of impulses in the afferent fibres of Hering's nerve ...." This hypothesis might now be elaborated to include the possibility either of a direct action on the endothelium or glomus cells of the carotid body, or as a result of increased O_2 consumption (e.g., by release of noradrenaline, as in brown adipose tissue by activation of a lipase, Chapter 15). The latter would be an effect complementary to a reduction in blood flow. If either hypothesis (vascular or otherwise) were correct, it should be possible to mimic the effect of tying the umbilical cord by stimulating the peripheral ends of the cervical sympathetic nerves, and Purves and Biscoe have recently found that sympathetic stimulation does indeed increase the activity in a group of fibres in the sinus nerve of foetal lambs having the latency and time course characteristic of chemoreceptors in adult cats.

If the maintenance of rhythmic breathing after birth were conditional on an increased sensitivity of the carotid chemoreceptors by this mechanism alone, then breathing should be arrested on blockade or section of the cervical sympathetic nerves. Administration of large doses of hexamethonium, sufficient to block autonomic ganglia, to newborn rabbits (Dawes, Handler, and Mott, 1957) did not cause respiratory arrest, nor did bilateral section of the carotid sinus/body nerves and/or cervical vagi (Blatteis, 1964). We, therefore, conclude that the presence of the systemic arterial chemoreceptors, whether or not their sensitivity is enhanced at birth, is not essential to the process which maintains rhythmic breathing, once started. What, then, is likely to be the function of the carotid chemoreceptors when they are activated after birth? In young rats, gasping in response to anoxia was entirely abolished when they were eliminated (Tschirgi and Gerard, 1947). This suggests that their presence may be essential to ensure the first deep gasping movements which are required to inflate the lungs, when these result from asphyxia. Tactile stimuli also cause gasping, and it is probable that this is a direct effect (rather than through the sympathetics and chemoreceptors).

There remains the problem of quiet rhythmic breathing. We can begin by eliminating certain possibilities. Its initiation is not due to removal of the nose from a fluid environment, otherwise all babies and lambs would breathe at once on delivery. It is possible that the maintenance of breathing, once established by a few vigorous gasps, might be due to a local feed-back mechanism. The most

obvious mechanism is by tracheobronchial receptors including the pulmonary stretch receptors and those excited by temperature and gas flow. Yet the afferent nerves for these run in the vagi, and bilateral section of the cervical vagi does not arrest breathing in the newborn rabbit or lamb, nor in the liquid-breathing lamb exposed to cold. The most likely explanation is based on Burns' (1963) view of central respiratory neurones as receiving a wealth of excitatory connections from nonrespiratory sources, on which their rhythmic activity is dependent. This could well explain the initiation of rhythmic breathing in the intact foetus exposed to cold; (the effect of carotid body denervation has not yet been explored in this preparation). It is less easy to explain the maintenance of normal rhythmic breathing in an infant which is not overtly stimulated other than by tying the umbilical cord. Probably the explanation lies in the summation of a number of subliminal stimuli. Delivery and exposure on a warm table alongside the mother may be insufficient to arouse respiratory movements, but when the cord is tied the subsequent transient asphyxia and the changes in the circulation may be adequate to set in train a respiratory rhythm which is self-perpetuating under those conditions. There is some evidence to support this view in that, occasionally, exposure of a newborn lamb to a warm environment (immersion at 38–40°C or exposure beneath an infrared lamp) will cause an otherwise unaccountable arrest of breathing which is, in that individual, repeatable. In fact, it has induced something which appears like a cyanotic attack in a premature infant. Similar observations have been made, rarely, upon healthy newborn human infants (see Cross, Dawes, and Karlberg, 1966).

General anaesthesia with urethane (Barcroft, 1946), chloralose, or pentobarbitone in animals may delay the onset of rhythmic breathing at birth but, unless the depth of anaesthesia is sufficient to cause very severe maternal hypoventilation (and hence foetal asphyxia), it does not preclude its final attainment. This should not be taken as indicating that deep surgical anaesthesia is or is not prejudicial to survival in clinical practice. The fact is quoted to demonstrate that rhythmic breathing can be established at birth in a deeply anaesthetized foetus. Conversely, animals within a few hours of birth can be deeply anaesthetized without respiratory arrest, though the dose of chloralose or barbiturate required by weight is a third to a quarter of that in adults. Thus, the external signs of arousal at birth, symptomatic perhaps of awakening consciousness,

TABLE 35.—Mean Time of the First Respiratory
Movement in Normal Mature Human Infants
According to Early and Late Clamping of the
Umbilical Cord (Oh, Lind, and Gessner, 1966)

	Mean Time (Secs ± S.E.) from Delivery on	
	Early Clamping	Late Clamping
First gasp	6.3 ± 0.6	9.2 ± 1.3
First cry	13.5 ± 2.5	15.0 ± 4.8

The mean birth weights and 5-minute Apgar scores of the two groups
were not significantly different.

are not necessary to the establishment of a respiratory rhythm. Normal infants, after a protracted delivery, may be comatose for many hours, and gross types of anencephaly are compatible with the establishment of normal rhythmic breathing. This merely indicates that we are dealing with a very primitive, and probably comparatively simple mechanism, whose analysis might well proceed more rapidly in species less sophisticated than mammals.

It is most difficult to control the conditions of human delivery. In the normal baby, the arterial Po_2 and pH are already reduced and the Pco_2 raised at the end of labour (Chapter 10) and during the first half-minute after delivery, although "there is no evidence of major respiratory efforts during the normal delivery process" (Engström, Karlberg, Rooth, and Tunell, 1966). During the first half-minute after delivery there is a considerable umbilical blood flow, if the cord is not tied (200–300 ml/min; Stembera, Hodr, and Janda, 1965), of relatively well oxygenated umbilical venous blood, yet it is at this time that spontaneous breathing normally begins whether the cord is tied early or late (Table 35). The difficulties in interpretation are obvious. Yet the fact seems agreed, that during the first half-hour after birth, the rectal temperature falls rapidly in normal infants, to a mean value of about 35°C (Edwards, 1824; Engström et al., 1966). A similar fall has been seen in newborn animals of several species.

The Fluid in the Foetal Lung

Before air breathing can be established the fluid in the tracheobronchial tree must be removed. It is interesting to consider how it gets there in the first place. It was for many years assumed to be aspirated amniotic fluid. However, Potter and Bohlender (1941) found alveolar fluid in 2 human foetuses

with malformations of the respiratory tract which precluded the entrance of amniotic fluid. The respiratory tract was also found to be distended with fluid in foetal rabbits whose necks had been ligated as a preliminary to intra-uterine decapitation some days previously, provided that the trachea remained occluded (Jost and Policard, 1948). There were also a number of observations on guinea pigs (Whitehead, Windle, and Becker, 1942), sheep (Reynolds, 1953; Dawes, 1954), and goats (Setnikar, Agostoni, and Taglietti, 1959), which suggested that foetal pulmonary fluid originated in the lungs. When a cannula was introduced into the trachea of foetal sheep or goats, delivered by caesarean section near term, a relatively large quantity of fluid drained out within the next few minutes (~5 ml/kg body weight); smaller quantities (~0.25 ml/kg min) continued to drain out over the next 1–2 hours in most instances. Occasionally, the flow of pulmonary fluid was reported to cease; it is not clear whether this was associated with a deterioration in the condition of the foetus or was related to the height of the fluid in the collecting tube above the foetus. The effect of the latter does not seem to have been studied systematically. Adams (personal communication) has recently found in foetal lambs delivered under spinal anaesthesia, with an intact umbilical cord, that the intratracheal pressure is considerably above that in the mouth, the communication between the two being cut off by the joint action of the thyro-arytenoid muscles and the epiglottis. Cineradiography showed that this sphincteric mechanism relaxed from time to time and allowed contrast medium, introduced into the trachea, to enter the pharynx and be swallowed. Thus pulmonary fluid does not normally appear to originate from, nor contribute to, the amniotic fluid.

Analysis of tracheobronchial and other foetal fluids are consistent with this conclusion (Adams, Fujiwara, and Rowshan, 1963; Adams, Moss and Fagan, 1963; Ross, 1963). The osmolarity and sodium and chloride content of amniotic fluid were considerably below that in the respiratory tract (Table 36), while the pH, viscosity, and the concentrations of urea, protein, and sugar were higher. The tracheobronchial fluid also contained material high in surface activity, presumed to originate from the alveoli (Adams and Fujiwara, 1963). The differences in composition do not exclude the possibility that the tracheobronchial and amniotic fluids might mix from time to time, but if so the amounts involved must be very small. Yet we cannot be sure that the observations of Table 36 were made under equilibrium conditions, since the mean value for

TABLE 36.—COMPARISON OF MATERNAL AND FOETAL FLUIDS IN MATURE FOETAL LAMBS

	MATERNAL ARTERY	UMBILICAL VEIN	FOETAL TRACHEA	AMNIOTIC FLUID	FOETAL URINE
From Adams, Fujiwara and Rowshan (1963)					
pH	7.44 ± 0.06	7.34 ± 0.07	6.43 ± 0.13	7.07 ± 0.22	6.84 ± 0.44
Osmolarity (mOsm/L)	302 ± 6	300 ± 6	300 ± 6	275 ± 14	264 ± 76
Sodium (mEq/L)	143 ± 5	140 ± 3	142 ± 5	110 ± 2	
Chloride (mEq/L)	108 ± 3	105 ± 5	144 ± 7	94 ± 10	
Lactic Acid (mEq/L)	2.3 ± 0.7	3.5 ± 0.6	0.6 ± 0.2	2.1 ± 0.8	0.8
Total CO_2 (mEq/L)	22.6 ± 3.6	22.1 ± 1.9	4.4 ± 1.6	18.4	18.8
From Adams, Moss and Fagan (1963)					
Urea (mg %)			46	118	
Protein (mg %)	6509	4439	327	699	
Sugar (mg %)	135	152	113	304	
Viscosity			1.25	2.11	

foetal blood sugar was very high (in foetal lambs and in other species it is normally half the maternal value; Shelley, 1960; Shelley and Neligan, 1966) and the blood lactate concentrations also were high (e.g., compared with those of Orzalesi *et al.*, 1965). The effects of reduction in pulmonary blood flow or asphyxia on the volume and composition of the fluid draining from the lung do not appear to have been studied, and would be worth investigation. Adams, Fujiwara, and Rowshan (1963), and Ross (1963) found that the osmolarity of foetal plasma and tracheal fluid were usually very similar. They suggested that the tracheobronchial fluid might originate as an ultrafiltrate of plasma with selective reabsorption or secretion of some components. Presumably, the composition of a pulmonary ultra-filtrate originating in the alveoli must be modified by the mucus-secreting glands of the tracheobronchial tree.

The presence of liquid in the foetal lung of itself results in there being a large resistance to inspiratory efforts, irrespective of a fluid-gas interface. The viscosity of water is 36 times that of air and its density a thousandfold. Consequently, when mature foetal lambs of 3–4 kg are induced (by the application of cold) to make rhythmic respiratory efforts, giving an intrapleural pressure change of 10–12 mm Hg (Fig. 59), these result only in trivial tidal volumes of 2–4 ml fluid. Gasping induced by transient asphyxia (as by brief occlusion of the umbilical cord) results in a larger fall in intrapleural pressure and a proportionate increase in the volume of fluid inhaled. But the volumes inhaled are still small unless the inspiratory effort is maintained for a longer period of time or is closely followed by a second gasp (Fig. 62). The major part of the pressure generated is resistive; part is due to inertance.

That due to the compliance of the foetal lungs is a trivial fraction of the whole (Howatt, Humphreys, Normand, and Strang, 1965). It should be noted that in all these experiments the trachea was cannulated; the presence of the larynx and epiglottis in the normal foetus is an additional complication.

These results also imply that admixture of tracheobronchial fluid with inhaled amniotic fluid is limited. It was calculated that 50 or more liquid breaths might be required to wash out 90% of the initial tracheobronchial fluid. Yet during asphyxia, over a period of 10 minutes or so, and particularly if the asphyxia were incomplete, the foetus might well gasp 50 times or more. The presence of amniotic debris and meconium in the periphery of the

Fig. 62.—Records of the flow **(above)** and change of volume **(centre)** of fluid in the airways and of pleural pressure in the foetal lamb to show how two gasps, closely spaced, result in the accumulation of pulmonary fluid. (Redrawn from Howatt, Humphreys, Normand, and Strang, 1965.)

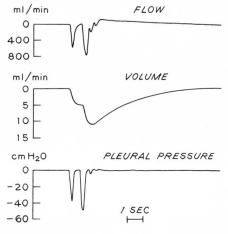

TABLE 37.—CHANGES IN MEAN LUNG WEIGHT AT BIRTH IN DIFFERENT SPECIES

SPECIES	WET LUNG WEIGHT: BODY WEIGHT RATIO		LUNG FLUID ABSORBED AFTER BIRTH (ML/KG BODY WEIGHT)	SOURCE
	Before Birth	After Birth		
Goats	0.040	0.017 (18–24 hours)	23	Avery and Cook (1961)
Dogs	0.031	0.020 (24 hours)	11	Avery (1961)
Mature rabbits (31 days)	0.024	0.018 (6 hours)	6	Aherne and Dawkins (1964)
Premature rabbits (28 days)	0.032	0.022 (6 hours)	10	Aherne and Dawkins (1964)
Lambs	0.033	0.018 (6 hours)	15	
Rhesus monkeys	0.019	0.010 (8–10 days)	9	

tracheobronchial tree is often noticed at autopsy after intra-uterine asphyxia. However, even introduction of large quantities of amniotic fluid into the lungs of foetal lambs did not disturb their surface-active properties (Howatt *et al.,* 1965).

We now have to consider how the fluid in the lung is removed after birth. Some is expelled from the mouth during normal human vertex deliveries, as the thorax is compressed in the birth canal, giving rise to an intrathoracic pressure of as much as 70 cm H_2O above atmospheric (Karlberg, 1960). The amount expelled is estimated as a quarter to a third of the gaseous functional residual capacity to be expected some days from birth, and this volume is replaced with air by the elastic recoil of the thorax on delivery. Some fluid must remain in the smaller airways, and this is presumably sucked into the alveoli at the first breath. How many alveoli are thus filled with fluid rather than air is not known; the proportion is likely to be higher after delivery by caesarean section because the chest is then not usually squeezed during delivery. This fluid must be gradually removed by evaporation or through the pulmonary blood capillaries or lymphatics. Some indication of the minimum amounts likely to be involved may be gained from Table 37, which shows the changes in lung weight at birth in different species. Removal is probably quite rapid because in man the functional residual capacity of the lungs rises to a near normal value of 25–30 ml/kg within 15 minutes from normal delivery.

Aherne and Dawkins (1964) suggested from histological observations of the lungs in newly delivered rabbits that much of the pulmonary fluid might be removed by the lymphatics. The periarterial tissues became distended with eosinophilic fluid similar to that disappearing from the alveoli at a time when the wet weight of the lung was falling. The reticular interstices of these tissues communicate freely with the lymphatic vessels of the lung, probably through large pores in their walls (Rusznyák, Földi, and Szabó, 1960). The periarterial tissues of the human newborn lung were similar to those in rabbits and the lymphatic spaces were so prominent that the pulmonary arterioles appeared to be suspended in distensible tunnels.

Direct evidence on the point was produced by Boston, Humphreys, Reynolds, and Strang (1965) who collected lymph from the heart and lungs via the right lymphatic duct (other lymph branches being tied) in foetal lambs. When the lungs were ventilated by positive pressure there was a very large increase in lymph flow, greater in mature (141–150 days gestation) than in immature (107–125 days) lambs (Fig. 63). It was computed that this could account for about a third of the water and all the protein lost from the lungs of mature lambs within the first 2 hours from delivery. It was also noticed that even in unventilated foetuses the rate of lymph flow was much greater than that in the young lamb or adult sheep. The protein concentrations were similar, so this suggested a greater capil-

Fig. 63.—Mean values of lymph flow from the heart and lungs, per kg body weight, in mature and immature lambs before and after the onset of ventilation. (Redrawn from Boston, Humphreys, Reynolds, and Strang, 1965.)

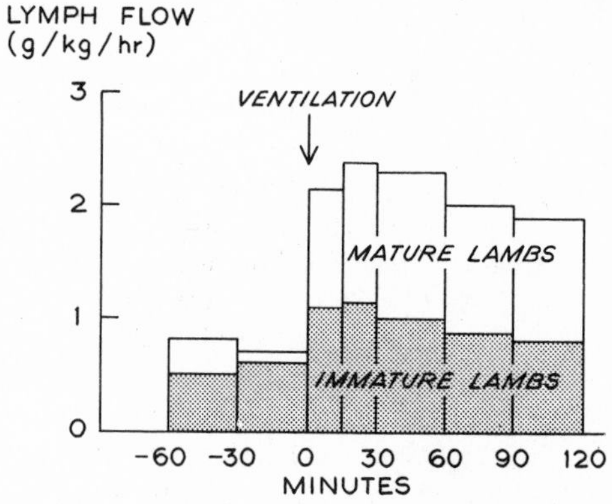

lary permeability. Thus assuming a plasma volume of 40 ml/kg, it was calculated that in a 24-hour period more than 20% of the plasma proteins were cleared through the right lymph duct in foetal lambs, as compared with 3–6% in lambs some while after birth or in the adult dog or sheep. This was the more remarkable because in the foetus there were no respiratory movements such as increase of the flow of lymph in adults.

These are a provocative series of observations which suggest another approach to some of the pathophysiological problems of the respiratory distress syndrome, from the point of view of pulmonary capillary permeability and of the close anatomical relation suggested between pulmonary arterioles and the drainage into the lymphatic system of the lung.

REFERENCES

Adams, F. H., and Fujiwara, T.: Surfactant in fetal lamb tracheal fluid, J. Pediat. 63:537–542, 1963.

Adams, F. H.; Fujiwara, T., and Rowshan, G.: The nature and origin of the fluid in the fetal lamb lung, J. Pediat. 63:881–887, 1963.

Adams, F. H.; Moss, A. J., and Fagan, L.: The tracheal fluid in the fetal lamb, Biol. neonat. 5:151–158, 1963.

Aherne, W., and Dawkins, M. J. R.: The removal of fluid from the pulmonary airways after birth in the rabbit, and the effect on this of prematurity and pre-natal hypoxia, Biol. neonat. 7:214–229, 1964.

Avery, M. E.: Mechanics of Respiration, in *Normal and Abnormal Respiration in Children,* 37th Ross Conference on Pediatric Research (Columbus, Ohio: Ross Laboratories, 1961), pp. 15–21.

Avery, M. E., and Cook, C. D.: Volume-pressure relationships of lungs and thorax in fetal, newborn and adult goats, J. Appl. Physiol. 16:1034–1038, 1961.

Avery, M. E., and Mead, J.: Surface properties in relation to atelectasis and hyaline membrane disease, Am. J. Dis. Child. 97:517–528, 1959.

Barcroft, J.: *Researches on prenatal life* (Oxford: Blackwell Scientific Publications, 1946).

Barcroft, J., and Karvonen, M. J.: The action of carbon dioxide and cyanide on foetal respiratory movements, the development of chemoreflex function in sheep, J. Physiol. 107:153–161, 1948.

Becker, R. F.; King, J. E.; Marsh, R. H., and Wyrick, A. D.: Intrauterine respiration in the rat fetus, Am. J. Obst. & Gynec. 90:236–246, 1964.

Bergström, R. M.: Prenatal development of motor functions, Ann. chir. gynaec. Fenniae Suppl. 112, 1962.

Bergström, R. M., and Bergström, L.: Prenatal development of stretch reflex functions and brain stem activity in the human, Ann. chir. gynaec. Fenniae Suppl. 117, 1963.

Blatteis, C. M.: Hypoxia and the metabolic response to cold in new-born rabbits, J. Physiol. 172:358–368, 1964.

Born, G. V. R.; Dawes, G. S., and Mott. J. C.: The viability of premature lambs, J. Physiol. 130:191–212, 1955.

Born, G. V. R.; Dawes, G. S.; Mott, J. C., and Rennick,

B. B.: The constriction of the ductus arteriosus caused by oxygen and by asphyxia in newborn lambs, J. Physiol. 132:304–342, 1956.

Boston, R. W.; Humphreys, P. W.; Reynolds, E. O. R., and Strang, L. B.: Lymph-flow and clearance of liquid from the lungs of the foetal lamb, Lancet 2:473–474, 1965.

Boyd, J. D.: The inferior aortico-pulmonary glomus, Brit. M. Bull. 17:127–131, 1961.

Bucher, V., and Reid, L.: Development of the intrasegmental bronchial tree: The pattern of branching and development of cartilage at various stages of intrauterine life, Thorax 16:207–218, 1961.

Buckingham, S., and Avery, M. E.: Tissue appearance of lung surfactant in the foetal mouse, Nature 139:688–689, 1962.

Burns, B. D.: The central control of breathing movements, Brit. M. Bull. 19:7–9, 1963.

Campiche, M.: Les inclusions lamellaires des cellules alvéolaires dans le poumon du raton. Relations entre l'ultrastructure et la fixation, J. Ultrastruct. Res. 3: 302–312, 1960.

Carter, W. A.; Becker, R. F.; King, J. E., and Barry, W. F.: Intrauterine respiration in the rat fetus, Am. J. Obst. & Gynec. 90:247–256, 1964.

Clements, J. A.: Air Space Dimensions, Geometry and Growth, in *Normal and Abnormal Respiration in Children,* 37th Ross Conference on Pediatric Research (Columbus, Ohio: Ross Laboratories, 1961), pp. 39–43.

Clements, J. A.: Pulmonary Surfactant, in Oliver, T. K. (ed.): *Neonatal Respiratory Adaptation* (Washington, D.C.: Public Health Service Publication 1432, 1963).

Clements, J. A.; Brown, E. S., and Johnson, R. P.: Pulmonary surface tension and the mucus lining of the lungs: Some theoretical considerations, J. Appl. Physiol. 12:262–268, 1958.

Cross, K. W.: Respiration in the new-born baby, Brit. M. Bull. 17:160–163, 1961.

Cross, K. W.; Dawes, G. S., and Karlberg, P.: Discussion, in Oliver, T. K. (ed.): *Neonatal Respiratory Adaptation,* (Washington D.C.: Public Health Service Publication 1432, 1966).

Cross, K. W., and Malcolm, J. L.: Evidence of carotid body and sinus activity in foetal and newborn animals, J. Physiol. 118:10, P., 1952.

Daly, M., de B.; Lambertsen, C. J., and Schweitzer, A.: Observations on the volume of blood flow and oxygen utilization of the carotid body in the cat, J. Physiol. 125:67–89, 1954.

Davis, M. E., and Potter, E. L.: Intrauterine respiration of the human fetus, J. A. M. A. 131:1194–1201, 1946.

Dawes, G. S.: Discussion, Cold Spring Harb. Symp. Quant. Biol. 19:164, 1954.

Dawes, G. S.: Oxygen Supply and Consumption in Late Fetal Life and the Onset of Breathing at Birth, in Fenn, W. O., and Rahn, H. (eds.): *Handbook of Physiology: Sec. 2. Respiration* (Washington, D.C.: American Physiological Society, 1965), pp. 1313–1328.

Dawes, G. S.: Initiation and Continuation of Respiration, in Oliver, T. K. (ed.): *Neonatal Respiratory Adaptation* (Washington, D.C.: Public Health Service Publication 1432, 1966).

Dawes, G. S.; Handler, J. J., and Mott, J. C.: Some cardiovascular responses in foetal, new-born and adult rabbits, J. Physiol. 139:123–136, 1957.

Dawes, G. S., and Mott, J. C.: Reflex respiratory activity in the new-born rabbit, J. Physiol. 145:85–97, 1959.

Edwards, V. F.: De l'influence des agens physiques (Paris: Crochard, 1824).

Engel, S.: *Lung Structure* (Springfield, Ill.: Charles C Thomas, Publisher, 1962).

Engström, L.; Karlberg, P.; Rooth, G., and Tunell, R.: *The Onset of Respiration* (New York: Association for the Aid of Crippled Children, 1966).

Fauré-Fremiet, E., and Dragoiu, J.: Le développement du poumon foetal chez le mouton, Arch. Anat. micr. 19:411–474, 1923.

Harned, H. S., Jr.; MacKinney, L. G.; Berryhill, W. S., and Holmes, C. K.: Effects of hypoxia and acidity on the initiation of breathing in the fetal lamb at term, Am. J. Dis. Child. 112:334–342, 1966.

Harned, H. S., Jr.; Rowshan, G.; MacKinney, L. G., and Sugioka, K.: Relationships of Po_2, Pco_2 and pH to onset of breathing of the term lamb as studied by a flow-through cuvette electrode assembly, Pediatrics 33:672–681, 1964.

Harned, H. S., Jr.; Wolkoff, A. S.; Pickrell, J., and Mac-Kinney, L. G.: Hemodynamic observations during birth of the lamb, Am. J. Dis. Child. 102:180–189, 1961.

Howatt, W. F.; Avery, M. E.; Humphreys, P. W.; Normand, I. C. S.; Reid, L., and Strang, L. B.: Factors affecting pulmonary surface properties in the foetal lamb, Clin. Sc. 29:239–248, 1965.

Howatt, W. F.; Humphreys, P. W.; Normand, I. C. S., and Strang, L. B.: Ventilation of liquid by the fetal lamb during asphyxia, J. Appl. Physiol. 20:496–502, 1965.

Joels, N., and Neil, E.: The excitation mechanism of the carotid body, Brit. M. Bull. 19:21–24, 1963.

Jost, A., and Policard, A.: Contribution experimentale à l'étude du développement prénatal du poumon chez le lapin, Arch. Anat. micr. 37:323–332, 1948.

Karlberg, P.: The adaptive changes in the immediate postnatal period, with particular reference to respiration, J. Pediat. 56:585–604, 1960.

King, J. E., and Becker, R. F.: Intrauterine respiration in the rat fetus, Am J. Obst. & Gynec. 90:257–263, 1964.

Klaus, M.; Reiss, O. K.; Tooley, W. H.; Piel, C., and Clements, J. A.: Alveolar epithelial cell mitochondria as source of the surface-active lung lining, Science 137: 750–751, 1962.

Loosli, G. C., and Potter, E. L.: Pre and postnatal development of the respiratory portion of the human lung, Am. Rev. Resp. Dis. 80: No. 1, part 2; 5–10, 1959.

Macklin, C. C. The pulmonary alveolar mucoid film and the pneumonocytes, Lancet 1:1099–1104, 1954.

McLain, C. R.: Amniography, a versatile diagnostic procedure in obstetrics, Obst. & Gynec. 23:45–50, 1964.

Mead, J. Mechanical properties of lungs, Physiol. Rev. 41:281–330, 1961.

Oh, W.; Lind, J., and Gessner, I. H.: The circulatory and respiratory adaptation to early and late cord clamping in newborn infants, Acta paediat. 55:17–25, 1966.

Orzalesi, M. M,; Motoyama, E. K.; Jacobson, H. N.; Kikkawa, Y.; Reynolds, E. O. R., and Cook, C. D.: The development of the lungs of lambs, Pediatrics 35: 373–381, 1965.

Pattle, R. E.: Properties, function and origin of the alveolar lining layer, Proc. Roy. Soc., B 148:217–240, 1958.

Pattle, R. E.: The formation of a lining film by foetal lungs, J. Path. & Bact. 82:333–343, 1961.

Pattle, R. E.: Lining layer of alveoli, Brit. M. Bull. 19: 41–44, 1963.

Potter, E. L., and Bohlender, G. P.: Intrauterine respiration in relation to development of the fetal lung: With report of two unusual anomalies of the respiratory system, Am. J. Obst. & Gynec. 42:14–22, 1941.

Purves, M. J., and Biscoe, T. J.: Development of chemoreceptor activity, Brit. M. Bull. 22:56–60, 1966.

Radford, E. P.: Method for estimating respiratory surface area of mammalian lungs from their physical characteristics, Proc. Soc. Exper. Biol. & Med. 87:58–61, 1954.

Reynolds, E. O. R., and Strang, L. B.: Alveolar surface properties of the lung in the new-born, Brit. M. Bull. 22:79–83, 1966.

Reynolds, S. R. M.: A source of amniotic fluid in the lamb: The nasopharyngeal and buccal cavities, Nature 172:307–308, 1953.

Reynolds, S. R. M., and Mackie, J. D.: Development of chemoreceptor response sensitivity: Studies in fetuses, lambs and ewes, Am. J. Physiol. 201:239–250, 1961.

Rosenfeld, M., and Snyder, F. F.: Stages of development of respiratory regulation and the changes occurring at birth, Am. J. Physiol. 121:242–249, 1938.

Ross, B. B.: Comparison of foetal pulmonary fluid with foetal plasma and amniotic fluid, Nature 199:1100, 1963.

Rusznyák, I.; Földi, M., and Szabó, G.: *Lymphatics and Lymph Circulation* (Oxford: Pergamon Press, 1960).

Setnikar, I.; Agostoni, E., and Taglietti, A.: The fetal lung, a source of amniotic fluid, Proc. Soc. Exper. Biol., & Med. 101:842–845, 1959.

Shelley, H. J.: Blood sugars and tissue carbohydrate in foetal and infant lambs and rhesus monkeys, J. Physiol. 153:527–552, 1960.

Shelley, H. J., and Neligan, G. A.: Neonatal hypoglycaemia, Brit. M. Bull. 22:34–39, 1966.

Snyder, F. F., and Rosenfeld, M.: Direct observation of intra-uterine respiratory movements of the fetus and the role of carbon dioxide and oxygen in their regulation, Am. J. Physiol. 119:153–166, 1937.

Sorokin, S. P.: Activities of the Great Alveolar Cell, in Oliver, T. K. (ed.): *Neonatal Respiratory Adaptation* (Washington, D.C.: Public Health Service Publication 1432, 1963).

Stembera, Z. K.; Hodr, Z., and Janda, J.: Umbilical blood flow in healthy newborn infants during the first minutes after birth, Am. J. Obst. & Gynec. 91:568–574, 1965.

Tschirgi, R. D., and Gerard, R. W.: The carotid-mandibular reflex in acute respiratory failure, Am. J. Physiol. 150:358–364, 1947.

von Neergaard, K.: Neue Auffassungen über einen Grundbegriff der Atemmechanik. Ztschr. ges. exper. Med. 66:373–394, 1929.

Whitehead, W. H.; Windle, W. F., and Becker, R. F.: Changes in lung structure during aspiration of amniotic fluid and during air-breathing at birth, Anat. Rec. 83: 255–264, 1942.

Willson, H. G.: Postnatal development of the lung, Am. J. Anat. 41:97–122, 1928.

Windle, W. F.; Becker, R. F.; Barth, E. E., and Schultz, M. D.: Aspiration of amniotic fluid by the fetus, Surg. Gynec. & Obst. 69:705–712, 1939.

Windle, W. F.; Monnier, M., and Steele, A. G.: Fetal respiratory movements in the cat, Physiol. Zoöl. 11: 425–433, 1938.

12

Birth Asphyxia, Resuscitation, and Brain Damage

THE REMARKABLE ABILITY of the foetus and newborn to withstand birth asphyxia or anoxia is well known. The first reference in the scientific literature (Boyle, 1670) was put in a characteristic 17th century style. Using "kitlings" in his pneumatical receiver " . . . it appears, that those Animals continued 3 times longer in the Exhausted Receiver, than other Animals of that bigness would probably have done." This difference between the adult and the foetus or newborn depends on several physiological factors, and varies very much in different environmental conditions, at different gestational ages, and in different species. Also, as Mott (1961) pointed out, the definitions of survival used by experimental workers have varied. Ultimately, we seek survival without permanent impairment of any function, particularly that of the brain; but in practice it is usually necessary to select some arbitrary endpoint such as the last gasp (in the absence of subsequent resuscitation), or the fall in arterial pressure or heart rate to a defined minimum. The means used to produce asphyxia also have varied, and have had a considerable influence upon the results.

In the early 19th century, curiosity about the natural phenomena associated with legal homicide resulted in some notable contributions to scientific medicine. The conditions for making useful observations were particularly favourable in Paris with the introduction of the guillotine. And it was natural for Le Gallois (1812) to extend the range of observations to the newborn of different species. He showed that newborn animals subjected to asphyxia survived for different periods of time according to their species, and recorded that this was particularly short for the guinea pig. He also produced quantitative evidence (summarized in Table 38) to show that the mean time to the last gasp decreased with increasing age from birth, and that interruption of the circulation was associated with a shorter time to the last gasp than when asphyxia was caused by submersion or opening the thorax. The decapitated head continued to gasp for 15 minutes, rather less than when the circulation was interrupted by removing the heart. He thus gave considerable weight to the importance of the circulation in survival during asphyxia. Le Gallois also made systematic measurements on the reflex responses to cutaneous stimulation in asphyxia and demonstrated that they failed shortly before spontaneous respiratory movements ceased. Finally, by serial sections of the spinal cord and brain stem, he demonstrated that gasping movements depended upon the integrity of the medulla oblongata. His book is illustrated by a figure which shows the syringe used for maintaining the vitality of the decapitated torso by positive pressure ventilation.

TABLE 38.—MEAN TIMES (MINUTES) TO THE LAST GASP DURING ASPHYXIA IN RABBITS OF DIFFERENT AGES* (LE GALLOIS, 1812)

AGE (DAYS)	ASPHYXIA BY SUBMERSION	ON OPENING THE THORAX	ON REMOVING THE HEART
1	27	30	20
5	16	16	9
10	5.5	7.5	4
15	4	5.5	2.8
20	3.3	3.5	2.3
30	2.5	2.3	1.3

* The environmental temperature was not stated.

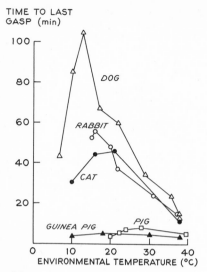

TIME TO LAST
GASP (min)

Fig. 64.—Observations on the times to last gasp in animals of different species exposed to 95% N_2 and 5% CO_2 at different environmental temperatures. (Redrawn from Miller and Miller, 1965.)

Perhaps the only criticism which could be made of these observations, which were remarkable for their thoroughness as compared with much of the anecdotal medical literature of that epoch, is that the temperature was not controlled. In 1824, Edwards remedied this deficiency. Among other observations he showed that newborn kittens, asphyxiated by excision of the heart, continued to gasp for 13.5 minutes in water at 20°C, but for only 7 minutes at 40°C, and 5 minutes at 0°C. There was, therefore, an optimal environmental temperature at which the duration of gasping was greatest, and the effect was independent of the circulation. He also recorded the fall in body temperature of 10 normal mature human infants after birth to a mean of 34.75°C, and in one premature 7-month baby (even though well swaddled and near to a fire) at 32°C. His observations on the effect of temperature on asphyxial survival have been confirmed by many subsequent investigations, particularly those of Bert (1870). Figure 64 summarizes some of the recent observations of Miller and Miller (1965), who for more than 12 years have made a systematic study of the effect of temperature. Their results show that the effect of a reduction in temperature in prolonging the duration of gasping in asphyxia depends upon the species. In those with a short time to last gasp at term, the effect is relatively smaller than in those with a longer time to last gasp, both absolutely and proportionately. The

maximum increase in time to last gasp in the pig was twofold, while in the dog it was more than eightfold.

When we come to compare the competence for asphyxial survival in different species it seems reasonable, in the first place, to study them at or shortly after birth and either in thermal conditions simulating those *in utero* or in a neutral thermal environment. Otherwise the propensity of small newborn animals to cool rapidly will lead to an exaggeration of their competence for survival, which will be enhanced by the species differences shown in Figure 64. Table 39 demonstrates the wide range in the time to last gasp of different species under these conditions, and illustrates the well-known fact that the newborn of species which are, in a very general sense, more mature at birth have a shorter time to last gasp. For instance, the newborn guinea pig which is mobile and eats solid food on its day of birth, survives total asphyxia for a time hardly as long as that of an adult.

There are some interesting differences in the times to last gasp recorded by different authors, using different methods, in the data of Table 39. Before these are examined in detail something must be said about the basis of comparison between animals asphyxiated by immersion (total or the head alone) and those exposed to either nitrogen alone or with 5% CO_2. On first exposure to nitrogen, a newborn animal hyperventilates and, hence, develops a respiratory alkalosis. Subsequent respiratory movements are infrequent although usually strong, and a metabolic acidosis then develops such that there is a large and rapid fall of arterial pH and rise of P_{CO_2} (often to exceed 150 mm Hg). In the newborn animal, therefore, the effects of asphyxia and of exposure to nitrogen are qualitatively similar in causing both hypoxaemia and hypercapnia. Quantitatively, one must suppose that they may be dissimilar, particularly in the early stages and, as we shall see, the initial alkalosis might create a situation in which gasping is prolonged. No systematic analysis of the results of this difference has been undertaken, probably because most authors have been concerned either with comparing results on different species or in analyzing physiological mechanisms in a single species, but using the same method of producing asphyxia. The mean time to last gasp of foetal rabbits within a day of term asphyxiated by delivery into saline at 37.5°C (22.5 minutes) was greater than that of newborn rabbits less than 2 days old exposed to nitrogen at 35°C (16 minutes), a difference which was ascribed to the rapid decrease in survival competence with age in

TABLE 39.—Species Variations in Times to Last Gasp on Asphyxia at Birth in a
Neutral Thermal Environment

SPECIES	METHOD OF ASPHYXIA	TIME TO LAST GASP (MIN)	SOURCE
Rat	Exposure to N_2 at 36°C	28	Stafford and Weatherall (1960)
	† Maternal uterine ischaemia	20	Becker, King, Marsh and Wyrick (1964)
Dog	Exposure to 95% N_2, 5% CO_2 at 36°C	23	Miller (1958)
	Exposure to N_2 at 35°C	28	Cassin, Swann and Cassin (1960)
Rabbit	Exposure to 95% N_2, 5% CO_2 at 36°C	20	Miller (1958)
	Exposure to N_2 at 35°C	26	Cassin, Swann and Cassin (1960)
	Immersion on delivery at 37.5°C	22.5	Campbell, Cross, Dawes and Hyman
	Exposure to N_2 at 35°C	16	(1966)
Cat	Immersion at 36°C	11.5	Bert (1870)
	Exposure to N_2 at 35°C	18	Cassin, Swann and Cassin (1960)
Rhesus Monkey	* Asphyxia on delivery	8.2	Dawes, Jacobson, Mott, Shelley and
Sheep	* Asphyxia on delivery	5.4	Stafford (1963)
Guinea Pig	Exposure to 95% N_2, 5% CO_2 at 36°C	3	Miller (1958)
	† Maternal uterine ischaemia	5.4	Becker, King, March and Wyrick (1964)

* By immersing the head in a fluid-filled bag.
† The foetus being left *in utero*, the uterus delivered into a warm saline bath.

this species (Campbell, Cross, Dawes, and Hyman, 1966). If the effect of anoxia were quantitatively different from that of asphyxia one might have expected a reversal of this result. The effect on the blood gases and pH of adding 5% CO_2 to the nitrogen used to cause anoxia (as in Miller's observations, Fig. 64), as compared with nitrogen alone, has not been examined.

The results obtained depend also on the method of applying the gas. Cassin, Swann, and Cassin (1960) used a flow of 10 litre/min, reduced to 5 litre/min after some seconds and which continued flowing past the animal's nose and mouth until death. The heads of newborn dogs, rabbits, and cats are small and may have been cooled by this very large airflow. This would account for the systematically and substantially higher times to last gasp recorded, as compared with those of other observers (Table 39). It is also interesting that in foetal rats subjected to asphyxia *in utero* (Becker *et al.*, 1964), the time to last gasp was less than that in newborn rats exposed to nitrogen at a flow of 2 liter/min in tubes with a diameter of about 6 cm (Stafford and Weatherall, 1960), even though the gas was warmed. It is thus possible that the ability to survive birth asphyxia has been somewhat exaggerated, in species which are immature at birth, by the use of anoxic newborn animals rather than asphyxiated foetuses.

The Physiological Mechanisms
CIRCULATION

The observation by Le Gallois (1812) that removal of the heart decreased the time to last gasp showed that the maintenance of the circulation during asphyxia was one factor in the prolonged survival of newborn animals. The fact that the isolated head also continued to gasp for many minutes demonstrated that there was a further factor by which newborn neural tissues differed from those of the adult. Both observations have been confirmed in other species (e.g., isolated or ischaemic head in mice, rats, rabbits, cats, and dogs; Enzmann and Pincus, 1934; Kabat, 1940; Selle and Witten, 1941; Hiestand, Tschirgi, and Miller, 1944; Thoms and Hiestand, 1947; Jílek, Fischer, Krulich, and Trojan, 1964: removal of heart in monkeys; Dawes, Jacobson, Mott, and Shelley, 1960), and the mechanisms involved have been investigated extensively.

Let us consider the effect of the circulation first. In adult animals asphyxia commonly causes, after a brief elevation of the arterial pressure, a relatively abrupt failure of the circulation with a rapid decline of pressure to very low levels, preceding the gradual cessation of gasping movements. But in foetal and newborn animals, the initial arterial pressure (before asphyxia) is less, and the decline during asphyxia is much slower. To take an extreme

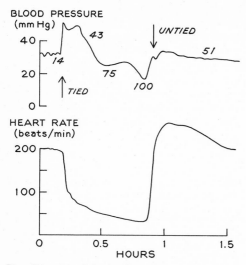

Fig. 65.—Foetal lamb of 88 days gestational age and 350 Gm weight. The umbilical cord was tied at the first arrow and untied at the second; the interpolated figures indicate the blood lactate concentration (mg/100 ml). (Redrawn from Dawes, Mott, and Shelley, 1959.)

later and the circulation recovered. Half an hour later the foetus began to make regular respiratory movements and moved its limbs. In all species the ability of the circulation to withstand asphyxia decreases with increasing age during late foetal and early neonatal life. For instance, in mature foetal lambs at term the arterial pressure fell, on tying the cord, from an initial value of ~65 mm Hg to ~15 mm Hg within 10 minutes.

The ability of the foetal and newborn circulation to withstand asphyxia is related inversely to the level of the systemic arterial pressure, both in different species and at different gestational ages. It is directly related to the pre-asphyxial glycogen concentration in the cardiac ventricles (Dawes, Mott, and Shelley, 1959; Shelley, 1960). Figure 66 shows the cardiac glycogen concentration in different species before and after birth. It is high early in foetal life (30–40 mg/Gm), and in most species is still high at term and falls slowly after birth as the arterial pressure rises. We do not know how it comes about that such large cardiac glycogen stores are laid down early in gestation, though we may guess that cardiac metabolism, which is more closely related to arterial pressure than to external work (Burton, 1965) is then less. The changes in the activity of cardiac enzymes during foetal development have been studied much less thoroughly than in the liver.

It seemed possible that the ability of the foetal

case, Figure 65 shows the changes in arterial pressure, heart rate, and blood lactate concentrations (mg/100 ml inserted as figures by the pressure record) in an immature lamb (at 0.6 of term) when the umbilical cord was tied at the first arrow. The cord was untied at the second arrow 40 minutes

Fig. 66.—Cardiac glycogen concentration in different species before and after birth (indicated by the vertical line). (Redrawn from Shelley, 1961.)

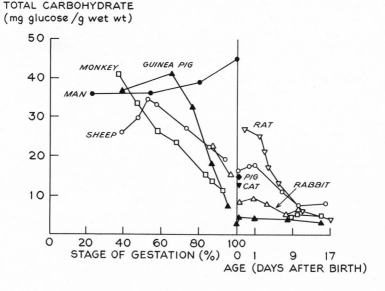

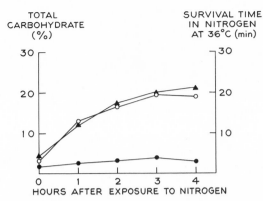

Fig. 67.—Litters of newborn rats were exposed to nitrogen for a period of time just short of lethal. The diagram shows the concentration of carbohydrate in the heart (▲) and liver (●) during recovery, and the survival times in nitrogen on subsequent exposure to nitrogen of littermates (○). (Redrawn from Stafford and Weatherall, 1960.)

or neonatal circulation to survive prolonged asphyxia was causally related to the high cardiac glycogen concentration, because in different species and at different gestational ages the time to the last gasp during asphyxia bore a linear relationship to the initial cardiac glycogen (Dawes, Mott, and Shelley, 1959), and because the latter was almost exhausted at this time. There was no correlation with liver glycogen. Stafford and Weatherall (1960) pursued the problem in newborn rats. They found that at a higher environmental temperature the rate of fall of total cardiac carbohydrate was greater than at a low one. When the cardiac carbohydrate was partially depleted by fasting or previous hypoxia, the survival time (to the last gasp) was decreased proportionately; it also increased proportionately during recovery from an anoxic episode. These latter experiments were particularly interesting because they showed that it required 3 hours for infant rats to recover their cardiac glycogen and their ability to survive asphyxia (Fig. 67). Repeated episodes of partial asphyxia in utero may, therefore, have an insidious cumulative effect in depleting cardiac glycogen, and hence the ability to withstand delivery, without causing any obvious sign.

Miller et al. (1964) have questioned the validity of the relation between cardiac glycogen and survival time on two grounds. First they point out that although newborn guinea pigs survive twice as long, the glycogen content of their ventricles is less than in adults. But neither newborn nor adult guinea pigs survive asphyxia for more than a few

minutes, and the figure for newborn guinea pigs reported by Miller (1958) is less than that given by Becker et al. (1964), using another method (Table 39). In this species any such difference in asphyxial survival as may exist between the newborn and adult might be explicable solely on neural grounds (see below); this would be a reasonable hypothesis which could be tested, as Le Gallois did in the rabbit more than 150 years ago, by removing the heart. Secondly, newborn pigs were reported as gasping for only 4 minutes at 39°C, a time less than that to be expected if their cardiac glycogen were 15 mg/Gm (Fig. 66), but this is consistent with some lower measurements in the literature (3.4 mg/Gm; Elneil and McCance, 1965), possibly resulting from exposure to cold. Miller and his colleagues have chosen to illustrate their argument two species (guinea pigs and pigs) in which asphyxial survival is small and the effect of cold is minimal (Fig. 64). They have consistently emphasized the direct effect of cold on the metabolism of the brain. It is possible that the large effect of cold in prolonging survival in the newborn cat, rabbit, and dog (Fig. 64) is as much due to slowing of cardiac metabolism as to its effect on the brain.

During asphyxia of foetal and newborn mammals, the arterial Po_2 falls rapidly and the O_2 content of the blood is virtually exhausted within 2 minutes. The ability of the heart to maintain some output, although much reduced, then depends on the production of energy by anaerobic glycolysis. If this is arrested by injection of sodium iodoacetate, the circulation fails as quickly in the newborn as in the adult. Thus the large initial supply of glycogen in the cardiac ventricles is a potential supply of energy which is made available by local glycolysis, a process which results in the accumulation of a high tissue lactate concentration during asphyxia. In foetal lambs a large proportion of the carbohydrate loss, and hence the lactate production, occurs in the heart (Table 40), which continues to perform active mechanical work. The blood lactate concentration rises rapidly (but less rapidly than in the

TABLE 40.—MEAN CARBOHYDRATE LOSS AND LACTATE PRODUCTION DURING ASPHYXIA IN FOETAL LAMBS (DAWES, MOTT, AND SHELLEY, 1959)

	0.6 OF TERM	0.9 OF TERM
Duration of asphyxia (min)	60	15
Total carbohydrate loss (mg)	179	878
Loss from heart (mg)	162 (90%)	375 (43%)
Total lactate production (mg)	181	642

heart) and the blood pH falls. Administration of extra glucose to asphyxiated immature foetal lambs did not reduce the rate of fall of heart rate or blood pressure, but when this was accompanied by an infusion of base (sodium carbonate or organic bases such as tris-hydroxymethylaminomethane or tri-ethanolamine) to prevent the fall in pH, survival was considerably prolonged (Dawes, Jacobson, Mott, Shelley, and Stafford, 1963). This was attributed to the maintenance of intracellular pH, so that glycolysis (as judged by tissue and blood lactate concentrations) continued at a much higher rate than in untreated lambs. It was necessary to provide glucose also as substrate in immature lambs whose liver glycogen stores were small and soon exhausted.

Total asphyxia causes a reduction in the energy available to maintain the normal ionic concentration gradients across cells and, therefore, the cells leak and the plasma potassium concentration rises. There is usually no significant change in plasma sodium during asphyxia, presumably because, although some enters the cells, this is accompanied by water to offset the rise in intracellular osmolarity as a result of lactate accumulation. As Battaglia, Meschia, and Barron (1958) point out, the osmolar changes in the plasma also are complicated by variations in blood glucose. There is always a small rise in haematocrit concentration during asphyxia.

Fig. 68.—To show the mean rise in plasma potassium in immature foetal lambs during asphyxia; untreated (○), or given an intravenous infusion of solutions of glucose and NaCl (□), glucose and Na_2CO_3 (●), or Na_2CO_3 alone (△). The vertical lines indicate ±S.E. where differences were significant. (Redrawn from Dawes, Mott, and Shelley, 1959.)

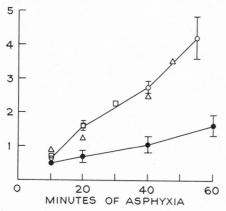

RISE IN PLASMA POTASSIUM (mEq/L)

MINUTES OF ASPHYXIA

Figure 68 demonstrates that the rise of plasma K^+ during asphyxia in immature foetal lambs was reduced by infusion of base (sodium carbonate), provided that an adequate quantity of glucose also was available. This is additional evidence for the beneficial effect of this treatment at the cellular level, although it is uncertain from which cells (cardiac, cerebral, or perhaps hepatic) the K^+ originated.

We also have to consider how it comes about that removal of the heart during asphyxia so much reduces the time to last gasp in foetal or newborn animals. Maintenance of the circulation does not prolong gasping by a continued supply of O_2 in foetal or newborn rabbits, dogs, lambs, or monkeys, because there is little or no O_2 left in the blood after 2 minutes. But maintenance of the circulation does ensure a continued supply of glucose (as a substrate for anaerobic glycolysis) to the brain, whose glycogen concentration during foetal life and at birth is as low as in the adult (<2 mg/Gm; Shelley, 1961). It also provides a sink into which lactate and hydrogen ions may drain and be redistributed throughout the blood and the tissues which are still perfused. It thus helps to buffer the pH and osmolar changes in the cerebral cells during asphyxia.

Scholander (1960) drew attention to a possible analogy between the ability of the adult seal to sustain life during a 20-minute dive, and that of the asphyxiated mammalian foetus, also in a liquid environment. It is true that both reduce and redistribute their cardiac outputs advantageously, largely restricting flow to the vital organs, the heart and brain. But, thereafter, the analogy breaks down. Whereas the foetus survives (after the first 2–3 minutes) by anaerobic glycolysis with a large rise in blood lactate concentration during asphyxia, the seal uses the large quantity of oxygen stored in its lungs and blood (particularly in a substantial vena caval reservoir) to supply its heart and brain, and the blood lactate concentration does not rise until blood flow is reinstituted to ischaemic parts of the body after surfacing. It would be interesting to know how the seal foetus behaves during asphyxia and whether the maternal blood supply to the placenta is maintained during a dive.

NEURAL AND OTHER TISSUES

As in the heart, so in the brain, anaerobic glycolysis is essential for survival in total asphyxia. Administration of sodium iodoacetate or fluoride, which

TABLE 41.—MEAN BLOOD pH DURING ASPHYXIA IN MATURE FOETAL LAMBS, MONKEYS, AND NEWBORN RABBITS

DURATION OF ASPHYXIA (MIN)	* LAMB	BLOOD pH IN ** MONKEY	† RABBIT
0	7.25	7.27	7.34
5	6.95	6.89	7.16
10	6.72	6.75	7.02
15			6.89

* Dawes, Jacobson, Mott, Shelley and Stafford (1963).
** Observations on 22 rhesus monkeys (unpublished).
† Campbell and Milligan (unpublished).

inhibits enzymes involved in glycolysis, reduces the time to the last gasp of asphyxiated or anoxic whole newborn animals (Himwich, Bernstein, Herrlich, Chesler, and Fazekas, 1942) or of isolated heads (Hiestand, Tschirgi, and Miller, 1944) to that observed in adults. Selle and Witten (1941) and Selle (1943) distinguished two series of gasping movements made by isolated heads, a first series of 6–12 gasps lasting for 20–80 seconds after decapitation or ligation of the cerebral vessels, and a second series beginning after an interval of 30–35 seconds. The first series of gasps was associated with continuing aerobic metabolism, and was blocked by administration of cyanide or general anaesthetics, but not by iodoacetate (Hiestand, Tschirgi, and Miller, 1944). The second series was associated with anaerobic glycolysis and was abolished by iodoacetate or by procedures which reduced blood glucose concentration before isolation of the head (starvation and insulin administration).

In 1931, Reiss suggested that the increased survival time and the large quantities of lactate produced in asphyxiated newborn animals might be due to an unusual capacity for glycolysis, which was lost with increasing age. However, the large lactate concentrations (up to 240 mg/100 ml in newborn rats) are only attained after many minutes of asphyxia. *In vitro* experiments on rat embryos

(Boell, 1957), foetal rat livers (van Rossum, 1963), and in kidney cortex slices from rats and rabbits (Whittam 1960, 1961) showed that the rate of glycolysis did decrease with increasing age. Yet in the heart and brain, similar studies showed that glycolysis increased with age in rats, cats, dogs, and man (e.g., Chesler and Himwich, 1944,a,b; DeHaan and Field, 1959). Also, *in vivo* observations demonstrated that the rate of lactate accumulation in the blood, heart, lung, brain, skeletal muscle, and kidney cortex was as great or greater during the first 15 minutes of asphyxia, in foetal lambs at 0.9 as at 0.6 of term (Dawes, Mott, and Shelley, 1959). In asphyxiated monkeys and lambs, which have a short time to last gasp, the rate of fall of blood pH was greater than in newborn rabbits which have a longer time to last gasp (Tables 39 and 41). An increased rate of glycolysis (say in the immature brain) would also be dependent on an increased carbohydrate supply, which is not available in the isolated head.

If an increased rate of glycolysis is not responsible for the survival of immature animals (by making relatively more energy available as compared with adults), it seems possible that a decreased rate of energy requirement might be the explanation, thus spinning out the available energy reserves. Most of the work on this idea has been carried out on rats during the first 3 weeks from birth because they are cheap, easily obtained, and show large changes. During this period, brain weight increases rapidly (Table 42), and the cells, although there are fewer per unit mass, grow larger and more complex. The water content decreases and measurements on the chloride space suggest that the extracellular volume is reduced (Lajtha, 1957). There is only a slight increase in vascularity during the first 5 days, but a very rapid increase between 10 and 21 days (Craigie, 1925) when myelinization is being completed. There is also a large decline in the mean time to the last gasp both of the anoxic whole animal and what is more pertinent to the present ques-

TABLE 42.—CHANGES IN THE RAT'S BRAIN WITH AGE

POSTNATAL AGE (Days)	BRAIN WEIGHT (Gm)	DRY WEIGHT (%)	DNA CONTENT (mg/Gm brain)	MITOCHONDRIAL PROTEIN (mg/Gm brain)	CELLULAR CONCENTRATION (per Gm brain $\times 10^8$)	O_2 UPTAKE/CELL (P atoms/hr)	RATE OF ATP UTILIZATION (μg/Gm sec)
1	0.25	12	2.56	11.0	4.2	0.04	1.8
5			1.89	11.8	3.1	0.07	
10	0.95		1.95	17.6	3.2	0.09	
20–21	1.15	22	1.73	24.4	2.8	0.14	10

Sources: Himwich, Baker, and Fazekas (1939); Dahl and Samson (1959); Samson, Balfour, and Dahl (1960).

TABLE 43.—MEAN TIMES TO THE LAST GASP OF
ISOLATED RAT HEADS

DAYS FROM BIRTH	TIME TO LAST GASP (MIN)	
	Selle (1941)	Jílek, Krulich, and Trojan (1963)
1	29	22
3		17
4	24	
5		10
7	16	
9		6
14	5	
21	2	1
25		

The environmental temperatures were not reported.

tion (because the influence of the circulation is then excluded) of the isolated head (Table 43).

Many authors have observed that the oxidative metabolism per unit weight in rat brains increases with age (e.g., Himwich, Baker, and Fazekas, 1939; Tyler and van Harreveld, 1942; Chesler and Himwich, 1944,a), but the quantitative correlation between this and the ability of the isolated head to continue gasping is poor. The former does not begin to rise significantly until 10 days from birth, when the latter has already fallen 75% (Table 43). However, O_2 uptake per cell does appear to increase during this period (Table 42). Samson, Balfour, and Dahl (1960) have estimated the energy utilization of anoxic rat brains *in vivo*, by measuring the rate of adenosine triphosphate (ATP) disappearance at different time intervals after the onset of anoxia, in the presence of iodoacetate (to inhibit anaerobic glycolysis). Utilization rose about fivefold between birth and 20 days (Table 42), but the change during the first 10 days was comparatively small. However, their observations have been repeated by Abdel-Latif and Abood (1964) who found that ATP-ase activity was distributed throughout all cellular fractions of rat whole brains (obtained by gradient centrifugation and cytologically identified by electronmicroscopy) and increased threefold between 14–16 days gestation (term is ~22 days) and 10 days postnatally. The increase was particularly large in the fraction which contained terminal boutons. The mitochondria of embryonic brain did not seem to differ morphologically or biochemically from those in neonatal or adult rats, while the specific activity of anaerobic glycolysis in particulate fractions was less (confirming previous results on whole brains). *In vitro*

measurements have shown that ATP-ase activity is already well developed at birth in the brain of the guinea pig (Flexner and Flexner, 1948) as compared with the rat (Potter, Schneider, and Lieb, 1945).

The conclusion that the high capability of anoxic survival in infant rat brains was related to the low rate of degradation of ATP was supported by experiments with paraldehyde and ether (Balfour, Samson, and Dahl, 1959). These both prolonged the time to the last gasp and decreased the rate of use of ATP. Dahl, Samson, and Balfour (1964) also observed in isolated nerve (the chicken vagus) that during energy deprivation (in the presence of anoxia and iodoacetate) electrical stimulation caused a decrease in the spike height and conduction velocity and accelerated the fall in ATP concentration. Thus we may guess that the continued activity of the respiratory centre during asphyxia causes a more rapid fall in its available energy reserves, and that these may be conserved under general anaesthesia which, initially at least, reduces the frequency of gasps (see p. 150). It would be interesting to know whether the same explanation can account for the greater susceptibility of some parts of the brain to asphyxia. For instance, does the respiratory centre, which continues to discharge for some while after most reflex responses have been extinguished by asphyxia, have a lower ATP utilization or a higher capacity for anaerobic glycolysis? And, conversely, do those brain-stem centres (e.g., the nuclei of the inferior colliculi), which in the rhesus monkey are most susceptible to permanent damage during asphyxia, have an unusually high rate of energy utilization corresponding to a greater cell elaboration, or do they have a small carbohydrate reserve and blood supply?

We may also speculate whether the same features which distinguish the tissues of the brain at birth (in the rat but not in the guinea pig) also pertain to the heart and liver. These tissues in immature animals are usually resistant to the effects of asphyxia, but less attention has been paid to the biochemical characteristics responsible for this. De-Haan and Field (1959) have shown that the buffer capacity of cardiac homogenates in newborn rats is somewhat less than that of adults, in conformity with their lower content of solid matter. There was no protein breakdown in cardiac homogenates until the pH <5, when the cathepsin activity was less in the newborn than the adult. The kidney has been studied by Whittam (1960, 1961), but the lung is hardly ever mentioned. This is an omission which should be remedied in view of the possibility that asphyxial damage may contribute to the aetiology of the respiratory distress syndrome.

Finally, we may consider the likely course of events in the brain cells during progressive asphyxia at birth. As time goes on, the rate of energy supply by glycolysis becomes inadequate. The possible limiting factors are twofold, exhaustion of substrate and fall of intracellular pH. The blood glucose concentration in the foetus is normally only half the maternal value and is often low in the first 2–3 days after birth (Shelley and Neligan, 1966), but provided there are adequate hepatic stores it rises during asphyxia. Hence, the level of blood glucose is rarely a limiting factor, although with a falling arterial pressure the level of cerebral blood flow may limit supply. The fall of intracellular pH is a more serious consequence of continued asphyxia. This may largely explain why infusion of base into asphyxiated newly delivered lambs and monkeys prolongs the duration of gasping and facilitates resuscitation (Dawes, Jacobson, Mott, Shelley and Stafford, 1963; Adamsons *et al.,* 1963) and prevents or mitigates permanent brain damage (Dawes, Hibbard, and Windle, 1964). Yet in these experiments there was also a beneficial effect upon the circulation which must have contributed to the outcome. Eventually, the cells must begin to suffer both from the lack of energy needed to maintain the ionic gradient across the cell membrane and from the osmolar effects of lactate accumulation. The first histological sign of damage is mitochondrial swelling (e.g., Hager, 1963). Ultimately, perhaps the proteases of the lysosomes are released and self-destruction proceeds (DeDuve, 1959). It is possible that this process may be detected by liberation of enzymes which are normally intracellular into the blood stream or cerebrospinal fluid. At what stage a cerebral cell loses its capacity for survival altogether is not known nor how, if recovery is possible, that process may best be facilitated in the immediate postasphyxial period.

The Natural History of Asphyxia and Resuscitation at Birth

When a normal foetal rhesus monkey is delivered without general anaesthesia near term, the umbilical cord is tied and the head is covered with a small bag of warm saline, a characteristic series of changes ensues (Fig. 69). Within about half a minute of tying the cord a short series of respiratory efforts begin, often of a rhythmic character. These are interrupted by a convulsion or series of clonic movements accompanied by an abrupt and profound fall in heart rate after which the animal lies inert with no muscular tone. The skin is by this time cyanosed and during the next few minutes becomes blotchy and finally white as vasoconstriction spreads to produce asphyxia pallida. The initial period of apnoea (primary apnoea) lasts for 0.5–1.0 minute. The monkey then begins to gasp, and 4–5 minutes after the onset of asphyxia the rate of gasping increases somewhat. Thereafter, there is little change in rate, the gasps merely becoming weaker terminally. There then follows *secondary* or *terminal apnoea* and, if resuscitation is not begun within a few minutes, death. If the arterial pH is low on delivery, as a result of placenta praevia, maternal hypotension or other causes (say 7.0–7.1) there are no rhythmic respiratory efforts preceding primary apnoea. If the initial pH is lower still (<6.8) there may be no gasps at all. The pH on delivery is the most powerful determinant of the time to the last gasp (when body temperature is maintained); sex is of no consequence in this respect and body

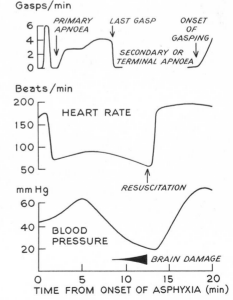

Fig. 69.—Schematic diagram of changes in rhesus monkeys during asphyxia and on resuscitation by positive pressure ventilation. Brain damage was assessed by histological examination some weeks or months later.

ARTERIAL

P_{O_2}	25	5	<2		
P_{CO_2}	45	100	150	200	40
pH	7.3	7.0	6.8	6.75	7.1

Gasps/min

PRIMARY APNOEA · LAST GASP · ONSET OF GASPING · SECONDARY OR TERMINAL APNOEA

Beats/min · HEART RATE

RESUSCITATION

mm Hg · BLOOD PRESSURE · BRAIN DAMAGE

TIME FROM ONSET OF ASPHYXIA (min)

weight or gestational age have only a comparatively small and barely significant effect during the last fifth of gestation in this species. In newborn rabbits the sequence of events is much the same, although rather more long drawn out in conformity with the longer time to the last gasp. There is, however, a pronounced terminal acceleration of gasping, which is heralded by the development of fine muscular movements of the cervical and thoracic muscles and a sentinel gasp of unusual vigour.

The phenomenon described as primary apnoea is of particular importance because, although normally of comparatively short duration, in individual rabbits it can be as long as 9 minutes (Fig. 70), and is greatly extended by anaesthetics such as pentobarbitone or analgesics such as meperidine (pethidine, demerol) or morphine. It then becomes almost impossible to distinguish from secondary or terminal apnoea. However, in primary apnoea uncomplicated by drugs a newborn animal will normally respond to tactile stimuli or to analeptics (such as lobeline) which will induce a gasp earlier than was otherwise to be anticipated, and hence shorten its duration. It seems clear that human infants which are apnoeic at birth, and which subsequently respond by gasping to resuscitative measures other than ventilation (and/or to the effects of increasing asphyxia on the systemic arterial or central chemoreceptors) were in primary apnoea. How does the human infant compare in other respects? We do not know for sure. Such measurements of cardiac carbohydrate as are available (Shelley and Neligan, 1966; Burnard, 1966) suggest that it may be as high at term (35–45

mg/Gm) as in other species at any period of gestation (Fig. 66). There are many anecdotal reports in the literature of human infants who have survived remarkable periods of asphyxia at birth, with survival after 10 minutes without oxygen or more (e.g., Bullough, 1958). Yet this evidence has to be viewed against the frequency distribution of gasping in infants of other species. Figure 70 shows this for 195 newborn rabbits (all runts, cool, unfed, or otherwise abnormal individuals or litters being excluded) which were exposed to nitrogen in uniform thermal ($\sim35°C$) conditions. Although the mean time to last gasp was 16 minutes there were several rabbits which gasped for more than 30 minutes. In the rhesus monkey, which has a shorter mean time to last gasp during asphyxia (8.2 minutes ±0.15, S. E., in 40 monkeys) the range of variation was less, with a maximum of only 10.2 minutes. We may guess that the average human baby lies somewhere in between (probably rather nearer to the rabbit than the monkey), as does its cardiac carbohydrate, though its arterial pressure at birth is higher than that of either of the others, Table 24, p. 98.

The sequence of events on successful resuscitation is qualitatively similar in all species including man (Cross, 1966). If the infant is still gasping, re-admission of air is usually sufficient to ensure rapid recovery unless the gasps have become feeble and the arterial pressure unusually low. If gasping has already stopped, i.e., in secondary apnoea, the first sign of recovery on rhythmic positive pressure ventilation is an acceleration of the heart. Following this the pressure rises, more rapidly if the last gasp is only just exceeded, more slowly if the duration of asphyxia has been greater, the skin becomes pink, and gasping then begins after an interval. This interval is greater the more the duration of asphyxia beyond the last gasp (Fig. 71), a fact which has some practical value in indicating at once, in a general way, the magnitude of the asphyxial insult which an infant has suffered. Rhythmic spontaneous respiratory efforts become established after a further interval which also is related to the duration of asphyxia. Not until some minutes after this do the spinal and corneal reflexes return. Muscular tone re-appears gradually over the course of the next hour or more.

The extinction of reflexes during asphyxia includes the respiratory reflexes. Yet Tschirgi and Gerard (1947) found that they could still elicit the linguo-mandibular reflex after the cessation of gasping in asphyxiated newborn rats, showing that

Fig. 70.—Frequency distribution of the duration of primary apnoea (●) and the time to the last gasp (○) in 195 newborn rabbits exposed to nitrogen at 35°C. (From the data of Campbell, Cross, Dawes, and Hyman, 1966.)

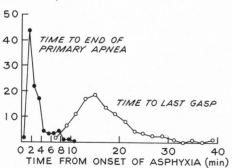

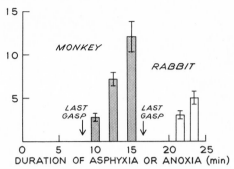

Fig. 71.—Mean times to the last spontaneous gasp, and from beginning positive pressure ventilation to the first gasp, for foetal monkeys asphyxiated for 10, 12.5, or 15 minutes, and for newborn rabbits exposed to nitrogen for 21.8 and 23.5 minutes. The vertical lines indicate ±S.E. (Redrawn from Campbell, Cross, Dawes, and Hyman, 1966.)

respiratory failure was central. Cross, Klaus, Tooley, and Weisser (1960) observed that the rise in intratracheal pressure during positive pressure inflation of the lungs in normal newborn human infants caused an inspiratory effort, a phenomenon analogous to the paradoxical reflex of Head (1889), whose afferent limb runs in the vagus. They surmised that this might assist in expansion of the lungs on resuscitation. It unquestionably does this when present, and is useful in accelerating recovery in primary apnoea, but Godfrey (1966) has shown that the inspiratory response to inflation only reappears late in recovery after resuscitation in secondary apnoea.

Methods of Resuscitation

The literature of this subject is littered with accounts of methods now discarded, from the Bloxam box to intragastric oxygen (James, Apgar, Burnard, and Moya, 1963), and it is important to recognize why this should be so. It seems to have resulted from two circumstances. First there was the failure to test new methods on animal preparations, so that their efficacy could be compared with other methods under controlled conditions, before using them on human infants. And secondly, human babies vary greatly in the degree of asphyxia with which they present at birth and this has not been easy to estimate quantitatively. Yet very few babies which are apnoeic on delivery are in secondary apnoea.

The vast majority are in primary apnoea and respond to a variety of stimuli. Thus the proponents of every new method of resuscitation which has been introduced have been able to claim a large measure of success, and to illustrate this with graphic stories of the apparent return to life from this condition, so dramatically described by a German author of the late 19th century as "Der Scheintod Neugeborener." This must not be taken to imply that any method will do. Recently, controlled trials in animals have shown that there are highly significant differences between the efficacy of different methods, and although the number of babies in serious danger of death may be small, the danger of permanent brain damage now appears to be greater than has been supposed.

POSITIVE PRESSURE VENTILATION.—The physiological principles in resuscitation are simple. The object is to restore the circulation, oxygen consumption, and the internal environment as quickly as possible. Time is important because the onset of brain damage is rapid. During asphyxia there is a large rise in pulmonary vascular resistance (Chapter 7) and the arterial pressure falls. The consequent decrease in pulmonary blood flow may thus become a limiting factor in oxygen uptake. Pulmonary vascular resistance may be reduced by gaseous ventilation of the lungs, raising the alveolar P_{O_2}, and decreasing the alveolar and pulmonary arterial P_{CO_2} and hydrogen ion concentration. The first two objectives may be achieved quickly by positive pressure ventilation with a high O_2 mixture. Elimination of CO_2 and restoration of a normal arterial pH after severe asphyxia is achieved slowly by ventilation alone (Fig. 69). Even 20 minutes after beginning resuscitation, when the arterial P_{CO_2} is reduced to 40 mm Hg, the metabolic acidosis may be so large that the pH is still only 7.1.

It is not always easy to judge the best ventilation for a monkey (or a human baby) after profound asphyxia, because the colour of the skin and the heart rate are not reliable guides. Underventilation is associated with a persistent high arterial pressure; overventilation is possible and results in persistent apnoea with a $P_{CO_2} < 25$ mm Hg. But if one is aware of these two possibilities they are usually avoided without the use of elaborate instruments, using the movement of the thoracic cage as a guide.

It is not at all difficult to expand the lungs of a severely asphyxiated mature foetus; the initial pressure required is high (20–35 mm Hg, as in unasphyxiated infants) but after the first inflations can be much reduced. The dangers of lung rupture with the production of pneumothorax in mature infants have plainly been greatly exaggerated. I have taken part in the resuscitation of many hundreds of severely asphyxiated rabbits, lambs, and monkeys without once encountering this complication. This is not to deny its occurrence in very premature infants, in association with inhaled meconium for instance, but there are well authenticated instances in spontaneously breathing children who have not received artificial ventilation (Donald, 1960; Chernick and Avery, 1963; Malan and Heese, 1966). So this complication is to be associated with the deficiencies of the infant rather than of the method, in competent hands.

The use of positive pressure ventilation in resuscitation has been widely practised for many years, and usually it is effective if there is a palpable heart beat. Objective evidence of its efficacy has recently been obtained by Hull and Segall (1966), who have measured the O_2 uptake *during* resuscitation of human infants and found that it rapidly increases to a level no different from that of a child during the first day of life. This confirmed in a striking manner similar measurements on animals (Adamsons, Behrman, Dawes, James, and Koford, 1964). However, there are reasons for believing that in some circumstances recovery is further facilitated by administration of base, to offset the metabolic acidosis.

INFUSION OF ALKALI.—The effect of infusions of alkali and glucose *during asphyxia* in preventing brain damage and in facilitating recovery has already been described. Ventilation alone only causes a gradual decline in arterial P_{CO_2} and hydrogen ion concentration. It was, therefore, expected that a rapid correction of arterial pH by injection of base and glucose during resuscitation might be an additional help by reducing pulmonary vascular resistance and by partial restoration of the normal cellular environment. Rapid infusion of alkali (0.5 M Tris) with glucose reduced the time required to establish rhythmic breathing and increased the immediate O_2 uptake in rhesus monkeys (Adamsons, Behrman, Dawes, James, and Koford, 1964); cautious clinical trials were advocated. Insofar as these have gone (and here I am indebted to numerous paediatric colleagues for reports of work in progress), they are encouraging, but no systematic study has been published.

Behrman (1966) has drawn attention to some potential dangers associated with rapid infusion of alkali, but these were exaggerated. Rapid correction of arterial pH by intravenous injection of sodium bicarbonate or Tris has been used for several years in Europe in the treatment of the human respiratory distress syndrome without evidence of an excessive sodium load, caustic effects upon the tissues, or other complications, nor have these been seen after use in more than 50 cases of asphyxia neonatorum (Tooley, personal communication).

CARDIAC MASSAGE.—In 2 of 110 foetal monkeys the heart stopped abruptly during asphyxia. It was restarted after positive pressure ventilation had been begun, by a few brief periods of external cardiac massage (in one instance after more than 4 minutes' arrest). Subsequent recovery was uneventful. This is an unusual complication but one worth remembering, for the arrest occurred after a period of asphyxia normally insufficient to cause widespread brain damage.

In many monkeys it was found that when the arterial pressure fell too low (usually <15 mm Hg) during asphyxia, positive pressure ventilation alone did not ensure immediate recovery, presumably because pulmonary blood flow was insufficient. This occurred when the heart rate was still above 50/min, but the pulse pressure was low and might have been imperceptible in a human infant. Once again, one or more brief periods of external cardiac massage were all that was required to initiate recovery. After a few experiences of this kind external cardiac massage was always performed on animals in which the heart did not accelerate, and maintain its acceleration, within 30–45 seconds of beginning ventilation. This is rarely necessary in human infants, but has been applied successfully (Moya, James, Burnard, and Hanks, 1962). Gupta and Scopes (1965) have published a striking illustration of the effect of cardiac massage on arterial pressure (recorded from an umbilical catheter) in a child whose heart stopped during a cyanotic attack. The effect of massage was almost identical to that seen in monkeys (Adamsons *et al.,* 1964), with rises in arterial pressure to about 40 mm Hg.

ANALEPTICS AND HYPOTHERMIA.—The use of analeptics in resuscitation has had a long and chequered career. Their use was abandoned in some centres partly as a result of clinical experience (they did not appear to work in many severely asphyxiated infants) (Resuscitation of Newborn Infants, 1956) and partly as a result of theory (that they were believed to act by stimulating the systemic arterial chemoreceptors, which were expected already to be strongly excited by asphyxia). Their use was continued in other centres, because there was no alternative and because from time to time they appeared to initiate gasps in some infants. Yet it is interesting that there is now evidence that the carotid chemoreceptors do not at once respond to cyanide in the foetus (Chapter 11). In newborn and adult monkeys, lobeline and nikethamide (coramine) do indeed excite respiratory efforts during primary apnoea, but so do many other stimuli. But in secondary apnoea they are not only ineffective, but cause a more rapid decline in blood pressure, whereas administration of alkali restores both the circulation (Fig. 72) and gasping, even in the presence of continuing asphyxia (Daniel, Dawes, James, and Ross, 1966). Clearly, these analeptics, in the infants which most need them, are not only valueless but dangerous.

The use of hypothermia in resuscitation has been advocated by Miller and his colleagues (Miller, 1949; Westin, Nyberg, Miller, and Wedenberg, 1962; Miller, Miller, and Westin, 1964; Miller and Miller, 1965). They argued that since cooling prolonged survival in asphyxiated animals it should also do so in man, a very reasonable proposition. They did not explain how prolongation of survival could lead to recovery, but proceeded to clinical trials. In foetal monkeys asphyxiated beyond the

last gasp, immersion in cold water did not cause gasping to begin again, although such monkeys can be resuscitated by other means, by positive pressure ventilation, or even by injection of alkali alone (Daniel, Dawes, James, Ross, and Windle, 1966). On immersion in water at 10°C, an asphyxiated monkey of 450 Gm takes more than 5 minutes to cool to 26°C (a newborn human infant of 2–3 kg takes longer still). So even when rapid cooling is begun before the last gasp (after only 6.5 minutes asphyxia) this does not prevent the development of brain damage. The time taken to cool a human infant effectively has to be set against the fact that positive pressure ventilation will restore oxygen uptake within a minute or two.

Miller and his colleagues reported that hypothermia was successful in human infants after other standard methods of resuscitation (including positive pressure ventilation) had failed. But their criterion of success was the appearance of gasping, rather than restoration of the circulation and oxygen uptake, during the first 4 minutes from birth. Their trial was weighted in favour of hypothermia because it is to be expected that even after 4 minutes, unventilated infants still in primary apnoea will gasp through the effects of continued

Fig. 72.—Observations on 2 foetal monkeys asphyxiated by tying the umbilical cord; the heads were covered by a bag containing a little saline. Drugs were injected during secondary apnoea, 1 minute after the last gasp. Injection of alkali (Tris) in **A** caused a rapid rise in heart rate (indicated by the numerals above the pres- sure record in beats per minute, and after 25 seconds the monkey began to gasp again. Injection of lobeline (2 mg/kg) in **B** caused the arterial pressure to fall more rapidly; heart rate continued to decrease, and there were no further respiratory efforts. Time scales in seconds. (Daniel, Dawes, James, and Ross, 1966.)

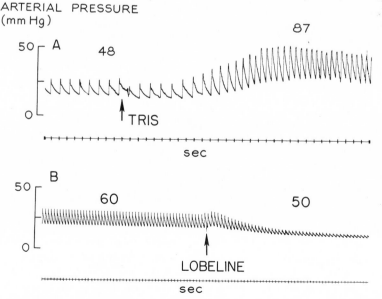

exposure and asphyxia; ventilated infants will be on the way to recovery. This is the logical defect in trials of asphyxia neonatorum using an infant as its own control. If an arbitrary time from birth is chosen, at which continuing apnoea is regarded as indicating failure of resuscitation, any method (or no method) of treatment will yield some apparent success.

HYPERBARIC OXYGEN.—Hutchison, Kerr, Williams, and Hopkinson (1963) have used hyperbaric oxygen as a means of resuscitation. They argued that raising the environmental Po_2 facilitated the uptake of O_2 by any available route, including the skin. The latter is a proposition that in mature warm-blooded animals deserves no more serious consideration than O_2 uptake from the gastrointestinal tract; the peripheral vessels are vasoconstricted in asphyxia, arterial pressure and blood flow are reduced and much of the O_2 absorbed is used locally. In the absence of pulmonary ventilation one has to be thin-skinned and small to survive long, even at 16 atmospheres oxygen pressure (Goodlin and Perry, 1966). Hence, if exposure to hyperbaric oxygen is to be effective, the lungs must be expanded either already or as a result of other stimuli (e.g., the effect of time and exposure in primary apnoea). This proposition was supported by experiments on foetal rabbits asphyxiated beyond the last gasp, and whose lungs had not been ventilated, which showed that exposure to hyperbaric oxygen (at 4 atmospheres absolute) failed to cause recovery while positive pressure ventilation was usually successful (Campbell, Cross, Dawes, and Hyman, 1966). Positive pressure ventilation has the additional advantage of immediate pulmonary ventilation and elimination of carbon dioxide. This explains why in anoxic newborn rabbits (whose lungs were already expanded) resuscitation by positive pressure ventilation caused a significantly higher survival rate (85%) as compared with exposure to hyperbaric oxygen (59%). There are also some practical considerations about the use of a hyperbaric oxygen chamber, which is expensive and, when the infant is once placed inside, precludes access to the mouth or to the chest for external cardiac massage.

In a clinical trial (Hutchison, Kerr, Inall, and Shanks, 1966), the mortality rates of human infants with birth asphyxia were almost (but not quite) the same, using either hyperbaric oxygen (19/107) or positive pressure ventilation (15/100). The composition of the two groups was similar as regards Apgar score, but this is a poor index of difference

in physiological conditions in severely asphyxiated infants. For instance, it does not differentiate between those which have or have not reached the last gasp, and its relation to arterial pH (which is of crucial importance) is uncertain. The fact that there was no statistically significant difference in mortality rate between the two groups should not be interpreted as meaning that resuscitation by exposure to hyperbaric O_2 is as good as on positive pressure ventilation; subsequent morbidity was not assessed. The results on a small number of babies in very severe asphyxia was swamped by those on a larger number resuscitated early in primary apnoea. And from the statistical point of view the numbers, and hence numbers of deaths, are inadequate for a valid comparison.

THE EFFECT OF GENERAL ANAESTHESIA AND ANALGESICS.—It is widely believed that anaesthesia, as given clinically in competent and experienced hands, has little effect on the infant at delivery. Animal experiments suggest that the results are rather more complex than at first appears, although one must take into account the fact that in the labour ward anaesthesia is often used only in small amounts and shortly before delivery, so that equilibration in the infant's brain may not be achieved. Yet there is good evidence that newborn animals of many species are unable to detoxicate some anaesthetics (barbiturates and chloralose) nearly as well as adults. The sleeping time is greatly extended and the LD 50 is less, mainly because the liver enzymes are poorly developed (Jondorf, Maickel, and Brodie, 1958; Fouts and Adamson, 1959; Weatherall, 1960; Arnfred and Secher, 1962; Yaffe 1962; Dawkins, 1966), even in the guinea pig which in other respects is so mature at birth.

In newborn animals of various species, administration of sodium pentobarbitone prolongs the duration of gasping during asphyxia (Snyder, 1946; Miller and Miller, 1962; Goodlin, 1965). When such experiments are performed in a neutral thermal environment (so that the effect of accelerated heat loss is minimized) the results are confirmed but are small. In asphyxiated foetal monkeys the time to last gasp was increased from 8.2 to 9.8 minutes (by 16%; Cockburn, Daniel, Dawes, James, Myers, Niemann, Rodriguez de Curet, and Ross, unpublished), and in anoxic newborn rabbits from 17.9 to 20.1 minutes (by 12%; Campbell and Milligan, unpublished). What is more striking is the great prolongation of primary apnoea, already referred to, and the fact that, nevertheless, in monkeys the total number of gasps is increased as a

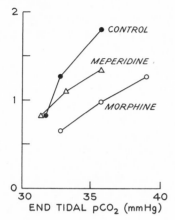

Fig. 73.—Effect of meperidine (0.5 mg/kg) and morphine (0.05 mg/kg) in reducing the ventilatory response to carbon dioxide in human infants 12–60 hours from birth. The dose is about one-third of that ordinarily used in adults on a weight basis. (Redrawn from Way, Costley, and Way, 1965.)

result of terminal acceleration and that resuscitation is facilitated. It is easy to establish rhythmic spontaneous breathing even though the monkey remains deeply anaesthetized. The reasons for the prolongation of survival and the relative ease of resuscitation are probably related to a reduction in the rate of ATP utilization and acid production both in the initial stages of asphyxia (when the animal lies inert instead of convulsing) and as a direct action of barbiturates upon the cells. These experiments were planned to find out more about the mechanisms of survival during asphyxia rather than in search of a possible therapeutic measure. The small effects of pentobarbitone and the difficulties encountered in nursing anaesthetized infants do not recommend it for practical use.

Way, Costley, and Leong Way (1965) observed the effect on newborn human infants of analgesics given as a preliminary to circumcision. Meperidine (pethidine, demerol) and morphine reduced the ventilatory response to carbon dioxide (Fig. 73). In the asphyxiated newborn rabbit they greatly prolong the duration of primary apnoea (Campbell and Milligan, unpublished). The time to last gasp is slightly prolonged, as with pentobarbitone, but resuscitability is not correspondingly increased. It is easy to measure the activity of analgesics in prolonging primary apnoea, which is their most

unfavourable feature in practice. It would be a good screening test in looking for analgesics in which this property was less.

Brain Damage at Birth

The reasons why so much effort has been put into understanding the physiological changes in birth asphyxia are that this is not only a good intellectual problem but also there is a strong suspicion that brain damage can result in human infants from abnormal events during or soon after birth. Far the most compelling evidence for this derives from the Collaborative Project studies, in which a close correlation has been found between the Apgar score at 1 minute and 5 minutes from birth, neonatal mortality, and the incidence of neurological abnormalities at one year of age (Drage and Berendes, 1966). A very striking feature is the association between birth weight and morbidity, the incidence of abnormality rising to 10.4% in infants of 1,001–2,000 Gm, and to 18.8% in those of this group which had an Apgar score of 0–3 5 minutes from birth (Fig. 74). This conclusion is reinforced by the observation that in a large group of infants weighing less than 1,800 Gm at birth, the incidence of cerebral palsy was 6.5%, most of them spastic diplegics (McDonald, 1963). This suggests that asphyxia and either prematurity or smallness-for-dates leads to an especially vulnerable association, which might be due to the effect of asphyxia

Fig. 74.—Proportion of human infants with neurological abnormalities at 1 year from birth, by birth-weight groups or by combinations of birth-weight and 5-minute Apgar score groups. (Redrawn from Drage and Berendes, 1966.)

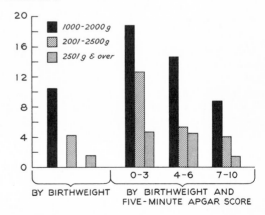

in the presence of inadequate metabolic and other resources. McDonald related the high incidence of abnormalities in her series to repeated cyanotic attacks during the first day or two from birth rather than to asphyxia during delivery. We also have to consider the possibility that neonatal hypoglycaemia is an equally potent factor.

When we come to review the detailed experimental evidence for the production of brain damage by these means, one must admit that it is incomplete (particularly in respect of hypoglycaemia). Ranck and Windle (1959) showed that in rhesus monkeys, as in guinea pigs, asphyxia on delivery can cause permanent brain damage, and their observations have been repeated and confirmed (Windle, 1963; Dawes, Hibbard, and Windle, 1964). But the duration of total asphyxia required is long and must exceed the time to the last gasp (Fig. 69). The anatomical distribution of lesions in the monkey is interesting. Haemorrhage is negligible. The lesions are bilaterally symmetrical and first appear (with increasing duration of asphyxia) in the nuclei of the inferior colliculus, then spreading to involve the other brain stem nuclei (particularly the gracile and medial cuneate) and, if asphyxia is prolonged to 12.5 minutes or more, to the cerebellum and thalamic nuclei. Involvement of the cerebral cortex as a result of acute birth asphyxia is unusual; it was seen only when recovery from asphyxia was complicated by prolonged cyanosis requiring resuscitative measures over several hours. The spinal cord also is usually spared.

Of monkeys which have been asphyxiated for 15 minutes or more, some show gross neurological signs, including ataxia, tremors, athetosis, and spastic paralysis. Many monkeys asphyxiated for 10 minutes or more prove difficult to feed during the first 2 weeks and appear to have some abnormalities of locomotion. But these abnormalities are hard to measure and disappear with increasing age. Such behavioural differences between asphyxiated and normal infant monkeys as have been observed also have not so far been satisfactorily measured or interpreted. Thus, despite the fact that at autopsy widespread brainstem lesions are found, the neurological signs so far observed have been indefinite and evanescent, perhaps because most of the lesions are subtotal and the capacity of the infant brain to compensate is considerable. Conventional neurological examination of muscular tone, reflex responses, and reaction to painful stimuli is singularly unproductive and one usually learns more by watching the infant monkey move about its cage or on the floor. Thus histological rather than clinical examination is a more reliable guide to the extent of brain damage in this species.

In the human infant, the diagnosis of cerebral palsy is not often made for sure until an age at which the child begins to move more vigorously, at 9–12 months. The chance of spotting minor damage is thus even less than in the monkey, which shows a remarkable variety of muscular activity during the first week after birth. If the pattern of damage were the same in both species one would guess that most of the minor instances in man would be overlooked. But we do not yet know whether the pattern is indeed the same, because it so rarely happens that a human infant with a well-authenticated and uncomplicated history of birth asphyxia or hypoglycaemia comes to autopsy within a short period after birth, and under circumstances which neither preclude good fixation and preservation of damaged brain nor could account for the damage (Courville, 1961; Spector, 1965). There is a further point. We do not yet know all the processes which continue to cause cell death, and these may differ in some respects from species to species. For instance, Lindenberg (1963) has emphasized the importance of the anatomical distribution of the blood supply, since local brain swelling may cause partial or complete obstruction to flow. If this is indeed an important contributory factor, it would be particularly susceptible to species variations. It might also be susceptible to therapeutic attack.

Thus while none would deny that very severe asphyxia at birth can cause death, or survival with brain damage, we do not yet know what proportion of neurological abnormalities in human infants can be directly attributed to this or to other pathological or genetic influences. Yet birth asphyxia and neonatal hypoglycaemia at least are conditions which are within our competence to control.

References

Abdel-Latif, A. A., and Abood, L. G.: Biochemical studies on mitochondria and other cytoplasmic fractions of developing rat brains, J. Neurochem. 11:9–15, 1964.

Adamsons, K.; Behrman, R.; Dawes, G. S.; Dawkins, M. J. R.; James, L. S., and Ross, B. B.: The treatment of acidosis with alkali and glucose during asphyxia in foetal rhesus monkeys, J. Physiol. 169:679–689, 1963.

Adamsons, K.; Behrman, R.; Dawes, G. S.; James, L. S., and Koford, C.: Resuscitation by positive pressure ventilation and Tris-hydroxymethylaminomethane of rhesus monkeys asphyxiated at birth, J. Pediat. 65:807–818, 1964.

Arnfred, I., and Secher, O.: Anoxia and barbiturates: Tolerance to anoxia in mice influenced by barbiturates, Arch. internat. pharmacodyn. 139:67–74, 1962.

Balfour, W. M.; Samson, F. E., and Dahl, N. A.: Effect of certain central nervous depressants on cerebral energy metabolism, Physiologist 2(3):5–6, 1959.

Battaglia, F. C.; Meschia, G., and Barron, D. H.: The effects of acute hypoxia on the osmotic pressure of the plasma, Quart. J. Exper. Physiol. 43:197–208, 1958.

Becker, R. F.; King, J. E.; Marsh, R. H., and Wyrick, A. D.: Intra-uterine respiration in the rat foetus, Am. J. Obst. & Gynec. 90:236–246, 1964.

Behrman, R. E.: Alkali therapy in the delivery room, J. Pediat. 69:173–174, 1966.

Bert, P.: Leçons sur la physiologie comparée de la respiration (Paris: J. B. Baillière et fils, 1870).

Boell, E. J.: In Lanman, J. T. (ed.): *Physiology of Prematurity*, Transactions of the 2d Conference (New York: Josiah Macy, Jr. Foundation, 1957), pp. 60–65.

Boyle, R.: New pneumatical experiments about respiration, Phil. Trans. R. Soc. 5:2011–2031, 1670.

Bullough, J.: Protracted foetal and neonatal asphyxia, Lancet, 1:999–1000, 1958.

Burnard, E.: Influence of delivery on the circulation, in Cassels, D. E. (ed.): *The Heart and Circulation in the Newborn and Infant* (New York: Grune and Stratton, Inc., 1966), pp. 92–97.

Burton, A. C.: *Physiology and Biophysics of the Circulation* (Chicago: Year Book Medical Publishers, Inc., 1965).

Campbell, A. G. M.; Cross, K. W.; Dawes, G. S., and Hyman, A. I.: A comparison of air and O_2, in a hyperbaric chamber or by positive pressure ventilation, in the resuscitation of newborn rabbits, J. Pediat. 68:153–163, 1966.

Cassin, S.; Swann, H. G., and Cassin, B.: Respiratory and cardiovascular alterations during the process of anoxic death in the newborn, J. Appl. Physiol. 15:249–252, 1960.

Chernick, V., and Avery, M. E.: Spontaneous alveolar rupture at birth, Pediatrics 32:816–824, 1963.

Chesler, A., and Himwich, H. E.: Comparative studies of the rate of oxidation and glycolysis in the cerebral cortex and brain-stem of the rat, Am. J. Physiol. 141:513–517, 1944,a.

Chesler, A., and Himwich, H. E.: Glycolysis in the parts of the central nervous system of cats and dogs during growth, Am. J. Physiol. 142:544–549, 1944,b.

Courville, C. B.: Clinical evaluation of brain damage in cases of cerebral palsy, Arch. Pediat. 78:127–142, 1961.

Craigie, E. H.: Postnatal changes in vascularity in the cerebral cortex of the male albino rat, J. Comp. Neurol. 39:301–324, 1925.

Cross, K. W.: Resuscitation of the asphyxiated infant, Brit. M. Bull. 22:73–78, 1966.

Cross, K. W.; Klaus, M.; Tooley, W. H., and Weisser, K.: The response of the newborn baby to inflation of the lungs, J. Physiol. 151:551–565, 1960.

Dahl, D. R., and Samson, F. E.: Metabolism of rat brain mitochondria during postnatal development, Am. J. Physiol. 196:470–472, 1959.

Dahl, N. A.; Samson, F. E., and Balfour, W. M.: Adenosinetriphosphate and electrical activity in chicken vagus, Am. J. Physiol. 206:818–822, 1964.

Daniel, S. S.; Dawes, G. S.; James, L. S., and Ross, B. B.: Analeptics and the resuscitation of asphyxiated monkeys, Brit. M. J. 2:562–563, 1966.

Daniel, S. S.; Dawes, G. S.; James, L. S.; Ross, B. B., and Windle, W. F.: Hypothermia and the resuscitation of asphyxiated fetal monkeys, J. Pediat. 68:45–53, 1966.

Dawes, G. S.; Hibbard, E., and Windle, W. F.: The effect of alkali and glucose infusion on permanent brain damage in rhesus monkeys asphyxiated at birth, J. Pediat. 65:801–806, 1964.

Dawes, G. S.; Jacobson, H. N.; Mott, J. C., and Shelley, H. J.: Some observations in foetal and newborn rhesus monkeys, J. Physiol. 152:271–298, 1960.

Dawes, G. S.; Jacobson, H. N.; Mott, J. C.; Shelley, H. J., and Stafford, A.: The treatment of asphyxiated mature foetal lambs and rhesus monkeys with intravenous glucose and sodium carbonate, J. Physiol. 169:167–184, 1963.

Dawes, G. S.; Mott, J. C., and Shelley, H. J.: The importance of cardiac glycogen for the maintenance of life in foetal lambs and newborn animals during anoxia, J. Physiol. 146:516–538, 1959.

Dawkins, M. J. R.: Biochemical aspects of developing functions in newborn mammalian liver, Brit. M. Bull. 22:27–33, 1966.

DeDuve, C.: The function of intracellular hydrolases, Exper. Cell. Res. (Suppl. 7) 169–182, 1959.

DeHaan, R. L., and Field, J.: Mechanism of cardiac damage in anoxia, Am. J. Physiol. 197:449–453, 1959.

Donald, I.: Asphyxia neonatorum, Brit. J. Anaesth. 32: 106–115, 1960.

Drage, J. S., and Berendes, H.: Apgar scores and outcome of the newborn, Pediat. Clin. North America 13:635–643, 1966.

Edwards, V. F.: De l'influence des agens physiques (Paris: Crochard, 1824).

Elneil, H., and McCance, R. A.: The effect of environmental temperature on the composition and carbohydrate metabolism of the newborn pig, J. Physiol. 179:278–284, 1965.

Enzmann, E. V., and Pincus, G.: The extinction of reflexes in spinal mice of different ages as an indicator of the decline of anaerobiosis, J. Gen. Physiol. 18:163–169, 1934.

Flexner, J. B., and Flexner, L. B.: Biochemical and physiological differentiation during morphogenesis. VII. Adenylpyrophosphatase and acid phosphatase activities in the developing cerebral cortex and liver of the fetal guinea pig, J. Cell. & Comp. Physiol. 31:311–320, 1948.

Fouts, J. R., and Adamson, R. H.: Drug metabolism in the newborn rabbit, Science 129:897–898, 1959.

Godfrey, S.: The loss of respiratory reflexes during asphyxia of newborn rabbits, J. Physiol. 184:78–80, P., 1966.

Goodlin, R. C.: Drug protection for fetal anoxia, Obst. & Gynec. 26:9–14, 1965.

Goodlin R., and Perry, D.: Fetal incubator studies, Am. J. Obst. & Gynec. 94:268–273, 1966.

Gupta, J. M., and Scopes, J. W.: Observations on blood pressure in newborn infants, Arch. Dis. Childhood 40: 637–644, 1965.

Hager, H.: Electron Microscopical Observations on the Early Changes in Neurons Caused by Hypoxidosis and on the Ultrastructural Aspects of Neuronal Necrosis in the Cerebral Cortex of Mammals, in Schadé, J. P., and McMenemy, W. H.: *Selective Vulnerability of the Brain in Hypoxaemia* (Oxford:Blackwell Scientific Publications, 1963), pp. 125–136.

Head, H.: On the regulation of respiration, J. Physiol. 10:1–70, 1889.

Hiestand, W. A.; Tschirgi, R. D., and Miller, H. R.: The influence of glycotropic substances on survival of the primitive respiratory center in the ischemic rat head, Am. J. Physiol. 142:153–157, 1944.

Himwich, H. E.; Baker, Z., and Fazekas, J. F.: The respiratory metabolism of the infant brain, Am. J. Physiol. 125:601–606, 1939.

Himwich, H. E.; Bernstein, A. O.; Herrlich, H.; Chesler, A., and Fazekas, J. F.: Mechanisms for the maintenance of life in the newborn during anoxia, Am. J. Physiol. 135:387–391, 1942.

Hull, D., and Segall, M. M.: Oxygen uptake during and after positive-pressure ventilation for the resuscitation of asphyxiated newborn infants, Lancet 2:1096–1099, 1966.

Hutchison, J. H.; Kerr, M. M.; Inall, J. A., and Shanks, R. A.: Controlled trials of hyperbaric oxygen and tracheal intubation in asphyxia neonatorum, Lancet 2:935–939, 1966.

Hutchison, J. H.; Kerr, M. M.; Williams, K. G., and Hopkinson, W. I.: Hyperbaric oxygen in the resuscitation of the newborn, Lancet 2:1019–1022, 1963.

James, L. S.; Apgar, V. A.; Burnard, E. D., and Moya, F.: Intragastric oxygen and resuscitation of the newborn, Acta. paediat. 52:245–251, 1963.

Jílek, L.; Fischer, J.; Krulich, L., and Trojan, S.: The Reaction of the Brain to Stagnant Hypoxia and Anoxia during Ontogeny, in Himwich, W. A., and Himwich, H. E.: The developing brain, Prog. Brain Res. 9:113–131, 1964.

Jílek, L.; Krulich, L., and Trojan, S.: The effect of sodium arsenate on the survival of spinal reflexes and the activity of the respiratory centre after decapitation in rats during their postnatal development, Physiol. Bohemoslov. 12:242–247, 1963.

Jondorf, W. R.; Maickel, R. P., and Brodie, B. B.: Inability of newborn mice and guinea pigs to metabolize drugs, Biochem. Pharmacol. 1:352–354, 1958.

Kabat, H.: The greater resistance of very young animals to arrest of brain circulation, Am. J. Physiol. 130:588–599, 1940.

Lajtha, A.: The development of the blood-brain barrier. J, Neurochem. 1:216–227, 1957.

Le Gallois, M.: Expériences sur le principe de la vie (Paris: Hautel, 1812).

Lindenberg, R.: Patterns of CNS Vulnerability in Acute Hypoxaemia, Including Anaesthesia Accidents, in Schadé, J. P., and McMenemy, W. H.: Selective Vulnerability of the Brain in Hypoxaemia (Oxford: Blackwell Scientific Publications, 1963), pp. 189–209.

Malan, A. F., and Heese H. deV.: Spontaneous pneumothorax in the newborn, Acta. paediat. 55:224–228, 1966.

McDonald, A.: Cerebral palsy in children of very low birth weight, Arch. Dis. Childhood 38:579–588, 1963.

Miller, J. A.: Factors in neonatal resistance to anoxia. I. Temperature and survival of newborn guinea pigs under anoxia, Science 110:113, 1949.

Miller, J. A.: In Windle W. F. (ed.): Neurological and Psychological deficits of Asphyxia Neonatorum with Consideration of Use of Primates for Experimental Investigations (Springfield, Ill.: Charles C Thomas, Publisher, 1958), p. 107.

Miller, J. A., and Miller, F. S.: Factors in neonatal resistance to anoxia, Am. J. Obs. & Gynec. 84:44–56, 1962.

Miller, J. A., and Miller, F. S.: Studies on prevention of brain damage in asphyxia. Develop. Med. Child Neurol. 7:607–619, 1965.

Miller, J. A.; Miller, F. S., and Westin, B.: Hypothermia in the treatment of asphyxia neonatorum, Biol. Neonat. 6:148–163, 1964.

Miller, J. A.; Zakhary, R., and Miller, F. S.: Hypothermia, asphyxia and cardiac glycogen in guinea pigs, Science 144:1226–1227, 1964.

Mott, J. C.: The ability of young mammals to withstand total oxygen lack, Brit. M. Bull. 17:144–147, 1961.

Moya, F.; James, L. S.; Burnard, E. D., and Hanks, E. C.: Cardiac massage in the newborn infant through the intact chest, Am. J. Obst. & Gynec. 84:798–803, 1962.

Potter, V. R.; Schneider, B. S., and Lieb, G. J.: Enzyme changes during growth and differentiation in the tissues of the newborn rat, Cancer Res. 5:21–24, 1945.

Ranck, J. B., and Windle, W. F.: Brain damage in the monkey, Macaca mulatta, by asphyxia neonatorum, Exper. Neurol. 1:130–153, 1959.

Reiss, M.: Das Verhalten des Stoffwechsels bei der Erstickung neugeborener Ratten und Mause, Ztschr. ges. exper. Med. 79:345–359, 1931.

Resuscitation of Newborn Infants Obst. & Gynec. 8:336–361, 1956.

van Rossum, G. D. V.: Respiration and glycolysis in liver slices prepared from rats of different foetal and postnatal ages. Biochim. et biophys. acta. 74:15–23, 1963.

Samson, F. E.; Balfour, W. M., and Dahl, N. A.: Rate of cerebral ATP utilization in rats, Am. J. Physiol. 198:213–216, 1960.

Scholander, P. F.: Experimental Studies on Asphyxia in Animals, in Walker, J., and Turnbull, A. C. (eds.) Oxygen Supply to the Foetus (Oxford: Blackwell Scientific Publications, 1960), pp. 267–274.

Selle, W. A.: A simple technic for studying the periodicity and survival of the respiratory center, Proc. Soc. Exper. Biol. & Med. 54:291–292, 1963.

Selle, W. A.: Influence of age on survival of respiration, spinal reflexes, pupillary responses and heart action, Proc. Soc. Exper. Biol. & Med. 48:417–419, 1941.

Selle, W. A., and Witten, T. A.: Survival of the respiratory (gasping) mechanism in young animals subjected to anoxia, Proc. Soc. Exper. Biol. & Med. 47:495–497, 1941.

Shelley, H. J.: Blood sugars and tissue carbohydrates in foetal and infant lambs and rhesus monkeys, J. Physiol. 153:527–552, 1960.

Shelley, H. J.: Glycogen reserves and their changes at birth, Brit. M. Bull. 17:137–143, 1961.

Shelley, H. J., and Neligan, G. A.: Neonatal hypoglycaemia, Brit. M. Bull. 22:34–39, 1966.

Snyder, F. F.: The effect of pentobarbital sodium upon the resistance to asphyxia in the newborn, Fed. Proc. 5:97–98, 1946.

Spector, R.: Neuropathology of prematurity, Clin. Develop. Med. 19:57–63, 1965.

Stafford, A., and Weatherall, J. A. C.: The survival of young rats in nitrogen, J. Physiol. 153:457–472, 1960.

Thoms, R. K., and Hiestand, W. A.: Relation of survival time of respiratory gasping mechanism of isolated mouse head to age, Proc. Soc. Exper. Biol. & Med. 64:1–3, 1947.

Tschirgi, R. D., and Gerard, R. W.: The carotid-mandibular reflex in acute respiratory failure, Am. J. Physiol. 150:358–364, 1947.

Tyler, D. B., and van Harreveld, A.: The respiration of the developing brain, Am. J. Physiol. 136:600–603, 1942.

Way, W. L.; Costley, E. C., and Leong Way, E.: Respiratory sensitivity of the newborn infant to meperidine and morphine, Clin. Pharmacol. Therap. 6:454–461, 1965.

Weatherall, J. C.: Anaesthesia in newborn animals, Brit. J. Pharmacol. 15:454–457, 1960.

Westin, B.; Nyberg, R.; Miller, J. A., and Wedenberg, E.: Hypothermia and transfusion with oxygenated blood in the treatment of asphyxia neonatorum, Acta paediat. (Suppl. 139) 51:1–80, 1962.

Whittam, R.: Sodium and potassium movements in kidney cortex slices from new-born animals, J. Physiol. 153:358–369, 1960.

Whittam, R.: Metabolic changes in rabbit kidney cortex during the first few weeks after birth, Biochim. et biophys. acta 54:574–576, 1961.

Windle, W. F.: Selective Vulnerability of the Central Nervous System of Rhesus Monkeys to Asphyxia During Birth, in Schadé, J. P., and McMenemy, W. H. (eds.) *Selective Vulnerability of the Brain in Hypoxaemia* (Oxford: Blackwell Scientific Publications, 1963), pp. 251–255.

Yaffe, S. J.: Strain Variation in Drug Response, in *Perinatal Pharmacology*, 38th Ross Conference on Pediatric Research (Columbus, Ohio: Ross Laboratories, 1962), pp. 48–52.

13

Changes in the Circulation After Birth

THE OUTWARD and visible signs of vitality, the arousal and crying of the infant, are the most obviously dramatic phenomena at birth. But the changes in the circulation, although less perceptible, are of equal importance to survival. They are dependent on two factors, the arrest of the umbilical circulation through the placenta and the increase of pulmonary blood flow on ventilation of the lungs. The latter has already been described in Chapter 7.

The Arrest of Umbilical Blood Flow and Placental Transfusion

In many species of animals the separation of the foetus from the mother is effected abruptly on delivery, by tearing of the umbilical cord as the infant falls away or by its struggles. The abrupt longitudinal tension on the cord is sufficient to cause the vascular smooth muscle to go into spasm, even if the whole cord is not torn (or bitten). In some species there is a sphincter, containing usually both longitudinal and circular smooth muscle, which loops around the cord vessels at their entry into the abdomen and extends to or just beyond the junction of the abdominal skin with the amnion (Parry, 1954). This sphincter is best developed in the horse, guinea pig, and rabbit and is less obvious in the cow and sheep. It is absent in the rat, cat, dog, rhesus monkey, and man. It is not innervated and is presumed to constrict as a result of mechanical stress, and thus to help in arresting blood loss from the torn cord. This conclusion is based mainly on anatomical studies. The structure would seem to have little functional purpose during foetal life.

The length of the umbilical cord varies greatly with species, being only about two-fifths of the body length in dogs and cats, and also in individuals within a species. If an infant with a cord of sufficient length is delivered gently, the vessels do not necessarily constrict at once. In man, some umbilical blood flow can continue up to several minutes after delivery, although usually at a rapidly decreasing rate (Štembra, Hodr, and Janda, 1965). The reason for the fall in flow rate is uncertain. It may be due to compression of umbilical vessels within the uterus, as a result of the change in shape of the uterine attachment of the placenta. Or it may be due to vasoconstriction in the vessels as a result of mechanical stimuli as the uterus contracts on delivery, or from exposure to cold and air. Or more likely it results from secretion into the blood stream of catecholamines acting directly on the cord vessels, and sympathetic stimulation of their innervated intra-abdominal portions, as a consequence of the central nervous activity generated when spontaneous breathing is established. Human cord vessels also constrict in response to bradykinin and angiotensin, as well as to a rise in transmural pressure (Davignon, Lorenz, and Shepherd, 1965), so there are several possibilities.

Presumably, a strong physical stimulus causes depolarization of the smooth muscle cells, and once in spasm the tension required to keep the vessels shut is low. But the smooth muscle does not behave as a syncytium. Partial constriction in a foetal lamb with an intact umbilical circulation can be seen as a result of rough handling or noradrenaline infusion, but the constriction does not necessarily spread and usually subsides after some minutes, if the physiological conditions are favourable. The human cord has one feature apparently unique to the species in that contraction of the smooth muscle after birth produces a deep indentation on one side of an artery or vein, limited to a short length of vessel, and producing folds first described by Hoboken (1669). There seems no anatomical reason why these folds appear at one point rather than another. The pressures developed by spontaneous vasoconstriction in six-inch lengths of human cord vessels clamped at both ends are remarkably high, up to 150 mm Hg in an artery and 45 mm Hg in a vein, the difference being attributable to the greater quantity of smooth muscle in the former (Hughes, 1966). The constriction is abolished by cyanide within a few minutes. The quantity of blood in the cord vessels on delivery is 10–15 ml, and their constriction no doubt tends to express blood in both directions, to the placenta or foetus, according to their relative intravascular pressures.

The value of transfer to the infant of the blood in the cord and placenta at birth has been an object of interest for a long while. Erasmus Darwin (1803) wrote that "another thing very injurious to the child is the tying and cutting of the navel-string too soon; which should always be left till the child has not only repeatedly breathed but till all pulsation in the cord ceases. As otherwise the child is much weaker than it ought to be, a part of the blood being left in the placenta, which ought to have been in the child." His distinguished grandson was somewhat critical of his grandfather's generalizations, "the proportion of speculation being so large to the facts given," although he may have been thinking more of the origin of species than the navel-string (Darwin, 1876). The same year that he wrote his autobiography, the volume of blood transferred at birth was recorded (Budin, 1876). Since that time many such measurements have been made in man (e.g., Cohnstein and Zuntz, 1884; and many others since), lambs, and foals (Barcroft, 1936; Rossdale and Mahaffey, 1958) by weighing the baby, by measurements of blood volume, and from the amount of blood obtainable from the placenta.

The amount of blood which may be transferred is roughly proportional to body weight (and hence to placental size, which are normally mutually related, Chapter 4) at a particular gestational age, but may be much greater in premature infants because the quantity of blood normally in the placenta is then so much more. Conversely, in premature infants a greater proportion of their normal blood volume may be sequestered in the placenta if the infant is held above the mother or the umbilical vein is compressed on delivery. Estimates in man of the volume of blood transferred when the cord is not clamped until pulsations have ceased, and when the baby is at or below the mother's level, have varied from 60 ml to as much as 200 ml at term. "Stripping" the cord (i.e., expressing the last drop of blood by milking it toward the baby) contributed a negligible amount. Measurements of blood volume per kg body weight in the newborn infant also have varied over a wide range (55–150 ml/kg; Mollison, Veall, and Cutbush, 1950; Sisson, Lund, Whalen, and Telek, 1959; Gairdner, Marks, Roscoe, and Brettall, 1958), no doubt in part because of differences in methods and because body weight is not necessarily the best estimate of metabolizing tissue (Gregersen and Rawson, 1959), but also as a result of variations in placental transfusion. The size of this can be a large fraction of blood volume, possibly as much as 50% at term (Usher, Shephard and Lind, 1963). A reasonable figure for normal blood volume at birth, taking all the facts into consideration and with neither blood loss into nor gain from the placenta, is 90 ml/kg; this is the mean blood volume in normal mature children 3 days from birth (Tooley, personal communication).

The possible advantages of placental transfusion (i.e., of making the infant hypervolaemic) have received more attention than the possible immediate disadvantages. This was originally due to the strong reaction to the establishment of "placental blood banks" in many countries in the late 1930s. The cord was tied promptly at birth and 100–125 ml blood were recovered from each placenta (e.g., Goodall, Andersen, Altimas, and MacPhail, 1938; Grodberg and Carey, 1938) for use in adult patients. This process of robbing little Peters to pay big Pauls was roundly condemned. Many authors (e.g., DeMarsh, Alt, Windle, and Hillis, 1941) drew attention to the large quantity of iron transferred to the baby in placental blood, which can be as much as is absorbed from the milk during the next month (Gunther, 1957). The 100 ml of fluid obtained was more than the average infant gets from breast-feeding alone in the first 2 days. Various guesses were made as to the hypothetical expansion of the pulmonary vascular bed when breathing starts. But these ignored the fact that changes in vascular resistance can be effected by small changes in vascular volume (because resistance is related to the fourth power of the radius) and that pulmonary arterial pressure falls after birth. (In the isolated lungs of foetal lambs, perfused at constant pressure, ventilation caused an increase in pulmonary blood volume of <5 ml, i.e., less than 2% of

TABLE 44.—THE EFFECTS OF EARLY (10–22 SECS) AND LATE (~5 MINS) CLAMPING OF THE UMBILICAL CORD ON BLOOD VOLUME,* PRESSURE, P_{CO_2} AND pH (MEANS ± S.E.) IN NORMAL FULL-TERM HUMAN INFANTS**

| | POSTNATAL TIME | UMBILICAL CORD CLAMPED | |
		Early	Late
Blood volume (ml/kg)	30 mins	78 ± 1	99 ± 3
	24 hours	86 ± 2	96 ± 2
Haematocrit (%)	30 mins	47	59
	24 hours	44	62
Arterial pressure (mm Hg)	5–10 mins	44 ± 3	69 ± 3
	4 hours	52 ± 5	71 ± 3
† Blood pH	30 mins	7.24 ± 0.01	7.30 ± 0.01
P_{CO_2} (mm Hg)	30 mins	55 ± 4	45 ± 1

* Estimated using I^{131} tagged human albumen.
** Usher, Shephad, and Lind, 1963; Buckels and Usher, 1965.
† Obtained from an unwarmed heel.

the normal blood volume of a lamb on delivery.)

With the passage of time, the placental transfusion pendulum has begun to swing the other way. It has been pointed out (Burnard and James, 1963; Usher, Shephard and Lind, 1963) that delayed clamping of the cord leads to an elevation in blood volume, haematocrit, and arterial pressure (Table 44), with a suggestion that the circulation may be overloaded (although interpretation was sometimes complicated by evidence of asphyxia). Urine flow, glomerular filtration rate, p-amino hippurate clearance, and effective renal flow were greater during the first 12 hours after delayed clamping, but not thereafter despite the persistent difference in blood volume and haematocrit (Oh, Oh, and Lind, 1966). Burnard (1966) estimated that the viscosity of whole blood is doubled at a haematocrit of 70%, so it is not surprising that, in less mature infants in which the placental transfusion has been greater, overt signs of cardiopulmonary difficulties sometimes appear, and are relieved by blood-letting.

Conversely, there is a risk of foetal blood loss to the placenta on delivery. This also is likely to be relatively greater in premature infants, and can result not only from elevation of the foetus above the mother (e.g., at caesarean section, as has been well publicized), but also from partial compression of the cord to obstruct venous return but not arterial flow. The consequence is a pale baby with a low blood pressure and a haematocrit which falls below 40% in the absence of respiratory distress. One may speculate that a moderate degree of placental transfusion is to be preferred and that the cord should be tied, say after not more than a minute.

Changes in the Heart and Lungs

Until the early 1950s, it was generally believed (in so far as the matter was considered at all) that the functional changes which took place in the circulation at birth were effected promptly. Although instances of continued patency of the ductus arteriosus or foramen ovale after birth had been recorded these were regarded as disturbances of the normal mechanism. The demonstration that the changes were not normally effected at once, but required hours or days for their completion, led to the realization that there was a period of time (varying with species, maturity at birth, and in health or disease) during which the newborn infant or animal had a circulation which was transitional in character between that of the foetus and adult (Born, Dawes, Mott, and Widdicombe, 1954). A great volume of work has been devoted to study of the special features of this transitional or neonatal circulation during the last 10 years. The gross architectural differences are illustrated diagrammatically in Figure 75. There are several features which distinguish it from the adult, viz:

1. Continued patency of the foramen ovale, with the possibility of a right-to-left shunt.
2. Continued patency of the ductus arteriosus, with the possibility of shunts in either direction.
3. The unusual characteristics of the pulmonary blood vessels which constrict vigorously in response to hypoxia and to hypercapnia or metabolic acidosis.
4. The fact that at birth the right ventricle is almost as thick as the left.

And perhaps we should add:

5. The lower systemic arterial blood pressure and the

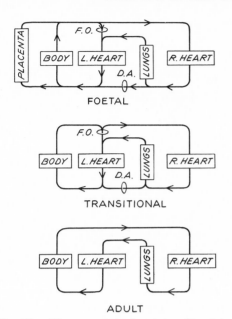

Fig. 75.—Diagrams of the foetal, transitional (neonatal), and adult types of circulation. (After Born, Dawes, Mott, and Widdicombe, 1954.)

unusual ability of the newborn to withstand severe hypoxaemia or asphyxia.

6. The relatively high O_2 consumption of newborn animals of many species at rest, because this entails a relatively large resting cardiac output.

Of these, the physiological behaviour of the pulmonary circulation after birth has been described in Chapter 7, the response to asphyxia in Chapter 12, and the changes in O_2 consumption will be dealt with in Chapter 15. This leaves us with the foetal blood channels and the changes in intravascular pressures and in cardiac muscle to be considered here.

Closure of the Foramen Ovale

The reasons for closure of the foramen ovale after birth are twofold. First, arrest of the umbilical circulation causes a decrease in the volume of blood flowing up the inferior vena cava, and hence both in the lateral pressure in this vessel and, perhaps of equal importance, in the momentum of blood impinging on the caval side of the valve to open it (see Fig. 48, p. 92). Thus occlusion of the cord reduces the inferior vena caval-left atrial pressure difference, whether or not the lungs are ventilated (Dawes, Mott, and Widdicombe, 1955,a). Secondly, the immediate increase in pulmonary venous return on ventilation is of itself sufficient to reverse the

pressure-difference across the foramen ovale. However, this effect is to some extent contingent upon the continued patency of the ductus arteriosus. When pulmonary vascular resistance is low there can be a large left-to-right shunt through the ductus arteriosus, which greatly increases pulmonary blood flow and hence left atrial pressure. So in the period which immediately follows birth the valve of the foramen ovale is held closed by haemodynamic changes, some of which can be reversed.

The anatomy of the valve varies greatly in different species. In the calf, for instance, it is tubular. It is not always complete even in man, while in the foal it is a thin delicate structure with multiple fenestrations (Barclay, Franklin, and Prichard, 1944). The valve usually becomes adherent to the edge of the foramen ovale within a few days of birth in most species, and the fenestrations become plugged with clot, but closure of the hole or holes (which with changes in the orientation of the heart eventually come to lie between the cavities of the atria) is not always completed. This is particularly so in man (Fig. 76). Thus effective prevention of a right-to-left shunt through the foramen ovale is mainly dependent on the reversal of the foetal pressure difference across it rather than on an anatomical barrier. A small left-to-right shunt at this point will normally have little functional significance. Such a shunt is sometimes present in human infants asphyxiated at birth (James, Burnard, and Rowe, 1961).

The establishment of the normal left-to-right atrial pressure gradient after birth is a matter of some importance on which little work has been done. Burnard and James (1963) found that in the normal human infant the pressure gradient soon

Fig. 76.—Closure of the special vascular channels of the foetus after birth, as judged by human postmortem material. (From the data of Scammon and Morris, 1918.)

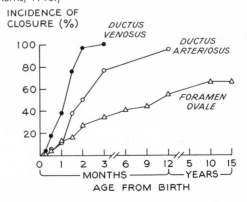

after birth was very small; at 24 hours it was hardly 2 mm Hg (see also Table 45). Van Harreveld and Russell (1956) showed that the difference between the pressures in the two atria was of doubtful significance in the newborn kitten, but increased with age so that at 2 months from birth left atrial pressure was about double that in the right atrium, as in the adult. This was roughly paralleled by the development of a large difference between the wall thickness and hence elasticity of the two ventricles. It was suggested that since a ventricle is filled against its own elastic resistance, this may largely determine mean atrial pressure. If this explanation is correct, it follows that the relative changes in atrial pressure after birth are in part a consequence of the atrophy of right ventricular muscle while the left ventricle hypertrophies. And in infants whose right ventricle does not atrophy after birth (e.g., when the outflow tract is narrowed or pulmonary vascular resistance is high) the circumstances continue to favour a right-to-left shunt across the foramen ovale.

The first functional observations by cineangiography suggested that a right-to-left shunt might be presented in newborn lambs (Barclay and Franklin, 1938). Barcroft, Kramer, and Millikan (1939) found that when a lamb was given oxygen to breathe, the arterial O_2 saturation rose to 95% in 5 minutes as measured by an oximeter, and this was "clearly inconsistent with the short-circuiting of any amount of blood through the foramen ovale so great as to be physiologically significant." Yet such indirect measurements of O_2 content, particularly when breathing pure O_2, are not always good guides to the presence or absence of moderate shunts. Condorelli, Dagianti, Polosa, and Guiliano (1957) and Stahlman, Merrill, and LeQuire (1962) injected small quantities of a dye intravenously and found dilution curves indicative of a right-to-left shunt through the foramen ovale in normal lambs for several days after birth. Observations on normal human infants by cineangiography (which usually involves a large fluid injection; Lind and Wegelius, 1954) or using a dye (with smaller quantities and hence less local rise in venous pressure; Prec and Cassels, 1955; Condorelli and Ungari, 1960) led to the same conclusion. The long-term consequences of a large interatrial communication, either as a result of defective development or function are difficult to assess. Diagnosis is not easy even in older infants, and the cardinal physical sign (a wide fixed split of the second heart sound) is rarely present in the newborn (Hoffman and Rudolph, 1966a). Although left-to-right atrial shunts occur, with pulmonary-to-systemic flow ratios of 3:1 or more within 2 weeks of birth, they seldom produce severe symptoms in early infancy.

Closure of the Ductus Arteriosus

The mechanism of closure of the ductus arteriosus has led to a great deal more discussion than that of the foramen ovale, ever since Hieronymus Fabricius of Aquapendente first published pictures of them in the lamb and human heart. He mentions that sheep and ox foetuses had been singled out for description by his predecessors, including Galen, because they were sufficiently large and easy to obtain, as no doubt they were in 16th century Padua. The same reasons today explain the widespread use of these species in experimental foetal and neonatal physiology.

The ductus arteriosus is a large vessel, almost as large as the aortic arch of a mature foetus, which it joins at an acute angle. It is hardly surprising that the complete closure of this great vessel within a day or two from birth should have attracted interest. More than a century ago, Virchow (1856) suggested that it must constrict and shorten after birth as a result of the contraction of the large quantity of smooth muscle in the vessel wall. And although we now recognize this as the correct explanation of the closure, as is obvious when studied *in vivo*, for more than 80 years the matter was one for vigorous dispute, the details of which have been summarized elsewhere (Born, Dawes, Mott, and Rennick, 1956). By the turn of the century, two important observations had been made. Continued patency of the ductus arteriosus, with its characteristic murmur, had been described (Gibson, 1898, 1900) and it was recognized that closure normally occurred in two stages, a rapid constriction after birth which was later followed by anatomical obliteration over a period of weeks (Gérard, 1900a,b). There was then a gap of many years before the reasons for the contraction of the smooth muscle were studied.

Barcroft, Kennedy, and Mason (1938), and Kennedy and Clark (1941, 1942) described the first systematic experimental studies on the stimulus to constriction in guinea pigs. A wide variety of procedures caused the ductus to constrict, including normal breathing on delivery, inflation of the lungs with a gas mixture containing oxygen, mechanical or electrical stimulation of the vessel itself or of various nerves, injection of adrenaline, and haemorrhage. The feature of these reports which later attracted most attention was the hypothesis that a rise in arterial Po_2 might be the immediate stimulus to closure. Yet at the time both Barron (1944) and Barcroft (1946) favoured other explanations. The Second World War had intervened and it was not until the early 1950s that the problem was tackled again. Then evidence accumulated in man that a higher incidence of persistent patency of the ductus arteriosus was associated with foetal distress at birth (Record and McKeown, 1953) or with delivery at high altitude (Alzamora *et al.,* 1953; Peñaloza *et al.,* 1964). Record and McKeown (1955) found that guinea pigs exposed to a reduced O_2 environment for 24 hours after birth had a wider ductus at postmortem than controls exposed to room air. And experiments on foetal lambs *in vivo* showed that the ductus constricted when the arterial O_2 saturation was raised by giving the ewe 100% O_2 to breathe, or by replacing the placenta by the lungs of a twin, or on ventilation of the lungs with air (Born, Dawes, Mott, and Rennick, 1956). This phenomenon was seen when the arterial pressure was controlled (so that the decrease in external diameter could not be due to a decrease in transmural pressure), on denervation of the ductus, and in an isolated heart-ductus-artificial lung preparation. These observations were verified in an isolated great vessel preparation perfused with blood (Assali, Morris, Smith, and Manson, 1963), or on perfusion with a saline solution and in isolated strips (Kovalčík, 1963). The observations of Kovalčík were particularly interesting because not only was he able to demonstrate *in vitro* that the reactivity of the ductus arteriosus to O_2 was peculiar to that vessel (in contrast to the adjacent pulmonary arteries, aortic arch, and descending aorta, which did not react), but the response persisted in the presence of dibenamine and atropine, which blocked the vasoconstrictor action of noradrenaline and acetylcholine, respectively. It was concluded that in the lamb and guinea pig O_2 caused the smooth muscle of the ductus arteriosus to contract by a direct action. Kovalčík also made the curious observation that this occurred even in the presence of 1–20 mM cyanide, which greatly reduced the O_2 uptake of isolated strips (although it was not possible to say whether it was decreased by more than 90%). This clearly demands further investigation, particularly as the contraction on exposure to O_2 was dependent on the presence of glucose in the bathing solution, suggesting that it was related to a normal metabolic pathway. The smooth muscle of the isolated ductus was unaffected by small changes in PCO_2 or pH.

There was one further oddity. Gillman and Burton (1966) have reported that of the several species which they studied, only the isolated ductus arteriosus of the dog failed to constrict on exposure to oxygen. The reason for this failure is uncertain. The vessel constricts in an apparently normal fashion after birth in intact puppies (Handler, 1956), and this process is delayed by exposure to a reduced atmospheric concentration of oxygen for the first few days after delivery (Wilcox, Roberts, and Carney, 1962). Otherwise there is no evidence of a species-specific variation.

Everyone who has used *in vivo* or *in vitro* preparations of ductus arteriosus has remarked on the fact that the contraction is slow in onset and does not reach equilibrium for 5–10 minutes after a stepwise change in PO_2. This may be due to the time required for equilibration of PO_2 in the smooth muscle both *in vitro* and *in vivo*. The vascular supply to the ductus arteriosus itself was studied by Prichard (personal communication), who found it was derived from the left coronary and first intercostal arteries. But while there are many vasa vasorum and capillaries in the adventitia and the outer part of the media, there are none in the inner media and intima (Kennedy and Clark, 1941; Slijper and deVries, 1965). Oxygen must diffuse there from the lumen of the vessel or from the vasa vasorum. When the environmental PO_2 is raised in successive steps from 0 to ~700 mm Hg the contraction of the smooth muscle of the ductus increases progressively. The data so far available are inadequate to determine the form of the relation (linear or otherwise) between PO_2 and muscle tension over this wide range. It seems to be a wider range than that over which changes in PO_2 affect coronary and cerebral arterioles. Perhaps the diffusion path for O_2 is greater in the thick smooth muscle wall of the ductus arteriosus.

Raising the O_2 tension is not the only means by which the ductus arteriosus may be caused to constrict *in vivo*. Infusion of large doses of adrenaline or noradrenaline (1.7–4.9 μg/kg min intravenously) caused it to constrict in foetal lambs. Underventilation after tying the umbilical cord, to cause asphyxia with a fall in arterial O_2 saturation below 30% (corresponding to a PO_2 ~13 mm Hg), had the same effect (Born, Dawes, Mott, and Rennick, 1956). This was probably due to release of catecholamines from the adrenals, since although nerve-endings have been described in close relation to the smooth muscle fibres of the ductus, their connection with the autonomic nervous system has not been established (Boyd, 1941). And stimulation of the left vagus and stellate ganglion had no effect on the ductus in guinea pigs (Kennedy and Clark, 1942).

The ductus arteriosus does not constrict wholly and at once after birth, but functional closure takes hours or days. Thus there is a period of time during which pulmonary vascular resistance has fallen considerably below that in the systemic circulation and the ductus is still patent. Under these circumstances there is a reversal in the direction of flow through the vessel. In the foetus this was right-to-left; it now becomes left-to-right (Dawes, Mott, Widdicombe, and Wyatt, 1953). If the velocity of flow is so great, because of partial constriction of the ductus, as to cause a sufficient degree of turbulence in the blood and vibration in the vessel wall, a murmur becomes audible through the chest wall (Dawes, Mott, and Widdicombe, 1955,b). This murmur is readily detected in the newborn lamb, and in the calf and foal (Amoroso, Dawes, and Mott, 1958), as a loud continuous roar, best heard in the interspace between the third and fourth ribs on the left side, radiating up into the axilla and persisting for many hours from birth. It is also present in the newborn piglet as a continuous, crescendo systolic or early systolic murmur (Evans, Rowe, Downie, and Rowsell, 1963). It is less easy to detect in puppies (Handler, 1956), and has not been recorded in rhesus monkeys. Thus it is less evident in animals which are of a smaller size at birth. In the human infant a soft inconstant murmur was found by Burnard (1958, 1959). It was present in a third of normal infants and usually disappeared within 10 hours. It was more often present when the baby was well warmed and in association with evidence of asphyxia. In the large farm animals the conditions for production and detection of the ductus murmur after birth are particularly favourable, because the pressure difference across the ductus becomes large and the pulmonary trunk is closely applied to the chest wall. It is also possible to open the chest and measure the external diameter of the vessel. These circumstances, with cineangiography and measurements of pressures and blood contents, have facilitated the study of the process of closure. In the normal lamb, calf, and foal this takes many hours and the murmur is sometimes present several days after birth. In the first few hours after delivery, hypoxia may cause the ductus to dilate again, but thereafter some further change normally occurs in the vessel, which makes it no longer sensitive to the changes in the O_2 tension of its environment. Strong contraction of the smooth muscle is associated with haemorrhage from and disruption of the vasa vasorum, and it may be that this is the process which jams the lock on the door. Eventually, flow through the vessel ceases as a result of muscular constriction, perhaps aided terminally by intimal swelling, and the wall is replaced by fibrous tissue.

In man, the evidence indicates a process of a similar nature. The postmortem evidence (Fig. 76) is consistent with this view, but is not necessarily a reliable guide as to what happens in normal healthy infants, as Barcroft (1946) emphasized. Yet even here the difference as compared with the closure of the foramen ovale is striking. Measurements of blood O_2 content *in vivo* showed that for the first hour or more from birth there was normally a right-to-left shunt through the ductus, i.e., continuing in the foetal direction (Eldridge and Hultgren, 1955; James, 1959; Saling, 1960; Oliver, Demis, and Bates, 1961). And in the past few years a wealth of evidence based on blood O_2 measurements, cineangiography, and indicator dilution methods has accumulated to show that this is followed by a reversal in flow direction, similar to that in animals, through a still patent ductus (Adams and Lind, 1957; James and Rowe, 1957; Condorelli and Ungari, 1960; Moss, Emmanouilides, and Duffie, 1963; Jegier, Blankenship, Lind, and Kitchin, 1964; Gessner *et al.*, 1965; Burnard, 1966).

The volume of blood flow, in either direction, depends on so many factors, on the cardiac output and the resistances of the pulmonary and systemic vascular beds as well as on the degree of constriction, length and orientation of the ductus arteriosus, that it is impossible to use this as a reliable index of the degree of patency. That is to say, we do not have a quantitative measure of the progressive constriction of the vessel in the first few hours or days from birth. But the indirect evidence would be consistent with a fairly rapid initial constriction during the first few hours after delivery, as in animals, followed by a more gradual final functional closure over 1–8 days. In infants delivered prematurely, this process may be spun out over some weeks (Burnard, 1959; Danilowicz, Rudolph, and Hoffman, 1966). In infants suffering from the respiratory distress syndrome, the ductus arteriosus remains widely patent during the most severe stage of the illness, and this is a complicating factor of importance in trying to understand the pathophysiology of the condition (Rudolph *et al.*, 1961; Stahlman, Shepard, Young, Gray, and Blankenship, 1966). The cause of the delay in closure of the ductus arteriosus in the respiratory distress syndrome is probably hypoxaemia. Individual children with cyanotic heart disease may show no delay in closure after birth (even when continued survival is dependent on its patency), but then their arterial Po_2 may still be raised well above the foetal level. The delay in closure in premature infants and in some other individuals is as yet unexplained.

The continued wide patency of the ductus arteriosus (unlike that of the foramen ovale) is not usually a benign condition in infancy. It can lead to left ventricular overload and failure. This occurs rapidly when an artificial ductus is opened in an adult dog (Rudolph, 1965). It sometimes happens within the first few days from birth (Auld, 1966) but not very often, probably because the changes are slower, pulmonary vascular resistance has not fallen as low as in adults, the systemic arterial pressure (and hence the level at which pulmonary arterial pressure is maintained) is less, and the heart is normally adapted to a large output toward the end of gestation.

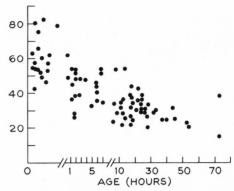

Fig. 77.—Measurements of pulmonary arterial pressure in normal human infants at different ages from birth. (From the data of Adams and Lind, 1957; Saling, 1960; Rudolph et al., 1961; and Emmanouilides et al., 1964.)

Pulmonary Arterial Pressure, Cardiac Output, and Vascular Shunts

Before birth, the pulmonary arterial pressure is greater than that in the descending aorta and is determined by the volume of cardiac output and the combined vascular resistances of the pulmonary, systemic, and umbilical circulations. After birth, when the ductus arteriosus is closed, it is determined by the volume of right heart output and pulmonary vascular resistance alone. The transitional period is one of great complexity, when pulmonary arterial pressure is determined by the output of the right heart, the vascular resistance of the lungs, and by flow in either direction through a partially constricted ductus. Transient pressure changes within the chest, a sigh, a cough, or a cry may then cause a brief reversal of the direction of flow. So long as the ductus arteriosus remains widely patent the pulmonary arterial pressure must approximate closely to that in the aortic arch. But as the ductus constricts, pulmonary arterial pressure comes to be determined more closely by pulmonary vascular resistance, so pulmonary arterial pressure is high after birth and falls gradually.

Figure 77 shows the decline in mean pulmonary arterial pressure after birth, as judged by the observations of various authors on individual normal newborn human infants. The results show a considerable variation, which may well be associated with variations in placental transfusion, as suggested by Arcilla, Oh, Lind, and Gessner (1966). They proposed that this might be related to continued pulmonary vasoconstriction; the facts can be explained as well by a high cardiac output and increased viscosity of the blood associated with a high haematocrit. Danilowicz, Rudolph, and Hoffman (1965) found a pressure gradient of 5–8 mm Hg between the main and peripheral pulmonary arteries in young human infants, which subsided during the first 4 months from birth. This was attributed to the acute angle at which the pulmonary arteries originate from the dome-like trunk left on contraction of the ductus.

Taking into account the species variations in arterial pressures at birth, the rate of decline in pulmonary arterial pressure in man is not very different from that observed in unanaesthetized animals (sheep, Polosa, Dagianti, Guiliano, and Condorelli, 1957; dog and goat, Rudolph, Auld, Golinko, and Paul, 1961; calf, Reeves and Leathers, 1964). There are minor differences. For instance, in the sheep, flow through the ductus is reversed (to become left-to-right) within 10 minutes from birth, whereas in man this normally takes about an hour. In all the species quoted, it takes a week or two for pulmonary arterial pressure to subside to adult levels. In the rabbit, the systemic arterial pressure is rising rapidly at this time; so it is perhaps not surprising that right ventricular systolic pressure (which is as near to pulmonary arterial as one can get in such small animals) falls to a minimum at about 3 days of age and then rises (Dennis, 1967). This observation is interesting because it shows that the net mean pulmonary arterial pressure observed at any one time is the result of several coincidental processes. Among them we may distinguish long-term changes such as the gradual decrease in the smooth muscle mass of the pulmonary arterioles after

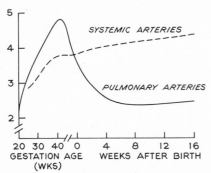

MEAN RATIO OF
AREA MEDIA : AREA INTIMA

Fig. 78.—Observations on arterioles of 5–30 μ luminal diameter from human autopsies to show the area of the muscular media relative to that occupied by the intima and internal elastic membrane in the pulmonary and systemic arterial beds at different ages. (Redrawn from Naeye, 1961.)

birth, and short-term changes such as the reaction to asphyxia or anoxia.

The decrease in the smooth muscle mass of the pulmonary arterioles after birth (in contrast with those in the systemic circulation, Fig. 78) is probably coincidental with a decreased response of the vessels, but it is interesting that no quantitative study of this relationship has been published. If there are changes at the same time in the smooth muscle of the pulmonary veins, these also have received no attention. The basic facts about the pulmonary vasoconstrictor response to asphyxia or anoxia in the newborn have been described in Chapter 7. Here we are concerned with the observation that underventilation, hypoxaemia, or acidaemia cause a rise in pulmonary arterial pressure in

the newborn of many species, accompanied by arrest or even reversal of the shunt through a patent ductus arteriosus from left-to-right to right-to-left. This represents a return to the condition which obtains during foetal life or immediately after delivery (e.g., in sheep, Born, Dawes, Mott, and Rennick, 1956; Condorelli, Guiliano, Dagianti, and Polosa, 1957; Cook, Drinker, Jacobson, Levison, and Strang, 1963; Stahlman, Shepard, Gray, and Young, 1964; and in man, Eldridge and Hultgren, 1955; James and Rowe, 1957; Saling, 1960; Moss, Emmanouilides, Adams, and Chuang, 1964). The large number of workers who have recently investigated this phenomenon, each of them using somewhat different methods in newborn animals and normal babies, indicates the keen interest in the problem because of the evidence that large vascular shunts are present in the respiratory distress syndrome.

When we look for quantitative measures of the size of the cardiac output and of the shunts in the neonatal period, there are not many. The figures of Burnard (1966), which appear in Table 45, are more detailed than, but agree with, those of other observers (e.g., Gessner et al., 1965) and are, therefore, chosen for illustration. The magnitude of the placental transfusion could well affect cardiac output, as it does pulmonary arterial pressure (Arcilla, Oh, Lind, and Gessner, 1966) in the first few hours after birth. Burnard does not specify whether the umbilical cords were clamped early or late, but the size of the haematocrit suggests that it must have been at an intermediate time (because the value observed, 54%, lies between those for early and late clamping in Table 44). The figures for cardiac output are high compared with those of adult man at rest ($\sim$70 ml/kg min), but O_2 consumption is

---

TABLE 45.—Average Values ($\pm$S.D.) on Normal Human Infants
(Burnard, 1966)

Age (hours)	10 ± 5 (range 2–28 hours)
Weight (kg)	3.2 ± 0.4
pH	7.39 ± 0.02
P_{CO_2} (mm Hg)	33 ± 2
Haematocrit (%)	54 ± 6
O_2 saturation (%), left atrium	97 ± 1.6
Systemic arterial pressure (mm Hg)	56 ± 8
Left atrial pressure (mm Hg)	2 ± 1.5
Right atrial pressure (mm Hg)	0 ± 1.4
O_2 consumption (ml/kg min)	6.9 ± 11
Left ventricular output (ml/kg min)	348 ± 42
Right ventricular output (ml/kg min)	233 ± 44
Pulmonary blood flow (ml/kg min)	305 ± 41
L to R shunt (% of L.V. output)	38 ± 11
R to L shunt (% of R.V. output)	20 ± 3

then relatively less ($\sim$3.7 ml/kg min). Both rise on exercise in adults (cardiac output to about 450 ml/kg min and O_2 consumption to 50 ml/kg min). The O_2 consumption in Burnard's babies was 50% more than that in a neutral thermal environment (4.6 ml/kg min; Scopes, 1966), so his infants were not in a basal condition either. Thus, although the figures for cardiac output may at first strike one as large, they are not unreasonably large. They are similar to those in newborn lambs (mean 325 ml/kg min; Cross, Dawes, and Mott, 1959).

The presence of shunts, presumably mainly through the foramen ovale and ductus arteriosus (though bronchial flow may not be entirely negligible), makes accurate measurement of cardiac output exceptionally difficult in the newborn infant. Thus Burnard used a thermal dilution method to measure left ventricular output (injection into the left atrium) and descending aortic flow (injection at the junction of ductus and aorta) while his detecting thermistor was at the bifurcation of the descending aorta. Right ventricular output was calculated by the Fick method and right-to-left shunt from measurements of blood O_2 content while breathing oxygen. These details are given to demonstrate the technical problems and, therefore, to warn against too great reliance on the figures quoted. Nevertheless, the estimates of the size of the shunts in the first few hours of life agree well with those of others.

The figures for cardiac output, both in the newborn sheep and man, suggest that there was a modest increase in the period immediately after birth as compared with that in the foetus near term. Even the highest mean figures for umbilical flow (Table 19, p. 77), which is at least 50% of the combined outputs of both ventricles, are less than those just quoted for sheep and illustrated in Table 45 for man. It is uncertain whether this apparent increase is mainly attributable to the conditions necessarily used to make the measurements, or whether it represents a true departure from the circumstances of intra-uterine life. It is tempting to suggest that such an increase, if real, might be associated with changes in environment and metabolism, with systemic vasodilatation in the infants' tissues, or with increased cardiac sympathetic activity.

Changes in Cardiac Muscle Before and After Birth

Spigelius (1626) and Harvey (1628) recognized that in the human foetus and newborn the wall of the right ventricle was approximately as thick as that of the left ventricle. Yet during the past century some doubt has arisen as to their exact equality. The reasons for these doubts have been ascribed to misinterpretation of the original measurements of Müller (1883), to selection of material (in the sense that the autopsy material available was not truly representative of normal individuals in the age-classes studied), and to variation in methods. Most recent investigators have concluded that the two ventricles are of equal thickness in midgestation but that the total mass of the right ventricle exceeds that of the left at term by about 25% (Hort, 1955, 1966; Emery and MacDonald, 1960; Recavarren and Arias-Stella, 1964). Keen (1955) used only the free walls of the ventricles (and even these vary in thickness along their length and breadth) and concluded they were of approximate equality at term. Hort (1966) also used the free walls of the ventricles and found that the left was smaller. The difference was ascribed to a difference in the plane of section, and Hort also concluded that at birth the external surface of the right ventricular wall was greater than that of the left. In freshly killed animal foetuses, which had not died from progressive asphyxia over a period of time as in man, there was no significant difference in the ventricular weights (lambs, Dawes, Mott, and Widdicombe, 1954; pigs, Yuan, Heymann, and Rudolph, 1966). Either there is a species difference or the apparent ventricular inequality in man at birth results from the mode of death or the methods used. The whole matter needs serious re-examination before we speculate about the possible physiological causes for a species difference.

After birth the left ventricular wall grows rapidly, while the right does not. The continued growth of the left ventricle is related to the growth of the infant and the rise in arterial pressure with age; the arrest of growth in the right ventricle is related to the closure of the ductus arteriosus and the fall in pulmonary arterial pressure. Keen (1955) and Hort (1955) both found that the free wall of the right ventricle fell in weight by 20% over the first month after birth (Fig. 79); the loss was not regained until the end of the first year. The number of fibres is approximately the same in both ventricles, and does not change from infancy with age in man, although they change in length and thickness (Linzbach, 1947; Hort, 1966). Boellaard (1952) found that the mean diameter of the muscle fibres of the human right ventricle decreased from 5.6–5.1 μ, while those of the left ventricle rose from 4.5–6.0 μ over the first 6 weeks from birth. There was a rapid rise in the concentration of RNA in the left ventricle in newborn rabbits during the first day from birth, but little change in the right ventricle (Gluck, Tal-

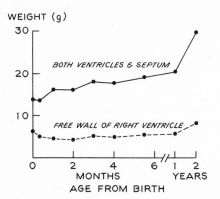

Fig. 79.—Measurements of the weight of the free wall of the right ventricle, and of both ventricles and septum. (From the data of Keen, 1955.)

ner, Gardner, and Kulovich, 1964). In rabbits delivered prematurely, there was no increase in RNA concentration in either ventricle during the first day; but, unfortunately, the pulmonary and systemic arterial pressures on premature delivery were not available for comparison. The changes in ventricular function after birth also appear to be accompanied by changes in myocardial blood flow. This was calculated from the cardiac output (estimated by a dye-dilution method) and the distribution of injected microspheres in newborn piglets (Yuan, Heymann, and Rudolph, 1966). Left ventricular myocardial flow (per unit weight of tissue) increased about 50% during the first few days from birth, while right ventricular myocardial flow fell. This is a reasonable adaptation to the change in the immediate needs of the two ventricles with changing intraventricular pressures.

There are also some interesting observations in the heart of the rat, which grows rapidly after birth and in which systemic arterial pressure rises particularly quickly during the first 3 weeks (Fig. 50). In this period there probably was an increase in the total number of cardiac muscle fibers (Rakušan, Jelínek, Korecký, Soukupová, and Poupa, 1965). The myoglobin concentration in the left ventricle also increased considerably, from 1.77–5.31 mg/Gm wet weight over the first 4 months (Rakušan, Radl, and Poupa, 1965). But the ratio between the number of muscle fibres and capillaries appeared to fall with age in rats, rabbits, and man, so that the calculated diffusion distance for oxygen increased. Of course, there is a large increase in arterial Po_2 at birth, and there is no doubt of an adequate O_2 supply. Yet these observations draw attention to the fact that the change in physical problems of gas diffusion in such young, very active, and rapidly growing tissues have generally been ignored.

Some Congenital Cardiovascular Malformations

Before we leave the changes in the heart and lungs at birth, it is timely to consider the origin and complications of some other congenital anomalies of the heart and great vessels, in addition to those already briefly considered.

COARCTATION OF THE AORTA.—The normal closure of the ductus arteriosus has already been described; we do not know why this fails in some individuals at sea level, who so far as is known received adequate oxygenation during the first few days from birth. Whereas a patent ductus results from failure of smooth muscle contraction at this critical period, coarctation of the aorta probably results from excessive muscular contraction. As Craigie (1841) wrote, describing his own experience and the preceding literature: "It seems, therefore, that the obliterating action, which had taken place in the ductus arteriosus, had been for some peculiar cause prolonged into the aorta, and had there given rise first to contraction and then to obliteration of that vessel." It is possible, but seems unlikely, that during foetal life there could be a severe constriction of the descending aorta at or near the entry of the ductus arteriosus; if this were postductal it would increase the vascular resistance of the hind part of the body and might reduce umbilical flow to the placenta. It has appeared more likely that coarctation results from the presence in the aorta of an unusual quantity of ductal tissue which has contracted when the arterial Po_2 rose after birth (see, for instance, Friedberg, 1942).

Gillman and Burton (1966) reasoned that if this were the correct explanation some ductal tissue might normally be present in the foetal aorta at birth, and that its presence might be manifest on exposure to a high Po_2. They perfused the isolated descending aorta (including the junction with the ductus arteriosus, which was occluded) of newborn rabbits, cats, guinea pigs, and pigs. When the Po_2 of the perfusion fluid was raised to a high value there was a large increase in resistance to flow, associated with local constriction of the aorta at the point of junction with the ductus. This very neat experiment provides a substantial basis for the view that coarctation can arise after birth, as a result of an unusual quantity of ductal muscle incorporated in the wall of the aorta during development.

TABLE 46.—AVERAGE VALUES (±S.E.) FOR
EFFECTIVE RENAL BLOOD FLOW AFTER BIRTH (OH, OH,
AND LIND, 1966)

| TIME AFTER BIRTH | EFFECTIVE RENAL BLOOD FLOW (ML/MIN PER 1.73M²) | |
	Cord Clamped Early	Late
Up to 12 hours	142 ± 11	259 ± 15
2–5 days	254 ± 3.5	350 ± 36

PULMONARY HYPERTENSION IN ASSOCIATION WITH SEPTAL DEFECT.—One interesting question which has been debated in the last 15 years has been the reason for the high pulmonary vascular resistance observed in children with a large ventricular septal defect. Civin and Edwards (1951) suggested that this might represent a persistence of the medial hypertrophy (as compared with adult lungs) of the small pulmonary arterioles observed at birth. Alternatively, it might result as a secondary change in the pulmonary vascular bed consequent on the high pulmonary arterial and left atrial pressure (Dammann and Ferencz, 1956). The elevated vascular resistance is found only in patients with a very large septal defect, in whom, therefore, pulmonary flow and arterial pressure are unusually high. The second hypothesis was favoured by the fact that in infants with a large uncomplicated ventricular septal defect, who died within the first 4 weeks after birth, the relative thickness of the muscular media was less than in infants who died some months later (Wagenvoort, Neufeld, DuShane, and Edwards, 1961). Also, Hoffman and Rudolph (1966,b) found a rise in pulmonary vascular resistance in some children with large septal defects. So it is more likely that pulmonary vascular resistance had fallen normally at birth in these children, that the pulmonary arterial pressure remained high because of the defect, and that subsequently, over a period of months, a progressive medial hypertrophy and rise

in pulmonary vascular resistance developed. The mechanism by which the resistance increases is uncertain. It could be related to the similar increase in mitral stenosis. None of the traditional mechanisms which regulate smooth muscle, such as the myogenic reflex, provide a satisfactory explanation. It is possible that prolonged perivascular oedema (West, Dollery, and Heard, 1965), as a result of the increased transmural pressures, may be the explanation.

Changes in the Peripheral Circulation

We know rather less about the changes after birth in the systemic circulation. Oh, Oh, and Lind (1966) observed that effective renal blood flow rose between 12 and 48 hours after birth (Table 46). The figures quoted are expressed in terms of surface area. In order to present them in terms of body weight (for a hypothetical infant of 3.5 kg weight, 50 cm length, and about 0.2 M²), they should be divided by 28. This would suggest that after the immediate transitional stage, from 2–5 days after birth, renal flow is not much more than 12 ml/kg min, i.e., a smaller fraction of resting cardiac output than flow through the adult kidney. During the period immediately after birth, renal flow increased by a greater proportion in the babies whose cords were clamped early. It is possible that this increase was due in part to a rise in arterial pressure (especially after early clamping of the cord), but more probably that it was associated with renal vasodilatation, perhaps as the effects of delivery and partial asphyxia subsided.

Celander (1966) has used an ingenious adaptation of venous occlusion plethysmography to measure blood flow in the calf and foot in sleeping newborn human infants. Resting blood flow (per 100 ml tissue) was higher in premature than full-term infants, and higher in full term than values calculated by similar methods in adult man (Table 47). Judg-

TABLE 47.—MEASUREMENTS OF BLOOD FLOW IN THE FOOT AND CALF OF
THE NEWBORN HUMAN INFANT (DATA DERIVED FROM CELANDER AND MÅRILD,
1962; CELANDER, 1966)

	PREMATURE	FULL TERM	ADULT
* Mean arterial pressure (mm Hg)	61	83	104
Resting blood flow (ml/min/100 ml tissue)	15	7.5	3.9
Flow during reactive hyperaemia or after exercise (ml/min/100 ml)	100	47	20–40

* Indirectly measured.

ing from published tracings the absolute volume of flow was ~5 ml/min, a small fraction of cardiac output. As Table 47 also shows, flow increased very greatly during reactive hyperaemia, by an amount roughly proportional to that in the forelimb or calf of adult man recovering from ischaemia or exercise. During the period of 2 hours or more after birth the most prominent change was an increase in blood flow to the calf or foot, attributable to a fall in vascular resistance. Conversely, after asphyxial delivery blood flow was reduced almost to zero because of peripheral vasoconstriction.

THE CLOSURE OF THE DUCTUS VENOSUS.—The ductus venosus constitutes a potential portal-caval shunt by-passing the liver, so its prompt closure at birth is a matter of some significance. Judging by human postmortem material (Fig. 76), closure is effected more consistently and more rapidly than that of either of the other special foetal vascular channels. But this is a difficult vessel to tackle, for anatomical reasons, so we have less direct evidence than is desirable. In both newborn lambs and human infants, radiopaque contrast medium, injected into the umbilical vein, may pass through it for a day or two after birth. It seemed to Peltonen and Hirvonen (1965) that this was unlikely to be due to the rise of pressure on injection because the same result was obtained in lambs on injection into vessels further from the ductus venosus, for instance, into a mesenteric artery; yet this is not a conclusive argument. Jegier, Blankenship and Lind (1963) thought it was functionally closed within 1–3 hours of birth in the human infant for two reasons. First, they and others found a mean pressure gradient between the umbilical venous recess (i.e., at the junction of umbilical vein and portal sinus) and inferior vena cava of about 6 mm Hg after cessation of umbilical flow; this was regarded as incompatible with a large patent communication between the two; but the range of values was large (0–12 mm Hg). Secondly, injection of a small quantity of dye into the right atrium or umbilical recess gave curves (recorded from an ear oximeter) which were utterly different. So probably little blood flows through the ductus venosus even an hour or two after birth in most infants, but it may be open in some or when portal venous pressure is raised.

From what has already been said about the structure of the ductus venosus (Chapter 8), and the doubts expressed about whether there is a true smooth muscle sphincter at its junction with the umbilical vein, it will have been anticipated that views as to the mechanism of closure are divided.

The view of Barcroft and his colleagues (1946) was that the sphincter contracted as a result of some stimulus, probably of autonomic nervous origin, after birth. Yet stimulation of the peripheral vagi, or injection of acetylcholine, adrenaline, or noradrenaline (but not saline or histamine) into the umbilical or jugular vein of lambs 3–6 days old caused the ductus venosus to reopen; the changes in venous pressure were small (Peltonen and Hirvonen, 1965). The fact that changes in vessel diameter were observed indicates either that the vessel contains elements which relaxed or that the transmural pressure altered (perhaps as a result of contraction of muscle within the liver tissue which encloses the ductus venosus). This latter proposal might reconcile some of the otherwise apparently contradictory reports. It is evident that more observations are needed both on the natural history and mechanism of closure.

The possible deleterious effects of continued patency of the ductus venosus in the neonatal period have not been defined in animals or in man. It has been suggested that liver function, and bilirubin excretion in particular, might be impaired; hepatic arterial flow presumably continues unaffected, but has not been measured. These possibilities are rarely considered, because there is no evidence.

Finally, it is perhaps just worth mentioning how little we know about the changes after birth in the distribution of cardiac output to other organs. A few observations have been made on coronary and cerebral flow in the sheep (as briefly mentioned in Chapter 8). Cerebral flow must form a much larger proportion of cardiac output in man, but there are no measurements in the neonatal period. Presumably, blood flow to the muscles of respiration must increase considerably after birth, and must be maintained during hyperpnoea, although it is unlikely that this is a large proportion of cardiac output. Increased flow to brown adipose tissue and to shivering muscles may also result from cold exposure, and to the gastrointestinal tract on feeding. No one of these changes is likely to be very large in a normal baby which is kept warm, but their cumulative effects may be considerable.

Conclusion

The complex nature of the transitional circulation in the period of a day or so after birth makes it less easy to detect heart failure (in the sense that venous pressure rises without an equivalent rise in output).

It would certainly be quite wrong to assume that because the infant heart is so much better at withstanding partial asphyxia than that of the adult, failure does not readily occur. There are three features which complicate the issue. First, there is the potential large size of the placental transfusion, or, conversely, placental blood loss. Individual newborn infants and animals may have very different blood volumes and systemic arterial and venous pressures after separation from their mothers. Consequently, the absolute level of venous pressure is not a reliable guide. Both this and the level of arterial pressure must be interpreted in relation to the haematocrit as well as the gestational age and size of the infant and the presence or absence of acidaemia. Secondly, there is the fact that the ventricles are of approximately equal thickness and that there may be relatively free communication between both sides of the heart. Thirdly, there is the fact that as failure occurs, arterial pressure begins to decline. The rise of venous pressure may thus be limited. So failure is characterized by a large heart, a small rise of venous pressure with increase in liver size and other signs of peripheral oedema (often not easy to detect, especially in animals) and, ultimately, a fall in arterial pressure. It would be hard to come to a firm conclusion about the presence and progress of cardiac failure in a human newborn infant without serial measurements of pressures. It is usually comparatively easy to tell whether a newborn human or animal is sick, but much more difficult to define what is wrong in physiological terms as a rational basis for treatment, even with all the available laboratory instruments.

REFERENCES

Adams, F. H., and Lind, J.: Physiologic studies on the cardiovascular status of normal newborn infants (with special reference to the ductus arteriosus), Pediatrics 19:431–437, 1957.

Amoroso, E. C.; Dawes, G. S., and Mott, J. C.: Patency of the ductus arteriosus in the newborn calf and foal, Brit. Heart J. 20:92–96, 1958.

Alzamora, V.; Rotta, A.; Battilana, G.; Abugattas, R.; Rubio, C.; Bouroncle, J.; Zapata, C.; Santa-Mariá, E.; Binder, T.; Subiria, R.; Parades, D.; Pando, B., and Graham, G. G.: On the possible influence of great altitude on the determination of certain cardiovascular anomalies, Pediatrics 12:259–262, 1953.

Arcilla, R. A.; Oh, W.; Lind, J., and Gessner, I. H.: Pulmonary arterial pressures of newborn infants born with early and late clamping of the cord, Acta paediat. 55: 305–315, 1966.

Assali, N. S.; Morris, J. A.; Smith, R. W., and Manson, W. A.: Studies on ductus arteriosus circulation, Circulation Res. 13:478–489, 1963.

Auld, P. A. M.: Delayed closure of the ductus arteriosus, J. Pediat. 69:61–66, 1966.

Barclay, A. E., and Franklin, K. J.: The time of functional closure of the foramen ovale in the lamb, J. Physiol. 94:256–258, 1938.

Barclay, A. E.; Franklin, K. J., and Prichard, M. M. L.: *The Foetal Circulation* (Oxford: Blackwell Scientific Publications, 1944).

Barcroft, J.: Foetal circulation and respiration, Physiol. Rev. 16:103–128, 1936.

Barcroft, J.: *Researches on Prenatal Life* (Oxford: Blackwell Scientific Publications, 1946).

Barcroft, J.; Kennedy, J. A., and Mason, M. F.: The relation of the vagus nerve to the ductus arteriosus in the guinea-pig, J. Physiol. 92:1–2, P., 1938.

Barcroft, J.; Kramer, K., and Millikan, G. A.: The oxygen in the carotid blood at birth, J. Physiol. 94:571–578, 1939.

Barron, D. H.: The changes in the fetal circulation at birth, Physiol. Rev. 24:277–295, 1944.

Boellaard, J. W.: Über Umbauvorgänge in der rechter Herzkammerwand während der Neugeborenen und Säuglungs-periode, Ztschr. Kreislaufforsch. 41:101–111, 1952.

Born, G. V. R.; Dawes, G. S.; Mott, J. C., and Rennick, B. R.: The constriction of the ductus arteriosus caused by oxygen and by asphyxia in newborn lambs, J. Physiol. 132:304–342, 1956.

Born, G. V. R.; Dawes, G. S.; Mott, J. C., and Widdicombe, J. G.: Changes in the heart and lungs at birth, Cold Spring Harb. Symp. Quant. Biol. 19:102–107, 1954.

Boyd, J. D.: The nerve supply of the mammalian ductus arteriosus, J. Anat. 72:146–147, 1941.

Buckels, L. J., and Usher, R.: Cardiopulmonary effects of placental transfusion, J. Pediat. 67:239–247, 1965.

Budin, P.: A quel moment doit-on pratiquer la ligature du cordon umbilicale, Bull. Gen. Thérap. 90:123–127, 1876.

Burnard, E. D.: A murmur from the ductus arteriosus in the newborn baby, Brit. M. J. 1:806–810, 1958.

Burnard, E. D.: The cardiac murmur in relation to symptoms in the newborn, Brit. M. J. 1:134–138, 1959.

Burnard, E. D.: A murmur that may arise from the ductus arteriosus in the human baby, Proc. Roy. Soc. Med. 52:77–78, 1959.

Burnard, E. D.: Influence of Delivery on the Circulation, in Cassels, D. E. (ed.): *The Heart and Circulation in the Newborn Infant* (New York: Grune & Stratton, Inc., 1966), pp. 92–97, 135–137.

Burnard, E. D., and James, L. S.: Atrial pressures and cardiac size in the newborn infant, J. Pediat. 62:815–826, 1963.

Celander, O.: Studies of the Peripheral Circulation, in Cassels, D. E. (ed.): *The Heart and Circulation in the Newborn Infant* (New York: Grune & Stratton, Inc., 1966), pp. 98–110.

Celander, O., and Mårild, K.: Reactive hyperaemia in the foot and calf of the newborn infant, Acta. paediat. 51: 544–552, 1962.

Civin, W. H., and Edwards, J. E.: The postnatal structural changes in the intrapulmonary arteries and arterioles, Arch. Path. 51:192–200, 1951.

Cohnstein, J., and Zuntz, N.: Untersuchungen über das Blut, den Kreislauf und die Athmung beim Säugethier-

Fötus, Pflüger's Arch. ges. Physiol. 34:173–233, 1884.

Condorelli, M.; Dagianti, A.; Polosa, C., and Guiliano, G.: Sulla persistenza di un fisiological corto circuito attraverso il forame ovale nei primi giorni della vita extrauterina. Atti XIX Congr. Soc. Ital. Cardiol. 165–170, 1957.

Condorelli, M.; Guiliano, G.; Dagianti, A., and Polosa, C.: Sulla funzionalita del dotto di Botallo nei primi giorni della vita extrauterina. Boll. Soc. Ital. Biol. Sper. 33:1599–1601, 1957.

Condorelli, S., and Ungari, C.: The period of functional closure of the foramen ovale and the ductus Botalli in the human newborn, Cardiologia 36:274–287, 1960.

Cook, C. D.; Drinker, P. A.; Jacobson, N. H.; Levison, H., and Strang, L. B.: Control of pulmonary blood flow in the foetal and newly born lamb, J. Physiol. 169:10–29, 1963.

Craigie, D.: Instance of obliteration of the aorta beyond the arch, illustrated by similar cases and observations, Edinburgh Med. & Surg. J. 56:427–462, 1841.

Cross, K. W.; Dawes, G. S., and Mott, J. C.: Anoxia, oxygen consumption and cardiac output in newborn lambs and adult sheep, J. Physiol. 146:316–343, 1959.

Danilowicz, D.; Rudolph, A. M., and Hoffman, J. I. E.: Vascular resistance in the large pulmonary arteries in infancy, Circulation 32(II):74, 1965.

Danilowicz, D.; Rudolph, A. M., and Hoffman, J. I. E.: Delayed closure of the ductus arteriosus in premature infants, Pediatrics 37:74–78, 1966.

Dammann, J. F., and Ferencz, C.: The significance of the pulmonary vascular bed in congenital heart disease, Am. Heart J. 52:210–231, 1956.

Darwin, C.: *The Autobiography of Charles Darwin* (1876), in Barlow, N. (ed.) (New York: Harcourt, Brace and Company, Inc., 1959).

Darwin, E.: *Zoonomia; or, the Laws of Organic Life* (Boston: Thomas and Andrews, 1803).

Davignon, J.; Lorenz, R. R., and Shepherd, J. T.: Response of human umbilical artery to changes in transmural pressure, Am. J. Physiol. 209:51–59, 1965.

Dawes, G. S.; Mott, J. C., and Widdicombe, J. G.: The foetal circulation in the lamb, J. Physiol. 126:563–587, 1954.

Dawes, G. S.; Mott, J. C., and Widdicombe, J. G.: Closure of the foramen ovale in newborn lambs, J. Physiol. 128:384–395, 1955,a.

Dawes, G. S.; Mott, J. C., and Widdicombe, J. G.: The cardiac murmur from the patent ductus arteriosus in newborn lambs, J. Physiol. 128:344–360, 1955,b.

Dawes, G. S.; Mott, J. C.; Widdicombe, J. G., and Wyatt, D. G.: Changes in the lungs of the new-born lamb, J. Physiol. 121:141–162, 1953.

DeMarsh, Q. B.; Alt, H. L.; Windle, W. F., and Hillis, D. S.: The effect of depriving the infant of its placental blood on the blood picture during the first week of life, J. A. M. A. 116:2568–2573, 1941.

Dennis, J.: Pressure measurements in the lesser circulation of the newborn rabbit, Unpublished.

Eldridge, F. L., and Hultgren, H. N.: The physiologic closure of the ductus arteriosus in the newborn infant, J. Clin. Invest. 34:987–996, 1955.

Emery, J. L., and MacDonald, M. S.: The weight of the ventricles in the later weeks of intrauterine life, Brit. Heart J. 22:563–570, 1960.

Emmanouilides, G. C., Ross, A. J., Duffie, E. R., and Adams, F. H.: Pulmonary arterial pressure changes in human newborn infants from birth to 3 days of age, J. Pediat. 65:327–333, 1964.

Evans, J. R.; Rowe, R. D.; Downie, H. G., and Rowsell, H. C.: Murmurs arising from ductus arteriosus in normal newborn swine, Circulation Res. 12:85–93, 1963.

Fabricius, H.: The Embryological Treatises. Tr. by H. B. Adelmann (Ithaca, New York: Cornell University Press, 1942).

Friedberg, C. K.: Coarctation of the aorta—a new theory as to its pathogenesis, J. Mt. Sinai Hosp. 8:520–533, 1942.

Gairdner, D.; Marks, J.; Roscoe, J. D., and Brettall, O. R.: The fluid shift from the vascular compartment immediately after birth, Arch. Dis. Childhood 33:489–498, 1958.

Gérard, G.: Le canal artériel, J. Anat. (Paris) 36:1–21, 1900,a.

Gérard, G.: De l'obliteration du canal artériel, les théories et les faits, J. Anat. (Paris) 36:323–357, 1900,b.

Gessner, I.; Krovetz, L. J.; Benson, R. W.; Prystowsky, H.; Stenger, V., and Eitzmann, D. V.: Haemodynamic adaptations in the newborn infant, Pediatrics 36:752–762, 1965.

Gibson, G. A.: *Diseases of the Heart and Aorta* (Edinburgh: J. Pentland Young, 1898), pp. 61, 303, 310–312.

Gibson, G. A.: Clinical lectures on circulatory affections —Lecture I. Persistence of the arterial duct and its diagnosis, Edinburgh M. J. 8:1–10, 1900.

Gillman, R. G., and Burton, A. C.: Constriction of the neonatal aorta to raised oxygen tension, Circulation Res., 19:755–765, 1966.

Gluck, L.; Talner, N. S.; Gardner, T. H., and Kulovich, M. V.: RNA concentrations in the ventricles of full-term and premature rabbits following birth, Nature. 202:770–771, 1964.

Goodall, J. R.; Andersen, F. O.; Altimas, G. T., and MacPhail, F. L.: An inexhaustible source of blood for transfusion and its preservation, Surg. Gynec. & Obstet. 66:176–178, 1938.

Gregersen, M. I., and Rawson, R. A.: Blood volume, Physiol. Rev. 39: 307–342, 1959.

Grodberg, B. C., and Carey, E. L.: A study of seventy-five transfusions with placental blood, New England J. Med. 219:471–474, 1938.

Gunther, M.: The transfer of blood between baby and placenta in the minutes after birth, Lancet 1:1277–1280, 1957.

Handler, J. J.: The foetal circulation and its changes at birth in some small laboratory animals, J. Physiol. 133:202–212, 1956.

Harvey, W.: *Exercitatio anatomica de motu cordis et sanguinis in animalibus* (Francofurti:Fitzeri, 1628).

Hoboken, N.: *Anatomia secundinae humanae* (Utrecht: Ribbius, 1669).

Hoffman, J. I. E., and Rudolph, A. M.: Physiologic and Clinical Aspects of Left to Right Shunts in the Newborn, in Cassels, D. E. (ed.): *The Heart and Circulation in the Newborn and Infant* (New York: Grune & Stratton, Inc., 1966,a), pp. 147–153.

Hoffman, J. I. E., and Rudolph, A. M.: Increasing pulmonary vascular resistance during infancy in association with ventricular septal defect, Pediatrics 38:220–230, 1966,b.

Hort, W.: Morphologische Untersuchungen am Herzen vor während und nach der postnatalen Kreislaufumschaltung, Virchows Arch. Path. Anat. 326:458–484, 1955.

Hort, W.: The normal heart of the fetus and its metamorphosis in the transition period, in Cassels, D. E. (ed.): *The Heart and Circulation in the Newborn and Infant* (New York: Grune and Stratton, Inc., 1966), pp. 210–224.

Hughes, T.: The role of the folds of Hoboken in the postnatal closure of the human umbilical vessels, Physiologist 9:207, 1966.

James, L. S.: In *Adaptation to Extrauterine Life,* 31st Ross Conference on Pediatric Research (Columbus, Ohio: Ross Laboratories, 1959), pp. 28–30.

James, L. S.; Burnard, E. D., and Rowe, R. D.: Abnormal shunting through the foramen ovale after birth, Am. J. Dis. Childhood 102:550, 1961.

James, L. S., and Rowe, R. D.: The pattern of response of pulmonary and systemic arterial pressures in newborn and older infants to short periods of hypoxia, J. Pediat. 51:5–11, 1957.

Jegier, W.; Blankenship, W., and Lind, J.: Venous pressure in the first hour of life and its relationship to placental transfusion, Acta paediat. 52:485–496, 1963.

Jegier, W.; Blankenship, W.; Lind, J., and Kitchin, A.: The changing circulatory pattern of the newborn infant studied by the indicator dilution technique, Acta paediat. 53:541–552, 1964.

Keen, E. N.: The postnatal development of the human cardiac ventricles, J. Anat. (Lond.) 89:484–502, 1955.

Kennedy, J. A., and Clark, S. L.: Observations on the ductus arteriosus of the guinea-pig in relation to its method of closure, Anat. Rec. 79:349–371, 1941.

Kennedy. J. A., and Clark, S. L.: Observations on the physiological reactions of the ductus arteriosus, Am. J. Physiol. 136:140–147, 1942.

Kovalčík, V.: The response of the isolated ductus arteriosus to oxygen and anoxia, J. Physiol. 165:185–197, 1963.

Lind, J., and Wegelius, C.: Human fetal circulation: Changes in the cardiovascular system at birth and disturbances in the post-natal closure of the foramen ovale and ductus arteriosus, Cold. Spring. Harb. Symp. Quant. Biol. 19:109–125, 1954.

Linzbach, A. J.: Mikrometrische und histologische Analyse hypertropher menschlichen Herzen, Virchows Arch. Path. Anat. 314:534–594, 1947.

Mollison, P. L.; Veall, N., and Cutbush, M.: Red cell and plasma volume in newborn infants, Arch. Dis. Childhood 25:242–253, 1950.

Moss, A. J.; Emmanouilides, G., and Duffie, E. B.: Closure of ductus arteriosus in newborn infant, Pediatrics 32:25–30, 1963.

Moss, A. J.; Emmanouilides, G. C.; Adams, F. H., and Chuang, K.: Response of ductus arteriosus and pulmonary and systemic arterial pressures to changes in oxygen environment in newborn infants, Pediatrics 33:937–944, 1964.

Müller, W.: Die Massenverhältnisse des menschlichen Herzens (Hamburg and Leipzig: Leopold Voss, 1883).

Naeye, R. L.: Arterial changes during the perinatal period, Arch. Path. 71:121–128, 1961.

Oh, W.; Oh, M. A., and Lind, J.: Renal function and blood volume in newborn infant related to placental transfusion, Acta paediat. 56:197–210, 1966.

Oliver, T. K.; Demis, J. A., and Bates, G. D.: Serial blood-gas tensions and acid base balance during the first hour of life in human infants, Acta paediat. 50:346–360, 1961.

Parry, H. J.: A comparative study of the umbilical sphincter, Proc. Zool. Soc. 124:595–604, 1954.

Peltonen, T., and Hirvonen, L.: Experimental studies on fetal and neonatal circulation, Acta paediat. Suppl. 161, 1965.

Peñaloza, D.; Arias-Stella, J.; Sime, F.; Recavarren, S., and Marticorena, E.: The heart and pulmonary circulation in children at high altitudes, Pediatrics 34:568–582, 1964.

Polosa, C.; Dagianti, A.; Guiliano, G., and Condorelli, M.: Valori tensivi del grande e del piccolo circolo in agnelli neonati, Boll. Soc. Ital. Biol. Sper. 33:1593–1596, 1957.

Prec, K. J., and Cassels, D. E.: Dye dilution curves and cardiac output in newborn infants, Circulation 11:789–798, 1955.

Rakušan, K.; Jelínek, J.; Korecký, B.; Soukupová, M., and Poupa, O.: Postnatal development of muscle fibres and capillaries in the rat heart, Physiol. Bohemoslov. 14:32–37, 1965.

Rakušan, K., and Poupa, O.: Changes in the diffusion distance in the rat heart muscle during development, Physiol. Bohemoslov. 12:220–227, 1963.

Rakušan, K.; Radl, J., and Poupa, O.: The distribution and content of myoglobin in the heart of the rat during postnatal development, Physiol. Bohemoslov. 14:317–319, 1965.

Recavarren, S., and Arias-Stella, J.: Growth and development of the ventricular myocardium from birth to adult life, Brit. Heart J. 26:187–192, 1964.

Record, R. G., and McKeown, T.: Observations relating to the aetiology of patent ductus arteriosus, Brit. Heart J. 15:376–386, 1953.

Record, R. G., and McKeown, T.: The effect of reduced atmospheric pressure on closure of the ductus arteriosus in the guinea pig, Clin. Sc. 14:225–233, 1955.

Reeves, J. T., and Leathers, J. E.: Circulatory changes following birth of the calf and the effect of hypoxia, Circulation Res. 15:343–354, 1964.

Rossdale, P. D., and Mahaffey, L. W.: Parturition in the thoroughbred mare with particular reference to blood deprivation in the newborn, Vet. Rec. 70:142–147, 1958.

Rudolph, A. M.: The effects of postnatal circulatory adjustments in congenital heart disease, Pediatrics 36:763–772, 1965.

Rudolph, A. M.; Auld, P. A. M.; Golinko, R. J., and Paul, M. H.: Pulmonary vascular adjustments in the neonatal period, Pediatrics 28:28–34, 1961.

Rudolph, A. M.; Drorbaugh, J. E.; Auld, P. A. M.; Rudolph, A. J.; Nadas, A. S.; Smith, C. A., and Hubbell, J. P.: Studies on the circulation in the neonatal period: The circulation in the respiratory distress syndrome, Pediatrics 27:551–566, 1961.

Saling, E.: Neue Untersuchungsergebnisse über den Kreislauf des Kindes unmittelbar nach der Geburt, Arch. Gynäk. 194:287–306, 1960.

Scammon, R. E., and Morris, E. H.: On the time of the post-natal obliteration of the fetal blood-passages (foramen ovale, ductus arteriosus, ductus venosus), Anat. Rec. 15:165–180, 1918.

Scopes, J. W.: Metabolic rate and temperature control in the human baby, Brit. M. Bull. 22:88–91, 1966.

Sisson, T. R. C.; Lund, C. J.; Whalen, L. E., and Telek, A. J.: The blood volume of infants. I. The full term infant in the first year of life, J. Pediat. 55:163–179, 1959.

Slijper, E. J., and deVries, R. J.: The closure of the foramen ovale and the ductus arteriosus Botalli in the domestic pig, Mammalia 29:602–609, 1965.

Spigelius, A.: *De formato foetu* (Patavy: Jo Bap. de Martinis et Liviu Pasquatu, 1626).

Stahlman, M. T.; Merrill, R. E., and LeQuire, V. S.: Cardiovascular adjustments in normal newborn lambs, Am. J. Dis. Childhood 104:360–365, 1962.

Stahlman, M.; Shepard, F. M.; Gray, J., and Young, W.: The effects of hypoxia and hypercapnia on the circulation in newborn lambs, J. Pediat. 65:1091–1092, 1964.

Stahlman, M.; Shepard, F. M.; Young, W. C.; Gray, J., and Blankenship, W.: Assessment of the Cardiovascular Status of Infants with Hyaline Membrane Disease, in Cassels, D. E. (ed.): *The Heart and Circulation in the Newborn and Infant* (New York: Grune & Stratton, Inc., 1966), pp. 121–129.

Štembra, Z. K.; Hodr, J., and Janda, J.: Umbilical blood flow in healthy newborn infants during the first minutes after birth, Am. J. Obst. & Gynec. 91:568–574, 1965.

Usher, R.; Shephard, M., and Lind, J.: The blood volume of the newborn infant and placental transfusion, Acta paediat. 52:497–512, 1963.

Van Harreveld, A., and Russell, R. E.: Postnatal development of a left-right atrial pressure gradient, Am. J. Physiol. 186:521–524, 1956.

Virchow, R.: Die Thrombosen der Neugebornen, in *Gesammelte Abhandlungen zur wissenschäftlichen Medicin* (Frankfurt: Verlag von Meidinger Sohn and Comp., 1856), pp. 591–597.

Wagenvoort, C. A.; Neufeld, H. N.; DuShane, J. W., and Edwards, J. E.: The pulmonary arterial tree in ventricular septal defect, Circulation 23:740–748, 1961.

West, J. B.; Dollery, C. T., and Heard, B. E.: Increased pulmonary vascular resistance in the dependent zone of the isolated dog lung caused by perivascular oedema, Circulation Res. 17:191–206, 1965.

Wilcox, B. R.; Roberts, W. C., and Carney, E. K.: The effect of reduced atmospheric oxygen concentration on closure of the ductus arteriosus in the dog, J. Surg. Res. 2:312–316, 1962.

Yuan, S. S. H.; Heymann, M., and Rudolph, A. M.: Relationship between ventricular weight, pressure and myocardial blood flow in the newborn piglet, Circulation 34(III):243, 1966.

14

Control of the Circulation and Breathing in the Newborn

The Circulation

THE PREVIOUS CHAPTER dealt with the principal changes in the circulation after birth. The present one is concerned with the competence of the circulation and respiration of the newborn animal or infant to cope with the tasks presented under a variety of conditions, as compared with adults of the same species.

Before discussing the competence of the circulation to react to gross stimuli such as haemorrhage, and changes in position or environmental conditions, we should take account of some general and specific features which must influence our final judgement. Among the general features which are relevant there is first the fact that the resting O_2 consumption, in a neutral thermal environment, of the newborn is larger than that of adults of the same species (see Table 50, p. 194). Secondly, although the arterial blood pressure is lower than that of adults at birth (for figures at birth see Table 24, p. 98), the distance which the blood must travel along the major arteries is less. Consequently, Mott (1965) calculated that in the newborn rabbit the mean velocity of blood flow was considerably less than that in the adult, although the circulation time was the same. The resistance to blood flow in some tissues also is less. For instance, Celander (1966) found that the peripheral vascular resistance (per 100 ml tissue) in the calf and foot of resting full-term newborn infants was less than half that observed in adult man, and in premature infants it was lower still. So although newborn animals and infants have a higher basal metabolic rate and a lower arterial pressure, the problem of O_2 transport is reduced by shorter distances, relatively greater vascularity in some organs, and in some species a higher haemoglobin concentration.

Measurements of blood volume in man and animals of different ages, newborn and adult, cover a moderate range when expressed in terms of body weight. In normal adult man blood volume is 63–85 ml/kg (Dittmer and Grebe, 1959; Altman and Dittmer, 1964), a range which almost covers that of the newborn when the large variations upward due to placental transfusion are eliminated (e.g., Mollison, Veal, and Cutbush, 1950; Usher, Shephard, and Lind, 1963). In the rat, rabbit, and guinea pig (Garcia, 1957; Constable, 1963; Mott, 1965, 1967) blood volume falls from about 70 ml/kg at birth to 40–60 ml/kg in adult life, the adult figures varying inversely with the haemoglobin concentration (i.e., being rather higher in anaemic individuals). According to Gotsev (1939), the blood volume in lambs at birth exceeds 150 ml/kg, falling to about 100 ml/kg over the first 3 weeks; his high values may be due in part to the use of a label which left the circulation rapidly. The moderate range in blood volume contrasts with the wide species variation in the size of organs or tissues at birth (Table 4, p. 16). The fall in blood volume per kg body weight after birth in some species is difficult to interpret because we do not know the changes in the proportion of actively metabolizing tissue or in the volume required to fill the great vessels at different ages.

When we turn to measurements of resting neonatal cardiac output, there are not many in normal human infants outside the immediate newborn

TABLE 48.—Observations on the Mean Resting Cardiac Output of Newborn and Adult Man and Animals

SPECIES	Newborn Age	Newborn Output	Adult	METHOD	SOURCES
Man			72 (resting) 450 (exercise)		Dittmer and Grebe (1959)
	<2 hours	(L) 240		Dye dilution	Gessner et al. (1965)
	7 hours– 4 days	(P) 181		Nitrous oxide	Klaus, Braun, and Tooley (1961)
	2–28 hours	(R) 233		Fick	Burnard (1966)
	1 hour– 11 days	210		Freon	Chu et al. (1965)
Sheep	∼10 days	‡ 270			Cross, Dawes, and Mott (1959)
	20–60 days	‡ 120	‡ 115		
			123	Dye dilution	Metcalfe and Parer (1966)
Rabbit	5–13 days	* 230		Fick	Dawes and Mestyán (1963)
			175–220	Fick and dye dilution	Edwards, Korner, and Thorburn (1959); Korner (1965)
Cows	1–12 months	142		Dye dilution	Kuida, Brown, Lange, and Hecht (1961)
			113	Dye dilution	Fisher and Dalton (1959)

(L) Left ventricular output; (R) right ventricular output; (P) pulmonary capillary flow.
‡ Chloralose anaesthesia.
* Urethane anaesthesia.

period (Table 48). The values observed using the nitrous oxide method for measuring pulmonary capillary flow or using Freon do not vary greatly over the first few days from birth (Tooley, personal communication), and during the first few hours agree well with those obtained by most other methods. Prec and Cassels (1955), using an umbilical venous injection of dye and an ear oximeter, obtained a mean figure of 1341 ml/min over 2–26 hours from birth. The infant weights are not available, but even so this appears higher than other measurements, probably because of the inaccuracy of the oximeter as a measure of absolute dye concentration. The values for cardiac output observed in newborn animals and man are on average greater than those in resting adults of the same species. Yet the most striking fact is the comparatively small variation, when expressed in terms of body weight, in animals varying in size from the newborn rabbit to the adult cow. The range is straddled by adult man at rest and on exercise.

The mean arterial pressure in the newborn period shows remarkable individual and species variations. The individual variations have been attributed to differences in the magnitude of blood gain from or loss to the placenta (Chapter 13), or to the effects of birth asphyxia. There is a further possible source of variation. Figure 80 shows that in foetal lambs of either 90 or 115 days gestation there was no significant variation in mean arterial pressure with weight. But near term, at a gestational age of 140 ± 2 days, there was a highly significant correlation between arterial pressure and weight. All these lambs were still attached to their mother, with an intact umbilical circulation, after delivery under light chloralose anaesthesia. Arterial pressure in the immediate neonatal period, after stabilisation from the changes at birth, may to some extent be dictated by the circumstances which prevailed during late intrauterine life (e.g., by the "settings" to which the baroreceptors and their central control had become adapted). It would hardly be surprising if mean arterial pressure were greater in heavier infants of the same conceptional and postnatal age, although this is not generally true of adults.

The variations in mean arterial pressure with age from birth in different species are shown in Figure 50 (rat, rabbit, dog, monkey, and sheep) and Figure 84 (man). The most striking feature is the relatively rapid rise in arterial pressure in species

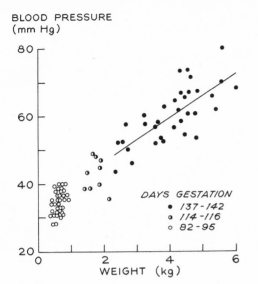

BLOOD PRESSURE
(mm Hg)

DAYS GESTATION
● 137 - 142
⊙ 114 - 116
○ 82 - 95

WEIGHT (kg)

Fig. 80.—Mean arterial blood pressures of anaesthetized foetal lambs at three different gestational ages. Near term there is a highly significant direct relation between arterial pressure and body weight.

which are very small at birth, such as the rat and rabbit, as compared with the more gradual increase in sheep and man. The reasons for this striking species difference do not appear to have been considered. It may possibly be related to the period of very rapid growth after birth in rats and rabbits, for instance, combined with their much greater metabolic rate both in a neutral thermal environment and on exposure to cold as compared with larger newborn animals or man. As will be seen (Chapter 15), a reduction in arterial pressure seriously impairs their ability to maintain a high metabolic rate.

CARDIOVASCULAR REFLEXES
IN THE NEWBORN

BARORECEPTORS.—Kellogg (1927), Clark (1932), and Bauer (1939) believed that the baroreceptor reflexes were not functional in newborn rats, rabbits, and dogs. The rabbit was chosen for further study because although small at birth ($\sim$50 Gm), it was possible to record arterial pressure with the new types of manometer introduced early in the Second World War and because in this species the depressor nerve is separate from the cervical vagus. Also, by all the usual criteria, the rabbit is very immature at birth and has a low mean arterial pressure ($\sim$30 mm Hg).

In the newborn rabbit stimulation of the pe-

ripheral end of the cut cervical vagus caused a profound bradycardia (Dawes, Handler, and Mott, 1957). Stimulation of the central end of one depressor nerve caused a small fall in arterial pressure and heart rate (Downing, 1960). And, more persuasively, when the static pressure was raised in one carotid sinus isolated from the rest of the circulation but with its afferent nerves intact, there was a fall in arterial pressure (Fig. 81). Single afferent nerve discharges were also identified, characteristic of baroreceptors, in the depressor and carotid sinus nerves of newborn rabbits (Downing, 1960). Bloor (1964) measured the threshold and sensitivity of the baroreceptor fibres in rabbits. The threshold was wide at every age, suggesting that similar mixed fibre-populations were present. The relation between discharge frequency and arterial pressure was linear, and sensitivity (as indicated by the change in discharge frequency per unit change in pressure) was of similar magnitude at all ages from birth to adult, with mean arterial pressures ranging from 30 to more than 100 mm Hg. The nerve endings are wrapped partly around the vessels, outside the muscular and elastic coats. If the latter grow in such a way as to contain the rise in transmural pressure, as they clearly do, the only adaptation required of the sensory endings would be to grow as the vessels increase in diameter. Presumably, the immediate stimulus to the receptors is the deformation of the vessel wall over which they are stretched, although attempts to prove this by direct experiment have so far been unsuccessful. If this explanation is correct it should follow that although baroreceptor dis-

Fig. 81.—Observations from 9 newborn rabbits to show the fall in the mean systemic arterial pressure at different pressures applied to the isolated left carotid sinus. The vertical lines represent $\pm$S.E. (Redrawn from Downing, 1960.)

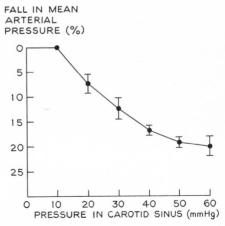

FALL IN MEAN
ARTERIAL
PRESSURE (%)

PRESSURE IN CAROTID SINUS (mmHg)

charges increase during an acute rise of arterial pressure they will not in chronic hypertension, provided that the vessel wall has hypertrophied to contain the pressure.

The afferent side of the reflex arc seems to be well developed at birth. On the efferent side, excitation of the sensory receptors caused a fall in arterial pressure, as in Figure 81, but section of the depressor and carotid sinus nerves in anaesthetised newborn rabbits caused a rise of arterial pressure which lasted only 5–15 minutes, with little change in heart rate. However, the same transient response also was seen in anaesthetised adult rabbits. In both newborn and adult rabbits administration of hexamethonium to block autonomic ganglia caused an immediate fall of blood pressure and heart rate, but these responses also were transient at all ages (Dawes, Handler, and Mott, 1957).

There is less direct evidence in other species. Carotid occlusion caused a large rise in arterial pressure (mean 25 mm Hg) in newborn monkeys, abolished by denervation of the carotid sinuses (Dawes, Jacobson, Mott, and Shelley, 1960). Cottom and Tooley (quoted by Brady and Tooley, 1966) produced bradycardia by massage of the carotid sinus area in 23 premature and mature human infants from 10 minutes to 5 days of age. They ascribe previous failures to observe this effect consistently to the position of the sinus close to the base of the skull. Their observation is undoubtedly compatible with that in animals, but does not clinch the point in man. If the sinus is so deep they might have massaged the vagus as well and hence produced bradycardia by direct stimulation of efferent nerve fibres.

TILTING.—In intact adult man various manoeuvres have been used to apply what has been regarded as a controlled stimulus to the baroreceptors of the cardiovascular system, including haemorrhage or sequestration of blood in the periphery, by tilting or applying cuffs to the limbs, or by the Valsalva manoeuvre. Yet these produce changes which are not confined to the baroreceptors of the aortic arch and carotid sinus. They certainly affect sensory receptors in the wall of the left ventricle and they cause changes on the venous side which must alter the discharge frequency of atrial receptors and possibly of pulmonary arterial baroreceptors. It is unlikely that they cause much immediate effect on the systemic arterial chemoreceptors, but they could alter their sensitivity if the stimulus were prolonged (haemorrhage is known to do this in the cat) or as a second order reflex (e.g., as a result of sympathetic efferent discharges). The consequences of these manoeuvres in man have

usually been explained as the result of a change in systemic arterial baroreceptor activity; while this is much the most likely explanation, the other possibilities are not excluded.

In adult men, tilting from a supine to a head-up, feet-down position causes an immediate fall in arterial pressure, and then a small increase in heart rate and peripheral vasoconstriction, which restore the mean arterial pressure to approximately normal values. On rapid return to the supine position the arterial pressure rises briefly above the initial level, because peripheral vasoconstriction is still present; neither the compensatory tachycardia and restoration of arterial pressure nor the overshoot on return to the supine position was present in tabetic patients whose sensory mechanisms were impaired (Sharpey-Schafer, 1956). It was believed that these patients had simply lost their baroreceptor reflexes, but there was no evidence that they had not lost other reflexes also.

When we try to compare the cardiovascular responses of newborn infants and adults, there is a further problem. The heights and shapes of the body are different, as are the distributions of blood volume between the trunk, head, and limbs. In the immediate newborn period, the foramen ovale and ductus arteriosus may still be patent; the arterial pressures also are different. Thus it may not follow that manoeuvres designed to present a specific stimulus to the circulation will do what is expected. Tilting a newborn infant from the supine into a head-up position did not cause an immediate fall of arterial pressure (as in the adult). There was a small rise of inferior vena caval pressure and either no change or an increase in aortic pressure (Moss, Duffie, and Emmanoulides, 1963; Gupta and Scopes, 1965; Young and Cottom, 1966) or, during a 35–40° tilt for 30–36 minutes, a fall of right atrial and aortic pressure (Oh, Arcilla, Oh, and Lind, 1966). In all instances, there was tachycardia, accompanied in different investigations by a decrease in forearm blood flow and a decrease in renal plasma flow. It is uncertain whether the latter were due to vasoconstriction or were passively associated with the fall in arterial pressure, where present. The duration of tipping is evidently of importance and it is possible that the angle of tilt is also. Greenberg, Lind, and von Euler (1960) strapped infants in the erect posture and observed an increased urinary output of noradrenaline. This could be due to the effect of gravity either on the circulation or in causing discomfort in an abnormal posture.

HAEMORRHAGE.—As tilting appeared to be an uncertain test stimulus in the newborn, attention was directed to blood-letting, which undoubtedly causes a fall of venous and arterial pressures. In newborn rabbits, haemorrhage was followed by a gradual recovery of arterial pressure toward the initial level, accompanied by haemodilution. An extensive investigation showed no evidence that the circulatory mechanisms which controlled the arterial pressure were less efficient in newborn than in adult rabbits, as judged by their capacity to maintain arterial pressure after removal of equal proportions of their blood volumes (Mott, 1965). The same conclusion still held on cutting the carotid sinus and depressor nerves, and stripping the carotid arteries to ensure removal of all systemic arterial baroreceptor afferent nerves (Mott, 1966,a). This suggests that other mechanisms, including haemodilution and perhaps the renin-angiotensin system, may be of greater importance in maintaining arterial pressure under these particular conditions.

Blood-letting in the normal human infant (withdrawal of up to 20 ml over 15 seconds) was followed by a rise in heart rate, but no consistent recovery of pressure during 40 seconds, after which the blood was returned (Young and Cottom, 1966). Yet, Wallgren, Barr, and Rudhe (1964) observed some degree of recovery during exchange transfusions in erythroblastotic infants, because when the same volume of blood was returned the pressure rose above the original level. The time factor is probably of crucial importance. If you are prepared to let a baby remain tilted or with a reduced blood volume for long enough it may well compensate. The fact that its heart accelerates within a few seconds of bleeding is the most direct evidence of a reflex response, probably indicating that the baroreceptors were discharging at the previously existing blood pressure level. Newborn rabbits, whose baroreceptors are undoubtedly working, show little rise of arterial pressure during the first 45 seconds after withdrawing a similar proportion of blood volume.

In neither newborn rabbits nor human infants has the simulated Valsalva manoeuvre, brief elevation of endotracheal pressure to reduce the transmural pressure of the thoracic aorta, produced positive results, characteristic of a baroreceptor reflex response. But as Mott (1966,b) has pointed out, this is yet another test which is relatively easy to perform, but which turns out to be more complex and less easy to interpret the more it is examined critically in young animals.

So much for the systemic baroreceptors. There is no reason to doubt that the systemic arterial chemoreceptors are active in newborn animals and man. Yet their contribution to cardiovascular control has not been systematically analyzed by localized stimulation. If they react as in the adult we would expect stimulation to cause reflex peripheral vasoconstriction and bradycardia, and secondary tachycardia as a second-order reflex associated with hyperpnoea. Generalized hypoxaemia or asphyxia has additional effects due to direct actions upon the central nervous system, heart, and peripheral vessels. Consequently, the gross effects of hypoxaemia are not easy to interpret, and I feel considerable diffidence about suggesting, even from our own experiments on newborn lambs and adult sheep, that one or the other is better able to withstand a low oxygen environment. If there is some small doubt about the chemoreceptors, there is a good deal more uncertainty about the cardiac atrial and ventricular receptors, whose functional significance in the adult is still a matter for debate. Neither they nor the pulmonary arterial receptors have yet been studied in the newborn; there should be a large reduction in the activity of pulmonary baroreceptors, due to the fall in pulmonary arterial pressure after birth, whose consequences might be worth examination.

EVIDENCE OF CARDIOVASCULAR RESPONSIVENESS

THE HEART.—Cardiovascular competence depends not only on the development of a sufficient range of sensory receptors, and on the capacity of the medullary centres to integrate the resultant information, but also on the ability of the executive arm of the circulation to respond. This consists of two parts, the heart and the peripheral blood vessels. Now it is curious that those who have challenged the competence of the circulation in the newborn have directed their attention mainly to the sensory receptors (already discussed) or the systemic vascular bed. They have taken the heart almost entirely for granted and ignored the pulmonary circulation. Perhaps this is understandable in view of the reputation of the infant heart for hardiness, and the fact that evidence of pulmonary vascular reactivity is of recent origin. In fact, there is not much systematised information about the functional capacity of the newborn heart in species other than the lamb (see p. 182). Heart rate can certainly increase to about 300 beats/min or more in many species, but whether this is always accompanied by a proportionate increase in output is not known. Hypoxaemia caused a large increase in cardiac output in adult sheep, but little alteration

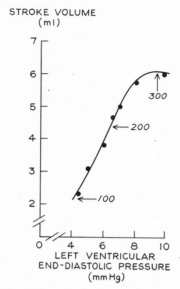

Fig. 82.—Left ventricular function in the heart of a 2-day-old lamb weighing 4.3 kg, at an aortic pressure of 60 mm Hg and heart rate of 200/min. Stroke volume reaches a maximum at a left ventricular end-diastolic pressure of 10 mm Hg, when cardiac output (indicated by the superimposed numerals) is 300 ml/min per kg foetal weight. (Redrawn from Downing, Talner, and Gardner, 1965.)

be about the maximum of which the newborn lamb's heart was capable, and that this corresponded well with the mean figure of 325 ml/kg min deduced from measurements *in vivo* (Cross, Dawes, and Mott, 1959). Infusion of noradrenaline (1 μg/kg min) caused a substantial increase in force and speed of contraction even when the blood pH was reduced from 7.24 to 6.84 by slow infusion of HCl. But it was not fair to compare this with the metabolic acidosis observed during asphyxia in the newborn, because in the latter circumstances there is a large accumulation of lactate and hydrogen ions intracellularly as well as in the blood. In fact, acidaemia is not synonymous with acidosis.

There is another feature of cardiac function in the newborn which deserves more attention, and I am indebted to Dr. T. N. James of Detroit for pointing this out. If a stimulus of sufficient strength is applied to the ventricle in the so-called vulnerable period (i.e., early during the recovery of excitability and before the end of the T-wave), the ventricles will fibrillate. The adult heart is protected from the possible dangers of a premature atrial contraction by the relatively slow rate of recovery of the transmission system, and this is attributed to the existence of a long refractory period in the atrioventricular node. The refractory period of the Purkinje system is less. But in suckling goats (4–6 kg), piglets

in anaesthetised lambs up to 60 days from birth (Cross, Dawes, and Mott, 1959), even though the dose of chloralose used was small. Yet in the rat and rabbit, 4 days from birth, on exposure to cold the O_2 consumption is maintained so high (~60 ml/kg min) that (as O_2 carrying capacity of the blood is 12–16 ml/100 ml) cardiac output must be about 500 ml/kg min, a figure which compares well with that in adult man on exercise.

Downing, Talner, and Gardner (1965) studied ventricular function in newborn lambs using a modified heart-lung preparation. With increasing venous return there was a linear relationship between left ventricular end-diastolic pressure (up to about 10 mm Hg) and stroke volume (up to a cardiac output of 300 ml/min per kg foetal weight), demonstrating a normal Frank-Starling relation (Fig. 82). Other ventricular functions (ejection rate, stroke work, and stroke power) behaved in a similar normal manner. Elevation of aortic pressure (at constant left ventricular end-diastolic pressure) from 50–75 mm Hg, which is the normal range for a newborn lamb, caused little change in stroke volume; but a further increase to 100 mm Hg caused a rapid fall (Fig. 83). The authors concluded that an output of about 300 ml/kg min seemed to

Fig. 83.—Influence of aortic pressure on stroke volume in the heart of a 12-hour-old lamb (5 kg weight; heart rate 250/min; left ventricular end-diastolic pressure 10 cm H_2O) receiving an infusion of noradrenaline 1 μg/min per kg body weight. Stroke volume falls as aortic pressure is raised above 80 mm Hg. (Redrawn from Downing, Talner, and Gardner, 1965.)

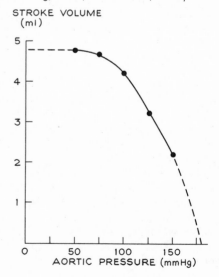

(4–7 kg), and young puppies (6–12 weeks old), the refractory periods of the atrioventricular node and the conducting system are insufficiently long to prevent an atrial premature beat from reaching the ventricle early in the recovery period (Preston, McFadden, and Moe, 1959). Consequently, atrial premature contractions can give rise to ventricular responses of bizarre configuration and, in some preparations, multiple responses and ventricular fibrillation. It was concluded that these phenomena were age-dependent rather than species-specific, because the young of all three species differed from the adult; and, cautiously, "whether these properties of the immature transmission system may account for sudden deaths in infants of these and other species is a question which cannot be answered from available data."

The risk of ventricular fibrillation resulting from premature atrial contractions in the young depends not only on the frequency and timing of atrial premature beats and on the delay in transmission, but also on the length of the ventricular Q-T interval. Fraser, Froggatt, and James (1964) have discussed a rare syndrome of congenital deafness, associated with electrocardiographic abnormalities, fainting attacks, and sudden death in infancy or childhood, of which the 9 cases examined all showed prolongation of the Q-T interval. Eight of the patients had experienced syncopal attacks, of which 3 were fatal. It was not established that these syncopal attacks arose from atrial premature beats, but the possibility is there. This is an interesting story which suggests that there is yet more to be found out about the normal development of the conducting mechanism in the young heart, which may be relevant to sudden death in infancy.

THE SYSTEMIC CIRCULATION.—Newborn rats, rabbits, and guinea pigs are highly specialized in their ability to produce heat on exposure to cold, as will be discussed in Chapter 15. One might not necessarily expect their skeletal muscles (for instance) to be developed to the same extent, either in respect of vascularity or of sympathetic control. On the other hand, the respiratory muscles are essential to continued survival, and the circulation to the skin also might be regulated to minimize heat loss in small animals. So we may inquire whether peripheral vascular control mechanisms are present in immature newborn animals or human infants and, if so, what form or forms such mechanisms take.

There seems little doubt that local mechanisms are already well developed at birth, such as those which cause vasodilatation in actively metabolizing tissues (e.g., in the heart or brain during hypoxaemia or hypercapnia, in the respiratory muscles during breathing, and in brown adipose tissue or shivering muscles on cold exposure). One may include in the same category the local mechanisms which are responsible for pulmonary vasoconstriction during hypoxia, and constriction of the ductus arteriosus when the arterial Po_2 is raised. These local mechanisms form an essential part of cardiovascular regulation. They ensure that blood flow is increased to working tissues and diverted away from ill-ventilated areas of the lungs. These local mechanisms have usually been ignored, and this has led to misapprehensions about the competence of the circulation in the newborn, for attention has been directed more to the capacity of the systemic circulation to constrict in response to noxious stimuli rather than to dilate when local metabolism increases.

It is also necessary to maintain the arterial pressure in order to make the most effective redistribution of cardiac output. This implies the capacity to reduce flow to areas which are not metabolizing actively and which are less essential to survival. Yet here one may speculate that the newborn may be at some advantage. Its arterial pressure is less than in adults of the same species, and if the slope of the pressure-flow regression line is non-linear and cuts the pressure axis at a finite value, a small fall in arterial pressure may cause a disproportionate reduction in flow to tissues which are not actively vasodilated. In other words, small blood vessels may close and limit flow as a result of a small fall in pressure. A spinal cat, in which central control of the circulation has been abolished by cutting the spinal cord in the neck and destroying the brain, will maintain its blood pressure at 40–60 mm Hg for many hours.

When we turn to active mechanisms for regulating arterial pressure there are some important ones which act generally and may be developed earlier than local systemic vasoconstriction. The capacity of the heart to accelerate and to increase its output is one factor. The general release into the circulation of adrenaline and noradrenaline from the adrenal glands, and perhaps the activation of the renin-angiotensin system, will cause a preferential degree of constriction in vessels which are not dilated from local metabolic causes. For instance, the vasoconstrictor action of adrenaline is much reduced in working as compared with resting skeletal muscle. It is true that this is a crude mechanism for redistributing cardiac output, and that nervous control of catecholamine release from the adrenals during hypoxaemia is developed late in foetal life or after birth in the lamb and calf (Comline and Silver, 1966). Yet catecholamines are released during hypoxia before nervous regulation is developed, and no one who has seen the skin of foetal or premature newborn animals or man blanch rapidly on acute asphyxia can doubt the effectiveness of this mechanism. In immature animals with thin skins it is also possible to see the blanching of the underlying skeletal muscle and viscera.

So we finally come to the problem of local autonomic nervous control. The evidence as to when this is first developed in the different organs of different species is incomplete. In adults, sympathetic denervation causes the blood vessels to become more sensitive to injections of adrenaline and noradrenaline, possibly because the latter are then removed or destroyed less rapidly at their site of action. We do not know whether the heart and blood vessels are relatively more sensitive before they are innervated, but this may be so. Sympathetic innervation is developed at different rates in different organs, because the heart will accelerate on stimulation of the stellate ganglion in the foetal lamb at 70 days gestation, while Comline and Silver (1966) found that splanchnic stimulation did not cause release of noradrenaline from the adrenals until about 120 days gestation. Yet, according to Greenberg and Lind (1961), the catecholamine concentrations in the human foetal heart, kidney, lungs, and adrenals near term were approximately similar to those in adults. Quite large changes in the content of acetylcholine, and in cholinesterase and choline acetyltransferase activity in the region of the sino-atrial node, continue after birth in different species (for references see Tuček, 1965).

As to direct experiments *in vivo* there is not much systematic quantitative evidence, even in animals. Boatman, Shaffer, Dixon and Brody (1965) opened the abdomen of dogs at different ages from birth, displaced the intestines, and inserted a constant outflow pump between the central and peripheral ends of the cut abdominal aorta. They assessed changes in vascular resistance of the hindquarters by alterations in perfusion pressure. Electrical stimulation of the lumbar sympathetic chain caused vasodilatation (abolished by atropine) in the hindquarters up to 2 weeks from birth. In older dogs, sympathetic stimulation caused vasoconstriction, increasing in magnitude with age. The local vasoconstrictor response on intra-arterial injection of adrenaline, noradrenaline, tyramine, and angiotensin also increased with age, suggesting that failure to respond on electrical stimulation in newborn

puppies was related to insensitivity of the receptor mechanism. This is different from observations in foetal lambs in which very small doses of noradrenaline cause vasoconstriction in the hindlimbs. There may be a species difference, yet comparisons of the vascular reactivity of animals at different ages are fraught with technical difficulties. Boatman *et al.* recorded the arterial pressures of their puppies, which were reasonable for their ages, but gave no flow measurements. The effect of operative manipulations is likely to be greater in newborn puppies (weighing 340–420 Gm at 1 day–1 week) than when a month old (1.1 kg). If there were already vasoconstriction in the hindlimbs of the newborn as a result of the operation, the effect of stimulating vasodilator nerve fibres would be relatively greater, and the effect of vasoconstrictor nerve fibres or drugs relatively less. Nor were the hindquarters truly isolated from the rest of the vascular system in their preparation. So these experiments cannot yet be regarded as conclusive.

In man the evidence is less direct. The ability to raise systemic arterial pressure during asphyxia is well authenticated. Many authors have now observed that arterial pressure declines after normal human birth, and both this and the fall from even higher values after gross evidence of asphyxia are attributed to the improvement in blood gas tensions on ventilation (Fig. 84). Recovery is accompanied by an increase in glomerular filtration rate (McCance and Widdowson, 1954) and in effective renal flow (Oh, Oh, and Lind, 1966), indicating that there must have been preceding renal vasoconstriction.

Fig. 84.—In human infants systolic arterial pressure is higher after overt asphyxial delivery than on normal delivery. In both instances, it falls during the first few hours and increases gradually during the next few months. (From the data of Neligan and Smith, 1960, and Young, 1961.)

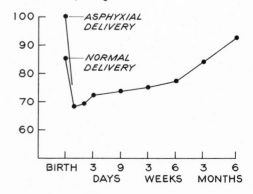

SYSTOLIC ARTERIAL
PRESSURE (mmHg)

Asphyxia also causes vasoconstriction in the calf and foot of newborn infants (Celander, 1966) and visibly in the skin. Vasomotor tone in the skin was demonstrated by Brück, Brück, and Lemtis (1957), and Young (1961) concluded from the response to the indirect heating test that the vasomotor sympathetic mechanisms were well developed, although skin vasodilatation was sluggish, during the first 3 days from birth (Young and Cottom, 1966). Infants also reacted vigorously to a cold pressor test (immersion of the foot in cold water for one minute) by a rise of arterial pressure of about 15%, but it is uncertain whether this was due to an increase in cardiac output, or to peripheral vasoconstriction as in adults (Moss, Duffie, and Emmanouilides, 1963). Without measurements of blood flow and pressure we cannot be sure that there has been vasoconstriction, and even when there has been vasoconstriction whether this was due to circulating noradrenaline or angiotensin or to local sympathetic nerve activity.

Breathing in the Newborn

The newborn lung is not an exact anatomical miniature of the adult (Table 49). It achieves functional similarity to the adult by variations in dimensions, so that the compliance of the lung and thoracic cage

TABLE 49.—MEASUREMENTS ON THE NEWBORN AND ADULT HUMAN LUNG

	NEWBORN	ADULT
Body weight (kg)	3.5	70
Surface area (M²)	0.21	1.90
Lung weight (Gm)	50	800
Tracheal diameter (mm)	8	18
Bronchiole diameter (mm)	0.1	0.2
Number of airways ($\times 10^6$)	1.5	14.0
Alveolar diameter (μ)*	50–100	200–300
Alveolar surface area (M²)	4	80
Number of alveoli ($\times 10^6$)	24	296
Vital capacity (ml/kg)	33	52
Functional residual capacity (ml/kg)	30	34
Dead space (ml/kg)	2.2	2.2
Tidal volume (ml/kg)	6	7
Respiratory rate at rest	40	20
Alveolar ventilation (ml/kg min)	100–150	60
Oxygen consumption at rest (ml/kg min)	6	3

Sources: Adult, Comroe *et al.* (1962), Comroe (1965): Newborn lung size, Altman (1958), Dunnill (1962); lung volumes, Avery (1964), Nelson (1966).

* Approximate and not taking into account possible variations between apex and base *in vivo.*

(per unit lung volume) is the same in the newborn and adult. The O_2 cost of breathing, even in the premature infant is, therefore, not great. It has been estimated as a mean of 0.9 ml/500 ml ventilated in a healthy infant at rest in a warm environment (Thibeault, Clutario, and Auld, 1966). This is equivalent to about 6% of total O_2 consumption as compared with 2% in adult man under analogous conditions. The greater proportion was attributed to the unsteady character of breathing in the newborn and to the greater alveolar ventilation (Table 49, p. 185). Alveolar ventilation is well distributed in the newborn as compared with the adult (Nelson, 1966), probably because the variation due to gravitational forces is less in the chest of a small infant than in a large man. For the same reason, the variation in perfusion of different parts of the lung, according to their height relative to the heart (West, 1965), must also be less in the infant; this is particularly so when pulmonary arterial pressure is still high, soon after birth. Studies of the mechanics of ventilation in the normal infant have shown no very remarkable features, but on the control of ventilation some interesting problems have emerged.

THE RESPONSE TO HYPOXIA

The first indication that there might be something unusual about the control of ventilation in the human infant came from the work of Cross and his colleagues (Cross and Warner, 1951; Cross and Oppé, 1952). They used an ingenious type of body plethysmograph to obtain an accurate measure of respiratory movements, with a soft seal around the head and jaw so that there was nothing covering the face and no increase in dead space. They observed that exposure to an hypoxic gas mixture (15% O_2 in N_2) caused a hyperpnoea which, unlike that in the adult, was sustained for a few minutes only in both premature and mature infants. The figure chosen to illustrate this point (Fig. 85, *a*) is not from Cross's original publication, but from a later study made under more closely controlled conditions for reasons which will appear. The hyperpnoea was attributed to excitation of systemic arterial chemoreceptors. The cause of the subsequent decline in ventilation was uncertain; depression of the medullary centres was proposed as a possible explanation. Exposure to 100% O_2 after breathing room air caused a decrease in ventilation; this decrease was greater if the infant was breathing the 15% O_2 mixture previously, in place of air. The interpretation put on these observations was that there was a continuing chemoreceptor discharge in normal infants

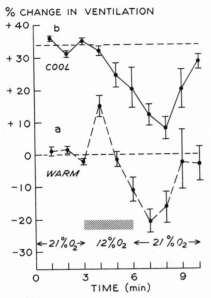

% CHANGE IN VENTILATION

Fig. 85.—Exposure of 10 normal human infants to 12% O_2 in a warm environment (a) caused a brief hyperpnoea followed by a reduction in the volume of respiration. In a cool environment (b) the hyperpnoea was absent. (Redrawn from Ceruti, 1966.)

breathing room air; both it and the greater discharge on breathing 15% O_2 were reduced or abolished by exposure to 100% O_2, with an appropriate decrease in ventilation. It was concluded that the chemoreceptors were working in a normal fashion after birth in the human infant. Cross soon found he was having to defend this proposition against attacks from both sides of the Atlantic.

In Kansas City, Miller and his colleagues (Miller and Behrle, 1954; Miller, 1954; Miller and Smull, 1955) were reluctant to accept this conclusion. They proposed that the chemoreceptor reflex mechanism gradually matured over several days after birth. Cross (1961) retorted that Miller's own data showed a significant fall in the volume of respiration of babies, less than 24 hours from birth, on changing the gas mixture breathed from 12% to 100% O_2. In Paris, Girard, Lacaisse, and Dejours (1960) were unable to demonstrate a fall in the volume of respiration when newborn human babies were given a single breath of oxygen. Cross (1964) replied that a single breath would not cause an increase in arterial Po_2 sufficient to inhibit the chemoreceptors in newborn infants in the first day or two when vascular shunts were still operating. Subsequent observations on newborn lambs in which a degree of venous admixture similar to that in babies was present, showed that this was indeed so (Purves

and Biscoe, 1966). One breath was evidently an inappropriate test of function at this age.

In the meantime, experiments on newborn rabbits and lambs showed that hypoxia or injection of small doses of cyanide caused hyperpnoea which was wholly abolished by denervation of the carotid bifurcations (Dawes and Mott, 1959; Cross, Dawes, and Mott, 1959; Purves, 1966,a). So in these species the carotid chemoreceptors were undoubtedly functional within a few hours of birth and, as in the adult, were largely if not entirely responsible for the ventilatory response to hypoxia. In both species the ventilatory response increased with age from birth, but even at birth, provided the animal was kept warm, it was well maintained for many minutes. In this respect it differed from the response of the human infant.

During the course of some experiments on newborn rabbits, Mott noticed that the increase in ventilation during hypoxia depended on the environmental temperature, being greater in a warm environment and less in a cold one. Exposure to cold in newborn rabbits and lambs produced a maintained increase in O_2 consumption and in the volume of respiration. In these circumstances, hypoxia caused a fall in O_2 consumption and little change in the volume of respiration (Dawes and Mott, 1959; Adamsons, 1959; Cross, Dawes, and Mott, 1959). The environmental temperatures had not been controlled in Cross's or Miller's studies on newborn human infants. So it was possible that the failure of hypoxia to cause a maintained hyperpnoea in the latter might be related to the temperature. However, when the original observations on human infants were repeated in a warm environment adjusted to be within the neutral thermal range, the hyperpnoea was still transient (Fig. 85, a; Brady and Ceruti, 1966). In a cool environment the hyperpnoea was absent as in animals (Fig. 85, b; Ceruti, 1966).

Brady and Ceruti (1966) also showed that in human infants older than 3 days of age the hyperpnoea during hypoxia was well maintained. The transience of the response in the newborn is, therefore, probably related to some phenomenon associated with the changes at birth. In some infants (i.e., newborn, in a warm environment, exposed to 18% O_2 in N_2) there was little or no hyperpnoea but merely a fall in the minute volume of respiration over 3 minutes (e.g., Brady and Ceruti, 1966). In these circumstances, the fall cannot be due to a reduction in alveolar Pco_2 consequent on preceding hyperpnoea, because the latter was absent. Even when it was present, the fall in respiratory volume still took place when the alveolar P_{CO_2} was maintained by adding CO_2 to the inspired gas mixture. The fall in respiratory volume during hypoxia was not related to the low alveolar P_{CO_2} which exists in the newborn period ($\sim$32 mm Hg in human infants and even less in lambs) because it was not observed in lambs, and was present in human infants in whom alveolar P_{CO_2} was raised and maintained (Cross, Hooper, and Lord, 1954; Brady and Ceruti, 1966).

Various other possibilities have been considered. It is most unlikely that the phenomenon is associated with a decrease in metabolism when breathing 18% or 15% O_2 in a warm environment (see Chapter 15). It is possible, but improbable, that this mild degree of hypoxia depresses the medulla. Brady and Ceruti (1966) found a small decrease in compliance during hypoxia in 2 newborn infants, but it is doubtful whether this would account for the fall in the volume of respiration. What is now needed is a measure of gas tensions in the blood supply to the carotid bodies and medullary centres (e.g., from a temporal artery) in order to determine whether there has been a redistribution of cardiac output during hypoxia sufficient to alter the stimulus, as, for instance, by a reduction in arterial P_{CO_2}. Any explanation proposed should also explain why this phenomenon is not seen in the newborn rabbit and lamb.

The Response to Carbon Dioxide, and Other Reflex Mechanisms

As in adults, the effect of carbon dioxide in causing hyperpnoea in the newborn is partly due to an effect on the systemic arterial chemoreceptors (because it is reduced by denervation of the carotid bifurcations; Purves, 1966,b), but mainly to an action on the central chemoreceptors in the ventro-lateral medulla. In the newborn lamb, hyperpnoea on exposure to carbon dioxide is enhanced by hypoxia until very low O_2 tensions are reached (Purves, 1966,b); measurements of comparable quality are not available in the human infant, but the observations of Brady and Ceruti (1966) suggest that the same may well be true. The quantitative analysis of the data in lambs in comparison with that in adult man suggested that the respiratory response to the combination of hypoxic and hypercapnic stimuli was identical (allowing for the difference in size).

In both man and sheep, during the first 2–3 days from birth there is at first a metabolic acidosis resulting from partial asphyxia (Graham and Wilson, 1954; Weisbrot *et al.*, 1958; Reardon, Baumann, and Haddad, 1960; Purves, 1966,b), followed by a compensated respiratory alkalosis such that the arterial pH is normal but the P_{CO_2} and bicarbonate concentration are reduced. The nature of the apparent excess stimulation to ventilation at this time is a little uncertain. Large doses of progesterone had no effect on alveolar P_{CO_2} in newborn infants, so it was not due to the stimulus alleged to be responsible for the low maternal P_{CO_2} toward the end of pregnancy (Stahlman, 1961). Arterial P_{O_2} in the newborn is less than in the adult and this could be a contributory factor. We also have to consider that the infant is newly delivered from a warm to a relatively cooler environment, and it may take some days for thermal receptors in the skin to adapt to the change.

Exposure to a cold environment is a strong stimulus to breathing in the newborn (e.g., rabbit, Dawes and Mott, 1959; lamb, Cross, Dawes, and Mott, 1959; human, Ceruti, 1966) as well as in the foetus. In animals the increase in breathing persists after denervating the carotid bifurcations and cutting the vagi, and in the human infant it is usually accompanied by a fall in alveolar P_{CO_2} (Ceruti, 1966). So it cannot be attributed to a change in the blood gases as a result of increased metabolism. It must be due mainly to an increase in peripheral sensory inflow because it begins soon after exposure to cold, before there has been any change in rectal temperature.

Other reflex mechanisms also are well-developed at birth and in infants delivered prematurely. The Hering-Breuer inflation and deflation reflexes are present in the liquid-breathing foetal lamb (Chapter 11), in the newborn rabbit (Dawes and Mott, 1959), monkey (Dawes, Jacobson, Mott, and Shelley, 1960), and man (Cross, Klaus, Tooley, and Weisser, 1960). The sensory mechanisms responsible for coughing or transient apnoea on presentation of a noxious stimulus (gaseous or tactile) to the airways also are functional. Lobeline causes rapid shallow breathing on injection into rabbits by an action on unidentified sensory receptors in the lungs, with an afferent pathway in the vagi; this mechanism also is present at birth (Dawes and Mott, 1959).

Conclusion

The first part of this chapter demonstrated that, as soon as the immediate changes after birth were completed, the circulation was remarkably competent at fulfilling the normal needs of the infant.

The same is evidently true of the lungs. If any further proof were required one only has to cite the astonishing ventilatory response of small newborn animals, such as rats, rabbits, and guinea pigs, on exposure to cold when they can sustain an O_2 consumption of 60 ml/kg min for many hours. The newborn human infant can increase its consumption to 12–15 ml/kg min; its maximal capacity has not been explored for obvious and proper reasons. Now this may be true of normal healthy animals and man, yet many of the troubles encountered in the period immediately after birth concern the heart and lungs. This apparent paradox results from the nature of the transition, which involves such large changes in function in these organs, and not in their inherent competence.

Their competence is impaired by anaesthetics, analgesics, and asphyxia. For instance, even very light anaesthesia greatly reduces the maximum O_2 consumption of a newborn animal exposed to cold. Quite small doses of analgesics reduce the ventilatory response to carbon dioxide. And progressively increasing hypoxaemia leads to an insidious deterioration which culminates in abrupt respiratory arrest. It is not easy to say how these effects compare with those in adults, yet most physiologists and paediatricians have been struck by the ability of the newborn to tolerate conditions which would rapidly prove fatal in an adult. In this respect, the newborn may be smaller, but it is not a less efficient miniature of the adult of its species, given the circumstances in which it normally lives.

REFERENCES

Adamsons, K.: Breathing and the thermal environment in young rabbits, J. Physiol. 149:144–153, 1959.

Altman, P. L.: *Handbook of Respiration* (Philadelphia: W. B. Saunders Company, 1958).

Altman, P. L., and Dittmer, D. S.: *Biology Data Book* (Washington, D.C.: Fed. Am. Soc. Exper. Biol, 1964).

Avery, M. E.: *The Lung and its Disorders in the Newborn Infant* (Philadelphia: W. B. Saunders Company, 1964).

Bauer, D. J.: Vagal reflexes appearing in the rabbit at different ages, J. Physiol. 95:187–202, 1939.

Bloor, C. M.: Aortic baroreceptor threshold and sensitivity in rabbits at different ages, J. Physiol. 174:136–171, 1964.

Boatman, D. L.; Shaffer, R. A.; Dixon, R. L., and Brody, M. J.: Function of vascular smooth muscle and its sympathetic innervation in the newborn dog, J. Clin. Invest. 44:241–246, 1965.

Bower, B. D.: Pink disease: The autonomic disorder and its treatment with ganglion-blocking agents, Quart. J. Med. 23:215–230, 1954.

Brady, J. P., and Ceruti, E.: Chemoreceptor reflexes in the new-born infant: Effects of varying degrees of hypoxia on heart rate and ventilation in a warm environment, J. Physiol. 184:631–645, 1966.

Brady, J. P., and Tooley, W. H.: Cardiovascular and respiratory reflexes in the newborn, Pediat. Clin. North America 13:801–821, 1966.

Brück, K.; Brück, M., and Lemtis, H.: Hautdurchblutung und Thermoregulation bei neugeborenen Kindern, Pflüger's Arch. ges. Physiol. 265:55–65, 1957.

Burnard, E. D.: In Cassels, D. E. (ed.): *The Heart and Circulation in the Newborn and Infant* (New York: Grune & Stratton, Inc., 1966), pp. 135–137.

Celander, O.: Studies of the Peripheral Circulation, in Cassels, D. E. (ed.): *The Heart and Circulation in the Newborn and Infant.* (New York: Grune & Stratton, Inc., 1966), pp. 98–110.

Ceruti, E.: Chemoreceptor reflexes in the newborn infant: Effect of cooling on the response to hypoxia, Pediatrics 37:556–564, 1966.

Chu, J.; Clements, J. A.; Cotton, E.; Klaus, M. H.; Sweet, A. Y.; Thomas, M. A., and Tooley, W. H.: The pulmonary hypoperfusion syndrome: A preliminary report, Pediatrics 35:733–742, 1965.

Clark, G. A.: Some foetal blood-pressure reactions, J. Physiol. 74:391–400, 1932.

Comline, R. S., and Silver, M.: Development of activity in the adrenal medulla of the foetus and new-born animal, Brit. M. Bull. 22:16–20, 1966.

Comroe, J. H., Jr.: *Physiology of Respiration* (Chicago: Year Book Medical Publishers, Inc., 1965).

Comroe, J. H., Jr.; Forster, R. E.; Du Bois, A. B., Briscoe, W. A., and Carlsen, E.: *The Lung* (Chicago: Year Book Medical Publishers, Inc., 1962).

Constable, B. J.: Changes in blood volume and blood picture during the life of the rat and guinea-pig from birth to maturity, J. Physiol. 167:229–238, 1963.

Cross, K. W.: Respiration in the newborn baby, Brit. M. Bull. 17:160–164, 1961.

Cross, K. W.: In Dickens, F., and Neil, E. (eds.): *Oxygen in the Animal Organism* (Oxford: Pergamon Press, 1964), p. 605.

Cross, K. W.; Dawes, G. S., and Mott, J. C.: Anoxia, oxygen consumption and cardiac output in new-born lambs and adult sheep, J. Physiol. 146:316–343, 1959.

Cross, K. W.; Hooper, J. M. D., and Lord, J.: Anoxic depression of the medulla in the new-born infant, J. Physiol. 125:628–640, 1954.

Cross, K. W.; Klaus, M.; Tooley, W. H., and Weisser, K.: The response of the new-born baby to inflation of the lungs, J. Physiol. 151:551–565, 1960.

Cross, K. W., and Oppé, T. E.: The effect of inhalation of high and low concentrations of oxygen on the respiration of the premature infant, J. Physiol. 117:38–55, 1952.

Cross, K. W., and Warner, P.: The effect of inhalation of high and low oxygen concentrations in the respiration of the newborn infant, J. Physiol. 114:238–295, 1951.

Dawes, G. S.; Handler, J. J., and Mott, J. C.: Some cardiovascular responses in foetal, new-born and adult rabbits, J. Physiol. 139:123–136, 1957.

Dawes, G. S.; Jacobson, H. N.; Mott, J. C., and Shelley, H. J.: Some observations on foetal and new-born rhesus monkeys, J. Physiol. 152:271–298, 1960.

Dawes, G. S., and Mestyán, G.: Changes in the oxygen consumption of newborn guinea-pigs and rabbits on exposure to cold, J. Physiol, 168:22–42, 1963.

Dawes, G. S., and Mott, J. C.: Reflex respiratory activity in the newborn rabbit, J. Physiol. 145:85–97, 1959.

Dittmer, D. S., and Grebe, R. M. (eds.): *Handbook of Circulation* (Philadelphia: W. B. Saunders Company, 1959).

Downing, S. E.: Baroreceptor reflexes in newborn rabbits, J. Physiol. 150:201–213, 1960.

Downing, S. E.; Talner, N. S., and Gardner, T. H.: Ventricular function in the newborn lamb, Am. J. Physiol. 208:931–937, 1965.

Dunnill, M. S.: Postnatal growth of the lung, Thorax 17:329–333, 1962.

Edwards, A. W. T.; Korner, P. I., and Thorburn, G. D.: The cardiac output of the unanaesthetized rabbit and the effects of preliminary anaesthesia, environmental temperature and carotid occlusion, Quart. J. Exper. Physiol. 44:309–321, 1959.

Fisher, E. W., and Dalton, R. G.: Cardiac output in cattle, Nature 183:829, 1959.

Fraser, G. R.; Froggatt, P., and James, T. N.: Congenital deafness associated with electrocardiographic abnormalities, fainting attacks and sudden death, Quart. J. Med. 33:361–385, 1964.

Garcia, J. F.: Changes in blood, plasma, and red cell volume in the male rat as a function of age, Am. J. Physiol. 190:19–24, 1957.

Gessner, I.; Krovetz, L. J.; Benson, R. W.; Prystowsky, H.; Stenger, V., and Eitzman, D. V.: Haemodynamic adaptations in the newborn infant, Pediatrics 36:752–762, 1965.

Girard, F.; Lacaisse, A., and Dejours, P.: Le stimulus O_2 ventilatoire à la période néonatale chez l'homme, J. Physiol. (Paris) 52:108–109, 1960.

Gotsev, T.: The blood volume in lambs, J. Physiol. 94:539–549, 1939.

Graham, B. D., and Wilson, J. C.: Chemical control of respiration in newborn infants, Am. J. Dis. Child. 87:287–297, 1954.

Greenberg, R. E., and Lind, J.: Catecholamines in tissues of the human fetus, Pediatrics 27:904–911, 1961.

Greenberg, R. E.; Lind, J., and von Euler, U. S.: Effect of posture and insulin hypoglycaemia in the newborn, Acta paediat. 49:780–785, 1960.

Gupta, J. M., and Scopes, J. W.: Observations on blood pressure in newborn infants, Arch. Dis. Childhood 40:637–644, 1965.

Kellogg, H. B.: Time of onset of vagal function in the heart of mammals. Proc. Soc. Exper. Biol. & Med. 24:839, 1927.

Klaus, M.: Braun, J., and Tooley, W. H.: Pulmonary capillary blood flow in the newborn infant, Am. J. Dis. Child. 102:466–467, 1961.

Korner, P. I.: The effect of section of the carotid sinus and aortic nerves on the cardiac output of the rabbit, J. Physiol. 180:266–278, 1965.

Kuida, H.; Brown, A. M.; Lange, R. L., and Hecht, H. H.: Cardiovascular studies on normal calves, Am. J. Physiol. 200:247–252, 1961.

McCance, R. A., and Widdowson, E. M.: The influence of events during the last few days *in utero* on tissue destruction and renal function in the first two days of independent life, Arch. Dis. Childhood 29:495–501, 1954.

Metcalfe, J., and Parer, J. T.: Cardiovascular changes during pregnancy in ewes, Am. J. Physiol. 210:821–825, 1966.

Miller, H. C.: Effect of high concentrations of carbon dioxide and oxygen on the respiration of full term infants, Pediatrics 14:104–113, 1954.

Miller, H. C., and Behrle, F. C.: The effects of hypoxia on the respiration of newborn infants, Pediatrics 14:93–103, 1954.

Miller, H. C., and Smull, N. W.: Further studies on the effects of hypoxia on the respiration of newborn infants, Pediatrics 16:93–103, 1955.

Mollison, P. L.; Veal, N., and Cutbush, M.: Red cell and plasma volume in newborn infants, Arch. Dis. Childhood 25:242–253, 1950.

Moss, A. J.; Duffie, E. R., and Emmanouilides, G.: Blood pressure and vasomotor reflexes in the newborn infant, Pediatrics 32:175–179, 1963.

Mott, J. C.: Haemorrhage as a test of the cardiovascular system in rabbits of different ages, J. Physiol. 181:728–752, 1965.

Mott, J. C.: The effect of cutting arterial baroreceptor nerves on the response to haemorrhage in rabbits of different ages, J. Physiol. 187:28–30, P., 1966,a. (in press).

Mott, J. C.: Cardiovascular function in newborn mammals, Brit. M. Bull. 22:66–69, 1966,b.

Mott, J. C.: The relation of blood volume to body weight and arterial haemoglobin levels in rabbits, J. Physiol., 1967 (in press).

Neligan, G. A., and Smith, C. A.: The blood pressure of newborn infants in asphyxial states and in hyaline membrane disease, Pediatrics 26:735–744, 1960.

Nelson, N. M.: Neonatal pulmonary function, Pediat. Clin. North America 13:769–799, 1966.

Oh, W.; Arcilla, R. A.; Oh, M. A., and Lind, J.: Renal and cardiovascular effects of body tilting in the newborn infant, Biol. Neonat. 10:76–92, 1966.

Oh, W.; Oh, M. A., and Lind, J.: Renal function and blood volume in newborn infant related to placental transfusion, Acta paediat, 56:197–210, 1966.

Prec, K. J., and Cassels, D. E.: Dye dilution curves and cardiac output in newborn infants, Circulation 11:789–798, 1955.

Preston, J. B.; McFadden, S., and Moe, G. K.: Atrioventricular transmission in young animals, Am. J. Physiol. 197:236–240, 1959.

Purves, M. J.: The effects of hypoxia in the new-born lamb before and after denervation of the carotid chemoreceptors, J. Physiol. 185:60–77, 1966,a.

Purves, M. J.: The respiratory response of the new-born lamb to inhaled CO_2 with and without accompanying hypoxia, J. Physiol. 185:78–94, 1966,b.

Purves, M. J., and Biscoe, T.: Development of chemoreceptor activity, Brit. M. Bull. 22:56–60, 1966.

Reardon, H. S.; Baumann, M. L., and Haddad, E. J.: Chemical stimuli of respiration in the early neonatal period, J. Pediat. 57:151–170, 1960.

Sharpey-Schafer, E. P.: Circulatory reflexes in chronic disease of the afferent nervous system, J. Physiol. 134:1–10, 1956.

Stahlman, M.: Ventilation control in the new-born, Am. J. Dis. Child. 101:216–227, 1961.

Thibeault, D. W., Clutario, B., and Auld, P. A. M.: The oxygen cost of breathing in the premature infant, Pediatrics 37:954–959, 1966.

Tuček, S.: Changes in choline acetyltransferase activity in the cardiac auricles of dogs during postnatal development, Physiol. Bohemoslov. 14:530–535, 1965.

Usher, R.; Shephard, M., and Lind, J.: The blood volume of the newborn infant and placental transfusion, Acta paediat. 52:497–512, 1963.

Wallgren, G.; Barr, M., and Rudhe, U.: Hemodynamic studies of induced hypo- and hypervolemia in the newborn infant, Acta paediat. 53:1–12, 1964.

Weisbrot, I. M.; James, L. S.; Prince, C. E.; Holaday, D. A., and Apgar, V.: Acid base homeostasis of the newborn infant during the first 24 hours of life, J. Pediat. 52:395–403, 1958.

West, J. B.: *Ventilation/Blood Flow and Gas Exchange* (Oxford: Blackwell Scientific Publications, 1965).

Young, M.: Blood pressure in the new-born baby, Brit. M. Bull. 17:154–159, 1961.

Young, M., and Cottom, D.: An Investigation of Baroreceptor Responses in the Newborn Infant, in Cassells, D. E. (ed.): *The Heart and Circulation in the Newborn and Infant* (New York: Grune & Stratton, Inc., 1966), pp. 111–120.

15

Oxygen Consumption and Temperature Regulation in the Newborn

NEWBORN ANIMALS and human infants, because they are smaller than adults of their species, have a larger surface to body weight ratio and hence a greater physical problem in maintaining their body temperature. To be sure, some of them are nursed in marsupial pouches, nest, or bassinets, or (like the rhesus monkey) clutch close to their mother, or (like the guinea pig and lamb) are born with a furry or woolen coat as a protection against cold. Even so, the problem of keeping up the body temperature is a serious one, which was recognized in human infants early in the 19th century soon after the introduction of the centigrade thermometer (Edwards, 1824). By the end of the century, a fall in rectal temperature in the newborn baby was associated with a great increase in mortality (Budin, 1900), and an incubator was designed to help in maintaining body temperature. It is odd that with the publication of Benedict's work on metabolic rate (Benedict and Talbot, 1915), his technique was not applied sooner to the analysis of heat production and heat loss in newborn human infants, sick or well. The tremendous increase of interest in this subject during the past 15 years has derived from several factors working simultaneously, among which we may count the recognition that cold was associated with an increased mortality rate in newborn piglets and lambs as well as in man, and that there were a number of interesting physiological problems still to be solved. Two of these have been of particular efficacy in stimulating research. First,

Cross, Tizard, and Trythall (1955) observed that a moderate degree of hypoxia (on breathing 15% O_2) caused a fall in O_2 consumption in normal mature newborn human infants, the reason for which was obscure. Secondly, there was the strong suspicion that the newborn of many species were able to increase their O_2 consumption by a mechanism which did not involve overt shivering (nonshivering thermogenesis), and which also was unknown.

Body temperature is maintained in homeothermic mammals by balancing heat production and heat loss. In small newborn animals or babies the capacity to limit heat loss, though not negligible, is small. This aspect of the problem will be taken up later. The capacity to increase heat production, as indicated by a rise in O_2 consumption, is large, as Figure 86 shows in 4 species of very different sizes at birth. Newborn rats weigh only 5 Gm and rabbits about 50 Gm, and the critical temperature (below which O_2 consumption increases) usually exceeds 35°C. O_2 consumption is 15–25 ml/kg min in a neutral thermal environment (i.e., when minimal) and increases greatly on exposure to cold. It also increases if the environmental temperature is raised too high, to 38°C or more. Newborn monkeys weigh about 500 Gm, the critical temperature is 35°C, and O_2 consumption in a neutral thermal environment is 9–10 ml/kg min at birth. Newborn human infants weigh more (~3.5 kg) and the critical temperature (32–35°C) and O_2 consumption in a neutral thermal environment (4.6 ml/kg min) are

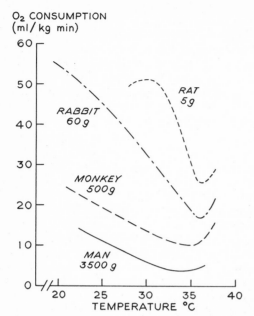

Fig. 86.—Changes in the rate of metabolism on exposure to different ambient temperatures in different species after birth.

less. So the smaller the animal, the larger the rate of O_2 consumption in a neutral thermal environment, the higher the critical temperature and, within limits, the greater the increase in metabolic rate on exposure to a cool environment. These phenomena are all related to the comparatively large surface area (compared with body weight) from which heat is lost in small animals.

Figure 86 also shows that when a newborn rat was exposed to a temperature below 30°C its O_2 consumption began to fall. Although its heat production was increased on exposure to cold, the thermal gradient between its body core and the surrounding environment also was increased, so that heat loss began to exceed heat production. Indeed, body temperature usually falls slightly in all small newborn animals on cold exposure even though heat production is raised. When the fall in core temperature is too great, O_2 consumption is reduced, presumably because of slowing of the rate of chemical reactions (although it must be admitted that the phenomenon has not been studied as thoroughly as it deserves). So the newborn rat can maintain only some small degree of thermal homeostasis within a limited range of environmental temperatures, about 30–37°C. The newborn rabbit, because it is larger, has a range of about 20–37°C. The newborn lamb, which is larger

still, has a range of about 5–35°C. Presumably, the newborn baby comes somewhere in between, but the lower limit of its capacity to withstand cold exposure has not been studied, for obvious reasons. The ability of the newborn to withstand cold exposure by increasing heat production is limited in two respects. First, since both insulation (fur and fat) and body size are usually small, body temperature begins to fall. And, secondly, increased heat production depends on an adequate supply of fuel; this varies in different species, but without suckling is rarely sufficient for more than 24–48 hours, often considerably less.

SOME DEFINITIONS AND TECHNICAL CONSIDERATIONS.—These facts set the scene for subsequent discussion, but before going into details the neutral thermal environment must be defined more closely. It is an environment in which, in a resting state and with a normal body temperature, O_2 consumption or heat production is minimal. The proviso about the body temperature is necessary because, as in the rat, O_2 consumption will fall yet further in a sufficiently cool environment. This definition, although easy to apply empirically if one can measure O_2 consumption or heat production, raises some problems when translated into practical terms. Heat loss occurs by evaporation, conduction, convection, and radiation, and so depends on the conductivity of the surface on which the subject lies, his posture, the wind speed, humidity, and the temperature and physical characteristics (heat capacity and emissivity) of surrounding radiant surfaces. Consequently, when an observer states that the neutral environmental temperature for a newborn rat is 35–37°C, this applies only to his particular equipment. Air temperature may be lowered without any change of O_2 consumption, if heat loss by radiation is reduced by increasing the temperature of surrounding radiant surfaces. This is why the term "neutral temperature" has been abandoned in favor of "neutral thermal environment." It is usually possible to make a fair comparison of the measurements of different observers provided that they have used an apparatus with the following characteristics:

1. The subject is wholly enclosed within a chamber whose walls are at a constant temperature.
2. The gas within the chamber is maintained at a constant (usually the same) temperature and is circulated at a speed sufficient to prevent rebreathing, but not so much as greatly to increase heat loss by convection.
3. The subject is placed in the chamber either on a support insulated from the walls or, if in contact with the floor of the chamber, in a posture which is defined.

4. The material of the walls (nowadays usually Perspex or Lucite) is defined.

If the subject is not wholly enclosed in a chamber or is exposed to radiation from multiple sources it becomes difficult to predict whether conditions will approximate to a neutral thermal environment.

Most newborn animals and human infants become restless when they are hungry, and activity is associated with a rise in O_2 consumption. So the convention has become established that measurements of O_2 consumption and calculations of minimal metabolic rate are made in a neutral thermal environment at rest or during sleep, and the fact that this almost always is shortly after they have been fed has had to be accepted (e.g., for human infants and rats). It is acknowledged that such measurements differ from those on fasting adults, but the difference due to the specific dynamic action of protein is probably small in comparison with other factors. In some other species, such as rabbits which normally feed only once or twice a day (Bernard and Hull, 1964), the problem does not arise.

Finally, there is a difference of opinion about the way in which O_2 consumption or metabolic rate is expressed, in terms of body weight, of some complex function of body weight (e.g., the two-thirds power) or of surface area. This should not give rise to any great difficulty at the moment. From the point of view of the physiologist or paediatrician who wishes to compare one animal or child with another, it seems more reasonable to use body weight as a standard of reference, because the capacity of different individuals and different species to maintain thermal balance is so variable. Only if attention is being specifically directed to heat balance, or to mechanisms of heat loss, does it become of the first importance to relate metabolic rate to surface area. I would plead most strongly that in the latter instance data should be presented in both forms (i.e., for kg body weight and for M^2 surface area) in order to facilitate comparison between different investigations.

In this book, metabolic rate is expressed in terms of O_2 consumption (which is usually what has been measured rather than heat production) because it is then easier to consider the consequences on the circulation and breathing. The effect of a change in the respiratory quotient (0.73–0.83 in lambs exposed to cold under different experimental conditions; Alexander, 1962) is comparatively small, and in transposing data it is assumed that 1 litre $O_2 \equiv 4.8$ Kcal.

Minimal O_2 Consumption After Birth

The first suggestion that minimal O_2 consumption (in a neutral thermal environment) might increase after birth was derived from observations on goats. Barcroft, Flexner, and McClurkin (1934) measured foetal cardiac output with a cardiometer and hence arrived at an indirect estimate of O_2 consumption. The sheep has been studied more thoroughly, and Figure 87 shows that O_2 consumption/kg body weight tends to fall somewhat toward the end of gestation, and then increases almost threefold during the first 24 hours after birth. Apart from these we do not have any reliable estimates of foetal O_2 consumption near term under good physiological conditions. But there are many observations on newborn infants and animals in a neutral thermal environment (Table 50). All this evidence suggested that minimal O_2 consumption at birth may be closely related to, but perhaps a little greater than, that of the nonpregnant adult, when expressed per kg body weight (Acheson, Dawes, and Mott, 1957). One would not expect it to be identical, because not only is the foetus growing more rapidly, but the relative weights of its component parts (e.g., skin, brain, skeleton) differ greatly from adults of the same species.

There are two reservations which may be made. First, the figures given in Table 50 have been arbitrarily selected as giving a reasonable indication of minimal O_2 consumption. In adults of the same species, basal metabolic rate is more closely related to surface area, or to a complex function of weight which also is closely related to surface area, than to body weight. There is, therefore, a large element

Fig. 87.—Observations on the resting O_2 consumption in a neutral thermal environment of anaesthetized lambs before and after birth. (Redrawn from Dawes and Mott, 1959.)

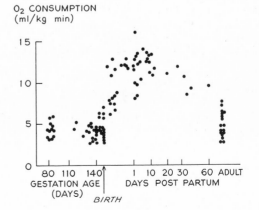

O$_2$ CONSUMPTION
(ml/kg min)

TABLE 50.—OXYGEN CONSUMPTION (ML/KG MIN) IN ADULT AND NEWBORN MAN AND ANIMALS

SPECIES	ADULT		NEWBORN		
	NEUTRAL THERMAL ENVIRONMENT	COLD (0–10°C)	NEUTRAL THERMAL ENVIRONMENT	COLD	
Man	3.7	19	4.6	15 (20–25°C)	Dill and Forbes, 1941; Adolph and Molnar, 1946; von Döbeln, 1956; Brück, 1961; Adamsons, Gandy, and James, 1965; Scopes, 1966.
Sheep	3.4–5		4.6† 12 *	58 (0–10°C)	Dawes and Mott, 1959; Cross, Dawes, and Mott, 1959; Alexander, 1962; Hemingway, Robinson, Hemingway, and Wall, 1966; Hemingway and Hemingway, 1966.
Pig	3.7–5.8		12.5	39 (4°C)	Altman, 1958; Mount and Rowell, 1960 and personal communication.
Monkey	6.1		10.7	27 (22°C)	Dawes, Jacobson, Mott, and Shelley, 1960.
Cat	6.7		16	60 (15°C)	Scopes and Tizard, 1963; Hull, 1965; Nadeau and Colebatch, 1965.
Guinea pig	13.5	35	18	50 (20°C) 70 (5°C)	Gosselin, 1949; Dawes and Mestyán, 1963; Brück and Wünnenberg, 1965,a.
Rabbit	10		18	63 (22–27°C)	Dawes and Mestyán, 1963.
Rat	16–20	80	20	50* (32°C)	Taylor, 1960; Bramante, 1961.
Mouse	27–47		30	47 (30°C)	Altman, 1958; Cassin, 1963.

† At birth.   * 24 hours old.

of variability in adults. Yet this might be used to test the hypothesis that minimal oxygen consumption in the foetus, or immediately after birth, may be related to that of the mother. The basal metabolic rate of sheep rises by 4–8% during pregnancy, varying with feeding, and the critical temperature is 27–35°C (Graham, 1964). Sheep of different breeds vary greatly in weight; Welsh mountain sheep weigh 30–35 kg while cross-bred Cluns or Suffolks weigh up to 100 kg. One would expect that in the same thermal environment, but depending on fleece length, the basal metabolic rate of the former would be greater than that of the latter. Shearing the fleece could be used to introduce another variable. In this way, it should be possible to find out to what extent, or under what circumstances, the basal metabolic rate of a lamb at birth is determined by that of its mother. The activity of the foetal thyroid has already been mentioned in Chapter 4, and it would seem a priori more reasonable to suppose that the basal metabolic rate of the foetus was largely independent of that of the individual mother, but the proposition has not been examined experimentally.

Secondly, it will be seen in Table 50 that minimal O_2 consumption in newborn pigs, cats, and rabbits appears to be much greater than that of adults. As to pigs, this may be due to selection of piglets which are some hours old; minimal O_2 consumption increases rapidly after birth in this species, which has no fur or wool. The results in cats and rabbits are unlikely to be due to this cause, although there is a curious feature in that increase in minimal O_2 consumption after birth is small, if it is present at all (Scopes and Tizard, 1963; Hull, 1965; Hill and Rahimtulla, 1965). The reasons for these variations need further exploration.

In other animal species, including the goat and sheep (already mentioned), the piglet (Mount, 1959), rhesus monkey (Dawes, Jacobson, Mott, and Shelley, 1960), and rat (Taylor, 1960) minimal O_2 consumption increases considerably soon after birth (Fig. 88). In the human infant there was at first some doubt (Brück, 1961), but recent measurements have shown a rise from about 4.6 ml/kg min at birth to 7 ml/kg min after 10 days (Hill and Rahimtulla, 1965; Scopes, 1966). The latter figure is not much less than that observed by Benedict

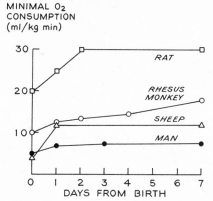

MINIMAL O₂
CONSUMPTION
(ml/kg min)

Fig. 88.—Changes in minimal O₂ consumption, in a neutral thermal environment, in different species after birth.

and Talbot (1915) in normal full-term infants at 4 weeks from birth (about 8 ml/kg min) in thermal conditions which were not defined.

The reasons for the rise in minimal O_2 consumption after birth have not been explored thoroughly. There are several possibilities, including a rise in the general level of sympathetic activity, the rise in arterial Po_2, increased tone in skeletal muscles, the greater activity of the gastrointestinal tract, the specific dynamic action of protein, and the work of breathing. The contribution from the last three items is probably quite small. One of the first things to exclude, if possible, was the effect of cold exposure after birth, and an attempt was made to do this. Newborn rhesus monkeys were used because, as Figure 88 shows, the increase in minimal O_2 consumption is spread out over 10 days in this species. They were removed from their mother as soon as practicable, and were hand reared in an incubator whose air temperature was maintained at 35 ± 2°C in conditions which were then believed to approximate to a neutral thermal environment; the rise in minimal O_2 consumption with age still occurred normally (Dawes, 1961). The possibility that heat loss by radiation to the incubator walls might be considerable was not appreciated at that time, and I now suspect that this was not really a neutral thermal environment. The experiment needs repeating under more stringent conditions.

The Metabolic Response to Cold

Table 50 shows the magnitude of the metabolic response to cold in the newborn of several species.

These observations should be interpreted with care because they have been made by different observers using different experimental conditions. In adults, two measures of the maximum metabolic response to cold have been described. Giaja (1929) described as summit metabolism the maximum rate attained at approximately normal body temperature, without voluntary muscle activity. This was distinguished from a greater rate of metabolism observed briefly during the first stage of hypothermia before body temperature began to fall. Alexander (1962) measured summit metabolism as the mean metabolic rate over a 20-minute period of cold exposure where there was only a small fall in rectal temperature, and this seems a reasonable definition for comparative purposes. Most of the observations on newborn animals exposed to cold in Table 50 approximate to this definition, although, naturally, the environmental temperature varied with species.

As compared with adults of the same species and on a straightforward weight basis, the capacity of the newborn to increase its O_2 consumption on cold exposure seems to be as good or better. The summit metabolism of the adult guinea pig is about 35 ml/kg min, while at birth it is 50–70 ml/kg min. The summit metabolism of the adult rat is 80 ml/kg min; that of a newborn rat is 50 ml/kg min 24 hours from birth, rising to 80 ml/kg min within 2 weeks. The summit metabolism of adult man (unacclimatized to cold), at 0°C in the nude, is about 19 ml/kg min, but his ability to maintain this for more than 2 hours is limited by fatigue from shivering (Adolph and Molnar, 1946). Figures of up to 15 ml/kg min have been recorded in newborn human infants on cold exposure. But when we take into consideration the small size of newborn animals the result is different. The solid symbols in Figure 89 indicate the maximum or summit metabolism in adults of various species (▲ birds, ● mammals), and it is clear that summit metabolism increases with decrease in body size. The open circles indicate the maximum rate of O_2 consumption in the newborn of various species from Table 50. Only the lamb (which is normally born in a cold and unprotected environment) comes out really well from this comparison. It is surprising that the newborn piglet also falls close to the adult line, because the piglet is notoriously susceptible to cold exposure. The explanation is that the piglet responds well at first, but only for a short time until its fuel reserves are exhausted. Apart from these two species the remainder are not able to raise their O_2 consumption as much as small adults of other species and the

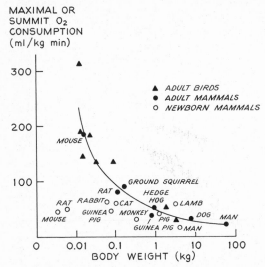

MAXIMAL OR
SUMMIT O₂
CONSUMPTION
(ml/kg min)

Fig. 89.—Maximum or summit O_2 consumption on cold exposure of adult birds (▲) or mammals (●) and in the newborn (○) of different species according to body weight. (From the data of Giaja (1929), Dill and Forbes (1941), Adolph and Molnar (1946), Gosselin (1949), Popovic (1959), and Table 50.)

same size. This goes a long way to explaining the apparent paradox that newborn rats, rabbits, monkeys, or human infants can increase their O_2 consumption so much on exposure to cold (as compared with adults of the same species) and yet their body temperature falls.

In the lamb, summit metabolism does not increase on suckling or with increasing age from birth (Alexander, 1962), presumably because it is already adequate. But it does increase with suckling and age in the newborn of some other species, particularly in the rat (Taylor, 1960), and to a lesser extent in puppies (Gelineo, 1957; McIntyre and Ederstrom, 1958) and monkeys (Dawes, Jacobson, Mott, and Shelley, 1960). This is probably due more to acquisition of fat from the milk than to other possible causes (see below).

We must now consider the mechanisms by which newborn animals and human infants increase their oxygen consumption, and so their heat production, on cold exposure. All the newborn of the species listed in Table 50 (except the rat and mouse, which are so small that it is uncertain) will shiver if they are subjected to a sufficiently cold environment. But overt shivering is not at all a prominent feature of the response to cold. So, in the decade before 1960, a strong suspicion developed that another mechanism (of nonshivering thermogenesis) was

involved. It was difficult to be sure about this because an increase in skeletal muscle tone might lead to an increase in metabolism without obvious movement. It was possible to record muscle potentials from a few points, but not from every muscle in the body. However, in newborn rabbits and guinea pigs, skeletal muscular paralysis caused by gallamine did not decrease the elevated O_2 consumption in a cold environment (Dawes and Mestyán, 1963). (Curare also was used, but this caused a fall in O_2 consumption in the cold, almost certainly because it partly blocked ganglionic as well as neuromuscular transmission.) This observation eliminated the skeletal muscles.

Meanwhile, the observations of Moore and Underwood (1960,a,b) had directed attention to the possible importance of sympathetic amines (which were already known to cause a small rise in O_2 consumption in adults). They found that very large doses of noradrenaline injected subcutaneously caused a large rise in the O_2 consumption of newborn kittens and that hexamethonium blocked the metabolic response to cold (Moore and Underwood, 1962). The latter observation was difficult to interpret, because hexamethonium, by blocking ganglionic transmission, might not only have interrupted sympathetic nerve discharges to a hypothetical site of thermogenesis, but might also have disturbed the distribution of cardiac output on which O_2 supply to the site of thermogenesis depended. Scopes and Tizard (1963) followed up Moore and Underwood's work and showed that intravenous infusion of noradrenaline in doses as low as 0.5 μg/kg min caused a large rise in O_2 consumption in newborn kittens and rabbits, but it required a dose of 2 μg/kg min to mimic the response to cold. This is a very large quantity of catecholamine and it hardly seemed possible that this amount could be continuously released (e.g., from the adrenal medulla) into the circulating blood of a young animal on exposure to cold. Indeed, Hull (1964) showed that the metabolic effect of noradrenaline infusion was blocked by pronethalol in a dose which hardly affected the response to cold. So, if the latter was due to sympathetic activity, it must be through direct nervous connection with the tissue responsible for thermogenesis.

Three other facts also were available by the early spring of 1963. First, it was apparent that in newborn animals noradrenaline and isoprenaline were more active in causing a rise of O_2 consumption (in a warm environment) than adrenaline, contrary to the situation in adults. Secondly, Scopes and Tizard (1963) had shown by functional evisceration, that the liver and gastrointestinal tract were not essential to the rise in O_2 consumption and rectal temperature on infusion of noradrenaline. And, thirdly, they also showed that in rabbits the response to noradrenaline decreased considerably during the 3 weeks after birth. So the intestines, liver, and skeletal muscles were eliminated and the search was on for some tissue whose response to noradrenaline declined with age. Dawkins, while doing autopsies on newborn rabbits for another purpose, observed that the brown adipose tissue between the scapulae became shriveled up after 2–3 weeks from birth, and Hull measured the temperature over this tissue and showed that it increased on infusion of noradrenaline and on exposure to cold (Dawkins and Hull, 1963). This strongly suggested that brown adipose tissue was a site of nonshivering thermogenesis in the newborn rabbit.

Several parallel lines of investigation came to meet at this time, from studies of nonshivering thermogenesis in the newborn, of the mechanism of cold acclimatization in adults, of thermal homeostasis during hibernation and arousal, and from investigations of fat metabolism *in vitro.* As has so often happened before in science, until the connection was finally established, the fact that there was a common problem was not generally recognized and there was little communication between the different groups. Yet Hatai, in 1902, had pointed out the similarity between the dorsal and cervical fat masses of the human foetus and the hibernating gland of mammals. Johansson (1959), and particularly Smith (1961), and Smith and Hock (1963), had proposed that brown adipose tissue might be important in body temperature regulation and as a site of heat production. And Ball and Jungas (1961) had suggested that this tissue might act as a heat generator, especially in hibernators, by a process involving triglyceride breakdown and resynthesis. Here, I shall consider the results in the newborn first and return to the wider issues later.

Brown Adipose Tissue as a Site of Heat Production in the Newborn Rabbit

The most interesting feature of brown adipose tissue is that it has turned out to be not so much a source of readily available fat to be burned elsewhere as a site of heat production in itself. This conclusion depends on three lines of evidence, first on knowledge of its anatomical distribution,

mass, and histological appearance, secondly, on physiological experiments *in vivo,* and thirdly on biochemical experiments mainly *in vitro.* It is remarkable how much evidence has accumulated in the last few years and how well it has dovetailed together, particularly in the rabbit.

Brown fat accounts for 5–6% of the body weight of a newborn rabbit and is concentrated around the neck and between the shoulder blades (Fig. 90). The human infant has a thin sheet of brown fat between the shoulder blades, around the neck, behind the sternum, and around the kidney and adrenals (Aherne and Hull, 1966). There are minor variations in the distribution in the newborn of other species studied (mouse, rat, kitten, and lamb); the coypu, for instance, has a particularly large interscapular pad.

Fig. 90.—The distribution of brown adipose tissue in the newborn rabbit and human infant. (After Dawkins and Hull, 1965.)

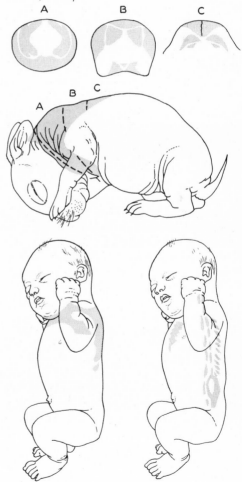

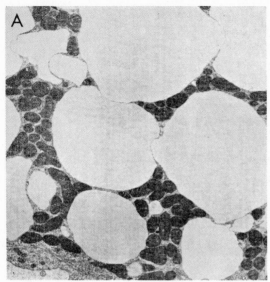

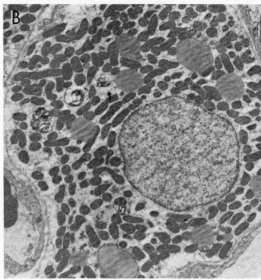

Fig. 91.—Electronmicrographs of brown adipose tissue from newborn rabbits. **(A),** Soon after birth, showing part of a cell in which mitochondria surround fat vacuoles; and **(B),** fasting for 2 days at 30°C, when the fat vacuoles have shrunk, and the endothelial cells of capillaries can be seen in 3 of the 4 corners. (From Hull, 1966.)

When full of fat, brown adipose tissue is yellow in colour. As it becomes depleted of fat it turns yellow-brown and finally red-brown because of the high content of mitochondrial cytochrome. The tissue has a very rich nerve and blood supply which also contributes to its relatively dark colour as compared with white adipose tissue. The cells of brown adipose tissue are distinguished by a granular cytoplasm and many small vacuoles of fat. The granularity is due to the presence of many large mitochondria adjacent to the fat vacuoles (Fig. 91, A). After feeding, the vacuoles may fuse, while when the cell is depleted of fat they decrease in size and the mitochondria then appear to pack the cytoplasm (Fig. 91, B). Each cell is supplied by a rich capillary network. Thus the cells of brown adipose tissue are very different from those of white adipose tissue, which have large droplets of fat surrounded by a narrow rim of cytoplasm and a relatively meagre blood supply.

In order to explore the local temperature response on exposure to cold, continuous recordings were made from subcutaneous thermocouples in newborn rabbits (Dawkins and Hull, 1964). One was placed over the brown adipose tissue between the scapulae, another over the sacrospinalis muscle in the lumbar region, and a third in the colon. At an ambient temperature of 35°C, all three tissue temperatures were similar (Fig. 92). When the

Fig. 92.—Observations on the effects of cold and hypoxia on a rabbit of 57 Gm 12 hours after natural birth. The subcutaneous temperature over brown adipose tissue exceeds that elsewhere on cold exposure, provided the supply of oxygen is adequate. (Redrawn from Dawkins and Hull, 1964.)

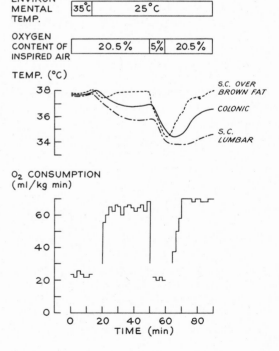

ambient temperature was reduced to 25°C both subcutaneous temperatures began to fall, followed shortly by a decrease in deep colonic temperature. But thereafter the subcutaneous temperature over the interscapular brown adipose tissue rose slightly to maintain a steady level, although the lumbar subcutaneous and deep colonic temperatures continued to decrease. After 30 minutes the temperature over the brown adipose tissue was more than 1°C higher than deep colonic and more than 2°C higher than lumbar subcutaneous temperature. It was also greater than that in the anterior abdominal wall over the liver. During this time the rabbit was breathing 20.5% O_2. When the O_2 content of the inspired air was reduced to 5%, all three temperatures fell and became approximately equal; this degree of hypoxia abolished the metabolic response to cold. Then, when the O_2 content was increased again, the temperature over the brown adipose tissue increased at once, before those over the lumbar region or in the colon. A similar result was obtained when the metabolism of newborn rabbits was increased on infusion of noradrenaline, instead of exposure to cold. The subcutaneous temperature over the brown adipose tissue rose more and more rapidly than that elsewhere (Fig. 93).

Excision of the cervical and interscapular deposits of brown adipose tissue, which contain about 72% of the total body store of brown fat in newborn rabbits, reduced the metabolic responses to cold and noradrenaline by 82 and 80%, respectively. In sham-operated rabbits the responses were reduced by 32 and 20%, suggesting that these responses were largely dependent on brown adipose tissue (Hull and Segall, 1965,a). Brown adipose tissue might be necessary for heat production either as a store of lipid required for metabolism elsewhere (e.g., in the liver, heart, or skeletal muscles), or as a site of heat production on its own account, as the measurements of local temperature suggested. It was desirable to obtain a quantitative measure of blood flow and hence of local O_2 consumption in brown adipose tissue to determine to what extent this hypothesis was correct. An extensive search was made for a preparation, in a variety of species of newborn animals, in which a good quantitative measurement of blood flow to brown fat could be obtained, at first without any success. Finally, Heim and Hull (1966) devised a very simple direct method, by which the outflow was collected from a vein draining the lateral and posterior cervical lobes of brown adipose tissue in newborn rabbits. Angiography demonstrated that the area drained was reasonably constant between individuals.

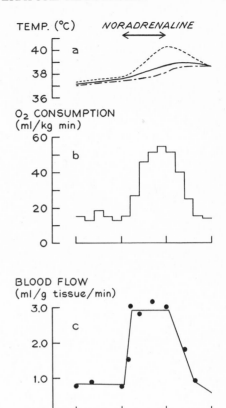

Fig. 93.—The effect of intravenous infusion of noradrenaline (2 µg/kg min) in the newborn rabbit, above (a, b) unanaesthetised; below (c) restrained and anaesthetised to facilitate measurement of blood flow. (Redrawn from Hull, 1966.) Noradrenaline infusion causes a greater rise in the temperature over brown adipose tissue (----------) than that over the lumbar muscles (— — — —) or in the colon (————).

Using this method, Heim and Hull were able to show that infusion of noradrenaline or exposure to cold produced quite remarkable changes in the circulation of newborn rabbits. During noradrenaline infusion there was a large increase in blood flow through brown adipose tissue (Fig. 93); on average it rose from 87 to 360 ml/100 Gm tissue (wet weight) per minute, and the mean O_2 consumption rose from 9.3 to 60 ml O_2/100 Gm tissue per minute. Similarly, on exposure to cold, blood flow more than tripled. Mean cardiac output was 266 ml/kg body weight per minute; it rose on noradrenaline infusion to 405 ml/kg min. At rest about one-tenth, and during noradrenaline infusion about one quarter of the cardiac output went to brown adipose tissue. Calculation suggested that more than two-thirds of the extra oxygen consumed during noradrenaline infusion or on cold exposure was used by brown adipose tissue. This is near to final proof of the theory that most of the metabolic response to cold in the newborn rabbit takes place in brown adipose tissue. It is also evident that any agent which alters the volume or distribution of cardiac output (e.g., general anaesthetics, haemorrhage, deep hypothermia, asphyxia, or hexamethonium) may for this reason alone reduce the metabolic response to cold exposure.

The efferent neural path by which the metabolic response to cold is effected is sympathetic. Unilateral section of the cervical sympathetic prevented fat depletion in part of the cervical brown adipose tissue, in newborn rabbits which were fasted and exposed to a cool environment (30°C). Removal of a stellate ganglion retarded fat depletion in the entire cervical mass of the same side (Hull and Segall, 1965,b). The distribution of sympathetic nerves to the interscapular brown adipose tissue was probably mainly through upper thoracic ganglia because removal of the stellate retarded fat depletion only in its cephalic part. Stimulation of the cervical sympathetic nerve caused a repeatable rise in the temperature of cervical brown adipose tissue in 9 of 27 experiments. This is a difficult procedure in small newborn rabbits, and the fact that it was not always successful is not surprising.

The metabolic response to cold is not arrested by dibenamine (which blocks so-called α-receptors), but is blocked by propranalol in a larger dose (5 mg/kg) than that required to inhibit the response to intravenous infusion of noradrenaline (1 mg/kg; Heim and Hull, 1966,b). The larger dose of propanalol probably blocked the effect of noradrenaline released at sympathetic nerve endings in brown adipose tissue by competition with the receptors (which must now be regarded as β-receptors). The alternative explanation, that this dose of propanalol caused a fall in O_2 consumption in the cold as a result of cardiovascular effects, is now unlikely, because it did not reduce the rise in O_2 consumption caused by intravenous infusion of either glucagon (4 μg/kg min) or corticotrophin (1 i.u./kg min) in newborn rabbits. Both the latter drugs caused an increase in the subcutaneous temperature over brown adipose tissue accompanied by a large increase in local blood flow and oxygen consumption (Heim and Hull, 1966,b). They must have acted directly upon the brown adipose tissue (rather than reflexly through the autonomic nervous system). And since all three, noradrenaline, glucagon, and corticotrophin, caused an increase in local blood flow comparable to the increase in O_2 consumption, it is probable that the increase in flow was secondary to the increase in local metabolism.

We now turn to the third line of evidence, which is biochemical. Adipose tissue has been thought of more as a store of lipid or as insulating material. But Cahill (1962) remarked, when white adipose tissue was found to possess considerable metabolic activity, that it should be thought of "not merely as a simple insulating blanket, but as an electric blanket." Brown adipose tissue is even better in this respect because of its much higher metabolic rate.

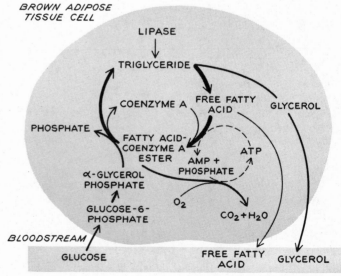

Fig. 94.—Schematic representation of the process of heat production in brown adipose tissue by the oxidation of fatty acids. (Redrawn from Dawkins and Hull, 1965.)

Slices and homogenates *in vitro* have an exceptionally high rate of O_2 consumption, as high or higher than that of cardiac muscle. It is proposed that sympathetic amines activate an adipose tissue lipase (Rizack, 1961) and thus split triglyceride (Fig. 94). The free fatty acids liberated have three possible routes in the adipose tissue cell. They may be released into the bloodstream, or re-esterified to triglyceride or oxidised. *In vitro* studies of brown adipose tissue slices from newborn rabbits suggested that about 60% were re-esterified and 30% oxidised, contributing to local O_2 consumption. Ball and Jungas (1961) draw attention to the fact that the local hydrolysis and resynthesis of triglycerides was potentially a highly exothermic process, which then seemed purposeless but is now seen to serve a vital function. Re-esterification requires a supply of α-glycerol phosphate derived from glucose, since adipose tissue is not able to phosphorylate the glycerol liberated; most of the latter enters the bloodstream. Hence a rise in plasma glycerol suggests that hydrolysis of triglyceride is taking place in adipose tissue. On exposure of newborn rabbits to cold the plasma glycerol concentration rose fourfold in 20 minutes, while the free fatty acid concentration rose only by about 50% (Dawkins and Hull, 1965). This also suggests that *in vivo* most of the heat production must take place locally in the brown adipose tissue. It is less good evidence than that from measurements of local blood flow and O_2 consumption, because we cannot be sure of the turnover rates of glycerol and free fatty acids under these circumstances.

Brown Adipose Tissue in Other Species

The evidence for the function of brown adipose tissue has been described in the newborn rabbit first, as a model whose validity must be examined in other species. There is good evidence for the role of brown adipose tissue as a site of heat production in hibernating animals (Smalley and Dryer, 1963; Smith and Hock, 1963) in which it has long been known to have a high O_2 consumption *in vitro* (Fleischmann, 1929; Hook and Barron, 1941). Infusions of noradrenaline caused a considerable increase in oxygen consumption in cold-adapted rats (Hsieh and Carlson, 1957), and in both the latter and in hibernators during arousal there was a selective increase in blood flow to brown fat as indicated by indirect methods (Johansen, 1959; Hannon, Evonuk, and Larson, 1963). The local temperature of interscapular brown adipose tissue rose more rapidly than that elsewhere in bats and ground squirrels during arousal from hibernation (Hayward, Lyman, and Taylor, 1965) and in normal (not cold-acclimatised) adult rats, guinea pigs, and ground squirrels on exposure to a cool environment (Donhoffer and Szelényi, 1965). This is the most direct evidence as yet available. Alternatively, it has been suggested that the tissues (liver, kidney, skeletal muscle) of cold acclimatised rats are well adapted to metabolise free fatty acids liberated from fat depots, presumably including brown fat, on cold exposure (Hannon and Larson, 1962; Jansky and Hart, 1963). And it has been proposed that accumulation of free fatty acid might be associated with uncoupling of oxidative phosphorylation (Havel, 1965). So local heat production in brown adipose tissue may not be the only mechanism of nonshivering thermogenesis.

Smith and Roberts (1964) have pointed out that the vascular supply to brown adipose tissue in the rat is such as to facilitate counter current exchange between the arteries and veins and to maintain the temperature of the sympathetic chain and upper spinal cord. The validity of this teleologically tempting hypothesis needs to be checked by measurements of intravascular temperatures.

In man, the evidence is incomplete. In adults, infusion of noradrenaline may increase O_2 consumption after cold acclimatisation (Joy, 1963; Budd and Warhaft, 1966) but the effect, if present, is evidently much smaller than in the newborn. The newborn human infant has a moderate supply of brown adipose tissue at term (Fig. 90), and there is a progressive fall in its fat content in infants coming to autopsy within the first few days of birth, attributed to cold exposure (Aherne and Hull, 1966). In babies dying of the cold syndrome and in adults admitted with gross hypothermia the brown adipose tissue was depleted of fat. Intravenous infusion of noradrenaline (0.4 µg/kg min) into newborn human infants caused a rise in O_2 consumption with a respiratory quotient ∼0.75, i.e., consistent with the oxidation of fat (Karlberg, Moore, and Oliver, 1965). In normal newborn infants exposed to a cool environment (ambient temperature 25–26°C), the nape of the neck where there is brown adipose tissue remained moderately warm, but was below colonic temperature (Silverman, Zamelis, Sinclair, and Agate, 1964). The observation that cold exposure caused plasma glycerol concentration to double, while there was no significant rise in plasma free fatty acids, also suggests that the human baby probably burns fat in brown adipose tissue rather than releasing free fatty acids to be burned elsewhere (Dawkins and Scopes, 1965); it does not prove it because we do not know the turnover rates.

This is the nub of the problem. We may be fairly confident that in the newborn rabbit some two-thirds of the extra O_2 consumption on cold exposure takes place in brown adipose tissue. It may be granted that the same mechanism is present in the newborn of other species, but most have less (often considerably less) fat available in brown adipose tissue than the rabbit. The rabbit was chosen as our model because it was cheap, easily available, easy to handle, and showed a large metabolic response to cold. But it would be quite wrong to presume that the same mechanisms obtain to the same extent in the newborn of other species. This remains to be tested, and will probably not be at all easy in the human infant.

The newborn lamb shivers violently on exposure to cold. It may be that this is a more important means of heat production in large farm animals at birth, whose skeletal musculature is already well developed. Shivering depends on coordinated activity to be most effective and in the rat, whose myelinization is grossly deficient at birth, this mechanism for increasing heat production may be imperfect. Postnatal development of motor neurons and their axons is also slow in kittens (see, e.g., Buller, 1966). Thus, provided the autonomic efferent nerve supply is adequate, nonshivering thermogenesis would seem more particularly appropriate to small animals, which are born in nests or burrows, than in a large animal whose physical problem in terms of thermal homeostasis is relatively less and which needs its skeletal muscles to accompany its mother. If this generalization is true, the human infant is probably more like a newborn rat, rabbit, or kitten than a lamb or foal.

The guinea pig is an interesting animal, because it appears to be so mature at birth, has a moderately thick pelt, and forages for solid food at once. But on cold exposure oxygen consumption is increased mainly by nonshivering thermogenesis, for which brown adipose tissue is most important (Brück and Wünnenberg, 1965,a). After a few weeks the thermogenic capacity of brown adipose tissue decreases (as in the rabbit) and shivering appears. Shivering could also be made to appear at birth when nonshivering thermogenesis was blocked by pronethalol (a β-blocking agent) or hexamethonium. But Brück and Wünnenberg (1965,b) concluded from comparisons of O_2 consumption before and after blockade that shivering was less effective than non-

shivering thermogenesis. So, evidently, the guinea pig, which is of a similar size to a rabbit at birth, behaves very much like a rabbit on exposure to cold despite its apparent maturity in other respects. Probably size is of great importance in determining the predominant mechanism in different species. Yet it would not be wise to overlook other environmental conditions since the coypu, which is a water rodent living along the banks of streams, weighs several hundred grams at birth and yet has an exceptionally well developed cervical and interscapular pad of brown adipose tissue. The newborn seal, which weighs several kilograms at birth, also has large quantities.

Oxygen Consumption and Hypoxia

IN THE WARM.—Cross, Tizard, and Trythall (1955, 1958) reported that exposure of normal newborn human infants to 15% oxygen caused a substantial decrease in O_2 consumption. It was not certain that their observations had been made in a strict neutral thermal environment, and Hill (1959) and many others subsequently pointed out from experiments in adult and newborn animals that when O_2 consumption is elevated on cold exposure it is particularly susceptible to hypoxia. Thus, provided the newborn animal is mature, healthy, and well-fed, a limited degree of hypoxia (e.g., exposure to 12% O_2 or slightly below) does not cause a fall in O_2 consumption in a neutral thermal environment (Fig. 95, ●).

Fig. 95.—Changes in the O_2 consumption of a young rabbit during hypoxia in a neutral thermal environment (●) and a cool environment (○). (Redrawn from Adamsons, 1959.)

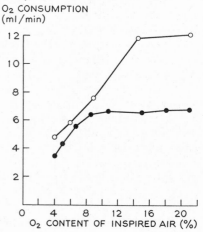

O_2 CONSUMPTION (ml/min)

Oliver and Karlberg (1963), and Cross, Flynn and Hill (1966) repeated the observations in a neutral thermal environment and found no change in O_2 consumption on exposing mature newborn human infants to 15% O_2. The explanation given of the previous observations is interesting. In order to be sure that the air breathed by the infants was pure and uncontaminated by expired gases in the nursery, it was drawn from outside the building. It was, therefore, almost certainly cooler than the mixture of 15% O_2 in N_2 which was made up in Douglas bags, and which remained at room temperature until required. Mestyán, Járai, Bata, and Fekete (1964,a) showed that application of cool air to the faces of premature infants caused an increase in their O_2 consumption. So in the original experiments by Cross *et al.* it seems probable that the higher O_2 consumption while breathing air was due to its lower temperature rather than to its higher O_2 content.

The only other apparent exception to the rule that the normal newborn can tolerate a moderate degree of hypoxia well is in rats, in which Taylor (1960) reported a fall of O_2 consumption when breathing 15–18% O_2 in a neutral thermal environment. At the time when these experiments were done, I found them quite convincing, but we were then much less aware of the importance of adequate nutrition and of litter variation in this species. Looking back on this evidence, I cannot be sure that these were really normal healthy rats, and the observations need repeating.

This conclusion, that in a neutral thermal environment the newborn tolerate moderate hypoxia well, should not be allowed to obscure the fact that they do not tolerate more severe degrees of hypoxia. Their O_2 consumption falls when the O_2 content of the inspired gas mixture is reduced below 10% in newborn rabbits (Fig. 95), lambs (Cross, Dawes, and Mott, 1959), kittens (Hill, 1959), and in other species. Most adults maintain, or even slightly increase, their O_2 consumption on exposure to inspired oxygen concentrations of 6% or even less. Their circulation and breathing then suddenly collapses. There are several possible reasons for this difference between the newborn and the adult. The newborn has a relatively higher O_2 consumption per kg body weight (Table 50), and in the immediate neonatal period there are complications from the nature of the transitional circulation and the ability (in some species) to survive despite severe hypoxaemia and a reduced O_2 consumption.

IN THE COLD.—We now have to consider the method by which hypoxia decreases O_2 consumption in a cold environment. It was tempting, from the work of Hill (1959), to suppose that hypoxia might specifically reduce the extra O_2 consumption on cold exposure, by whatever means (shivering or nonshivering thermogenesis) that was effected. Yet we have to take into consideration the fact that when the inspired O_2 content falls below about 10%, O_2 consumption is reduced even in a neutral thermal environment (Fig. 95). In newborn lambs, exposed to even 10% O_2 in a neutral thermal environment, the O_2 consumption of the hindquarters fell by about 25% despite an increased blood flow to those parts and although total O_2 consumption was not significantly reduced (Cross, Dawes, and Mott, 1959). In fact, there was a redistribution of O_2 consumption, and it was possible that the effect of hypoxia in reducing O_2 consumption was a simple result of the fall in arterial O_2 content (Dawes, 1961). Yet there were other possibilities to consider.

In adult animals, hypoxia abolishes shivering and the observations of von Euler and Söderberg (1958), and Mott (1963) have shown that this can be due to excitation of systemic arterial chemoreceptors. Acute hypoxia also arrests shivering in the newborn lamb (Cross, Dawes, and Mott, 1959). Foetal lambs shiver violently on cold exposure despite a relatively low arterial Po_2; presumably, their systemic arterial chemoreceptors are relatively quiescent. So here is a specific method by which one of the efferent mechanisms of the metabolic response to cold may be turned off. But it does not apply to nonshivering thermogenesis. Bilateral section of the carotid sinus and/or vagus nerves in the newborn rabbit did not affect the immediate fall in O_2 consumption caused by hypoxia in a cool environment (Blatteis, 1964).

Some of Blatteis' other observations are also relevant. For instance, he found that during prolonged exposure to hypoxia and cold, up to 4 hours, newborn rabbits began to shiver and O_2 consumption rose (although not so much as when breathing air). But another variable had then entered the picture; the rectal temperature fell to a new low level (about 32°C). Possibly this additional factor allowed the temperature regulating centres in the hypothalamus to respond by throwing in the shivering mechanism despite the low arterial Po_2 (and consequent chemoreceptor excitation).

We must also consider the possibility that hypoxia reduces the blood supply to thermogenic tissue (e.g., brown adipose tissue) either by local or pulmonary vasoconstriction. Heim and Hull (1966) have eliminated both these possibilities in newborn rabbits so far as the response to noradrenaline is concerned. Hypoxia greatly reduced the local O_2 consumption and heat production in brown adipose tissue, but not the increase in local blood flow caused by noradrenaline infusion. The oxygen content of arterial blood was much reduced and that of the venous effluent from brown adipose tissue averaged only 0.7 ml/100 ml. So the extraction was almost maximal. Thus hypoxia decreased local O_2 consumption simply as a result of the fall in the O_2 content of arterial blood. Heim and Hull also suggest that brown adipose tissue is unlikely to produce much heat anaerobically, since the local temperature dropped abruptly during hypoxia.

Lastly, there is the question at what level of oxygenation O_2 consumption begins to decline in the cold. This obviously will depend on the degree of cold exposure, and whether O_2 extraction from the circulating blood is near maximal. Cross, Flynn, and Hill (1966) concluded, after reconsideration of the observations of Oliver and Karlberg (1963), that exposure of human newborn infants to 15% O_2 did not cause a fall in O_2 consumption in a moderately cool environment. They also quoted observations on other species to support the contention that there was little fall until the O_2 content of the inspired air was reduced to about 10%. Reference to the papers cited shows that their generalization is not justified. Both Moore (1959), using kittens, and Dawes, Jacobson, Mott, and Shelley (1960), using monkeys, found a decrease in O_2 consumption at a considerably higher inspired O_2 content (as high as 16% in monkeys), when they were exposed to cold. Whether this is also true of normal human infants exposed to an ambient temperature lower than that used by Oliver and Karlberg is unknown, and would be an undertaking hard to justify.

The effect of hypercapnia alone (while breathing 21% O_2) upon O_2 consumption in the cold has not been examined directly, but Scopes and Tizard (1963) found that it did not alter the rise in rectal temperature caused by infusion of noradrenaline in newborn rabbits.

Heat Loss on Cold Exposure

The partition of heat loss on cold exposure has been illustrated very nicely by Mount (1964,a) in experiments on newborn pigs, which are naked and of a size at birth similar to that of a premature human infant. Table 51 shows the results obtained on exposure to a cool air or wall temperature, or both together. Rectal temperature was maintained, but skin temperature fell and this of itself reduced heat loss by convection and radiation. The total heat loss doubled over the range of environments studied, but there was no significant change in evaporative heat loss (in any event, a small proportion of the whole) despite the increased ventilation required for the doubling of metabolic rate. Of nonevaporative heat loss, radiation comprised half to three-quarters, depending on the wall temperature of the environmental chamber. We shall return to this point later.

The methods by which a human or animal infant can reduce its heat loss on cold exposure are limited. And it is interesting that Mount (1964,a) found evidence that shivering can actually increase heat loss by convection. Brück (1961) observed that cold thermal stimulation of the whole body or the face alone of a newborn human infant caused a fall in blood flow through the skin of the heel. Celander (1966) observed a large decrease in blood flow through the calf and foot. These reactions are present in very premature infants and newborn animals (e.g., Mount, 1964,b) and should reduce heat loss by convection and radiation. Newborn animals on

---

TABLE 51.—PARTITION OF HEAT LOSS IN A NEWBORN PIG WEIGHING 2 KG WITH A TRUE SURFACE AREA OF 0.15 M^2 (DATA FROM MOUNT, 1964,a)

	TEMPERATURE (°C) OF			EFFECTIVE SURFACE AREA (M^2)	HEAT LOSS (K CAL/HR)			
Air	Chamber Wall	Rectum	Skin*		Total†	Evaporative	Radiant	Convective
30	30	39.6	37.0	0.114	9.5	1.2	4.9	3.4
30	20	39.7	35.3	0.108	13.1	1.2	9.1	2.8
20	20	39.6	33.1	0.101	15.7	1.1	7.3	7.3
20	10	39.5	31.2	0.095	18.2	1.0	10.2	7.0

*Weighted for difference between ear and mid-back skin temperatures.
†Estimated from measurements of O_2 consumption in a steady thermal state.
Note: The critical temperature for the newborn pig is 34–35°C, so these environments are below the neutral thermal zone but above the animal's cold limit, about 5°C in still air. Air movement was < 15 cm/sec near the piglet.

exposure to cold hunch themselves up, tuck their extremities in, and hence reduce their effective radiating surface area (Table 51). Mount (1964) calculated that the rate of heat loss on cold exposure of newborn piglets was reduced by a third from what it otherwise would have been, mainly as a result of the fall in skin temperature and skin vasoconstriction, partly because of the decrease in effective surface area. When several animals of a single litter are exposed to cold they huddle together and thus reduce their effective surface area still further. Consequently, the critical temperature of the group is lowered and their rate of heat loss becomes more like that of a single large animal (Mount, 1959). So a litter of piglets on cold exposure reacts more like a grown-up pig of 90 kg (Fig. 96). This is a vivid illustration of the fact that the thermal problem is primarily physical. In a single individual, the changes in skin blood flow and posture can do little to compensate for the physical disadvantage of the small size of the newborn animal, with its relatively large surface area and low thermal insulation. The only really effective steps it can take to achieve thermal homeostasis is to grow larger and acquire an insulating layer of subcutaneous fat. Alternatively, heat loss can be minimized by clothing.

The data of Table 51 show that, within a limited range of cold thermal environments, the various responses (such as increase in heat production and decrease in effective surface area) are associated with a fall in skin temperature, but no change in core temperature. Consequently, the principal sensory receptor site must be in the skin. A similar conclusion has been reached in newborn human infants (Mestyán, Járai, Bata, and Fekete, 1964; Adamsons, Gandy, and James, 1965) and in other species. The nature of the effective stimulus is probably a thermal gradient across the skin rather than the absolute skin temperature, since heat production falls so rapidly in hypothermic infants in a warm environment (Brück, 1961; Mestyán, Varga, Fohl, and Heim, 1962). There are some interesting points which still need to be explored on the distribution of thermal receptors in the skin and their effects on stimulation. As already mentioned, cooling of the gas flowing over the face causes both peripheral vasoconstriction (Brück, 1961) and an increase in O_2 consumption (Mestyán, Járai, Bata, and Fekete, 1964,a). Plunging the limb of a newborn child into cold water causes a rise of arterial pressure (the cold pressor test). There is a strong possibility that in the newborn local cold stimulus

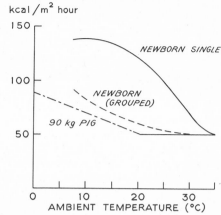

Fig. 96.—Changes in the metabolic rate on exposure to cold of newborn piglets studied singly, or allowed to huddle together as compared with a 90 kg pig. (Redrawn from Mount, 1964, c.)

to various areas, the limbs, trunk, and face, may have relatively different effects upon the circulation, breathing, and metabolism, as in the adult. The integration of these responses is complex, because a cold stimulus affects the circulation and breathing both directly, and secondarily as a result of the increase in metabolic rate. It may well be that the face is a predominant sensory receptor area in man, in which case swaddling would seem both to preserve sensitivity to ambient thermal changes and to improve thermal insulation in the newborn infant.

Heat loss in the naked newborn infant is commonly minimized by nursing in an incubator. This facilitates examination by the paediatrician and nursing staff, but the cost is often high, both financially and in terms of loss of thermal stability. Although it was evident from older work (such as that of Day, 1943) that a large proportion of heat loss in the newborn is by radiation, the implications of this for incubator design have only recently been realised. Glass and Perspex or Lucite (the materials usually used for the transparent walls of incubators) are opaque to radiation of the wavelength of about 9 μ emitted from the skin. The work of Mount (1964; see Table 51) on piglets, and of Adamsons, Gandy, and James (1965) on human infants, shows that in order to minimize heat loss the temperatures of the walls as well as of the gas in an incubator must be controlled. Otherwise the same effect can be achieved by the use of a radiant heat shield, e.g., composed of 1 mm thick transparent Perspex sheet, raised from the wall surface so as to attain thermal equilibration with the circulating air (Hey and

Mount, 1966). Yet infant incubators have already become too complex. Many have water containers (which increase humidity but are a potential site of bacterial proliferation), fans, and heat exchangers which are difficult to clean, and elaborate barriers between infant and nurse, and even so they do not always produce an adequate thermal environment for a very small premature infant. Paediatricians in the Western world have now got so used to seeing such infants naked that it is probably too much to suggest that they should use swaddling clothes. Yet a mini-swaddle, perhaps using transparent material, to give the child a micro-climate of its own should improve thermal stability and a simpler type of incubator would then be adequate. Alternatively, a radiant heat cradle of transparent plastic, with thin heating wires embedded between laminations, and servo-controlled from a sensor on the infant's abdomen, is simpler and equally effective (Levison, Linsao, and Swyer, 1966).

Some Practical Implications

In human infants which were small at birth, either as a result of premature delivery or because they were small for their dates, minimal O_2 consumption in a neutral thermal environment was the same as that of mature infants of normal size (Scopes, 1966). Very small premature babies had a consistently low metabolic rate (Mestyán, Fekete, Bata, and Járai, 1964). Small-for-dates babies had a significantly higher minimal O_2 consumption after the first 4 days from birth (Scopes and Ahmed, 1966). The fact that minimal O_2 consumption and critical temperature can vary so much in the first few days after birth suggests that an arbitrary selection of conditions described as thermoneutral is liable to be misleading. It cannot yet replace an empirical test by measurement of O_2 consumption by a direct recording method at several ambient temperatures. Sinclair and Silverman (1966) lumped together all the measurements in 79 infants between 2 and 10 days from birth, and their conclusion that there was an increase in minimal O_2 consumption per kg body weight with increase in birth weight or gestational age is, therefore, both suspect and in conflict with the observations of Adamsons, Gandy, and James (1965), Hill and Rahimtulla (1965), and Scopes (1966), all of whom recorded a lower mean minimal O_2 consumption. It is also evident that the rate of O_2 consumption is affected by other variables than the thermal environment, including the depth of sleep and the level of the plasma bilirubin, as well as hypoglycaemia and hypothyroidism. But

minimal O_2 consumption in a neutral thermal environment is not necessarily reduced in the respiratory distress syndrome when they are well oxygenated (Scopes, 1966), nor in well-compensated cyanotic heart disease (Brück, Adams, and Brück, 1962; Levison, Delivoria-Papadopoulos, and Swyer, 1965).

The potential consequences of inadequate warmth in newborn human infants and animals are serious. Mortality and morbidity are increased, especially in premature babies (Silverman, Fertig, and Berger, 1958; Buetow and Klein, 1964; Day, Caliguri, Kamenski, and Ehrlich, 1964) and piglets. In human infants the mortality does not appear to be affected by the humidity if the temperature is properly controlled. But at high altitude a low humidity contributes to the high neonatal mortality in rats (Fenton Kelly; personal communication). The difference is not yet explained, but is probably related to the smaller size of the newborn rat and its need to maintain a greater metabolic rate.

The reasons for the increased mortality rate in a cold environment are probably simple exhaustion of the fuel needed to maintain heat production and hence hypothermia. This seemed to be true in piglets (McCance and Widdowson, 1959). In newborn rabbits, fasted for 48 hours, the fat content of brown adipose tissue fell to very low levels and their capacity to increase heat production in the cold was grossly reduced (Hull and Segall, 1965,c). Newborn rabbits which were undernourished or exposed to a cool environment (e.g., 25°C as compared with a normal nest temperature ~32°C) lost the ability to suck and became hypothermic (Bernard and Hull, 1964). Presumably, this is also the reason why lambs born at term with a body weight <2.5 kg rarely survive; they are deficient both in size and fuel. This, then, is the reason that it is now proposed that sick newborn human infants should be nursed in a neutral thermal environment. But, as should now also be clear, an exact prescription for this environment, suitable for any infant and translated readily into practical terms, is not available. Various attempts have been made, ranging from maintenance of skin or rectal temperatures at arbitrary values to specification of air and wall temperatures in incubators, but further practical experience is still required.

REFERENCES

Acheson, G. H.; Dawes, G. S., and Mott, J. C.: Oxygen consumption and the arterial oxygen saturation in foetal and newborn lambs, J. Physiol. 135:623–642, 1957.

Adamsons, K., Jr.: Breathing and the thermal environment in young rabbits, J. Physiol. 149:144–153, 1959.

Adamsons, K., Jr., Gandy, G. M., and James, L. S.: The influence of thermal factors upon oxygen consumption of the newborn human infant, J. Pediat. 66:495–508, 1965.

Adolph, E. F., and Molnar, G. W.: Exchanges of heat and tolerances to cold in men exposed to outdoor weather, Am. J. Physiol. 146:507–537, 1946.

Aherne, W., and Hull, D.: Brown adipose tissue and heat production in the newborn infant, J. Path. & Bact. 91:223–234, 1966.

Alexander, G.: Temperature regulation in the newborn lamb. V. Summit metabolism, Australian J. Agric. Res. 13:100–121, 1962.

Altman, P. I.: *Handbook of Respiration* (Philadelphia: W. B. Saunders Company, 1958).

Ball, E. G., and Jungas, R. L.: On the action of hormones which accelerate the rate of oxygen consumption and fatty acid release in rat adipose tissue *in vitro,* Proc. Nat. Acad. Sc. (Washington) 47:932–941, 1961.

Barcroft, J.; Flexner, L. B., and McClurkin, T.: The output of the foetal heart in the goat, J. Physiol. 82:498–508, 1934.

Benedict, F. G., and Talbot, F. B.: The Physiology of the Newborn Infant. Character and Amount of the Katabolism (Washington, D.C.: Carnegie Inst. Publ. 233, 1915).

Bernard, E., and Hull, D.: The effect of the environmental temperature on the growth of newborn rabbits reared in incubators, Biol. Neonat. 7:172–178, 1964.

Blatteis, C. M.: Hypoxia and the metabolic response to cold in newborn rabbits, J. Physiol. 172:358–368, 1964.

Bramante, P. O.: Quantitation of oxygen consumption and spontaneous muscular activity of the rat, J. Appl. Physiol. 16:982–990, 1961.

Brück, K.: Temperature regulation in the newborn infant, Biol. Neonat. 3:65–119, 1961.

Brück, K.; Adams, F. H., and Brück, M.: Temperature regulation in infants with chronic hypoxemia, Pediatrics 30:352–360, 1962.

Brück, K., and Wünnenberg, B.: Untersuchungen über die Bedeutung des multilokulären Fettgewebes für die Thermogenese des neugeborenen Meerschweinchens, Pflüger's Arch. ges. Physiol. 283:1–16, 1965,a.

Brück, K., and Wünnenberg, B.: Blockade der chemischen Thermogenese und Auslösung von Muskelzittern durch Adrenolytica und Ganglienblockade beim neugeborenen Meerschweinchen. Pflüger's Arch. ges. Physiol. 282:376–389, 1965,b.

Budd, G. M., and Warhaft, N.: Cardiovascular and metabolic responses to noradrenaline in man, before and after acclimatization to cold in Antarctica, J. Physiol. 186:233–242, 1966.

Budin, P.: *Le Nourrisson. Alimentation et hygiene des enfants debiles nés à term* (Paris: Octave Doin & Cie, 1900).

Buetow, K. C., and Klein, S. W.: Effect of maintenance of "normal" skin temperature on survival of infants of low birth weight, Pediatrics 34:163–169, 1964.

Buller, A. J.: Developmental physiology of the neuromuscular system, Brit. M. Bull. 22:45–48, 1966.

Cahill, G. F.: Adipose Tissue as an Organ, in Kinsell, (ed.): *Deuel Conference on Lipids* (Springfield, Ill.: Charles C Thomas Publisher, 1962), p. 126.

Cassin, S.: Critical oxygen tensions in newborn, young and adult mice, Am. J. Physiol. 205:325–330, 1963.

Celander, O.: Studies of the Peripheral Circulation, in Cassels, D. E. (ed.): *The Heart and Circulation in the Newborn and Infant* (New York: Grune & Stratton, Inc., 1966).

Cross, K. W.; Dawes, G. S., and Mott, J. C.: Anoxia, oxygen consumption and cardiac output in newborn lambs and adult sheep, J. Physiol. 146:316–343, 1959.

Cross, K. W.; Flynn, D. M., and Hill, J. R.: Oxygen consumption in normal infants during moderate hypoxia, Pediatrics 37:565–576, 1966.

Cross, K. W.; Tizard, J. P. M., and Trythall, D. A. H.: The metabolism of newborn infants breathing 10% oxygen, J. Physiol. 129:69, P., 1955.

Cross, K. W.; Tizard, J. P. M., and Trythall, D. A. H.: The gaseous metabolism of the newborn infant breathing 15% oxygen, Acta. paediat. 47:217–237, 1958.

Dawes, G. S., in Wolstenholme, G. E. W., and O'Connor, M. (eds.): Oxygen Consumption and Hypoxia in the Newborn Animal, *Ciba Foundation Symposium on Somatic Stability in the Newly Born* (London: J. & A. Churchill, Ltd., 1961), pp. 170–182.

Dawes, G. S.; Jacobson, H. N.; Mott, J. C., and Shelley, H. J.: Some observations on foetal and newborn rhesus monkeys, J. Physiol. 152:271–298, 1960.

Dawes, G. S., and Mestyán, G.: Changes in the oxygen consumption of newborn guinea pigs and rabbits on exposure to cold, J. Physiol. 168:22–42, 1963.

Dawes, G. S., and Mott, J. C.: The increase in oxygen consumption of the lamb after birth, J. Physiol. 146:295–315, 1959.

Dawkins, M. J. R., and Hull, D.: Brown fat and the response of the newborn rabbit to cold, J. Physiol. 169:101, P., 1963.

Dawkins, M. J. R., and Hull, D.: Brown adipose tissue and the response of newborn rabbits to cold, J. Physiol. 172:216–238, 1964.

Dawkins, M. J. R., and Hull, D.: The production of heat by fat, Scient. Am. 213:62–67, 1965.

Dawkins, M. J. R., and Scopes, J. W.: Non-shivering thermogenesis and brown adipose tissue in the human newborn infant, Nature 206:201–202, 1965.

Day, R.: Respiratory metabolism in infancy and childhood XXVII. Regulation of body temperature of premature infants, Am. J. Dis. Child. 65:376–398, 1943.

Day, R. L.; Caliguiri, L.; Kamenski, C., and Ehrlich, F.: Body temperature and survival of premature infants, Pediatrics 34:171–181, 1964.

Dill, D. B., and Forbes, W. H.: Respiratory and metabolic effects of hypothermia, Am. J. Physiol. 132:685–697, 1941.

Donhoffer, S. Z., and Szelényi, Z.: The role of brown adipose tissue in thermoregulatory heat production in the non cold-adapted adult rat, guinea pig, ground squirrel and in the young rabbit, Acta. physiol. Hung. 28:349–361, 1965.

Edwards, V. F.: *De l'influence des agens physiques* (Paris: Crochard, 1824).

von Euler, C., and Söderberg, V.: Coordinated changes in temperature thresholds for thermoregulatory reflexes, Acta. physiol. Scandinav. 42:112–129, 1958.

Fleischmann, W.: Beiträge zur Physiologie der Gewebsatmung nach Untersuchungen an Winterschläfern, Pflüger's Arch. ges. Physiol. 222:541–547, 1929.

Gelineo, S.: Dévellopement ontogénétique de la thermoregulation chez le chien, Bull. Acad. Serbe Sc. 18:97–102, 1957.

Giaja, J.: Le metabolisme de sommet, C. R. Soc. Biol. Paris 101 (Réunion Plénière):3–36, 1929.

Gosselin, R. E.: Acute hypothermia in guinea pigs, Am. J. Physiol. 157:103–115, 1949.

Graham, N. M.: Influence of ambient temperature on the heat production of pregnant ewes, Australian J. Agric. Res. 15:982–988, 1964.

Hannon, J. P.; Evonuk, E., and Larson, A. M.: Some physiological and biochemical effects of norepinephrine in the cold-acclimatised rat, Fed. Proc. 22:783–787, 1963.

Hannon, J. P., and Larson, A. M.: Fatty acid metabolism during norepinephrine induced thermogenesis in the cold-acclimatised rat, Am. J. Physiol. 203:1055–1061, 1962.

Hatai, S.: On the presence in human embryos of an interscapular gland corresponding to the so-called hibernating gland of lower mammals, Anat. Anz. 21:369–373, 1902.

Havel, R. J.: Autonomic Nervous System and Adipose Tissue, in *Handbook of Physiology: Adipose Tissue* (Washington, D.C.: American Physiological Society 1965), pp. 575–582.

Hayward, J. S.; Lyman, C. P., and Taylor, C. R.: The possible role of brown fat as a source of heat during arousal from hibernation, Ann. New York Acad. Sc. 131:441–446, 1965.

Heim, T., and Hull, D.: The blood flow and oxygen consumption of brown adipose tissue in the newborn rabbit, J. Physiol. 186:42–55, 1966,a.

Heim, T., and Hull, D.: The effect of propranalol on the calorigenic response in brown adipose tissue of newborn rabbits to catecholamines, glucagon, corticotrophin and cold exposure, J. Physiol. 187:271–283, 1966,b.

Hemingway, A., and Hemingway, C.: Respiration of sheep at thermoneutral temperature, Resp. Physiol. 1:30–37, 1966.

Hemingway, A.; Robinson, R.; Hemingway, C., and Wall, J.: Cutaneous and brain temperatures related to respiratory metabolism of the sheep, J. Appl. Physiol. 21:1223–1227, 1966.

Hey, E., and Mount, L.: Temperature control in incubators, Lancet 2:202–203, 1966.

Hill, J. R.: The oxygen consumption of newborn and adult mammals: Its dependence on the oxygen tension in the inspired air and on the environmental temperature, J. Physiol. 149:346–373, 1959.

Hill, J., and Rahimtulla, K. A.: Heat balance and the metabolic rate of newborn babies in relation to environmental temperature; and the effect of age and of weight on basal metabolic rate, J. Physiol. 180:239–265, 1965.

Hook, W. E., and Barron, E. S. G.: The respiration of brown adipose tissue and kidney of the hibernating and non-hibernating ground squirrel, Am. J. Physiol. 133:56–63, 1941.

Hsieh, A. C., and Carlson, L. D.: Role of adrenaline and noradrenaline in chemical regulation of heat production, Am. J. Physiol. 190:243–246, 1957.

Hull, D.: Pronethalol and the oxygen consumption of newborn rabbits, J. Physiol. 173:13–23, 1964.

Hull, D.: Oxygen consumption and body temperature of newborn rabbits and kittens exposed to cold, J. Physiol. 177:192–202, 1965.

Hull, D.: The structure and function of brown adipose tissue, Brit. M. Bull. 22:92–96, 1966.

Hull, D., and Segall, M. M.: The contribution of brown adipose tissue to heat production in the newborn rabbit, J. Physiol. 181:449–457, 1965,a.

Hull, D., and Segall, M. M.: Sympathetic nervous control of brown adipose tissue and heat production in the newborn rabbit, J. Physiol. 181:458–467, 1965,b.

Hull, D., and Segall, M. M.: Heat production in the newborn rabbit and the fat content of the brown adipose tissue, J. Physiol. 181: 468–477, 1965,c.

Jansky, L., and Hart, J. S.: Participation of skeletal muscle and kidney during non-shivering thermogenesis in cold-acclimatized rats, Canad. J. Biochem. Physiol. 41:953–964, 1963.

Johansen, K.: Distribution of blood in the arousing hibernator, Acta physiol. scandinav. 52:379–386, 1961.

Johansson, B.: Brown fat: A review, Metabolism 8:221–240, 1959.

Joy, R. J. T.: Responses of cold-acclimatized men to infused norepinephrine, J. Appl. Physiol. 18:1209–1212, 1963.

Karlberg, P.; Moore, R. E., and Oliver, T. K.: Thermogenic and cardiovascular responses of the newborn baby to noradrenaline, Acta paediat. 54:225–238, 1965.

Levison, H.; Delivoria-Papadapoulos, M., and Swyer, P.: Variations in oxygen consumption in the infant with hypoxemia due to cardiopulmonary disease, Acta paediat. 54:369–374, 1965.

Levison, H.; Linsao L.; and Swyer, P. R.: A comparison of infra-red and convective heating for newborn infants, Lancet, 2:1346–1348, 1966.

McCance, R. A., and Widdowson, E. R.: The effect of lowering the ambient temperature on the metabolism of the newborn pig, J. Physiol. 147:124–134, 1959.

McIntyre, D. G., and Ederstrom, H. E.: Metabolic factors in the development of homeothermy in dogs, Am. J. Physiol. 194:293–296, 1958.

Mestyán, J.; Fekete, M.; Bata, G., and Járai, I.: The basal metabolic rate of premature infants, Biol. Neonat. 7:11–25, 1964.

Mestyán, J.; Járai, I.; Bata, G., and Fekete, M.: The significance of facial skin temperature in the chemical heat regulation of premature infants, Biol. Neonat. 7:243–254, 1964,a.

Mestyán, J.; Járai, I.; Bata, G., and Fekete, M.: Surface temperature versus deep body temperature and the metabolic response to cold of hypothermic premature infants, Biol. Neonat. 7:230–242, 1964,b.

Mestyán, G., Varga, F.; Fohl, E., and Heim, T.: Oxygen consumption of hyper- and hypo-thermic premature infants, Arch. Dis. Childhood 37:466–469, 1962.

Moore, R. E.: Oxygen consumption and body temperature in newborn kittens subjected to hypoxia and reoxygenation, J. Physiol. 149:500–518, 1959.

Moore, R. E., and Underwood, M. C.: Noradrenaline as a possible regulator of heat production in the newborn kitten, J. Physiol. 150:13–14, P., 1960,a.

Moore, R. E., and Underwood, M. C.: Possible role of noradrenaline in control of heat production in the newborn mammal, Lancet 278:1277–1278, 1960,b.

Moore, R. E., and Underwood, M. C.: Hexamethonium, hypoxia and heat production in the newborn and infant kittens and puppies, J. Physiol. 161:30–53, 1962.

Mott, J. C.: The effects of baroreceptor and chemoreceptor stimulation on shivering, J. Physiol. 166:563–586, 1963.

Mott, J. C.: Haemorrhage as a test of the cardiovascular system in rabbits of different ages, J. Physiol. 181:728–752, 1965.

Mount, L. E.: The metabolic rate of the newborn pig in relation to environmental temperature and age, J. Physiol. 147:333–345, 1959.

Mount, L. E.: The thermal insulation of the newborn pig, J. Physiol. 168:698–705, 1963.

Mount, L. E.: Radiant and convective heat loss from the newborn pig, J. Physiol. 173:96–113, 1964,a.

Mount, L. E.: The tissue and air components of thermal insulation in the newborn pig, J. Physiol. 170:286–295, 1964,b.

Mount, L. E.: The Young Pig and Its Physical Environment, in Blaxter, K. L. (ed.): *Symposium on Energy Metabolism,* 3rd Troon, Scotland (London: Academic Press, Inc., 1964,c), pp. 379–385.

Mount, L. E., and Rowell, J. G.: Body-weight and age in relation to the metabolic rate of the young pig, Nature 186:1054–1055, 1960.

Nadeau, R. A., and Colebatch, H. J. H.: Normal respiratory and circulatory values in the cat, J. Appl. Physiol. 20:836–838, 1965.

Oliver, T. K., and Karlberg, P.: Gaseous metabolism in newly born human infants, Am. J. Dis. Child. 105:427–435, 1963.

Popovic, V.: Lethargic hypothermia in hibernators and non-hibernators. Ann. New York Acad. Sc. 80:320–331, 1959.

Rizack, M.: An epinephrine-sensitive lipolytic activity in adipose tissue, J. Biol. Chem. 149:217–227, 1961.

Scopes, J. W.: Metabolic rate and temperature in the human baby, Brit. M. Bull. 22:88–91, 1966.

Scopes, J. W., and Ahmed, I.: Minimal rates of oxygen consumption in sick and premature infants, Arch. Dis. Childhood 41:407–416, 1966.

Scopes, J. W., and Tizard, J. P. M.: The effect of intravenous noradrenaline on the oxygen consumption of newborn animals, J. Physiol. 165:305–326, 1963.

Silverman, W. A.; Fertig, J. W., and Berger, A. P.: The influence of the thermal environment upon the survival of newly born infants, Pediatrics 22:876–886, 1958.

Silverman, W. A.; Zamelis, A.; Sinclair, J. C., and Agate, F. J.: Warm nape of the newborn, Pediatrics 33:984–987, 1964.

Sinclair, J. C., and Silverman, W. A.: Intrauterine growth in active tissue mass of the human fetus, with particular reference to the undergrown baby, Pediatrics 38:48–62, 1966.

Smalley, R. L., and Dryer, R. L.: Brown fat: Thermogenic effect during arousal from hibernation in the bat, Science (New York) 140:1333–1334, 1963.

Smith, R. E.: Thermogenic activity of the hibernating gland in the cold-acclimated rat, Physiologist 4:113, 1961.

Smith, R. E., and Hock, R. J.: Brown fat: Thermogenic effector of arousal in hibernators, Science (New York) 140:199–200, 1963.

Smith, R. E., and Roberts, J. C.: Thermogenesis of brown adipose tissue in cold-acclimated rats, Am. J. Physiol. 206:143–148, 1964.

Taylor, P. M.: Oxygen consumption in newborn rats, J. Physiol. 154:153–168, 1960.

Van Döbeln, W.: Human standard and maximal metabolic rate in relation to fat-free body mass, Acta physiol. scandinav. 37 (Suppl. 126):7–79, 1956.

16

Energy Metabolism in the Foetus and After Birth

BEFORE BIRTH the foetus receives a continuous supply of glucose from its mother through the placenta, and its principal metabolic fuel is carbohydrate. Toward the end of gestation, the normal foetus accumulates large reserves of carbohydrate in its liver and skeletal muscle and these help to tide it over the transitional period after birth until efficient suckling is established. Thereafter, its principal fuel is fat. So there is a major change in metabolism at birth, as well as in the functions of the heart and lungs.

Carbohydrate and Fat Metabolism in the Foetus

The conclusion that carbohydrate was the principal metabolic fuel of the foetus originally derived from measurements of uncertain significance for mature foetal mammals, in invertebrates, birds, or reptiles, or in rats very early in gestation (Needham, 1931; Dickens and Šimer, 1930; Brachet, 1950). Measurement of the respiratory quotient in mammalian foetuses *in vivo* near term is difficult, because of the technical problem of maintaining a steady state and so ensuring that the observed umbilical O_2 and CO_2 arteriovenous differences are fair estimates. The new methods of obtaining foetal blood samples from indwelling catheters *in utero*, or for maintaining an isolated foetus with replacement of the placenta by an extracorporeal artificial lung (see Appendix), may make it easier to calculate how closely the respiratory quotient approaches 1.0. In immature isolated foetal lambs (which have only small carbohydrate reserves in the liver), there is a

very rapid disappearance of blood glucose and little change in plasma amino-nitrogen with time (Alexander, Britton, and Nixon, 1966). The rate of disappearance of blood glucose (8 mg/kg min) was not wholly adequate to account for the normal O_2 consumption of an isolated foetal lamb (4.5 ml/kg min) if all were oxidized; but some carbohydrate may have been mobilized from reserves.

There are a number of measurements of the respiratory quotient in man soon after birth, but while some approximate to 1.0 others are 0.8 or less (Smith, 1959). Cross, Tizard, and Trythall (1958) have pointed out the difficulties in interpreting the respiratory quotient derived from such measurements, even when made in an apparently steady fasting state and in a neutral thermal environment. It is difficult to be sure that the excretion of carbon dioxide is wholly through the lungs; and the rate of excretion can be altered either by preceding metabolic acidosis or concurrent lipogenesis, for example. So measurements of the respiratory quotient must be examined with considerable caution.

Alternatively, we may consider whether fat is available or is used as an energy source. Ahlfeld (1877) observed that lipaemia in the human mother was not associated with lipaemia in the foetus, which suggested that fat did not cross the placenta rapidly. The transfer of maternal plasma lipids to the foetus has been studied with radioisotope techniques, which have shown that the placenta is relatively impermeable to lipids which circulate as constituents of lipoproteins of large molecular size, such as cholesterol, phospholipids, and triglyceride esters of fatty acids (Goldwater and Stetten,

1947; Popják and Beeckmans, 1950; McBride and Korn, 1964). Analysis of the fatty acid composition of maternal and foetal blood and tissue triglycerides and phospholipids suggested that some unsaturated fatty acids could cross the placenta, although there was also evidence of species differences (Satomura and Söderhjelm, 1962; Body and Shorland, 1964). The fact that the major plasma total fatty acids of newborn unsuckled lambs, kids, calves, and piglets were palmitic, palmitoleic, stearic, and oleic acids was consistent with the synthesis of most of the fatty acids from non-lipid sources in the foetus (Leat, 1966). Yet there were large amounts of linoleic and linolenic acids in the triglycerides of brown and white adipose tissue from unsuckled newborn rabbits, suggesting placental transfer of these essential acids (Dawkins and Stevens, 1966). There are large differences in the relative maternal and foetal blood concentrations of free fatty acids (Table 52), the foetal value approximating to that of the mother in the rabbit, but being considerably less in man and particularly in sheep. These observations were made under different experimental circumstances, and the foetal blood glucose concentrations in the sheep foetus were rather low, while those in the human foetus were close to maternal values presumably due to the stress of delivery (see below). Whether the variations in the conditions of observations will have affected the free fatty acid concentrations is uncertain. Measurements of the rate of transfer of isotope-labeled free fatty acids across the placenta have shown that this is comparatively slow in the sheep and rat (van Duyne, Parker, Havel and Holm, 1960: Koren and Shafrir, 1964), but moderately rapid in the rabbit (van Duyne, Havel and Felts, 1962), which is consistent with the relative blood concentrations observed. So, evidently, free fatty acid is not readily available in large quantities as a metabolic fuel in the foetuses of most species. In the rabbit, where it is available, Popják and Beeckmans (1950) concluded that fat was not used as a main source of energy.

There is also evidence from *in vitro* studies. For instance, Wittels and Bressler (1965) showed that the cardiac tissues of newborn rats were less able to metabolize long-chain fatty acids than those from adults, but had a greater capacity for oxidizing glucose. *In vitro* measurements on tissue slices or homogenates must be interpreted alongside observations on living tissues *in vivo*. For instance, Heim and Hull (1966) found that the maximum O_2 consumption of brown adipose tissue *in vivo* was three times greater than that to be expected from observations *in vitro*. This applies with even greater force when the metabolism of the whole body is being considered.

It is likely that proteins are used mainly for synthesis rather than for oxidation or gluconeogenesis in the foetus, but direct evidence is lacking. In fasting newborn babies and animals (McCance and Strangeways, 1954; McCance and Widdowson, 1959; Hahn, Koldovský, Krěcěk, Martínek and Vacek, 1961), protein utilization was slow. None of the evidence considered above excludes the possibility that small quantities of fat or protein are normally oxidized by the foetus. Using an isolated foetus, it should now be possible to determine whether glucose may be replaced as a metabolic fuel by free fatty acids or protein, and to what extent. The general conclusion that carbohydrate is

TABLE 52.—MEAN MATERNAL AND FOETAL PLASMA CONCENTRATIONS IN VARIOUS SPECIES AT TERM OR ON DELIVERY

SPECIES		FREE FATTY ACID (mEQ/L)	TRIGLYCERIDE FATTY ACID (mEQ/L)	GLUCOSE (MG/100 ML)	AUTHORS
Sheep*	Mother	1.0	0.31	74	van Duyne, Parker, Havel and
	Foetus	0.1	0.13	7	Holm (1960)
Human†	Mother	0.9–1.22		83	van Duyne and Havel (1959);
	Foetus	0.27–0.42		76	Keele and Kay (1966)
Rabbit*	Mother	0.65	1.12	152	van Duyne, Havel and Felts
	Foetus	0.51	2.41	64	(1962)
Rat	Adult	0.8			Novák, Hahn, Koldovský, and
	At birth	0.5			Melichar (1965)

* Delivered by caesarean section near term under spinal or general anaesthesia.
† Foetal samples obtained from umbilical vessels after normal vaginal delivery.

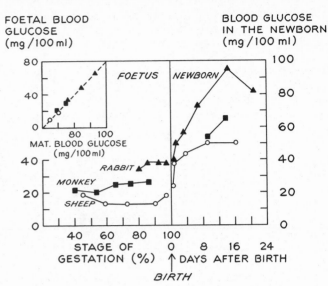

Fig. 97.—Changes in blood glucose concentration with age in foetal and newborn animals (▲ rabbit; ■ rhesus monkey; ○ sheep). The inset indicates the relation between maternal and foetal blood glucose levels; the line represents the relation foetal level = half the maternal level. (Redrawn from Shelley and Neligan, 1966.)

the main fuel of the foetus is not yet seriously challenged, but there is need for better quantitative information.

The level of the blood glucose concentration in the foetus is relatively low (Fig. 97). It is less than and fluctuates with that of the mother. Glucose is continuously removed by the foetal tissues and supplied from the placenta, which it crosses by a process of facilitated transfer (Widdas, 1961). Early work in animals of different species suggested that foetal blood sugar rose toward that of the mother late in gestation, but when consideration is restricted to measurements of true glucose concentration (rather than total reducing substances), under good physiological conditions, it was found to be about half the maternal level throughout the latter half of gestation (Fig. 97). The apparent rise in blood glucose previously observed was attributable to mobilization of hepatic glycogen reserves, which are large near term, mainly as a result of partial asphyxia. With the same precautions, the concentrations in the umbilical artery of human infants at birth also are 50–60% of the maternal values (Cornblath *et al.*, 1961). In normal human infants and animals within a few days from birth, the blood glucose concentration is regulated at a new higher level, probably because fat is then being used preferentially. This raises an interesting point about the regulation of blood glucose concentration in the foetus. Presumably, it can be regulated because Alexander, Britton, and Nixon (1966) found that the blood glucose level did not fall in isolated foetal lambs (maintained by an extracorporeal artificial lung in place of a placenta), provided the lambs were near term

and thus had a large hepatic carbohydrate reserve; also, this reserve is rapidly depleted on asphyxia or after birth. If so, then the regulating mechanism must be reset, as it is for arterial blood gas tensions, breathing, and temperature regulation after birth. During the first half of this century, ideas about the regulation of breathing were dominated by blood gas tensions, and it is only quite recently that the importance of other sensory mechanisms has been appreciated. It is worth considering whether the change in blood glucose levels also results not merely from an alteration in the internal environment (when fat is absorbed from the gastrointestinal tract), but also as a result of the change in the external environment. For instance, it might be interesting to see whether the application of cold to a foetal lamb still attached by an intact placenta to its mother, which initiates breathing movements (Chapter 11), also affects blood glucose and free fatty acid levels.

The level of foetal blood glucose concentration is the net result of supply from the placenta, by glycogenolysis (e.g., in the foetal liver) and by gluconeogenesis and of demand by the foetal tissues. In the early stages of embryonic life the chick heart is freely permeable to glucose, and uptake is limited only by the rate of intracellular phosphorylation. But at a later stage of development, long before hatching, an insulin-sensitive barrier develops which regulates glucose uptake, and the transport mechanism then becomes rate-limiting (Guidotti, Kanameishi, and Foà, 1961). To what extent this is true of other foetal tissues and in other species appears to be uncertain.

Although the blood of foetal ungulates contains large concentrations of fructose (50–150 mg/100 ml in sheep), which is synthesized in the placenta, this is not readily metabolized. Much of the plasma fructose is excreted in the urine after delivery (Dawes and Shelley, 1962) and in the isolated sheep foetus maintained by an extracorporeal artificial lung (Alexander, Britton, and Nixon, 1966). So the direct contribution of fructose to foetal oxidative metabolism is trivial, even in those species in which the blood concentration is large.

Glycogen and Lipid Hoards in the Foetus

It is now more than a century since Bernard (1859) isolated glycogen from foetal tissues, described its distribution in foetuses of different ages, and suggested that it might have an important biological function. During the next 50 years, it was supposed that some embryonic tissues were particularly rich in glycogen because they were necessary for growth and differentiation. But Needham (1931) concluded that "this belief died out when it came to be found that glycogen is not present in embryonic tissues to a greater extent than in adult ones." This is so, yet recent work has shown that large glycogen reserves are accumulated late in foetal life, and these have an important function as sources of metabolic fuel in asphyxia and when the infant is separated from its placental source of glucose at birth.

During late foetal life, large glycogen reserves are built up in the liver, where the concentration rises to 40–100 mg/Gm (Fig. 98), more than double the values in adults of the same species. Generally speaking, the rise in hepatic glycogen content occurs relatively late in species with a short gestational period, and relatively earlier in those with a longer gestation (e.g., man and rhesus monkey). In the rat and rabbit, the rise is prevented by decapitation, which removes the hypophysis, combined in the rat with maternal adrenalectomy since adrenal steroids cross the rat placenta (Jost and Jacquot, 1955). Glycogen appears normally if adrenocorticotrophic hormone (ACTH) is implanted at the time of decapitation. So at least we know that the accumulation of foetal liver glycogen is under hormonal control, even if we are uncertain about the control of foetal blood glucose.

It was to be anticipated that changes in the activity of the liver enzymes concerned with glycogen synthesis and breakdown might be associated with the rise in hepatic glycogen during gestation, but the results have turned out to be somewhat frustrating (Dawkins, 1966). The possible precursors as judged by *in vitro* studies are glucose, fructose, amino acids, glycerol, lactate, and (in the lamb but not the rat) pyruvate. Of the several enzymes involved in glycogen synthesis, phosphoglucomutase, uridine diphosphoglucose pyrophosphorylase, and uridine diphosphoglucose-α-glucan glucosyltransferase increase in activity at or preceding the time of hepatic glycogen accumulation, in different species (e.g., Ballard and Oliver, 1963; Kornfeld and Brown, 1963; Jacquot and Kretchmer, 1964). Con-

LIVER GLYCOGEN OR
TOTAL CARBOHYDRATE
(mg glucose/g wet wt)

Fig. 98.—Changes in liver glycogen concentration in different species before and after birth. (Modified from Shelley, 1961.)

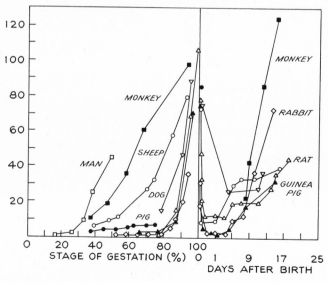

versely, the activities of glucose-6-phosphate dehydrogenase, glucose-6-phosphatase, and α-glucan phosphorylase are usually low (Nemeth, 1954; Dawkins, 1961; Ballard and Oliver, 1963; Kornfeld and Brown, 1963, to give only a few references). Yet the correspondence between enzyme activity *in vitro* and the time of glycogen accumulation is not exact, and no particular step in the enzyme chain has been identified as rate-limiting. Perhaps this is because *in vitro* activities imperfectly represent potential activity *in vivo,* or because hormonal factors and the level of the blood glucose have not been taken into account.

Here a digression will be made to describe the fascinating changes in the activity of hepatic glucose-6-phosphatase, which is necessary to the breakdown of glycogen to glucose. The remarkable changes in its activity after birth at first suggested that it might determine the rate of glycogenolysis. The activity is low in the livers of many species early in gestation (Fig. 99), increasing to near adult levels in some near term. Yet in man (Villee, 1953) and the rhesus monkey (Dawkins, 1963,a), it is already close to adult levels at 0.5–0.75 of term, (and yet liver glycogen accumulates to high levels in these species, Fig. 98). After birth, in all species examined, there is a rapid rise in activity to levels considerably higher than in the adult, a rise which was suppressed in the rat by ethionine, an inhibitor of protein synthesis (Dawkins, 1963,a). It was also suppressed by administration of glucose, demonstrating that this enzyme induction was dependent on glucose lack. The stable door was shut after the horse had bolted since there was little change in glucose-6-phosphatase activity at the time of maximum glycogen mobilization after birth, and glycogen mobilization still occurred normally when the rise was suppressed by ethionine in rats. So despite the remarkable changes which normally take place, and although these are in the direction which would appear to facilitate function, it is not evident that they are of crucial significance. This has been disappointing, for it seemed a few years ago a likely explanation of the rise and fall in liver glycogen at birth.

Glycogen also accumulates in relatively large quantities in some other tissues during gestation. The heart has been discussed elsewhere (Chapter 12). In the skeletal muscles, the concentration reaches adult levels at an early stage of gestation, and varies greatly with different species at term, from 10–70 mg/Gm (Fig. 100). It is most in the piglet, which is born with little fat; it is least in the rabbit, which has a moderate reserve of fat (Table 53). It will be noticed that the proportion of carbohydrate in the liver as compared with that in the skeletal muscles varies greatly in different species. Muscle glycogen is not mobilized for use elsewhere during asphyxia, unlike liver glycogen, but is used rapidly with increased muscular activity after birth.

During gestation, glycogen also accumulates in the placenta and the foetal lung. The time course of these processes is different from those in other tissues. In the lung, the glycogen is concentrated in the epithelium of the foetal alveoli, rising there to a peak concentration of about 75 mg/Gm halfway through gestation in the sheep (Fauré-Fremiet and Dragoiu, 1923), and falling when this epithelium disappears. In the rat and guinea pig, in which pulmonary maturation occurs relatively later, the

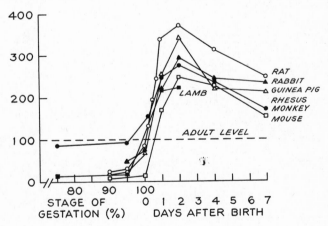

PERCENTAGE OF
ADULT LEVEL

Fig. 99.—Changes in the activity of hepatic glucose-6-phosphatase activity in different species before and after birth. (From Dawkins, 1966.)

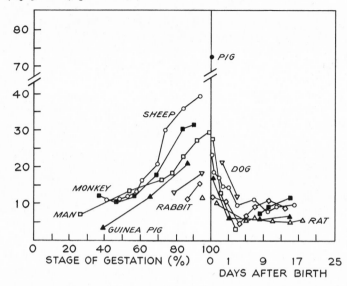

MUSCLE GLYCOGEN OR
TOTAL CARBOHYDRATE
(mg glucose/g wet wt)

Fig. 100.—Changes in skeletal muscle glycogen concentration in different species before and after birth. (From Shelley, 1961.)

peak occurs nearer term, while primates resemble the sheep. The placenta of the rabbit contains up to 36 mg/Gm at 0.6 of term (Huggett, 1929), mostly on the maternal side, and falling rapidly thereafter. In other species there is less placental glycogen. There is no evidence that either pulmonary or placental glycogen is mobilized on intravenous infusion of adrenaline, hypoglycaemia, or asphyxia. The cause of their accumulation may be a casual result of local changes in enzyme activity or structural alterations; it is not necessary to find some teleological significance in every such variation.

Table 53 also shows the great variation in the total body lipid reserves with species at birth. The newborn rat comes off particularly badly as regards both carbohydrate and fat, especially as some of

the latter must be structural and not available as fuel for energy metabolism. In the rabbit much of the lipid is in brown adipose tissue. Hull and Segall (1966) have pointed out that brown and white adipose tissue are clearly distinguishable functionally, as well as on embryological grounds and histologically. Brown adipose tissue is primarily heat producing, while white adipose tissue is a fat store. Hence the lipid of brown adipose tissue is depleted on exposure of newborn rabbits to cold, but not during fasting in a neutral thermal environment. Conversely, white adipose lipid is depleted during a fast but not on cold exposure. So the rabbit is comparatively well endowed at birth with metabolic reserves to maintain its body temperature, but less well equipped to face starvation. In the normal human infant, on full term delivery the lipid stores of both brown and white adipose tissue are quite large. This explains why some infants can survive several days without food although, as will be seen, the hazards of neonatal hypoglycaemia are such as to make early feeding desirable.

Changes in Energy Metabolism After Birth

In all species there is a period between birth and the establishment of suckling during which the infant is dependent for energy metabolism on its own resources. If suckling is established soon the blood glucose concentration rises to adult levels at a rate

TABLE 53.—METABOLIC FUEL RESERVES IN SOME
SPECIES AT BIRTH

SPECIES	TOTAL LIPID (GM/KG)	SKELETAL MUSCLE AND HEPATIC CARBOHYDRATE (GM/KG)	PROPORTION OF CARBOHYDRATE IN LIVER (%)
Man	161	11	33
Sheep	30	11	20
Pig	11	23	9
Rabbit	58	5	54
Rat	11	8	76

From the data of Widdowson (1950), Alexander (1962), and Dawkins and Hull (1964).

which varies in different species, from 7–10 days in lambs, and 2–3 weeks in rabbits (Fig. 97). In mature human infants, the fasting blood glucose usually begins to rise after 2–3 days from birth, but in premature infants it may take several weeks. In infants fasted from birth, from maternal neglect, oesophageal atresia, or other causes, there is a profound fall in blood glucose levels, usually within 1–4 days, depending on the ambient temperature, species, and maturity at birth (Goodwin, 1957; McCance and Widdowson, 1959). In the premature human infant or the pig, it may fall considerably within 48 hours, whereas the starved calf can maintain its blood sugar for more than a week.

The rapid fall in liver glycogen concentration after birth, in so many different species (Fig. 98), suggests that it is mobilized rapidly in order to maintain the blood glucose level in the interval before other sources of energy supply become available, or, perhaps, partly as a result of asphyxia on delivery. The former explanation is supported by the fact that the blood sugar concentration is usually maintained until the liver glycogen is reduced below 5 mg/Gm (Alexander, 1962; Elneil and McCance, 1965).

It seems reasonable to assume that the mobilization of liver glycogen after birth is due to secretion of adrenaline or glucagon, since there is evidence that these activate phosphorylase in slices of newborn rat liver, although the activation is relatively less than in slices of adult liver (Dawkins, 1963,b). In the foetal lamb, Dawkins (1964) found that intravenous injection of a large dose of adrenaline (25 μg/kg) caused only a small rise of blood glucose (from a mean of 29 up to a peak of 46 mg/100 ml). This may have been due to the fact that the injection was made into a jugular vein, so that much might have been removed from the blood before it reached the liver through the hepatic artery, portal vein, and umbilical vein. Yet in newborn lambs also, as in newborn human infants (Desmond, 1953; Cornblath et al., 1961) and puppies (Allen, Kornhauser, and Schwartz, 1966), the rise in blood glucose was less and less rapid than in older individuals. This cannot be attributed to an increased rate of glucose utilization, because when glucose was infused intravenously the concentration fell less rapidly in newborn human infants and puppies. Injection of glucagon likewise caused a slower rise in blood glucose in the newborn. The reasons for this difference in response have not been identified with certainty. Dawkins (1964) was inclined to attribute it to the relatively low level of hepatic

glucose-6-phosphatase activity in lambs at birth, but this hardly explains the small response in the human baby where it is already high (Fig. 99). The other enzymes concerned in glycogenolysis, including the debranching enzyme, clearly need further study in this respect. It seems to be hard to identify the rate-limiting step or steps from conventional *in vitro* enzyme studies, and it may well be necessary to proceed to a preparation analogous to the isolated perfused rat heart, which has proved so useful in unraveling the control points of carbohydrate utilization in the adult.

Other hormonal mechanisms, the secretion of insulin and growth hormone in response to rapid changes in blood glucose concentrations, or of glucocorticoids and catecholamines, are all of reasonable magnitude, taking into account the smaller size of the newborn infant (Cornblath et al., 1966). So it would seem that the rather leisurely rise in blood glucose concentration to adult levels in the days or weeks after birth may be due to relative lack of central regulation and/or to a smaller peripheral response to sympathetic stimulation (as compared with adults). This is the more likely, because when the rise does occur it is associated with the development of a greater capacity for gluconeogenesis, e.g., from galactose and 3-carbon compounds.

During the first two hours from birth the plasma free fatty acid concentrations rise to values of 0.6 mEq/L in sheep (van Duyne et al., 1960), and 1.1–1.3 mEq/L in rats and man (Novák et al., 1961, 1964, 1965; Keele and Kay, 1966). This represents a threefold to sixfold increase over foetal levels (compare Table 52). The rabbit may represent an exception to the rule that plasma free fatty acid always rises rapidly after birth, since Dawkins and Hull (1964) found a mean value of 0.45 mEq/L 2 hours from birth, which is not significantly different from the value recorded by van Duyne, Havel and Felts (1962) on delivery. This needs further examination. It is also noteworthy that Dawkins and Scopes (1965) observed a mean plasma free fatty acid concentration of only 0.33 mEq/L at 6–30 hours from birth in healthy newborn human infants. This variant from other published figures already quoted is unexplained, although it is possible that their infants had received glucose, which might have reduced the plasma free fatty acid concentration. In man, the rise in plasma free fatty acid continues for some hours (Fig. 101) and then gradually declines over a long period of time; at 12 months of age the level was still higher than that in

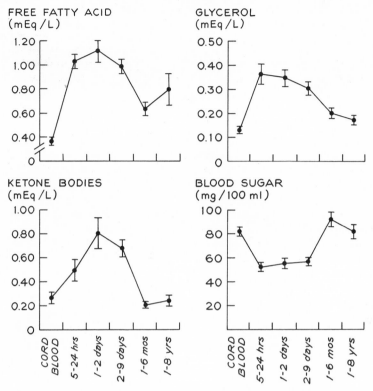

Fig. 101.—Changes in blood concentrations in human infants of different age groups, the vertical lines indicating ±S.E. of the mean. (Redrawn from Persson and Gentz, 1966.)

adults. The immediate rise at birth was attributed to mobilization of depot fat and was accompanied by a rise in blood glycerol and ketone levels.

The abrupt rise in plasma free fatty acid concentration after birth was attributed by van Duyne, Parker, Havel, and Holm (1960) to an increase in sympathetic efferent nervous activity, such as has already been discussed in relation to chemoreceptor function in Chapter 11. The speed of the response, its occurrence only in vigorous lambs, and its blockade by hexamethonium (van Duyne, Parker and Holm, 1965) all suggested a nervous mechanism (Havel, 1965). It did not appear to be related to reduced availability of carbohydrate, since there was a large increase in plasma free fatty acid concentration before the blood glucose concentration fell. Cold exposure leading to sympathetic stimulation of adipose tissue has been proposed as a possible mechanism. According to Dawkins and Scopes (1965), this is accompanied by a rise in plasma glycerol in the human infant, but hardly any increase in plasma free fatty acids; however, cold

exposure at birth commonly causes a larger fall in rectal temperature than was observed in their experiments (0.1–0.5°C) and may, therefore, have been a greater stimulus. We also have to take into account the high level of growth hormone in foetal blood on delivery at term (Table 15, p. 56). The effect of growth hormone in raising plasma free fatty acid concentrations is of slow onset, with a peak after 2 hours or more in man (Raben and Hollenberg, 1959) and sheep (Manns and Boda, 1965), and this could certainly contribute to the rise which is seen on delivery. The reserves of fat at birth are comparatively small except in man, but as soon as suckling is established the infant is provided with a generous supply of lipid. The lipid content of milk is higher in many animal species than in man. It is 22% in rat colostrum (Luckey, Mende, and Pleasants, 1954), a fact which may be related to the low metabolic reserves in this species at birth. After suckling, the newborn rat acquires within a few hours the ability to increase its O_2 consumption very considerably on exposure to cold, and the fat content of its brown adipose tissue increases (Novák, Hahn, Koldovský, and Melichar, 1965). The rat shows these changes to an exaggerated degree, but in all species efficient thermoregulation after birth is dependent on an assured supply of energy, principally from fat.

Hypoglycaemia in the Newborn

Most of our detailed knowledge of hypoglycaemia and its consequences in the newborn comes from observations on man, who has been studied more intensively than other species. The blood glucose concentration in normal mature infants delivered at term and kept warm is 60 ± 17 (S.D.) mg per 100 ml, as compared with 45 ± 14 in infants allowed to cool (Cornblath and Schwartz, 1966). The mean values in infants of low birth weight are less. It is not uncommon for the blood glucose level to fall below 30 mg per 100 ml after premature delivery, and signs of hypoglycaemia are then liable to occur. These signs, which range from enhanced activity (twitching, a high-pitched cry, and, rarely, convulsions) to reduced activity (limpness, difficulty in feeding, apnoeic episodes, and finally coma), are not specific for hypoglycaemia. A low blood glucose may result from various pathological conditions, and may thereby contribute to their symptomatology and to residual brain damage, or it may occur as an isolated entity. The latter is a particularly interesting condition, because not only is its incidence associated with conditions which on physiological grounds go far to explain its origin, but it seems to be an unusually clear experiment of nature by which to judge the capacity of the infant brain to withstand low glucose concentrations.

According to Cornblath and Schwartz (1966), more than a hundred cases of transient symptomatic hypoglycaemia have now been described in newborn infants, with an incidence calculated in Sweden, England, and the United States as 2–3 per 1,000 live births. The susceptible infants were predominantly males (2:1) of low birth weight for their gestational age, often the smaller of twins if less than 2 kg weight and 25% or more discordant (Cornblath, Joassin, Weisskopf, and Swiatek, 1966). Of these, only 15% had primary central nervous system damage or anomalies, none of the mothers had diabetes mellitus, about half had an uneventful pregnancy, and most had a normal delivery of a lively child who cried and breathed spontaneously. It appeared that in most instances the condition resulted from undernourishment *in utero;* most were underweight (70% under the tenth percentile of birth weight for their age) and undergrown (44%

under the tenth percentile of length for age). Symptoms usually appeared from 24–72 hours from delivery and were rapidly relieved by intravenous administration of glucose. The hyperglycaemic response to adrenaline and glucagon was much reduced (Cornblath and Schwartz, 1966), suggesting that the condition was related to reduced hepatic glycogen stores at birth. There was no evidence of deficiency in the hepatic enzymes associated with carbohydrate metabolism, since once the condition was relieved the normal response to glycogenolytic hormones was restored.

One of the most interesting points which has emerged from this and other work is that the newborn infant is able to tolerate remarkably low blood glucose concentrations without coma or convulsions. It has been suggested that this might be due partly to the ability of the brain at birth to metabolize large amounts of other substrates. Thus Edwards (1964), in newborn calves, and Scopes (1964), in the human infant, found that clinical signs of hypoglycaemia were absent as long as the blood lactate concentration was high. In calves, hypoglycaemia caused a rise of blood lactate by adrenaline release; when the splanchnic nerves were cut, protection could still be obtained by infusion of 1 (+)-lactate and glycerol in physiological amounts (Edwards, quoted by Shelley and Neligan, 1966). Yet Cornblath, Joassin, Weisskopf, and Swiatek (1966) found no relief of signs in two hypoglycaemic human infants given sodium lactate (5 mEq per kg) alone intravenously, sufficient to cause a large rise in blood lactate concentration. More evidence is needed to see whether lactate and glycerol would be effective, or whether there is a species difference. There is also the possibility that the newborn brain may be able to use quantities of other substrates such as acetoacetate (Mourek, 1965,a,b). Both glycerol and ketone bodies are available in relatively large quantities in the newborn (Fig. 101).

The brain of the newborn is able to tolerate comparatively low blood glucose concentrations for many hours even when the blood lactate and glycerol concentrations are not elevated. Shelley and Neligan (1966) point out that the brains of newborn animals are also better able to tolerate anoxia than adults, an ability which cannot be attributed to a high concentration of substrates such as lactate or glycerol, as these are not metabolized without oxygen. They propose, as an alternative explanation of the tolerance to hypoglycaemia, the reputed low energy requirement of the newborn brain, associated with low cerebral adenosine triphosphatase activity (see Chapter 12). The evidence on this point mainly relates to the ability of the new-born brain to survive a relatively short period of acute total oxygen lack, lasting half an hour or less (varying with species) at normal body temperatures. Moreover, the newborn lamb and calf appear to tolerate comparatively low blood glucose concentrations, although their capacity to withstand acute oxygen lack is hardly greater than that of adults. A simpler explanation would be that the cells of the newborn brain are able to absorb and use glucose at a low blood glucose concentration. What we need now is a measure of glucose utilization by the brain *in vivo* at different blood glucose concentrations in animals of different ages and in the presence of different concentrations of possible alternative substrates. The blood glucose concentration in normal foetuses near term is only about half that in the maternal blood (Fig. 97), and carbohydrate is then the main source of energy. So it would not be surprising if the foetal brain were well adapted to make use of a low blood glucose concentration.

Finally, there is the problem of whether permanent brain damage may result from neonatal hypoglycaemia. The data so far available are very suggestive of this, but as Cornblath *et al.* (1966) cautiously remarked, it is still too early for a final conclusion. If brain damage does result from hypoglycaemia alone (i.e., in circumstances where asphyxia due to transient apnoea can be positively excluded), its distribution would be most interesting for comparison with that resulting from asphyxia alone. But it is worth noting that the brain is especially vulnerable to the combination of asphyxia with hypoglycaemia, because in the absence of adequate carbohydrate reserves it cannot derive energy from glycolysis. So, in practice, it is unlikely that we shall be able to distinguish the results; transient apnoea and cyanotic attacks are commonly associated with hypoglycaemia. Neligan (quoted by Shelley and Neligan, 1966) suggests that asymptomatic hypoglycaemia is unlikely to cause cerebral damage in newborn infants, but there is little evidence available on this point yet.

The Effects of Intra-uterine Growth Retardation

Intra-uterine growth retardation is believed to result from the operation of several different factors, genetic (in association with chromosomal abnormalities), as a result of maternal disease (e.g., pre-eclamptic toxaemia with placental infarction), or when the placental mass is unusually small (see Chapter 4) and in the case of grossly discordant multiple pregnancy. Here we are concerned with some of the consequences.

Such infants are not always easy to distinguish from children of equal weight who are delivered prematurely. They are commonly described as being small and thin with dry, wrinkled, peeling, and often meconium-stained skin on delivery. Skeletal and epiphyseal growth is delayed, so cannot be used with certainty as a diagnostic criterion. Various external features may indicate that this is an older infant, despite its small weight. These are, in descending order of value, the complexity of the creases on the soles of the feet, the size of the breast nodule (which appears after 33 weeks), the change in the texture of the cephalic hair from woolly to silky (from 36 weeks), and changes in the ear cartilage and scrotum, also near term (Mitchell and Farr, 1965; Usher, McLean and Scott, 1966). Such infants tend to be more lively and alert than less mature children, and neurological examination may help to distinguish them. Thus some reflex responses appear at predictable times toward the end of the normal period of gestation and are independent of age from birth. They include pupillary responses at 27–29 weeks, the blink response to a glabellar tap at 30–32 weeks, and the traction response at 31–34 weeks (Robinson and Tizard, 1966). Very premature infants also differ from those at term in their patterns of sleep and activity, in posture and muscle tone, and in their electroencephalograms (particularly in respect of episodic sleep activity). Hence several clinical criteria serve to distinguish the infant of low birth weight (for other reviews see Dawkins and McGregor, 1965; Koenigsberger, 1966). There is, therefore, no doubt that we are dealing here with a separate entity, which is of great clinical interest because of its association with a high morbidity and mortality.

When such infants come to autopsy they are found to have characteristic changes in their organ weights and structure as compared either with normal infants of similar gestational age or with infants of the same body weight but lesser age (Gruenwald, 1963; Naeye and Kelly, 1966). The weight of the brain is affected least of any organ, and the heart, kidneys, and the lungs next least. The spleen, liver, adrenals, and thymus are, relatively speaking, very much reduced in size. Consequently, as Dawkins (1964,b) has pointed out, the change in brain:liver ratio is a particularly powerful index of malnutrition *in utero*, the brain being spared most and liver almost the least. Histological investigation shows that the lungs (in which at term cuboidal epithelial cells are present at sites only where alveolar growth is continuing; Short, 1950) and kidneys (where glomeruli normally continue to form beneath the capsule until ~35 weeks; Potter, 1965) continue to develop normally in small-for-dates babies. In other tissues, haemopoietic, nervous, and cardiovascular, the normal variations are great and information is limited, but it does not appear that cell differentiation is abnormal. According to Naeye and Kelly (1966), both cell size and number may be reduced, especially in the thymus, adrenal cortex, and the exocrine part of the pancreas. The fact that cell size is reduced, and that there is little or no subcutaneous fat, probably accounts for the significantly higher O_2 consumption per kg body weight in a neutral thermal environment, in small-for-dates human infants after the first 4 days from birth (Scopes and Ahmed, 1965). They have a relatively greater mass of metabolizing tissue and presumably can make up some of the growth retardation which had occurred *in utero,* once the transition to an extra-uterine environment is successfully accomplished.

It is this transitional period which is especially hazardous for the small-for-dates baby, as is shown by its propensity to hypoglycaemia. The relatively high brain:liver weight ratio would aggravate the effect of a lower liver glycogen concentration (Dawkins, 1964). Harding and Shelley (1966) found that, in foetal rabbits whose mothers' food was restricted to 25% of normal during the last third of gestation, the total quantity of carbohydrate in the liver of the smallest foetuses per Gm of brain was only a quarter that in foetuses of normal weight from normal litters. At autopsy, small-for-dates babies also have little fat, and in 10 of birth weight <2 S.D. from the mean, dying 3–4 days from birth, the brown adipose tissue was wholly depleted of lipid (Aherne and Hull, 1966).

There is another interesting feature of these small infants which appear to have suffered from partial starvation *in utero.* One might have expected that their arterial blood pressure would be less than normal, on account of their lower weight (see Chapter 14 and Fig. 80, p. 179). Yet it was noted that in immature foetal lambs with small placentas, arterial pressure was unusually high, and this was attributed to their need to maintain a greater umbilical blood flow to make the best use of the limited area of placental exchange (Chapter 6). In many small-for-dates babies the arterial blood pressure is above normal for age and/or size, several days after birth, when the immediate effects of delivery are past and blood volume is stabilized at

a normal level, and it remains elevated for some weeks (Tooley, personal communication). This accords with the observation that when such infants come to autopsy, some have unusually well developed muscular coats to the systemic arterioles (Naeye, 1965). So it is possible that their arterial pressure has become set by their intra-uterine misadventure. In any event, it is an important practical point as the normal high pressure may be attributed incorrectly to hypervolaemia due to placental transfusion on delivery.

Whether the future growth and development of these infants is already compromised, even though they escape the immediate hazards of asphyxia and hypoglycaemia after birth, remains to be seen. Undernutrition in the neonatal period can cause permanent stunting in rats (Jackson, 1932; Widdowson and McCance, 1960), pigs, and cockerels (McCance, 1960), so this is a possibility. Yet the complexities of human life and development will make it unlikely that we can be sure that a higher incidence of neurological abnormalities in early childhood (for instance) in a group of small-for-dates babies can be attributed solely to intra-uterine malnutrition, rather than to a genetic disturbance or to asphyxia and hypoglycaemia during or shortly after birth.

REFERENCES

Aherne, W., and Hull, D.: Brown adipose tissue and heat production in the newborn infant, J. Path. & Bact. 91: 223–234, 1966.

Ahlfeld, F.: Zur Frage über den Uebergang geformter Elemente von Mutter auf Kind, Zentralbl. Gynäk. 1:265–267, 1877.

Allan, D. T.; Kornhauser, D., and Schwartz, R.: Glucose homeostasis in the newborn puppy, Am. J. Dis. Child. 12:343–350, 1966.

Alexander, G.: Energy metabolism in the starved newborn lamb, Australian J. Agric. Res. 13:144–164, 1962.

Alexander, D. P.; Britton, H. G., and Nixon, D. A.: Maintenance of the isolated foetus, Brit. M. Bull. 22:9–12, 1966.

Alexander, D. P.; Britton, H. G., and Nixon, D. A.: Observations on the isolated foetal sheep with particular reference to the metabolism of glucose and fructose, J. Physiol. 185:382–399, 1966.

Ballard, F. J., and Oliver, I. T.: Glycogen metabolism in embryonic chick and neonatal rat liver, Biochim. et biophys. acta 71:578–588, 1963.

Bernard, C.: De la matière glycogène considérée comme condition de développement de certains tissues chez le foetus avant l'apparition de la fonction glycogenique de foie, C.R. Acad. Sc. 48:673–684, 1859.

Body, D. R., and Shorland, F. B.: Maternal and foetal lipids of sheep, Nature 202:769, 1964.

Brachet, J.: *Chemical Embryology* (New York: Interscience Publishers, Inc., 1950).

Cornblath, M.; Ganzon, A.; Nicolopoulos, D.; Baens,

G. S.; Hollander, R. J.; Gordon, M. H., and Gordon, H. H.: Studies of carbohydrate metabolism in the newborn infant. III. Some factors influencing the capillary blood sugar and the response to glucagon during the first hours of life, Pediatrics 27:378–389, 1961.

Cornblath, M.; Joassin, G.; Weisskopf, B., and Swiatek, K. R.: Hypoglycemia in the newborn, Pediat. Clin. North America. 13:905–920, 1966.

Cornblath, M., and Schwartz, R.: *Disorders of Carbohydrate Metabolism in Infancy* (Philadelphia: W. B. Saunders Company, 1966).

Cross, K. W.; Tizard, J. P. M., and Trythall, D. A. H.: The gaseous metabolism of the newborn infant breathing 15% oxygen, Acta paediat. 47:217–237, 1958.

Dawes, G. S., and Shelley, H. J.: Fate of glucose in newly delivered foetal lambs, Nature 194:296–297, 1962.

Dawkins, M. J. R.: Changes in glucose-6-phosphatase activity in liver and kidney at birth, Nature 191:72–73, 1961.

Dawkins, M. J. R.: Glycogen synthesis and breakdown in fetal and newborn rat liver. Ann. New York Acad. Sc. 111:203–211, 1963,a.

Dawkins, M. J. R.: Glycogen synthesis and breakdown in rat liver at birth, Quart. J. Exper. Physiol. 48:265–272, 1963,b.

Dawkins, M. J. R.: Changes in blood glucose and non-esterified fatty acids in the foetal and newborn lamb after injection of adrenaline, Biol. Neonat. 7:160–166, 1964,a.

Dawkins, M. J. R.: Discussion, Proc. Roy. Soc. Med. 57: 1063–1064, 1964,b.

Dawkins, M. J. R.: Biochemical aspects of developing function in newborn mammalian liver, Brit. M. Bull. 22:27–33, 1966.

Dawkins, M. J. R., and Hull, D.: Brown adipose tissue and the response of newborn rabbits to cold, J. Physiol. 172:216–238, 1964.

Dawkins, M. J. R., and McGregor, W. G.: Gestational Age, Size and Maturity, Clin. Develop. Med., vol. 19, 1965.

Dawkins, M. J. R., and Scopes, J. W.: Non-shivering thermogenesis and brown adipose tissue in the human newborn infant, Nature 206:201–202, 1965.

Dawkins, M. J. R., and Stevens, J. F.: Fatty acid composition of triglycerides from adipose tissue, Nature 209:1145–1146, 1966.

Desmond, M. M.: Observations related to neonatal hypoglycaemia, J. Pediat. 43:253–262, 1953.

Dickens, F., and Šĭmer, F.: CXLIII. The metabolism of normal and tumour tissue. II. The respiratory quotient, and the relation of respiration to glycolysis. Biochem. J. 24:1301–1326, 1930.

Edwards, A. V.: Resistance to hypoglycaemia in the newborn calf, J. Physiol. 171:46, P, 1964.

Elneil, H., and McCance, R. A.: The effect of environmental temperature on the composition and carbohydrate metabolism of the newborn pig, J. Physiol. 179: 278–284, 1965.

Fauré-Fremiet, E., and Dragoiu, J.: Le développement du poumon foetal chez de mouton, Arch. Anat. Micr. 19:411–474, 1923.

Goldwater, W. H., and Stetten, DeW.: Studies in fetal metabolism, J. Biol. Chem. 169:723–738, 1947.

Goodwin, R. F. W.: The relationship between the concentration of blood sugar and some vital body functions in the newborn pig, J. Physiol. 136:208–217, 1957.

Gruenwald, P.: Chronic fetal distress and placental insufficiency, Biol. Neonat. 5:215–265, 1963.

Guidotti, G.; Kanameishi, D., and Foà, P. P.: Chick embryo heart as a tool for studying cell permeability and insulin action, Am. J. Physiol. 201:863–868, 1961.

Hahn, P., Koldovský, O.; Krěcěk, J.; Martínek, J., and Vacek Z., in Wolstenholme, G. E. W., and O'Connor, M. (eds.): *Ciba Foundation Symposium on Somatic Stability in the Newly Born* (London: J. & A. Churchill, Ltd., 1961), pp. 131–148.

Harding, P. G. R., and Shelley, H. J.: Some effects of intrauterine growth retardation in the foetal rabbit, in *Symposium de laesione foetus intrauterina* (Amsterdam: Excerpta Medica Foundation, 1967).

Havel, R.: Autonomic nervous system and adipose tissue, in *Handbook of Physiology—Adipose Tissue* (Washington, D.C.: American Physiological Society, 1965), pp. 575–582.

Heim, T., and Hull, D.: The blood flow and oxygen consumption of brown adipose tissue in the newborn rabbit. J. Physiol. 186:42–55, 1966.

Huggett, A. St. G.: Maternal control of placental glycogen, J. Physiol. 67:360–371, 1929.

Hull, D., and Segall, M. M.: Distinction of brown from white adipose tissue, Nature. 212:469–472, 1966

Jackson, C. M.: Structural changes when growth is suppressed by undernourishment in the albino rat, Am. J. Anat. 51:347–379, 1932.

Jacquot, R., and Kretchmer, N.: Effect of fetal decapitation on enzymes of glycogen metabolism, J. Biol. Chem. 239:1301–1304, 1964.

Jost, A., and Jacquot, R.: Recherches sur les facteurs endocriniens de la change en glycogène du foie foetale chez le lapin (avec des indications sur le glycogène placentaire), Ann. endocrinol. 16:849–872, 1955.

Keele, D. K., and Kay, J. L.: Plasma free fatty acid and blood sugar levels in newborn infants and their mothers, Pediatrics 37:597–604, 1966.

Koenigsberger, M. R.: Judgment of fetal age. I. Neurological evaluation, Pediat. Clin. North America 13: 823–833, 1966.

Koren, Z., and Shafrir, E.: Placental transfer of free fatty acids in the pregnant rat, Proc. Soc. Exper. Biol. & Med. 116:411–414, 1964.

Kornfeld, R., and Brown, D. H.: The activity of some enzymes of glycogen metabolism in fetal and neonatal guinea pig liver, J. Biol. Chem. 238:1604–1607, 1963.

Leat, W. M. F.: Fatty acid composition of the plasma lipids of newborn and maternal ruminants, Biochem. J. 98:598–603, 1966.

Luckey, T. D.; Mende, T. V., and Pleasants, V.: The physical and chemical characterization of rat's milk, J. Nutrition 54:345–359, 1954.

Manns, J. G., and Boda, J. M.: Effects of ovine growth hormone and prolactin on blood glucose, serum insulin, plasma nonesterified fatty acids and amino nitrogen in sheep, Endocrinology 76:1109–1114, 1965.

McBride, O. W., and Korn, E. D.: Uptake of free fatty acids and chylomicron glycerides by guinea pig mammary gland in pregnancy and lactation, J. Lipid. Res. 5:453–458, 1964.

McCance, R. A.: Severe undernutrition in growing animals, Brit. J. Nutrition 14:59–73, 1960.

McCance, R. A., and Strangeways, W. M. B.: Protein katabolism and oxygen consumption during starvation in infants, young adults and old men, Brit. J. Nutrition 8:21–32, 1954.

McCance, R. A., and Widdowson, E. M.: The effect of lowering the ambient temperature on the metabolism of the newborn pig, J. Physiol. 147:124–134, 1959.

Mitchell, R. G., and Farr, V.: The meaning of maturity and the assessment of maturity at birth. Clin. Develop. Med. 19:83–99, 1965.

Mourek, J.: Concerning the metabolic substrate of central nervous activity during early postnatal development of the rat, Physiol. Bohemoslov. 14:379–382, 1965,a.

Mourek, J.: Oxidative metabolism in the medulla oblongata of the rat in relation to age and metabolic substrates, Physiol. Bohemoslov. 14:502–506, 1965,b.

Naeye, R. L.: Cardiovascular abnormalities in infants malnourished before birth, Biol. Neonat. 8:104–113, 1965.

Naeye, R. L., and Kelly, J. A.: Judgment of fetal age. III. The pathologist's evaluation, Pediat. Clin. North America 13:849–862, 1966.

Needham, J.: *Chemical Embryology* (London: Cambridge University Press, 1931).

Nemeth, A. M.: Glucose-6-phosphatase in the liver of the fetal guinea pig, J. Biol. Chem. 208:773–776, 1954.

Novák, M.; Hahn, P.; Koldovský, O., and Melichar, V.: Postnatal changes in the blood serum content of glycerol and fatty acids in human infants. Biol. Neonat. 7:179–184, 1964.

Novák, M.; Hahn, P.; Koldovský, O., and Melichar, V.: Triglyceride and free fatty acid content of serum, lungs, liver and adipose tissue during postnatal development of the rat, Physiol. Bohemoslov. 14:38–45, 1965.

Novák, M.; Melichar, V.; Hahn, P., and Koldovský, O.: Level of lipids in the blood of newborn infants and the effects of glucose administration, Physiol. Bohemoslov. 10:488–491, 1961.

Novák, M.; Melichar, V.; Hahn, P., and Koldovský, O.: Release of free fatty acids from adipose tissue obtained from newborn infants, J. Lipid. Res. 6:91–95, 1965.

Persson, B., and Gentz, J.: The pattern of blood lipids, glycerol and ketone bodies during the neonatal period, infancy and childhood, Acta paediat. 55:353–362, 1966.

Popják, G., and Beeckmans, M.: Synthesis of cholesterol and fatty acids in foetuses and in mammary glands of pregnant rabbits, Biochem. J. 46:547–561, 1950.

Potter, E. L.: Development of the human glomerulus, Arch. Path. 80:241–255, 1965.

Raben, M. S., and Hollenberg, C. H.: Effect of growth hormone on plasma fatty acids, J. Clin. Invest. 38:484–488, 1959.

Robinson, R. J., and Tizard, J. P. M.: The central nervous system in the newborn. Brit. M. Bull. 22:49–55, 1966.

Satomura, K., and Söderhjelm, L.: Deposition of fatty acids in the newborn in relation to the diet of pregnant guinea pigs, Texas Rep. Biol. & Med. 20:671–679, 1962.

Scopes, J. W.: Hypoglycaemia in childhood, Proc. Roy. Soc. Med. 57:1063, 1964.

Scopes, J. W., and Ahmed, I.: Minimal rates of oxygen consumption in sick and premature newborn infants, Arch. Dis. Childhood 41:407–416, 1966.

Shelley, H. J.: Glycogen reserves and their changes at birth, Brit. M. Bull. 17:137–143, 1961.

Shelley, H. J., and Neligan, G. A.: Neonatal hypoglycaemia, Brit. M. Bull. 22:34–39, 1966.

Short, R. H. D.: Alveolar epithelium in relation to growth of the lung, Phil. Tr. Roy. Soc. (B)234:35–42, 1950.

Smith, C. A.: *The Physiology of the Newborn Infant* (Springfield, Ill.: Charles C Thomas, Publisher, 1959).

Usher, R.; McLean, F., and Scott, K. E.: Judgment of fetal age. II. Clinical significance of gestational age and an objective method for its assessment, Pediat. Clin. North America 13:835–862, 1966.

van Duyne, C. M., and Havel, R. J.: Plasma unesterified fatty acid concentration in fetal and neonatal life, Proc. Soc. Exper. Biol. & Med. 102:599–602, 1959.

van Duyne, C. M.; Havel, R. J., and Felts, J. M.: Placental transfer of palmitic acid —1—C^{14} in rabbits, Am. J. Obst. & Gynec. 84:1069–1074, 1962.

van Duyne, C. M.; Parker, H. R.; Havel, R. J., and Holm, L. W.: Free fatty acid metabolism in fetal and newborn sheep, Am. J. Physiol. 199:987–990, 1960.

van Duyne, C. M.; Parker, H. R., and Holm, L. W.: Metabolism of free fatty acids during perinatal life of lambs, Am. J. Obst. & Gynec. 91:277–285, 1965.

Villee, C. A., and Hagerman, D. D.: Effect of oxygen deprivation on the metabolism of fetal and adult tissues, Am. J. Physiol. 194:457–464, 1958.

Widdas, W. F.: Transport mechanisms in the foetus, Brit. M. Bull. 17:107–111, 1961.

Widdowson, E. M.: Chemical composition of newly born mammals, Nature 166:626–628, 1950.

Widdowson, E. M., and McCance, R. A.: Some effects of accelerating growth, Proc. Roy. Soc. (B)152:188–206, 1960.

Wittels, B., and Bressler, R.: Lipid metabolism in the newborn heart, J. Clin. Invest. 44:1639–1646, 1965.

17

Some Other Aspects of Developmental Physiology

THE PRECEDING CHAPTERS have been concerned primarily with cardiovascular and respiratory functions and with energy metabolism and growth in late foetal and early neonatal life. The subject has been treated almost as if cell differentiation and organogenesis were complete. But this is not so. Growth and development continue throughout this period of life, although less rapidly than in the embryonic period; the dividing line between the two is vague. Most anomalies of development have their origin wholly in embryonic life, other than those especially related to the changes at birth (e.g., the closure of the ductus arteriosus and, perhaps, preductal coarctation of the aorta). There is some basis for believing that each organ or organ-system has a critical period of development, marked by rapid cell differentiation, changes in form and sometimes in function, and by susceptibility to noxious influences which can cause congenital malformations and lead to crippling or death. Yet when we examine more closely the times and features of these critical periods, in different organs and different species, they are found to be widely variable. In some instances, there is good evidence to suggest that crucial changes are subject to hormonal or other physiological influences, as well as being dependent on genetic factors.

Critical Phases in Development
THE HEART

The most critical phase for the development of the heart is in the embryonic period, but it is evident that during foetal and neonatal growth the heart

and peripheral vasculature are continually moulded and adapted as nervous control is established, the systemic blood pressure rises, pulmonary respiration is begun, and pulmonary arterial pressure falls. Presumably, the processes involved are similar to those with which we are more familiar in later life. The high pressure to which the pulmonary arteries are subjected in the last third of gestation in the lamb and calf do not result in medial degeneration, and it is uncertain whether this is simply a question of time or of a difference in the tissues. It is presumably the medial degeneration which results in the fixity of pulmonary hypertension in some children a year or more from birth.

The structural changes in the ventricles after birth at first sight appear to resemble those in adults in which, for instance, the transmural pressures have altered as a result of systemic hypertension or its relief. But this is probably too simple a conclusion, as shown by the fact that in several species the safeguard to the ventricles (afforded by the relatively long refractory period of the atrioventricular node) against premature excitation by atrial irregularities is not yet established at birth (Chapter 14). The morphological and cellular reasons for this need further study. Conversely, a developmental anomaly which arises earlier in life, such as inter-atrial or ventricular septal defect, or a patent ductus arteriosus persisting a week or more from birth, may be repaired by natural processes. These channels may narrow and close spontaneously during the next year or two; the mechanisms responsible for these late corrections of earlier malfunction have not been elucidated.

223

The Lung

The normal growth of the lung appears to be dependent on the availability of space in which it may grow. The best known example of pulmonary hypoplasia is in association with diaphragmatic hernia, when the occupation of part of the pleural cavity by small bowel (probably after it has wholly returned to the abdominal cavity from the omphalocoele) reduces the space available (Cohn, 1939; Liebow and Miller, 1940; Roe and Stephens, 1956; Gruenwald, 1957; Potter, 1962). The reduction in lung weight (as compared with infants of the same size and age) is much greater on the ipsilateral side. Pulmonary hypoplasia is also seen in association with conditions which grossly impair the development of the thoracic cage (anencephaly and spina bifida) as well as other space-occupying lesions, e.g., pleural effusion (Potter and Bohlender, 1941). It also occurs in renal agenesis or with polycystic kidneys, and we may guess that this is because the consequential paucity of amniotic fluid does not permit normal development of the chest cavity. This seems a more likely explanation than a genetic defect causing both renal agenesis and pulmonary hypoplasia by a direct action. It is a proposition which could be put to experimental test by removal of the kidneys of normal foetal animals early in gestation.

The histology of the congenitally hypoplastic lung has been studied extensively, and there is general agreement that the appearance suggests a relative excess of bronchial structures as compared with distal parenchyma. The bronchi are distorted and the terminal airspaces are in many places lined with cuboidal epithelium even at 42 weeks gestation (Butler and Claireaux, 1962). Yet although there is so much bronchial tissue, the number of bronchial branchings is greatly reduced, more so on the ipsilateral side in instances of diaphragmatic hernia, with counts of bronchial branches along axial pathways of half the normal value or less (Areechon and Reid, 1963). Surprisingly, therefore, (as compared with conventional histological appraisal) these measurements show that the principal failure must have been in development of the bronchial tree; the alveoli were relatively less affected. It was concluded that bronchial development was arrested at a stage normally reached at 10–12 weeks gestation. It would be interesting to know whether such a lung retains a sufficient potential for further bronchial, as well as alveolar, development after birth to make up for what was lost. Most human infants with pulmonary hypoplasia either die in the immediate neonatal period or survive indefinitely, so recourse must be had to animal experiments to study the question.

These observations are interesting because they suggest that limitation of space for growth, even during the foetal stage, can cause a gross modification of structure. The final form of expression of these congenital malformations may not be entirely the direct result of the agent (genetic or otherwise) which was responsible for the primary maldevelopment, but may be in part the consequence of factors operating later in gestation.

The Neuromuscular Junction, Skeletal Muscle, and Spinal Reflexes

The activity of spinal reflexes and responses to cortical stimulation are dependent on adequate development of the peripheral nerves and muscles. The nerves are excitable before myelinization begins but conduction velocity is then low. Myelinization occurs at a rather leisurely pace in man (from 12–22 weeks gestation to achieve an axonal diameter of about 2.5μ; Gamble, 1966), rather more rapidly in sheep (from about 80 days gestation onward; Änggård and Ottoson, 1963), and in the rat even more rapidly but wholly after birth. Similarly, in the kitten the conduction velocities of peripheral nerves increase greatly after birth.

The normal development of the skeletal muscles depends upon their innervation. Thus after denervation in foetal rats, muscle spindles are not formed (probably because of the absence of sensory nerve fibres), motor end-plates do not appear (Zelená, 1962), and the entire length of the muscle fibre remains sensitive to acetylcholine, instead of the neuromuscular junction only as in the adult (Diamond and Miledi, 1962). In the kitten, rat, and mouse at the time of birth, all the skeletal muscles studied have a similar twitch speed (Buller, 1966). Over a period of several weeks after birth there is a progressive shortening of the contraction time of those muscles which are destined to become "fast" as compared with those which remain "slow"; the former are innervated by motor nerves which finally attain a relatively higher conduction velocity. From these and cross-innervation experiments it appears likely that the motor neurones are functionally differentiated before the muscles which they innervate, and that it is the central organization of the neurones which determines the pattern of "fast" and "slow" skeletal muscle. It would be interesting to know whether this differentiation of function occurs before birth in species which are more mature on delivery, such as the guinea pig, sheep, or rhesus monkey.

The development of spinal reflexes has been studied most extensively in cats (Malcolm, 1955; Skoglund, 1960a), because this species was chosen by Sherrington and his colleagues as the subject of their original investigations of the integrative action of the central nervous system in the adult. Skoglund (1960b) concluded that γ-efferent control was developed at 17–20 days after birth, moving in a cranio-caudal and proximo-distal direction on the trunk and limbs, as judged by the reactions to electrical stimulation. This process naturally influenced the development of the tonic stretch reflexes, decerebrate rigidity, and the fine coordination of locomotion. By 3 weeks of age the adult pattern of innervation was already established, as determined by intracellular recordings from spinal neurones of potentials generated by volleys applied to afferent and efferent nerve fibres (Eccles, Shealy, and Willis, 1963), but the central latency was still double that in the adult. The relatively smaller size of the motorneurones and paucity of dendrites probably accounted for the increased size of the monosynaptic excitatory-post-synaptic potentials. The gradual appearance of the different reflex mechanisms correlated well with the maturity of the peripheral nerves and of their central connexions (Skoglund and Romero, 1966).

In 1902, Huber drew attention to the abundant distribution of muscle spindles in the intercostal muscles and suggested that they might be concerned in the nervous regulation of breathing. This hypothesis has been abundantly confirmed (Critchlow and von Euler, 1963; Sears, 1964). There is no doubt that the γ-efferent mechanism is closely involved in the fine adjustment of the intercostal muscles in respiratory movement in the adult. Section of the cervical and thoracic dorsal roots weakens respiratory movements in animals and man. Yet newborn kittens can maintain an O_2 consumption of as much as 60 ml/kg min (Table 50, p. 194) which involves an extreme degree of hyperpnoea. It remains to be seen whether the γ-efferent mechanism to the respiratory muscles is already developed at birth in this and other species.

THE CEREBRAL CORTEX

The idea of a critical period of development in the brain was first clearly enunciated by Flexner, who gave a succinct summary of the evidence available in 1954. The differentiation of neuroblasts into neurones in the cerebral cortex, particularly of the guinea pig, was examined in considerable detail. He defined a critical period at 41–45 days gestation (i.e., 0.61–0.67 of term), at which time cell processes (probably dendrites) and Nissl bodies first appear and the nucleus ceases to increase in volume. Simultaneously, there is a rapid increase in the activity of many enzymes, including ATP-ase, cytochrome oxidase, and succinic dehydrogenase; the activity of acetylcholinesterase begins to increase a few days earlier. These cytological and chemical changes are accompanied by the earliest evidences of function, as judged by muscular responses to cortical stimulation and the appearance of spontaneous electrical potentials of cortical origin. Spontaneous electroencephalographic activity first appears at 46 days gestation in the foetal guinea pig, and becomes continuous at 55 days. In the pig, a similar series of changes in the cerebral cortex are seen at the beginning of the last trimester, whereas in the rat they do not occur until about 10 days postnatally (Flexner, 1954; Bŭres, 1957). Microscopic and other studies of the cerebral cortex suggest that the corresponding period in man is 12–16 weeks gestational age, and in the cat during the second to fourth week after birth (Bergström, 1962; Pappas and Purpura, 1966; Purpura, Shofer, Housepian, and Noback, 1966). Intracellular recordings from the sensorimotor cortex of the newborn kitten show postsynaptic potentials of unusually long latency and duration, as compared with adults (Purpura, Shofer and Scarff, 1965). And the conduction velocity of pyramidal neuronal axons increases greatly after the first 3 weeks postnatally, some while after myelinization has begun. In sheep, cortical activity first appears at 80–100 days gestation (Bernhard, Kaiser, and Kolmodin, 1959). This is the age at which epileptiform cortical activity can first be evoked by electrical stimulation, although it can be excited by administration of metrazol earlier (Bernhard, Kaiser, and Kolmodin, 1962). A steady positive potential between the pial surface of the cortex and a reference electrode can first be detected at about 60 days gestation (Eidelberg, Kolmodin, and Meyerson, 1965).

Table 54 summarizes these observations on the development of cortical functional activity in different species. A word of warning must be given, that this summary depends on the interpretation of work using somewhat different criteria of activity in different species, although where a more thorough assessment has been made (e.g., by Flexner using histological and biochemical as well as func-

TABLE 54.—PROBABLE CRITICAL PERIOD OF
DEVELOPMENT FOR CEREBRAL CORTICAL ACTIVITY IN
DIFFERENT SPECIES

		PROPORTION OF FULL TERM
Man	12–16 weeks gestation	0.3–0.4
Pig	~80 days gestation	0.66
Sheep	80–100 days gestation	0.54–0.68
Cat	2–4 weeks after birth	>1
Guinea pig	41–45 days gestation	0.61–0.67
Rat	10 days after birth	>1

For criteria and sources see the text.

tional evidence in the guinea pig) the agreement is good. There are some notable gaps in the evidence available. The rabbit appears to have been relatively neglected as compared with other species; judging from its poor neuromuscular coordination (other than of its respiratory muscles) at birth, we may guess that its cortical development will prove to take place mainly after birth, like the cat and rat (Table 54). Conversely, we would guess that the cortex of the rhesus monkey would be already well developed at birth. Esquivel de Gallardo, Fleischman, and Ramirez de Arrellano (1964) reported that the electroencephalogram of the monkey foetus a few days before term showed a small spontaneous activity, increasing greatly with arousal on delivery. Yet the contralateral hemiplegia caused by hemidecortication of a newborn rhesus monkey lasts only a short while (Peacock and Coombs, 1965). Other areas must take over the function of those that were removed, when the operation is performed at a sufficiently early age. So evidence of functional activity in the cortex does not necessarily imply that allocation of function to a specific area is as yet rigidly determined.

In those species which are mature at birth (e.g., guinea pig, sheep) the development of the cerebral cortex, by Flexner's criteria, occurs well before term. But man is relatively immature at birth, despite development of cortical function relatively early in gestation. In man, the development of particular reflex motor responses to appropriate stimuli is spread out over many months pre- and postnatally (see e.g., Bergström and Bergström, 1963; Humphrey, 1964; Robinson and Tizard, 1966). Whereas some reflexes appear to be solely dependent on conceptual age, the development of others is contingent upon the time of delivery and hence, presumably, on usage.

SEXUAL DIFFERENTIATION OF THE BRAIN

The concept of a critical phase of neuronal development seems to have meant different things to different authors. To Flexner it meant a point of time at which the broad outline of cellular development approached completion, the activity of neuronal enzymes rapidly increased, and evidence of function was first detectable. To others it has implied a time when neuronal development was most likely to be disrupted, a period of enhanced vulnerability. To others, again, it has implied an epoch during which some change takes place in the nervous system which, once passed, can never be corrected. A good example of this is provided by the mechanism for the determination of sex behaviour.

During adult life the hormones of the gonads appear to act upon the central nervous system in an excitatory or inhibitory way, and thus take part in the neural regulation of gonadotrophic secretions and in the determination of the overt expression of sexual behaviour. But during foetal or early neonatal life, differing in this respect with species, they appear to act inductively on the as yet undifferentiated brain, to give rise to a male or female type of neural apparatus. The first suggestion that this might be so came from the work of Pfeiffer (1936), who showed that transplantation of testicular tissue into newborn female rats led to sterility and absence of the oestrous cycle in adult life. Conversely, castration of the newborn male led to an adult in which there was cyclical release of gonadotrophin, as shown by its effect on ovarian transplants in the anterior chamber of the eye. From these and other experimental results, it was suggested that newborn male and female rats possess an undifferentiated neural mechanism, which becomes differentiated in the former by the action of the testicular hormone. Subsequent evidence for this conclusion has been well documented in recent reviews (e.g., Harris, 1964; see also Harris and Levine, 1965). What concerns us here is the time and place at which sexual differentiation is imprinted on the brain of different species. In the rat, this occurs after birth, experiments are thus considerably easier and probably more is known in this than other species. Administration of testosterone to a female rat 1–10 days from birth (but not thereafter) causes masculinization of the nervous system, as shown by subsequent lack of a rhythmic mechanism regulating gonadotrophic secretion and by male patterns of behaviour, both sexual and otherwise. Conversely, castration of a male rat during the first 1–2 days from birth (but not thereafter) results in the retention of female characteristics. The reason for this difference in the critical period for neural differentiation in males and females is still under investigation. In the guinea pig, the critical period is probably between days 30–65 of foetal life, commensurate with the development of other functions of the nervous system in this species (compare Tables 33, p. 129 and 54, p. 226). The anterior pituitary does not undergo sexual differentiation, since transplantation of male anterior lobe tissue beneath the hypothalamus of hypophysectomized female rats enabled female reproductive function to continue (Harris and Jacobsohn, 1952). Hence the site of action is probably the hypothalamus, which controls anterior lobe function by the liberation of releasing factors (probably polypeptides; Harris, Reed, and Fawcett, 1966) from hypothalamic nerve-endings; these reach the gland through the hypophysial portal blood supply.

This is a fascinating story and it suggests that the critical period for sexual differentiation of the brain may in a given species approximate in time to that defined as a critical period for cortical neurones by Flexner. Indeed, it would not be altogether surprising if the period during which hypothalamic neurones (if these are indeed the cells responsible) are approaching full size and their enzymes are maturing, is that at which they are most susceptible to environmental influences, including the level of circulatory testosterone. The mechanism by which the cells are changed arouses one's curiosity. One possible analogy is narcotic addiction, in which some other cells of the central nervous system become dependent upon a relatively constant concentration of a complex molecule. In this instance, however, tolerance is lost on gradual withdrawal (even in infants who have acquired tolerance during foetal life), whereas sexual differentiation of the brain, once acquired, is retained throughout life.

This particular example of a critical period of neural development is one which is susceptible to the design of exact experiments in animals by which the site of action may be located and the mechanisms defined. There is another example, probably of less immediate importance to the newborn human infant than to some other species, and more difficult to study. This is the recognition of its mother or foster-parent by a young bird or animal after birth. This is particularly necessary to newborn fledglings or animals which are mobile, and the mechanism is obviously dependent on the proper development of distance receptors. Thus,

in instances in which recognition is established rapidly after birth, the infant must be born in a relatively mature condition. This would seem to imply a more advanced state of neural development than that required for sexual differentiation. Yet it may still be a critical period for survival in some species.

To summarize, then, differentiation and development of function is a process continuing throughout the embryonic, foetal, and the neonatal period, but varying in point of time relative to birth in different species. The processes which influence development may vary from the quite simple consequences of internal or external pressures (in the circulation and heart or upon the lungs) to the more subtle effects of hormones or the integrative action of the central nervous system. And it may well be worth considering whether there are other examples in any of these categories still to be discovered. The idea that normal development during embryonic and foetal life is in part dependent on the functional physiology of each successive epoch is worth further detailed examination in respect of each organ system.

The Integration of Physiological Responses in Different Species

So we approach what appears at first as a conflict between two different points of view. On the one hand, there is the proposition that, although in many species the development of various functions is mature long before birth, these functions are normally inhibited or held in abeyance until delivery. On the other hand, it is suggested that physiological function during foetal life may, especially in some instances, directly affect development. The conflict is perhaps more apparent than real. The foetus *in utero* is normally well insulated from sensory stimuli, other than occasional mechanical and acoustic sensations (including the uterine souffle). It is, therefore, not surprising that, apart from quickening movements, respiratory and locomotor activity is small until arousal after birth. Yet this limited amount of movement, superimposed on some degree of resting muscle tone, may well be sufficient to influence development. When we come to consider the autonomic nervous and the hypothalamic-pituitary glandular systems, some parts are active and others appear to be relatively inactive. In the foetus, heart rate and cardiac output are high, suggesting considerable activity in the cardiac branches of the sympathetic system, while it seems very likely that the sympathetic efferent nerves to brown adipose tissue are quiescent. (Both these propositions are susceptible of direct test, but neither has yet been examined.) Similarly, there is evidence for secretion of growth and thyrotrophic hormones in foetal life, but urinary secretion is copious and dilute, suggesting that secretion of antidiuretic hormone is minimal and/or that the concentrating power of the kidney is limited. Perhaps the situation can be summarised in the conclusion that certain physiological functions are especially highly developed in late foetal and early neonatal life, to a degree which may equal or even exceed those in adults of the same species (e.g., as regards the circulation and the capacity for heat production), whereas other functions (particularly locomotor) are less mature.

When we now compare the relative development of different species at birth, some interesting points emerge. For instance, various of the integrative functions of the central nervous system may be separated by choice of species or of individuals, without other experimental interference. Shield (1966) has shown that the newborn of a species of marsupial (the quokka or *Setonix Brachyurus*) are wholly poikilothermic at birth, unlike normal eutherian mammals (Table 50, p. 194). The young quokka or "joey" spends about 180 days from birth in the maternal pouch, growing from 0.4 to 500 Gm. During the first 100 days it does not increase its O_2 consumption on exposure to cold, but by the time it leaves the pouch its minimal O_2 consumption in a neutral thermal environment has risen to 17 ml/kg min (comparable to that of a 10-day-old rhesus monkey of the same size) and it is homeothermic. So in this species at birth the mechanism for temperature control by heat production is absent, although the infant breathes, feeds, and survives indefinitely. An anencephalic human infant studied by Cross, Gustavson, Hill, and Robinson (1966) also was a poikilotherm; it was acyanotic, appeared well, and breathed without dyspnoea for several hours from birth. Yet most anencephalic infants die within a day or two, and this one was no exception, suggesting that without proper integration of other functions (e.g., possibly hypothalamic control of the circulation and metabolism) independent survival after birth is not possible. Presumably, so far as they are necessary, these functions are already sufficiently developed in the quokka "joey" at birth.

All the species with which we have been concerned have a common mammalian origin, perhaps some 60 million years ago (see frontispiece). So although marsupials, mice, and men belong to different orders of mammals they are originally of the same stuff, and the physical problems which they face after birth are of the same kind, varying only in degree. A phylogenetic chart of the type shown in the frontispiece must be interpreted with caution. The mere passage of time does not necessarily imply an equal degree of differentiation from their common ancestor by all species. The solutions to the problem of survival, of the species and the individual, which we find today in modern mammals show a very wide range of variation, in body size, in length of gestation, care of the young, and habit of life. So it is very natural to wonder to what extent physiological observations on other species are applicable to man. There is no simple answer to this question. It is plain that a physiological mechanism, if demonstrated in more than one mammalian species, probably applies to all, provided it is not related to a specialised adaptation (e.g., in a hibernating or a diving aquatic mammal). Yet any analogy must be drawn with care and with knowledge of the natural history of the species. For instance, the observation that undernourishment of the rat for the first 3 weeks after birth leads to permanent stunting (McCance, 1962) has suggested that a similar effect may be seen in human infants. But in the latter the period of most rapid growth and cellular differentiation is already passed at birth. If the same phenomenon does occur in man it is most likely between the tenth and thirtieth week of gestation, i.e., as a result of malnutrition *in utero*. There is no clear evidence that severe malnutrition in children after birth causes permanent retardation in growth (see e.g., Garrow and Pike, 1967).

Biological measurements before or shortly after birth in different species fall roughly into two classes:

1. Those in which there is comparatively little variation, as in body temperature and (in the adult) blood pressure, in the plasma levels of ions, proteins, and glucose, in the pH and partial pressure of O_2 and CO_2 in the blood of normal foetuses or after birth. These represent the conditions necessary for an internal environment most favourable for cell life and multiplication. It is reasonable to suppose that the general mechanisms required for their maintenance are common to all mammals, and that these must be present at the minimum age of viability for any species at birth.

2. Those in which there is great variation, which comprise mainly external form and structure, the framework for the cells of the body, adapted to its particular habit of life, carnivorous or herbivorous,

predatory or slothful, in a temperate or exacting climate. So we expect and find great variations in size, basal metabolic rate, and capacity for temperature regulation, in the normal period of gestation, in longevity and the usual number of young, and in the degree of maturity at normal birth. Yet even within these wide variations there appears to be some constraint. For instance, small animals usually have a shorter expectation of life, a shorter period of gestation, and more young at a single birth than larger ones of other species. On the other hand, relative maturity at birth does not appear to be related to size (the newborn rabbit and human infant are less mature than the guinea pig or rhesus monkey) or to the mammalian order to which a species belongs.

We may expect that a careful study of the physiology of different mammalian species at the minimum age for viability would demonstrate the presence of the minimum control mechanisms required for survival, integrated through the lower parts of the central nervous system. Yet apart from man, we know comparatively little about the consequences of premature delivery.

Most human infants delivered at 36 weeks gestation (0.9 of term) survive, some survive when delivered at 30 weeks (0.75 of term), and very occasionally as early as 24 weeks (0.6 of term). So in the human species, when conditions are favourable and with good nursing care, the essential requirements can be met almost as soon as the lungs become expansible. In non-human primates we know most about the rhesus monkey; in this species survival at 150 days gestation (0.9 of term) is usual, and survival as early as 135 days gestation (0.8 of term) has been recorded. So, bearing in mind the much smaller numbers available for study as compared with man, survival after premature birth would appear to follow a similar pattern. But in the sheep, although the normal duration of pregnancy (147 days) is not very different from that in the rhesus monkey (168 days), premature delivery at 140 days gestation or less (0.95 of term) is associated with a very high mortality rate, rising to 100% at 0.9 of term (Dawes and Parry, 1965). This appears to be a remarkable species difference, and needs further study. It is also worth mentioning that premature delivery also seems to be less common than in the rhesus monkey or man. I do not know of large scale systematic studies of premature deliveries in other species, although the rabbit is said to be capable of survival after delivery at 29 days gestation (0.94 of term).

Until these figures are established with greater certainty, there seems little point in attempting a detailed comparison of the minimum physiological requirements for survival in different species. Yet this is a field which permits study of the integration of physiological mechanisms under conditions different from that in adult life, in circumstances which can be less complex and, provided that the problem of dealing with very small animals can be overcome, more susceptible of experimental manipulation. The period when physiological function first emerges is one which offers special opportunities.

REFERENCES

Änggård, L., and Ottoson, D.: Observations on the functional development of the neuromuscular apparatus in fetal sheep, Exper. Neurol. 7:249–304, 1963.

Areechon, W., and Reid, L.: Hypoplasia of the lung with congenital diaphragmatic hernia, Brit. M. J. 1:230–233, 1963.

Bergström, R. M.: Prenatal development of motor functions, Ann. chir. et gynaec. Fenniae Suppl. 112:1–48, 1962.

Bergström, R. M., and Bergström, L.: Prenatal development of stretch reflex functions and brain stem activity in the human, Ann. chir. et gynaec. Fenniae Suppl. 117:1–21, 1963.

Bernard, C. G.; Kaiser, I. H., and Kolmodin, G. M.: On the development of cortical activity in fetal sheep, Acta physiol. scandinav. 47:333–349, 1959.

Bernard, C. G.; Kaiser, I. H., and Kolmodin, G. M.: On the epileptogenic properties of the fetal brain, Acta paediat. 51:81–87, 1962.

Buller, A. J.: Developmental physiology of the neuromuscular system, Brit. M. Bull. 22:45–48, 1966.

Büres, J.: The ontogenetic development of steady potential differences in the cerebral cortex in animals, Electroencephalog. & Clin. Neurophysiol. 9:121–130, 1957.

Butler, N., and Claireaux, A. E.: Congenital diaphragmatic hernia as a cause of perinatal mortality, Lancet 1:659–663, 1962.

Cohn, R.: Factors affecting the postnatal growth of the lung, Anat. Rec. 75:195–205, 1939.

Critchlow, V., and von Euler, C.: Intercostal muscle spindle activity and its γ-motor control, J. Physiol. 168:820–847, 1963.

Cross, K. W.; Gustavson, J.; Hill, J. R., and Robinson, D. C.: Thermoregulation in an anencephalic infant as inferred from its metabolic rate under hypothermic and normal conditions, Clin. Sc. 31:449–460, 1966.

Dawes, G. S., and Parry, H. B.: Premature delivery and survival in lambs, Nature 207:330, 1965.

Diamond, J., and Miledi, R.: A study of foetal and newborn rat muscle fibres, J. Physiol. 162:393–408, 1962.

Eccles, R. M.; Shealy, C. N., and Willis, W. D.: Patterns of innervation of kitten motorneurones, J. Physiol. 165:392–402, 1963.

Eidelberg, E.; Kolmodin, G. M., and Meyerson, B. A.: Ontogenesis of steady potential and direct cortical response in fetal sheep brain, Exper. Neurol. 12:198–214, 1965.

Esquivel de Gallardo, F. O.; Fleischman, R. W., and Ramirez de Arrellano, M. I. R.: Electroencephalogram of the monkey fetus in utero and changes in it at birth, Exper. Neurol. 9:73–84, 1964.

Flexner, L. B.: Enzymatic and Functional Patterns of the Developing Mammalian Brain, in Waelsch, H. (ed.): *Biochemistry of the Developing Nervous System* (New York: Academic Press, Inc., 1954), pp. 281–300.

Gamble, H. J.: Further electron microscope studies of human foetal peripheral nerves, J. Anat. 100:487–502, 1966.

Garrow, J. S., and Pike, M. C.: The long-term prognosis of severe infantile malnutrition, Lancet 1:1–4, 1967.

Gruenwald, P.: Hypoplasia of the lungs, J. Mt. Sinai Hosp. 24:913–919, 1957.

Harris, G. W.: Sex hormones, brain development and brain function, Endocrinology 75:627–648, 1964.

Harris, G. W., and Jacobsohn, D.: Functional grafts of the anterior pituitary gland, Proc. Roy. Soc., London, B 139:263–276, 1952.

Harris, G. W., and Levine, S.: Sexual differentiation of the brain and its experimental control, J. Physiol. 181: 379–400, 1965.

Harris, G. W.; Reed, M., and Fawcett, C. P.: Hypothalamic releasing factors and the control of anterior pituitary function, Brit. M. Bull. 22:266–272, 1966.

Huber, J. C.: Neuro-muscular spindles in the intercostal muscles of the cat, Am. J. Anat. 1:520, 1902.

Humphrey, T.: Some Correlations Between the Appearance of Human Fetal Reflexes and the Development of the Nervous System, in Purpura, D. P., and Schadé, J. P.: *Growth and Maturation of the Brain.* Progress in Brain Research (Amsterdam: Elsevier Press, Inc., 1966) Vol. 4, pp. 93–135.

Liebow, A. A., and Miller, H. C.: Congenital defects in the diaphragm, Am. J. Path. 16:707–738, 1940.

Malcolm, J. L.: The Appearance of Inhibition in the Developing Spinal Cord of Kittens, in Waelsch, H. (ed.): *Biochemistry of the Developing Nervous System* (New York: Academic Press, Inc., 1955), pp. 104–109.

McCance, R. A.: Food, growth and time, Lancet 2:621–626, 671–675, 1962.

Pappas, G. D., and Purpura, D. P.: Electron Microscopy of Immature Human and Feline Neocortex, in Purpura, D. P., and Schadé, J. P.: *Growth and Maturation of the Brain.* Progress in Brain Research (Amsterdam: Elsevier Press, Inc., 1966), Vol. 4, pp. 176–186.

Peacock, J. H., and Coombs, C. M.: Retrograde cell degeneration in diencephalic and other structures after hemidecortication of rhesus monkeys, Exper. Neurol. 11:367–399, 1965.

Pfeiffer, C. A.: Sexual differences of the hypophyses and their determination by the gonads, Am. J. Anat. 58: 195–225, 1936.

Potter, E. L.: *Pathology of the Fetus and the Newborn* (2d ed.; Chicago: Year Book Publishers, Inc., 1962).

Potter, E. L., and Bohlender, G. P.: Intrauterine respiration in relation to development of the fetal lung: With report of two unusual anomalies of the respiratory system, Am. J. Obst. & Gynec. 42:14–22, 1941.

Purpura, D. P.; Shofer, R. J.; Housepian, E. M., and Noback, C. R.: Comparative Ontogenesis of Structure —Function Relations in Cerebral and Cerebellar Cortex, in Purpura, D. P., and Schadé, J. P.: *Growth and Maturation of the Brain.* Progress in Brain Research (Amsterdam: Elsevier Press, Inc., 1966), vol. 4, pp. 187–221.

Purpura, D. P.; Shofer, R. J., and Scarff, T.: Properties of synaptic activities and spike potentials of neurons in immature neocortex, J. Neurophysiol. 28:925–942, 1965.

Robinson, R. J., and Tizard, J. P. M.: The central nervous system in the new-born, Brit. M. Bull. 22:49–55, 1966.

Roe, B. R., and Stephens, H. B.: Congenital diaphragmatic hernia and hypoplastic lung, J. Thoracic Surg. 32:279–290, 1956.

Sears, T. A.: Efferent discharges in alpha and fusimotor fibres of intercostal nerves of the cat, J. Physiol. 174: 295–315, 1964.

Shield, J.: Oxygen consumption during pouch development of the macropod marsupial *Setonix Brachyurus*, J. Physiol. 187:257–270, 1966.

Skoglund, S.: On the postnatal development of postural mechanisms as revealed by electromyography and myography in decerebrate kittens, Acta physiol. scandinav. 49:299–317, 1960,a.

Skoglund, S.: The activity of muscle receptors in the kitten, Acta physiol. scandinav. 50:203–221, 1960,b.

Skoglund, S., and Romero, C.: Postnatal growth of spinal nerves and roots, Acta physiol. scandinav. 66:Suppl. 260, 1966.

Zelená, J.: In Gutmann E. (ed.): *The Denervated Muscle* (Prague: Czechoslovak Academy of Sciences, 1962).

Appendix:
Some Experimental Methods

THE METHODS MENTIONED in early chapters will be less familiar to some readers than to those who regularly work with foetuses and flowmeters. There is no adequate account readily available in the literature, so a synopsis is given here.

Sheep: Management and Delivery for Acute Experiments

In order to provide a steady supply of pregnant sheep throughout spring, ewes are introduced into a field with a ram from late September for the next 3–4 months (in England). It is tempting to try to extend the period of experimental work by using sheep with two breeding seasons a year (e.g., Dorset Horns, but these are expensive) or by hormonal treatment (but this also is expensive and not yet wholly reliable). On the other hand, with reasonable planning a limited period of intensive experimentation has something to be said for it; this book is being written between seasons. It is convenient to add a new group of ewes to the ram every two weeks, usually 5–10 in number but varied according to estimated future needs. The oestrus cycle is 16–17 days in sheep, so most of the new group will be tupped during the first 2 weeks after they have been introduced. A harness holding a coloured dye is strapped around the ram's chest, so that when a ewe is tupped her fleece is marked. Each ewe is identified by a numbered ear-tag, and also by the same number stencilled on her fleece to aid identification at a distance. The shepherd inspects the flock once a day and notes which, if any, ewe is freshly tupped. The colour of the dye is changed once a month so that any ewe which is tupped a

second time (after an infertile first mating) can be spotted. Up to about 115 days gestation, the variation in foetal weights is small and the rate of weight gain is large, so that the duration of gestation can readily be checked on delivery if the characteristics of the breed are known. Measurements of crown-rump length can also be used but do not appear to improve discrimination. After 115 days, the individual variation in weights becomes larger, but there are many external features (such as the thickness and markings of the skin and the development of the fleece and hoofs) which are used to check the observational accuracy of the shepherd.

Radiological examination is helpful in confirming pregnancy and in determining the number of foetuses from about 50 days gestation onwards (Ardran and Brown, 1964). Using a standard apparatus, so that distortion due to the distance of the foetus from the film is minimized, the duration of gestation can usually be estimated to within ± 5 days from 75–115 days gestational age, and with a rather larger possible error thereafter. In some breeds of sheep the fleece is so thick and the body so massive that it is not easy to be sure of pregnancy, without vaginal or rectal examination, until near term when the mammary glands begin to swell. When we first started doing experiments on pregnant sheep each was radiographed to confirm pregnancy and gestational age. This proved an uneconomic proposition, not so much on account of the cost of plates, but because of the numbers of men and the time required and because the less the ewes are handled the better (see p. 232). Most commercial flocks have a high fertility rate and, provided that one does not use an infertile ram (a misfortune which soon becomes apparent), infertile matings are uncommon. Radiological examination is now reserved for special circumstances as, for instance, when a twin pregnancy is essential for the experiment. Most breeds of sheep have been selected for multiple pregnancy, so that the twinning rate in many flocks is 80–100%, triplets are not at all uncommon, and I have seen two sets of quintuplets in the last 15 years. The presence of twins is not unfavourable to the experimental physiologist unless they are large toward term and in the same horn of the uterus. Otherwise it is usually possible to do two experiments. When there is more than one large foetus in a horn, and particularly if there are triplets (two in one horn and one in the other), the blood supply to the first-born may become impaired by the pressure of a second foetus *in utero;* it may then be better to deliver and abandon the others to ensure at least one good preparation. There are often small communications between the circulations of two foetuses which share one or two cotyledons in common, a fact which must be remembered when giving drugs which are not rapidly destroyed, or in some types of experiment on the circulation.

Towards term sheep are peculiarly susceptible to a disease called toxaemia of pregnancy, but probably different from that in man (Parry, 1950). This condition is precipitated by abnormal handling, removal from the normal pasture, or abrupt deprivation of food (as occasioned by a heavy snowfall). The resultant deterioration in maternal condition usually takes a few days to develop. If ewes near term are to be brought in from a farm this should be done as soon as possible before use in an acute experiment. They may be accustomed to handling for chronic experiments.

Sheep are also liable to develop bloat if given green food or hay within 24 hours of anaesthesia. Even when fed only on solid food the stomachs sometimes become distended with gas, and so one must always keep an eye on the abdominal girth. The condition is quickly relieved by inserting a tube or trochar (Hardy, 1874), which Shepherd Oak is said to have used "with a dexterity that would have graced a hospital surgeon."

The general anaesthetics in most common use for acute experiments are pentobarbitone (Nembutal) and chloralose. Anaesthesia with pentobarbitone can be induced by transcutaneous puncture of an external jugular vein with a dose of about 30 mg/kg, but it is then usually wise to introduce a venous catheter since further additional doses will be required when the depth of anaesthesia

decreases after 30–45 minutes. Some commercial solutions of pentobarbitone contain as a solvent propylene glycol which causes haemolysis and haematuria in sheep, and these should be avoided (Potter, 1958). Chloralose anaesthesia is usually induced by running in a 1–2% solution, warmed to increase solubility, through a jugular catheter introduced under local anaesthesia. An initial dose of 40 mg/kg is usually sufficient to maintain anaesthesia for 2–3 hours early in pregnancy, after which a further dose of 10 mg/kg may be required at intervals of 1–2 hours. Toward term an initial dose of 30 mg/kg is sufficient. These doses are less than those usually used in cats or dogs (60–70 mg/kg) and very much less than those observed by Bass and Buckley (1966) to depress ventricular function in dogs (>100 mg/kg). Table 48 (p. 178) shows that cardiac output was similar in adult sheep unanaesthetised or lightly anaesthetised with chloralose. In general, the use of chloralose leads to maternal respiratory alkalosis, well maintained arterial pressure, and lively cardiovascular reflexes with some peripheral vasoconstriction, while pentobarbitone often gives a preparation with some degree of hypoventilation and peripheral vasodilatation.

It is, of course, essential to maintain a clear airway from the onset of anaesthesia, by inserting an endotracheal tube or by tracheotomy. Sheep are very liable to regurgitate stomach contents and also produce thick bronchial mucus. A Rahn-Otis end-tidal gas sampler, with measurement of Po_2 and Pco_2 has, in general, proved a more useful guide to maternal condition than continuous measurement of arterial pressure, although obviously there are circumstances when both are desirable. Sheep do not tolerate a supine position well, and even when placed on their sides under general anaesthesia there is usually extensive atelectasis in the lower parts of the lungs at postmortem. They are large pronograde animals, and the unusual posture in which they are put for convenience of surgery places both ventilation and perfusion of the lungs at a disadvantage. It is, therefore, not surprising that the arterial Po_2 can be reduced from 85–95 mm Hg (unanaesthetised and erect) to 65–90 mm Hg when pregnant, anaesthetised, and laid on one side. It is unnecessary, and may even be undesirable, to tie a carotid artery for taking blood samples or measuring pressure. In sheep the internal carotids are vestigial and the external carotids provide the main supply to the brain via the carotid rete, flow in the basilar artery normally being in a caudal direction (Baldwin and Bell, 1963). The medial plantar artery is easily accessible beneath the retinaculum just above the forehock. If a yet larger vessel is required, the brachial artery is more accessible than the femoral in adult sheep.

The alternatives to general anaesthesia for caesarean section are local or spinal anaesthesia. Access to the lower part of the spinal canal in the sheep is possible only at the lumbosacral space, at or just below the level of the iliac crest, with the needle directed obliquely cephalad and the spine extended. For some purposes, conventional local anaesthetics have too transient an effect. In acute experiments, Huggett and his colleagues used alcohol. Alternatively, there are local anaesthetics with a long duration of action suitable for use in animals if not in man (Davies, 1963).

There are many ways of delivering a sheep by caesarean section. It may be partially immersed in a warm saline bath (as first described for goats by Huggett, 1927, and used by Barcroft for sheep) in order that the foetus, once delivered, may remain in a warm fluid environment. Or the ewe may be placed on the floor or a table and the foetus delivered alongside her and kept warm by other means. This makes cineangiography (as first used by Barclay, Barcroft, Barron, Franklin and Prichard in 1938–1939) a practical possibility; it also facilitates other operations upon the foetus and the intracardiac localization of catheters by radiology. After various trials, I and my colleagues have used for the last few years for acute experiments an operating table 3¼ feet high and 3 × 6½ feet wide, with an aluminum top which can be removed for cleaning. The ewe is placed on it on her side, and an abdominal incision is made approximately in the midline but so as to avoid the swollen abdominal veins. This incision is carried down to the mammary tissue, and the abdominal wall and peritoneum is slit open behind the mammary glands to the pubis to minimize pressure on the uterus when it is partially delivered. The length of this incision is of some importance and is adjusted to the size of the uterus; if it is extended too far cephalad the other abdominal viscera will deliver themselves. Some authors have marsupialized the uterus to the abdominal incision to prevent this. A secondary (foetal) table is then clamped to large horizontal bars running between the two front vertical supports of the operating table. It can thus be adjusted laterally. It slopes slightly toward the mother's abdominal midline (to drain amniotic fluid into a gutter) at a height of 4 inches above the operating table. For lambs at term the dimensions of the foetal table top are 44 × 12 inches; for immature lambs one of 30 × 12 inches is adequate. These table tops are slotted on the outer sides so that uprights can be inserted to hold manometers, and they have cleats to hold cords; heating elements underneath maintain the aluminum top at about 40°C (the rectal temperature of normal sheep). The umbilical cord is covered with a warm saline pack on delivery, and this and as much of the foetus as possible is covered with a cheap cotton wool substitute to minimize heat loss. Additional heat by radiation is provided to exposed parts. Rectal and oesophageal temperatures are recorded; it is surprising how much the exposed forepart of a foetus can cool while the hindpart remains warm. The ewe, if anything, tends to become too hot from the lights and electronic equipment close at hand, even in an English laboratory. She is adapted to a cold environment and has a heavy fleece, so as soon as she is anaesthetised most of the fleece is shorn; the sale of the wool reduces the cost of the sheep by about 5%. For experiments involving radiology, a foetal table top is used which has a radiotranslucent Perspex window, usually 5 inches in diameter to fit over an image-intensifier, the tube being located above the foetus.

There are a few other practical details which although useful, are rarely mentioned. The use of a cautery makes dissection of fragile tissues easier in very immature foetuses of any species. As in the ewe, so in the foetal lamb, it is not always necessary to tie a carotid artery. The foetus is usually laid supine, so the brachial artery is readily available when the forelimb is extended; in foetuses at term, a small catheter can be easily passed into one of the thyroid branches of the carotid. The femoral artery is large and easily located at term; but there is also an artery available behind the hock of the hindlimb, which may be delivered alone through a purse-string suture on the uterus. For a venous catheter, even in lambs of 75–90 days, the posterior auricular branch of the external jugular is very convenient and as easy to handle as a femoral vein. So there is a wide variety of routes of access to the branches of the venae cavae and aorta, even without the cotyledonary umbilical vessels. Catheterization of vessels has been so facilitated by the introduction during the last 10 years of plastic tubing which can be modelled to fit, that those who remember shaping their own glass cannulae may be forgiven for thinking this a major advance in medical technology. Hard plastics such as Perspex or Lucite also may be bent to the needs of the investigator by gentle traction in an oven, to make curved cannulae with a short lip which offer little resistance to blood flow and have revolutionized rapid cannulation of small vessels when space is tight.

Methods for Improving Accessibility to the Foetus

During the past 20 years a wide variety of operations have been performed on foetuses *in utero,* with survival, in small animals (rats, rabbits, and guinea pigs) as well as relatively large ones (rhesus monkeys and lambs). They have ranged in complexity from injections of antigens and drugs and intraperitoneal transfusions (in human infants), through transplantation of skin (for assessment of immunological competence), decapitation, hypophysectomy, and complex intrathoracic operations. Most organs (except the heart) have been removed, cardiographic and encephalographic electrodes have been placed in position, and chronic indwelling catheters have been introduced into the major blood vessels. It is clear that with patience, skill, and good anaesthesia almost any surgical procedure is practicable upon the foetus *in utero.* It might then be thought that there would be little need for the development of methods for maintaining an extra-uterine pregnancy. This is not so. Easy accessibility of the foetus and its orifices will facilitate many types of investigation, of the formation of amniotic fluid, of quantitative measurements on placental transfer, and of foetal metabolism, for example.

The intra-uterine position of the foetus is at the same time a safeguard to itself and a cause of frustration to the physiologist. There are a number of possibilities for improving accessibility. We could introduce fertile eggs into the abdomen to produce artificial ectopic pregnancies, as Bland and Donovan (1965) have done for other purposes in guinea pigs. But then the site of implantation and the vascular supply to the placenta would be abnormal. Rupture of the uterus, with a surviving intraperitoneal pregnancy, has occurred in man (e.g., Pauwen, 1964). It is thus possible to improve accessibility without removing the foetus from its mother, provided this is done early in gestation so that the uterus does not contract and expel the placenta. This is practicable in sheep and would be most useful as a chronic preparation in the rhesus monkey, in which access to the umbilical vein for measurement of flow is difficult *in utero.*

Alternatively, it is possible to maintain a foetus outside the uterus, replacing the placenta by an extracorporeal circulation which includes a gas exchanger, and sometimes also a dialysis chamber for the exchange of glucose and urea, for example. A wide variety of such machines have been used, with successful maintenance of an extra-uterine foetus in reasonably good physiological condition for some hours (Table 55). There was probably some advantage in keeping the foetus immersed in a warm fluid to prevent drying of the skin and to mimic the intra-uterine environment. It is evident from a study of these observations, which were reviewed recently by Alexander, Britton, and Nixon (1966), that the principal difficulty in using the umbilical vessels to join the foetal and extracorporeal circulations is that they are long and tend to constrict with time, so that ultimately they offer

TABLE 55.—MAINTENANCE OF ISOLATED FOETUSES BY EXTRACORPOREAL PERFUSION THROUGH A GAS EXCHANGER

SPECIES	AGE	CONNECTING VESSELS	EXTRACORPOREAL CIRCUIT	FLOW (ML/KG MIN)	SURVIVAL	AUTHORS
Sheep	Unstated	Umbilical	Bubble oxygenator and Sigmamotor pump	Unstated	1 hour	Harned *et al.* (1957)
Man	Previable	Umbilical	Gas exchanger and Archimedean screw	50	3–4 hours	Westin, Nyberg, and Enhörning (1958)
Sheep	Late foetal	Umbilical	Disc oxygenator and pump	13–60	3/10* after 40 min	Callaghan *et al.* (1963)
Pig	Late foetal	Umbilical	Gas exchanger only	100–200 at first, falling soon	Unstated	Lawn and McCance (1964)
Sheep	Late foetal	Umbilical	Gas exchanger and roller pump	30–200	Up to 9 hours	Alexander, Britton, and Nixon (1966)
Sheep	Late foetal	R. atrial drainage; carotid arterial infusion	Membrane oxygenator and roller pump	Mean 104	Several hours	Tchobroutsky, Clauvel, and Laurent (1966)

* Independent spontaneous breathing established.

a large resistance to blood flow. To some extent, this problem can be overcome by passing plastic tubes through the umbilical vessels to the aorta and by using a pump in the external circuit. Even so, it appears to be difficult to maintain a blood flow sufficient for foetal O_2 consumption (i.e., greater than 100 ml/kg min) for more than a few hours. Otherwise it is possible to use other vessels (see Tchobroutsky, Clauvel, and Laurent, 1966; last line of Table 55). Whether these methods ever prove useful in maintaining a premature human infant, they should certainly be invaluable in studying the metabolism of whole foetuses separated from the placenta, and so without the complication of variations in maternal or placental metabolism or hormone secretion. They are worth perfecting for that reason alone. The reasons for gradual vasoconstriction of the umbilical vessels, and particularly of their innervated intra-abdominal portions, on removal of the foetus from the uterus are, therefore, of some practical interest.

Another method has been to place small immature foetuses in a hyperbaric oxygen chamber at 16 atmospheres absolute, either with the umbilical cord tied or still attached to the placenta. Using foetal rabbits weighing 19–62 Gm (22–29 days gestation), delivered from mothers which had received pentobarbitone, respiratory movements were observed for as long as 6 hours. The mean duration of respiratory movements was greater when the foetuses were immersed in a saline solution than when placed in a gaseous environment with a tube in the trachea (both at high O_2 pressure; Goodlin and Perry, 1966). This was attributed to the efficacy of fluid breathing in promoting O_2 absorption by the lungs. Yet there can be no doubt that the conditions of these foetuses, both as regards their circulation, arterial blood gases, pH, and electrolytes are substantially different from those in utero (Goodlin, 1965). So this is not an acceptable alternative.

Placental Perfusion

This seems an appropriate point at which to consider, briefly, methods of placental perfusion. A method of perfusing the umbilical (foetal) side of the placenta, using sheep, was described by Huggett, Warren, and Warren (1951), and was improved by Alexander, Andrews, Huggett, Nixon, and Widdas (1955). A similar method was used in guinea pigs by Money and Dancis (1960), and Ely (1966). The essential feature of these methods is

that the placenta is left in situ, the foetus is discarded, and the umbilical circulation is maintained by a perfusion pump, using either blood or dextran-and-saline solutions, recirculated through a warmed reservoir or running continuously to waste.

The principal use made of these preparations so far has been to study placental transfer of various sugars, polyols, and other substances, under conditions in which foetal metabolism is excluded. There are some problems in interpretation, because it is not known how the preparation affects maternal blood flow through the placenta, or umbilical blood flow through those parts of the foetal side of the placenta which are either within or outside the principal area of exchange (e.g., the cotyledons and the extracotyledonary chorionic membrane in sheep). And it is often uncertain to what extent metabolism within the placental tissues is responsible for the results. For many purposes, it would be desirable to use an isolated placenta, perfused by independent systems from both maternal and foetal sides. This should provide both a better measure of placental metabolism than perfusion of the isolated placenta from the umbilical vessels alone, and a more reliable estimate of the transfer capacity of the placenta under varying conditions. But, unfortunately, the anatomy of the placenta makes such a preparation difficult, particularly in primates in which perfusion of the intervillous space separate from the myometrium seems impossibly difficult. There is a better chance of perfusing an isolated sheep's cotyledon from both sides, but even in this species the presence of arteriovenous anastomoses (Steven, 1966) may confuse interpretation. There is also the problem of vascular spasm to be overcome. So it may be some while before we have a wholly satisfactory isolated placental preparation, whose behaviour is reasonably similar to that of a placenta in situ.

Electromagnetic Flowmeters

During the past 10 years, electromagnetic flowmeters have been used increasingly for blood flow measurement, either incorporated into cannulated flow systems or on intact blood vessels. The principle is simple and attractive (Shercliff, 1962). If blood flows in a tube through an electromagnetic field, a potential difference is observed at right angles to the direction of flow and to the magnetic field, whose magnitude is directly proportional both to the field strength and the volume of blood flow, provided that flow is axially symmetrical. Given the volumes of blood flow which are required to be measured in small experimental animals, of the order of 20–1,000 ml/min, and having regard to the problem of heat dissipation (which restricts the field strength in a practical flowmeter head), the signal voltage is low, commonly only a few microvolts. Cannulated flowmeter heads of high fidelity (maximum error ±1% of full scale) have been designed and proved reliable over several years' use in many different experimental applications (e.g., Wyatt, 1961).

The design of satisfactory small cuff electromagnetic flowmeters has proved very much more difficult. There are many reasons for this, related to the fact that the cuff head is immersed in a conducting fluid and the impossibility of using efficient screens with the requirement of small size and high sensitivity. Nine sources of base-line error have been described (Wyatt, 1966,a), and in each case the magnitude of the error depends upon a complicated combination of circumstances. Also a practical cuff flowmeter head is between 100 and 1,000 times more sensitive *in vivo* to main power supply interference than a cannulated head, because of the presence of the blood vessel and consequent asymmetry in the conducting medium (Wyatt, 1966,b). Nevertheless, by careful attention to design, it is possible to make a sinusoidally-excited cuff flowmeter with reasonable band width and signal-to-noise ratio, of high fidelity within the range of flows required to be measured. Indeed, it turns out that sinusoidal excitation is not only simpler to handle but inherently less noisy than trapezoidal excitation. Thus the final selection of a practical cuff flowmeter design depends on the assessment of very many complex and interacting factors, which are certainly beyond the scope of this discussion. But if the experimental physiologist may not wish to follow the nuances of design considerations, he needs guidance in the practical qualities to be expected in a completed instrument.

There are two types of cuff electromagnetic flowmeter, iron-cored and air-cored. The typical iron-cored head has a U-shaped core, with curved pole-pieces to improve the homogeneity of the magnetic field. With this arrangement the field strength is accurately predictable. Air-cored heads provide a relatively small magnetic field, and so are more suitable for measurement of large flows (>500 ml/min). They are relatively small and light in weight and are more easily implanted chronically. On the other hand, more care is needed in their construction to obtain the predicted mag-

netic field. Axial potential gradients in phase quadrature with the magnetic field are produced by eddy currents. These potential gradients are greater when the head is immersed in a conducting material and are several times greater for conventional iron-cored heads than for air-cored heads because of the difference in flux distribution. So the greater sensitivity achieved by using an iron core carries disadvantages with it, but is necessary for the accurate measurement of low flows.

The quality of the head largely determines the performance of cuff electromagnetic flowmeters. In particular, accurate construction is necessary to avoid unwanted quadrature potentials either from electrode loops or axial misalignment of the electrodes. It is now well known that some instruments have proved to have possible baseline errors of 20–50% of signal, and that this may vary apparently erratically. These errors can be minimized by careful construction of the gauge head, by electronic design to provide adequate phase stability, by the use of quadrature suppression, low impedance platinized cavity electrodes, and neutralized leads (Wyatt, 1966,a). Manual adjustment of the gating-circuit is unnecessary and an indication either that phase stability is inadequate (e.g., because of thermal changes in circuit elements) or that there are potential baseline errors. The change in baseline on switching the magnet on and off when there is no flow should in no circumstances exceed 1% of scale, when the head is immersed in a beaker of saline or *in vivo*. Identification of zero flow by arresting the heart or otherwise is unnecessary and an unacceptable procedure, because if you are driven to use this manoeuvre it must imply that the instrument has a large potential baseline error, and the probability is that it is then variable from time to time.

Similarly, the need to calibrate a cuff electromagnetic flowmeter head *in vivo* must almost always be an admission of failure in design. The sensitivity of a given gauge head can be calculated from knowledge of the interelectrode distance and field strength, when end-shorting (Shercliff, 1962), and the effect of the bloodvessel (Gessner, 1961) are negligible. The r.m.s. signal voltage is $Vs = 4BQ10^{-8}/\pi d$, where B is the magnetic flux density in gauss r.m.s., Q the flow in ml/sec, and d the flowmeter internal diameter in cm. In practice, the effects of end-shorting, of the annulus of conducting material composed of the blood vessel wall, and of inhomogeneity of magnetic field can be small and calculable. Thus, while it is desirable from time to time to check the performance of a gauge head in a test rig and *in vivo,* the check should be against its calculated theoretical sensitivity. The electromagnetic flowmeter is an absolute instrument, and deviation from its theoretical performance indicates a failure in design or construction.

Any cuff electromagnetic flowmeter is potentially susceptible to external interfering currents, at the mains frequency or harmonics of that frequency. The magnet excitation frequency should never be at main supply frequency. If excitation frequency differs from mains harmonics, mains interference can still produce a difference frequency. This will increase noise at this frequency, but is much to be preferred to a baseline error. By appropriate design, interference can be minimized, but the performance of each head in this respect can be readily tested. The sensitivity to interference is greater with bright than with platinized electrodes, whose impedance is less. A meter which records interference is of considerable practical value.

The fit and symmetry of the blood vessel in the gauge head is another point of practical importance. A poor fit, or application of the head to a vessel on which there are ecchymoses (with consequent variations in conductivity) cause an increase in the spurious voltage in phase quadrature with the magnetic field. If this quadrature voltage is detected for the purpose of quadrature suppression by a negative feedback system, its magnitude can be indicated by an auxiliary meter which then gives an index of goodness of fit to the vessel. Experience with this system has proved it to be of considerable value. A number of instances have been observed where an iron-core cuff flowmeter head of high sensitivity gave an erroneous reading due to an imperfect fit not visible on external inspection, but clearly indicated by the auxiliary meter.

It is evident that the cuff electromagnetic flowmeter can be used as an absolute instrument of high fidelity, with a maximum probable error which can be as little as 2% when used on veins and 3% on arteries (e.g., on the external jugular or common carotid of adult sheep with a mean flow of 50–150 ml/min). Comparisons with other methods are not readily made. For instance, although there are many comparisons between indicator-dilution and Fick methods in the literature, these are of doubtful value for our purpose. Changing conditions are encountered even in an apparently steady state through small variations in breathing and stroke volume. Even simultaneous comparisons of these two methods are hardly meaningful, because such variations will affect the two types of measurements in different ways. Thus to assess the variation of another method it is necessary to measure it against a flow measurement of unquestioned accuracy. Lüthy and Galletti (1966) used an open-chest dog in which left ventricular output was set at a fixed value by an extracorporeal pump. They found that four thermodilution measurements were required to estimate cardiac output within 10%, at a 95% confidence limit. This gives an idea of the range of variation in one particular experimental situation, using one system of injection and sampling site. It does not follow that the variation will fall within the same range in another set of physiological and experimental conditions. Most workers would not now claim that a single indicator dilution measurement gives a measure of flow or cardiac output better than within $\pm 15\%$.

If I have written extensively of the electromagnetic flowmeter it is because I have used it a great deal (and have not had personal experience of the ultrasonic flowmeter, for instance). It has acquired in the last 10 years an undeservedly bad general reputation, because of the unreliability of some models. And as with any instrument, even the most reliable model has its limitation. Some surgical exposure is necessary, and if the cuff is applied to an artery it may damage the nerve supply to the area under study. When applied to a vein, the cuff head usually needs support if the vessel is not to be distorted. And it is always necessary to ensure that blood flow is axially symmetrical. Although cuff flowmeters have often been applied to the ascending aorta, aortic arch, or pulmonary trunk, this point is rarely considered. Yet, despite these limitations, it is an instrument which has already proved most useful in both acute and chronic experiments and seems to be capable of considerable further exploitation.

REFERENCES

Alexander, D. P.; Andrews, R. D.; Huggett, A. St. G.; Nixon, D. A., and Widdas, W. F.: The placental transfer of sugars in the sheep: Studies with radioactive sugar, J. Physiol. 129:352–366, 1955.

Alexander, D. P.; Britton, H. G., and Nixon, D. A.: Maintenance of the isolated foetus, Brit. M. Bull. 22:9–12, 1966.

Alexander, D. P.; Britton, H. G., and Nixon, D. A.: Observations on the isolated foetal sheep with particular reference to the metabolism of glucose and fructose, J. Physiol. 185:382–399, 1966.

Ardran, G. M., and Brown, T. H.: X-ray diagnosis of pregnancy in sheep with special reference to the determination of the number of foetuses, J. Agric. Sc. 63: 205–207, 1964.

Baldwin, B. A., and Bell, F. R.: The anatomy of the cerebral circulation of the sheep and ox. The dynamic distribution of the blood supplied by the carotid and vertebral arteries to cranial regions, J. Anat. 97:203–215, 1963.

Baldwin, B. A., and Bell, F. R.: Blood flow in the carotid and vertebral arteries of the sheep and calf, J. Physiol. 167:448–462, 1963.

Baldwin, B. A., and Bell, F. R.: The effect on blood pressure in the sheep and calf of clamping some of the arteries contributing to the cephalic circulation, J. Physiol. 167:463–479, 1963.

Bass, B. G., and Buckley, N. M.: Chloralose anaesthesia in the dog: A study of drug actions and analytical methodology, Am. J. Physiol. 210:854–862, 1966.

Bland, K. P., and Donovan, B. T.: Experimental ectopic implantation of eggs and early embryos in guinea-pigs, J. Reprod. Fertil. 10:189–196, 1965.

Callaghan, J. C.; Angeles, J.; Boracchia, B.; Fisk, L., and Hallgren, R.: Studies of the first successful delivery of an unborn lamb after 40 minutes in the artificial placenta, Canad. J. Surg. 6:199–206, 1963.

Davies, F. G.: A spinal anaesthetic with long duration of action, Nature 198:390, 1963.

Ely, P. A.: The placental transfer of hexoses and polyols in the guinea-pig, as shown by umbilical perfusion of the placenta, J. Physiol. 184:255–271, 1966.

Gessner, U.: Effects of the vessel wall on electromagnetic flow measurement, Biophys. J. 1:627–637, 1961.

Goodlin, R. C.: Fetal incubator studies. III. Factors associated with breathing in fetal rabbits, Biol. Neonat. 8:274–280, 1965.

Goodlin, R., and Perry, D.: Fetal incubator studies. II. Fetal alveolar electrolyte excretion, Am. J. Obst. & Gynec. 94:268–273, 1966.

Hardy, T.: *Far from the Madding Crowd,* 1874.

Harned, H. S.; Tandysh, M. A.; McGarry, M.; Keeve, J., and Kusserow, B.: The use of the pump oxygenator to sustain life during neonatal asphyxia of lambs, Am. J. Dis. Child. 94:530, 1957.

Huggett, A. St. G.: Foetal blood-gas tensions and gas transfusion through the placenta of the goat, J. Physiol. 62:373–384, 1927.

Huggett, A. St. G.; Warren, F. L., and Warren, N. Y.: The origin of blood fructose in the foetal sheep, J. Physiol. 113:258–295, 1951.

Lawn, L., and McCance, R. A.: Artificial placentae, Acta paediat. 53:317–325, 1964.

Lüthy, E., and Galletti, P. M.: In vivo evaluation of the thermodilution technique for measuring cardiac output, Helvet. physiol. et pharmacol. acta 24:15–23, 1966.

Money, W. L., and Dancis, J. D.: Technique for the in situ study of placental transport in the pregnant guinea-pig, Am. J. Obst. & Gynec. 80:209–214, 1960.

Parry, H. B., in Hammond, J.; Browne, F. J., and Wolstenholme, G. E. W. (eds.): Pregnancy Toxaemia in Sheep, *Ciba Foundation Symposium on Toxaemias of Pregnancy: Human and Veterinary* (London: J. & A. Churchill, Ltd., 1950).

Pauwen, J.: Über eine ausgetragene extrauterine Schwangerschaft mit leben dem Kind nach einer Uterusruptur im 3. Schwangerschaftsmonat, Zentralbl. Gynäk. 86: 1514–1516, 1964.

Potter, B. J.: Haemoglobinuria caused by propylene glycol in sheep, Brit. J. Pharmacol. 13:385–389, 1958.

Shercliff, J. A.: *The Theory of Electromagnetic Flow Measurement* (London: Cambridge University Press, 1962).

Steven, D. H.: Arteriovenous anastomoses in the uterus of the sheep, J. Physiol. 187:18, P., 1966.

Tchobroutsky, C.; Clauvel, M., and Laurent, D. N.: Extracorporeal oxygenation in puppies and in newborn and fetal lambs, Am. J. Obst. & Gynec. 96:367–381, 1966.

Westin, B.; Nyberg, R., and Enhörning, G.: A technique for perfusion of the previable human fetus, Acta paediat. 47:339–349, 1958.

Wyatt, D. G.: A 50 c/s cannulated electromagnetic flowmeter, Electronic Engng. 33:650–655, 1961.

Wyatt, D. G.: Baseline errors in cuff electromagnetic flowmeters, M. Biol. Engng. 4:17–45, 1966,a.

Wyatt, D. G.: Noise in electromagnetic flowmeters, M. Biol. Engng. 4:333–347, 1966,b.

Index